W9-BCB-703

GERMANY AND ENGLAND

DD 120
G 7
S 6
1964

GERMANY AND ENGLAND

Background of Conflict

1848-1894

By RAYMOND JAMES SONTAG

NEW YORK
RUSSELL & RUSSELL · INC
1964

AUG 1964

90619

COPYRIGHT, 1938, BY
D. APPLETON–CENTURY COMPANY, INC.
REISSUED, 1964, BY RUSSELL & RUSSELL, INC.
BY ARRANGEMENT WITH APPLETON-CENTURY (AFFILIATE OF MEREDITH PRESS)
L. C. CATALOG CARD NO: 64—15034

Reprinted from a copy in the collections of
The New York Public Library

PRINTED IN THE UNITED STATES OF AMERICA

To

WILLIAM E. LINGELBACH

327.120913
So59

PREFACE

In the summer of 1938, Neville Chamberlain's foreign policy proceeded on the assumption that if an amicable understanding with Germany could be achieved, the position of England was secure, not only on the Continent, but in the Mediterranean and in Asia. Adolf Hitler was no less eager for an understanding; *Mein Kampf* made the alienation of England the cardinal error of the Second Reich, and promised that the Third Reich would not repeat this ruinous blunder.

Forty years earlier Joseph Chamberlain, Neville's father, was a powerful member of Lord Salisbury's cabinet. Father, like son, believed an understanding with Germany necessary for British security in Europe and in the world. William II, like Hitler, wished alliance with England, thought an Anglo-German alliance the inevitable expression of the interests of the two countries.

The negotiations of forty years ago broke down. England and Germany, from natural allies, became natural enemies. The result of that enmity was a war which was ruinous to these two strongest of European nations. In 1938 it was recognized that a second failure would complete the ruin wrought by the World War.

The Chamberlains were proud of the fact that they were business men who could measure costs and make a balance sheet. They argued that a business-like estimate of relative costs, enmity against accord, demonstrated that agreement was the sensible course. The Kaiser, like Hitler, knew the risks of challenging the island empire. The dangers and advantages were known, in 1898 and 1938. And yet there were few to prophesy that the efforts of Neville Chamberlain would, over the long run, be more successful than those of Joseph Chamberlain.

The explanation of failure in the past, and the barrier to success in the present, is to be found only partly in vital conflicts of interest or in faulty statesmanship. Account must be taken of barriers to understanding which cannot be accurately set down in a business man's balance sheet. They are to be found in what Bismarck called the imponderables of politics, in the realm of history and in the realm of ideas. Just as the period of the American Revolution continued to affect relations between England and the United States for generations, so the half century after 1848 left a lasting mark on Anglo-German relations.

In 1848, Britain was incomparably the strongest and the richest European power. Many elements had built up power and wealth, but Englishmen thought freedom was the essential element in their success, and they also thought that what had been good for England would be good for the rest of the world. In the years following, the liberal tradition was built up by men of thought and action, men like Cobden and Palmerston, Herbert Spencer and William Gladstone. The tradition was firmly grounded in the conviction that mankind was groping toward conformity with eternal, universal, and beneficent natural laws; misery and evil followed from the breach of these laws, whether through ignorance or short-sighted selfishness. The sum of these laws was, on the one hand, the right of the individual to freedom from coercion by other individuals or by governments, and on the other hand, the interdependence and community of interest between individuals and nations. In the distance loomed the vision of a day when all men would be free, and when the community of mankind would be realized. The enemy was, first of all, ignorance, and beyond that, selfishness, the selfishness alike of vested, privileged interests within nations, and the selfishness of the rulers of states in their dealings with other nations. The enemies were powerful; but law, working through the great masses of mankind, must win in the end, not only because the battle was between the many and the few, but because the irresistible power of nature's god was the ally of the many.

Englishmen thought nationalism a subordinate manifestation of liberalism. People should be freed from foreign, no less than domestic, oppressors. The advance of nationalism was confidently expected to hasten the coming of world peace. Free peoples would want only to be left alone so that they might enjoy the blessings of peace. Progress towards individualism and cosmopolitanism, progress towards freedom, with England leading and the Continent following, though often reluctantly—such roughly and approximately was the creed of mid-nineteenth century English liberalism, the creed which Germans were preparing to challenge.

In 1848, Germany was divided and weak. German nationalists were usually liberals and admirers of their English cousins. Already, however, many German patriots were, like Friedrich List, disillusioned with individualism and cosmopolitanism as the road to national progress. Having no national state, wanting a national state above all other earthly desires, they could not dismiss nationalism as a minor expression of liberalism, or the state as a necessary but dangerous mechanism of administration. After the failure of the Revolution of 1848, German liberalism became increasingly heretical to Englishmen. The individual and mankind fell into the background; the national state became the center of human aspirations. The state seemed no longer a mechanical contrivance, but became a living personality with a will capable of coercing citizens, and other states. Nature's laws were dismissed as a figment of the imagination; every nation was a law unto itself, bound only by national character as determined through historical evolution. Force, war, from being a temporarily necessary but ultimately doomed evil, became a positive good when used to further national interests.

German liberalism, retreating from English doctrines, steadily approached an understanding with conservatives like Bismarck who were disillusioned with monarchical and aristocratic doctrines which, in practice, kept Prussia in servitude to Austria. Conservatives like Bismarck continued to exalt order and mistrust freedom, but they also were deserting cosmopolitanism to worship at the altar of the national state, and seeking a basis for law in the history of the nation rather than in the eternal and universal dictates of nature. When, through his wars with Denmark, Austria, and

France, Bismarck made the dream of unity a reality, German liberalism sloughed off the last remnants of individualism and cosmopolitanism: freedom came to mean the freedom of the German nation, freedom for the nation to live and to grow. Bismarck himself was now satisfied; for him the new Reich was a satiated state. Even his enormous prestige, however, could not completely restrain the national craving for new victories. In 1884 and 1885 he launched Germany on a career of colonial expansion, partly to keep his hold on public opinion. When he attempted to revert to a policy of stability, there was discontented murmuring. William II took advantage of popular discontent to dismiss the old Chancellor; but when the Kaiser and his new advisers showed themselves no less reluctant to continue colonial expansion, murmuring began anew. By 1894, William II was coming to realize that the one sure way to win popular favor was to demonstrate that Germany was a growing nation. He had learned also that the popular imagination was most easily captured by growth in rivalry with England.

That German admiration for England should prompt a desire to emulate the imperial triumphs of England was not strange. The aspiration to grow in rivalry to England was explained partly by the necessity of demonstrating German emancipation from British tutelage, partly by the lack of sympathy shown by England to the rise of Germany from impotence to continental supremacy and imperial power. British statesmen opposed Bismarck at every step in the 'sixties; British publicists had few good words to say for the Second Reich; British statesmen and publicists alike were slow to admit the right of Germany to a share of the imperial spoils. Germans attributed both criticism and opposition to jealousy, jealousy of a poor relation who had come up in the world, jealousy of a people who had learned that English talk of freedom and the rights of mankind was a hypocritical cloak to perpetuate British world supremacy. There was some truth, at least in the first half of the allegation. Englishmen could not quite recognize that parvenu Germany had climbed above the older powers of the Continent, up to equality with

England. But even the reluctance to admit the changed status of Germany was in large part reluctance to admit that such methods could produce such results. The ideal of the national state which Bismarck carried to triumph was in every way the antithesis of British liberalism. Watching from across the Channel, men like Gladstone knew that if the rest of Europe accepted the state ideal dominant in Germany, liberalism was doomed. They also knew that success was the best argument for an ideal. Therefore, English liberals refused to believe that Bismarck could win; when he did win unity, they refused to believe the state he had created could endure; when it did endure, they insisted Germans were slaves.

So it was that, even in the 'eighties, when it was usual to speak of England and Germany as "natural allies," when there was real community of interest, and when there were few conflicts of interest, relations between the two countries were precarious. Divergent political ideals, broadening out through economics and social life to the boundaries of the national culture, made it impossible for either people to see the other objectively, much less sympathetically. Friction, the inevitable result of misunderstanding, produced a host of minor explosions which the imagination of suspicious and resentful publicists like Treitschke transformed into major upheavals. When real conflict of interests appeared, compromise was excluded by the excited temper of both countries.

Such was the background of the failure of Joseph Chamberlain, the story told in the pages which follow. It is a story which bears a depressing resemblance to the situation today. Again, the conflict of ideals bars understanding. Again, Englishmen see Satan at war with God's unalterable law, and pray for his overthrow. Again, Germans can be happy in the consciousness of a strong national life only if growth, never ending growth, is the evidence of life, and again there are many Germans who can be happy only if the growth is in rivalry with Britain. The parallel is impressive.

The story here is only of England and Germany, but the story has more general implications. The Germany of Bismarck, like the Germany of Hitler, seemed reactionary to Englishmen. And yet, in the field of ideas, is it not the Germans who have been innovators? In all that concerns the relations of the individual to the state, of the state to the world community, and, more broadly, of law to force, the world of today is closer by far to the ideals of the German nationalists of Bismarck's day than to the Gladstonian liberals. This fact may, to many, seem more impressive than the similarity of the problem confronting the two Chamberlains.

Such, briefly, are the reflections suggested by a study of the relations between Britain and Germany in the second half of the nineteenth century. As a student, the fatal rivalry of these great peoples in the two decades immediately preceding the World War has long held my attention; as an observer of the contemporary scene, the recurrence of rivalry seems to me the most ominous development for the future of Europe. In studying the evidence, post-war as well as pre-war, I have been continually impressed with the fact that the difficulty of accommodating the conflicts of interest between England and Germany was out of all proportion to the importance and complexity of the interests at stake. As Joseph Chamberlain said, and as his son said, accommodation on a business-like basis would be easy—if it were possible to be business-like. In all negotiations, however, there has been an intangible but irremovable barrier to sober discussion. The search for that barrier took me back to the years when there were no vital conflicts of interest, back of the creation of the German Empire. In the search, I examined newspapers and magazines, pamphlets and scholarly studies, the works of poets and novelists, the dispatches of statesmen, tables of commerce and industry. The search was not exhaustive or exhausting. I went as deep and as far as appeared necessary to find the missing element. The search was exciting because it illumined for me, not merely the past and present relations between these two greatest of European nations, but because it forced me to confront the greatest political problem of the century, the problem of the relation of the national state to the individual citizen and to the community of nations. To enable the reader to follow me without weariness in the search, I have dispensed with the paraphernalia of scholarship. Footnotes have been suppressed, except where there is direct quotation. More drastic and hazardous was the decision not to build up the argument like a mosaic from many scattered fragments of evidence, but to recreate the scene through the use of a few individuals and situations. Throughout I have been troubled by knowledge of the pitfalls awaiting any student of public opinion today when the standards of measurement and analysis are not only primitive but diverse. Undoubtedly, I have fallen into many traps, and certainly the result cannot be called a definitive study of Anglo-German relations. It is intended merely to suggest that the statesmen of England and Germany negotiated, and still negotiate in a room darkened by misunderstanding and haunted by the ghosts of men and actions long past.

Like all students, I have incurred heavy obligations in the course of my work. In Europe, I am indebted to the officials of the German Foreign Office, the Prussian state library, the university libraries of Munich, Freiburg i.B., and Heidelberg, and the British Museum; of the many men in England and Germany who gave wise counsel there is opportunity to mention only the late Dr. Otto Hammann. My indebtedness to institutions and individuals in the United States is no less great. My study of Anglo-German relations was begun many years ago when I was a Harrison Fellow at the University of Pennsylvania, and was steadily encouraged by Professor William E. Lingelbach, who gave many suggestions for the improvement of this book. Equally valuable were the comments of Dr. Edward M. Earle of the Institute for Advanced Study, Princeton, Professor E. A. Beller of Princeton University, and of my wife, Dorothea Agar Sontag. To Princeton University, I owe more than can be here detailed. The release from teaching duties made possible by the Benjamin D. Shreve Fellowship and the History Alumni Fund are only the most obvious of many forms of encouragement. Less tangible, but no less valuable, was the help of my colleagues and students. For this assistance, I am very grateful.

R. J. S.

TABLE OF CONTENTS

PART I

THE POOR RELATION, 1848–1871

PART II

NATURAL ALLIES, 1871–1894

PART I

THE POOR RELATION

1848–1871

List of Abbreviations

B.D.	Great Britain. *British Documents on the Origins of the War, 1898–1914.*
F.Z.	*Frankfurter Zeitung.*
G.P.	Germany. *Die Grosse Politik der Europäischen Kabinette, 1871–1914.*
Ges. Werke.	Bismarck. *Die gesammelten Werke.*
K.Z.	*Kölnische Zeitung.*
M. & B.	Monypenny and Buckle, *Life of Disraeli.*
Origines	France. *Les Origines diplomatiques de la guerre de 1870–1871.*
V.Z.	*Vossische Zeitung.*

INTRODUCTION

IN JANUARY, 1871, the German Empire was proclaimed at Versailles. It was the moment of which patriots had dreamed. "As on the raised benches of an amphitheatre the nations will group themselves around Germany to behold the great tournament," Heine had prophesied a generation before; and now the nations were indeed watching this scene in the palace of Louis XIV. By proclaiming their empire in the Hall of Mirrors, the Germans were paying back old scores, not merely to the Bourbons but to the medieval Capetian and Valois rulers of France. "Once in a beer-cellar at Göttingen," Heine had warned, "I heard a young Teuton say that revenge must be had on the French for Conradin of Hohenstaufen whom they beheaded at Naples [in 1268]. You have long forgotten that. But we forget nothing." Those old wounds inflicted by France could, in victory, be forgiven. Forgiven were the Danes, too, since Schleswig-Holstein had been won for the new Germany. Habsburg Austria, so triumphantly vanquished in 1866, could be Germany's friend. Russia had won the gratitude of Germans by preventing the intervention of other powers when Bismarck was creating united Germany. Even in the flush of victory, Germans forgot no wrongs, real or fancied, inflicted on their divided country in centuries past, by France, by Austria, by Russia; but in victory they could forgive much.

England had been neither Germany's friend nor Germany's conquered foe during these years past; so the sins of England were neither forgotten nor forgiven. Patiently and meticulously, German students recounted the old tale. The ruthlessness of the medieval Hanseatic League was forgotten; but the blows struck at the Hanse merchants by the Tudors were remembered. The Machiavellianism of Frederick the Great was ignored when the "shameful desertion" of Frederick by England during the Seven Years' War was described. The pusillanimous and greedy German princes of the Napoleonic period were bad, but worse was England's refusal to insist on German unity in 1815. After 1815 it was the same story. England had done all in her power to check the growth of the Prussian Zollverein, the customs union which had laid the economic foundations of German unity. During the revolution of 1848 and in the three wars, with Denmark in 1864, with Austria in 1866, with France in 1870, always England had been on the side of those who opposed German unity. Germany had won out despite England; but Germans must never forget. German students were ceaselessly reminded by mighty scholars and by obscure textbook writers that their old scores against England must be paid off.

Across the Channel, events left a very different impression. There, Frederick the Great was remembered as a trickster, ready to break his most sacred promise when the chance of conquest appeared. Bismarck was another Frederick, ruthless, cynical, and insatiably ambitious, first isolating, then despoiling, the neighbors of Prussia. England had not opposed German freedom. On the contrary, England had expected and desired the liberation of the Germans from selfish, despotic princes. But in English eyes, the scene at Versailles did not represent the liberation of Germany; it represented the subjection of Germans, high and low, to reactionary, treacherous Bismarck. Englishmen did not believe the coronation at Versailles was the end of the story. Alarmed, ashamed that Bismarck had so long been unchecked by England, they watched suspiciously, determined to act when Prussian lust for conquest appeared again.

These interpretations had only a remote connection with the events they purported to describe. Both were attempts to rationalize a more fundamental, less tangible antagonism between the English and German peoples. Englishmen of 1871 saw in Germany a people who had not only deserted the path of progress, but closed the path to the world. Germans of 1871 were somewhat confused: their dominant feeling was one of satisfaction at their emancipation from English ideas; but at times the very intensity of their satisfaction suggested the uneasy conscience of the renegade. The mark of this spiritual divorce is on subsequent relations of the English and German peoples. It is, therefore, necessary to go back of 1871, not to wrangle about the meaning of this or that action, as the two peoples did, but to try to understand why the habit of quarrelling about meanings arose.

CHAPTER I

COBDENITE ENGLAND

IN LONDON, May 1, 1851, was a day of alternate sun and shower. Despite the uncertain weather, the streets were crowded from dawn, everyone hurrying to Hyde Park for the opening of the Great Exhibition in the vast, cathedral-like Crystal Palace. Great cheers went up whenever a famous arrival was sighted. The Duke of Wellington—it was his eighty-second birthday—arrived amid an ovation which contrasted strangely with the abuse hurled at him by Londoners twenty years before in the days of the Reform Bill agitation. The Duke stood talking with Richard Cobden, waiting for the arrival of the royal party. At last Queen Victoria arrived, and the privileged guests inside the Crystal Palace stood and took up the cheers of those outside. "The sun, too, for a moment emerged from the envious clouds that for some time previously had dimmed his lustre, and a flood of light pouring in through the glittering dome of the transept illuminated this imposing spectacle of loyalty." [1] Prince Albert stepped down to join the other members of the Exhibition Committee in turning over their handiwork to the Queen. After a tour of the building, the royal party left. The Exhibition was opened; and the prophets of disaster who had expected riots, starvation, revolution, were forced to admit that London had shown, instead, good nature and quiet order.

It had seemed a fearsome undertaking, not merely this thirty-three million cubic feet enclosed with glass, iron, and wood, but the problem of organizing the transportation, housing, and feeding of the hordes who, it was estimated, would double the size of London for six months. Coöperative organization on a na-

[1] *Times,* May 2.

tional scale was exactly what Prince Albert, the driving personality of the Committee, wished to effect; but was exactly what individualistic Englishmen thought strange, foreign—German. Yet it had been achieved, and in face of the accomplished fact, Englishmen were proud. Thackeray's Ode for the occasion was not great poetry, but it did say what Englishmen were thinking.

But yesterday a naked sod,
The dandies sneered from Rotten-row
And cantered o'er it to and fro;
And see, 'tis done!
As though 'twere by a wizard's rod
A blazing arch of lucid glass
Leaps like a fountain from the grass
To meet the sun!

He continued with descriptions of the peoples, and objects, assembled

From Mississippi and from Nile—
From Baltic, Ganges, Bosphorus . . .

And concluded with the distinctively English contribution:

Look yonder where the engines toil;
There England's arms of conquest are,
The trophies of her bloodless war:
Brave weapons these.
Victorious over wave and soil
With these she sails, she weaves, she tills,
Pierces the everlasting hills,
And spans the seas.[2]

Engines made possible the Exhibition; more important, engines made possible the England of 1851. Applied to production, the engine had made the factory the usual center of production; applied to communication in the railroad, it had brought about a redistribution of population, a shift from the south to the west and the north, and from the country to the city. "And along the iron veins that traverse the frame of our country, beat and flow the fiery pulses of its exertions, hotter and faster every hour. All

[2] *Times,* April 30, 1851—Thackeray's *May Day Ode.*

vitality is concentrated through those throbbing arteries into the central cities; the country is passed over like a green sea by narrow bridges, and we are thrown back in continually closer crowds on the city gates." [3] Finally, applied to ocean transport, the engine was slowly winning preponderance over the sail. From the outset, England had taken the lead in the transformation of production and communications. In 1851 she no longer had a monopoly on the engine, but as yet she had no serious competitor. In industry, commerce, and finance she was not only the first, but by far the first power in the world. In ocean transport the United States was a competitor, but Britain carried half the world's commerce. In industry, a few observers like Cobden foresaw an age when the United States might equal or surpass the mother country, but that day was thought to be far in the future. Other potential rivals in mechanical production or transport there seemed none.

In 1851 the industrialization of England was still far from complete. Half her population was urban, a situation previously unparalleled. Moreover, population was increasing rapidly, less from an increase in births than from the decline in the death rate brought about by improved sanitation. Nevertheless, had it been forced to do so, native agriculture could still have fed the islanders, and, even though that necessity did not exist, agriculture remained the largest and one of the most prosperous British industries. It was also one of the most highly centralized: more than half of the land was owned by a few thousand families. The fruits of agriculture, increasingly supplemented by industrial and commercial holdings, supported an aristocracy which retained great prestige and power. The growth of industry, commerce, and finance had been brought about by a middle class which increased in numbers, power, and self-confidence as industry grew. The workers in the factories shared in the prosperity of the times; real wages increased greatly in the middle years of the century. Englishmen boasted that in the transformation of their country no one had fallen. All had risen, and were still rising.

[3] Ruskin, *Seven Lamps*, 187.

Little wonder that Englishmen greeted complacently the visitors who came in 1851. The Exhibition was a place of pilgrimage, drawing from all the world people who would carry back to their own lands the inspiration to accomplish what England had accomplished. "We challenge contradiction," the *Times* declared proudly on the opening day, "when we say that this is the first morning since the creation that all peoples have assembled from all parts of the world and done a common act. Happily that act is an act of peace, of love, and of religion."

Few Englishmen would have been willing to admit that the steam engine alone explained the greatness of their country. Far more important was British reasonableness. For two generations continental Europe had been swept by revolutionary disturbances which were fatal to peace, prosperity, and progress. Inevitably, revolution on the Continent had repercussions in England; the marvel was that the repercussions were so slight. Again and again, sober men had held their breath, fearing that the fabric of British institutions could not stand the double strain of rapid change at home and the example of violence offered by neighboring peoples. The most severe crisis was only just past. The Revolution of 1848 which swept Europe from Naples to Kiel, from Paris to Budapest, had coincided with the Chartist agitation for democratic political reform. Yet while continental governments were fighting for their existence, the sum of British difficulties had been a few easily handled riots. The failure of Chartism seemed final proof of English intelligence, an intelligence which had recognized the inevitability of change at a time when the ruling classes of other countries were blindly resisting change. To be sure, the victory of reason over stupidity had been hard won, and was still far from complete. But at least victory had come soon enough and had been complete enough to save England from the convulsive upheavals which were a commonplace on the Continent.

The expression "mid-Victorian" is not as easy to define as men once thought. No one who knows anything would now make it synonymous with stodgy and smug, or would claim that there was even approximate agreement among Englishmen about the problems of government and society. What common denominator united Thomas Carlyle, John Stuart Mill, Richard Cobden, Charles Kingsley, Matthew Arnold, and Lord Palmerston? Nothing except their earnestness and their eagerness; vigorous purposefulness was certainly a general characteristic of the age. Beyond, there was little agreement. If, however, we confine our attention to "the middle and industrious classes," as they liked to call themselves, at least approximate agreement can be attained. These were the men who had made industrial and commercial England, who had forced the aristocracy to admit them to a share in the government; and they were regarded by the outside world as the whole of England. Their view of the age was best summed up by Gladstone when, looking back, he said: "It has been predominantly a history of emancipation—that is of enabling man to do his work of emancipation, political, economical, social, moral, intellectual." Opening doors and windows, he called it on another occasion. The figure might change, but always freedom is the objective: "It is liberty alone which fits men for liberty. This proposition, like every other in politics, has its bounds; but it is far safer than the counter-doctrine, wait till they are fit." Again, at the end of his life, he summed up his career in words which might well be applied to the generation of his youth: "I was brought up to distrust and dislike liberty, I learned to believe in it. That is the key to all my changes." [4] Despite the felicity with which he could express middle class ideals, Gladstone always shrank from the full implications of belief in liberty. His eagerness to preserve the authority of Christian teachings, and his conviction that landed property was an essential element in social stability, show his fear lest liberty drift over into anarchy. As Balfour remarked, "He is, and always was, in everything except essentials, a tremendous Tory." [5] Tory may be too strong a word, but certain it is that Gladstone sought, in religion and an aristocratic sense of responsibility, authorities

[4] Morley, *Gladstone,* III, 58, 475, 535.
[5] Dugdale, *Balfour,* I, 159.

which would temper liberty. Again and again we meet these doubts. John Stuart Mill's essay is the classic defence of liberty, but it is full of reservations and hesitations, fear that men could not safely be allowed full freedom from restraint; and in the end it seems almost as if Mill would not so fervently have praised liberty if he had not been convinced that most men were too much the slaves of custom and ignorance ever really to use this freedom.

The very tentativeness of Gladstone and Mill help to explain the hold which they had on Englishmen in the middle of the century, the one as a rising liberal statesman, the other as the most respected liberal thinker. More dogmatic men, although their dogmatism makes them representative of only part of the middle class mind, enable us to form a clearer picture.

Richard Cobden was neither a closet philosopher nor a narrowly selfish business man. He had made a success of his business, but he unhesitatingly allowed his business to fall into decay while he busied himself in the campaign for the repeal of the Corn Laws. In that campaign he showed himself to be one of the earliest masters in the art of mass propaganda. Further, there were not many members of Parliament who possessed his intimate knowledge of foreign countries. He had travelled in, and studied, the United States, Continental Europe, North Africa, and the Near East, always trying to grasp conditions peculiar to each region, always preaching his doctrine of free trade, but never betraying a narrowly insular point of view. He was full of praise for the United States, where the middle and industrious classes were in the ascendant. On the other hand, he could see the advantages of the Prussian system of government, its efficiency, economy, sobriety. He was one of the first Englishmen to grasp the fact that the economic unification of Germany through the Zollverein must lead to political unity. He perceived, too, the superior education of the German middle class, which was to be of such importance later. "Our countrymen, if they were possessed of a little of the *mind* of the merchants and manufacturers of Frankfort, Chemnitz, Uberfeld, etc., would become the de' Medicis, and Fuggers, and De Witts of England, instead of glorying in being the toadies of a clod-pole aristocracy, only less enlightened than themselves!" [6]

This capacity for self-sacrifice, and this breadth of understanding are of importance because Cobden's plump little figure and round face, with the inevitable halo of whiskers, embodied the German idea of English middle class cant. Middle class and self-made he proudly was, and he was sure that England would be better off if it were ruled by men like himself. "The sooner the power in this country is transferred from the landed oligarchy, which has so misused it, and is placed absolutely—mind, I say 'absolutely'—in the hands of the intelligent middle and industrious classes, the better for the condition and destinies of this country." [7] Why? Because these were men who asked only to be left alone; at least, the best of them did. Cobden was worried by the tendency of business men to ape the aristocracy; he was alarmed by the attempts of demagogues to win the support of workers "by holding out flattering and delusive prospects of cheap benefits to be derived from Parliament, rather than by urging them to a course of self-reliance." [8] Nevertheless, once government had been wrested from the landed oligarchy, conditions were bound to improve for the good and simple reason that the majority, once in power, would consult their own interests, and not the interests of a minority. "It takes time with us English people to make up our minds, but when great material interests can be appealed to on the side of principles of freedom and humanity, the eventual result in this country is not doubtful." [9]

This was not cant. It was an act of faith, of faith in the beneficent laws of nature. This faith, badly discredited among Englishmen during the French Revolution, had slowly revived in the years after Waterloo in new and native forms. Englishmen did not talk about the rights of man, and they, in theory at least, avoided large abstractions such as Revolutionary France had

[6] Morley, *Cobden*, I, 129 *ff*.
[7] *Speeches*, I, 256.
[8] Morley, *Cobden*, I, 467.
[9] *Ibid.*, II, 399.

propagated. Instead, they clung to tangible facts, and the most tangible facts they saw were the individual and the individual's pursuit of his interest or happiness. All their arguments began with and returned to the individual; groups or classes of men they dismissed as conventional or traditional abstractions. Let everyone pursue his own interest. Will not inevitably the sum of individual interests be the public interest? Of course, some men will seek to further themselves by despoiling or enslaving others, whether by the theft of a purse or by using the state as a class instrument. Such unfair practices must be stopped. But for the rest—let the individual alone. He is doing what nature tells him to do. To interfere with nature is to replace harmony by strife and inefficiency. In a variety of forms, this rationalistic and naturalistic individualism flourished in England. In the form of Utilitarianism, it measured the laws of England by the yardstick of the greatest good to the greatest number, and found most of the laws worthless or vicious. Therefore, in the name of Utility the corrupt and cruel legal code was overhauled, simplified, made less an instrument of aristocratic privilege. In the form of Manchesterism, an attack was made on the whole system of government protection and supervision of commerce and industry, an attack which had achieved almost complete success by the middle of the century.

It was the campaign against protection which made Cobden's reputation, and in his own career can be seen the reasons for the success of the rationalistic and individualistic doctrines of the Utilitarians and the Manchester school. He asked privileges of no one, and his class asked no privilege. His class had risen as he had, fighting every inch of the way against aristocratic paternalism and privilege. His class had made England rich and prosperous. Meanwhile, the aristocrats sat back and gathered the high rents their lands could command because of the increased wealth which they had not only done nothing to bring about, but had hampered in every way possible. Cobden had made his money in textiles, a trade peculiarly hampered by the protective system: raw cotton must be imported, and finished cloth demanded a market abroad. Still he had gone ahead. But how much further, and how much more rapidly, everyone could go ahead if every Englishman were allowed to use his strength unhampered. From experience Cobden drew the conclusions attained deductively by the economists from Adam Smith to young John Stuart Mill.

What the economists called laissez-faire, Cobden called nonintervention. Here was a world governed by natural laws. Production, distribution, profits, wages, and rent, all were subject to fixed and immutable laws. If nature's laws were obeyed, everything went smoothly; if nature's laws were violated, the result was waste and inefficiency, want and misery. In England and in the rest of the world, nature's laws had been and were being violated, partly through ignorant attempts to improve on nature, but largely because governments were controlled by minorities who used their power to oppress the majority and to give privileges to themselves. Even the unprivileged, influenced by aristocratic example, sought to better their condition by vicious means like the formation of trade unions. "There is a desperate spirit of monopoly and tyranny at the bottom of all these trade unions," Cobden warned. Laboring men should be taught that they could not influence the rate of wages in the slightest degree by coercion. "They might as well attempt to regulate the tides by force, or change the course of the seasons, or subvert any of the other laws of nature—for the wages of labor depend upon laws as unerring and as much above our coercive power as any other operations of nature." [10] Let workers be taught that their hope of progress lay rather in securing obedience to natural law through the abolition of privilege. That was what the middle class had done by their successful educational campaign against the Corn Laws. In this agitation the middle classes were furthering their own interests. Of course. But as always when interests are furthered by removing privileges, the interests of one class were the interests of the whole community. "Free trade! What is it? Why, breaking down the barriers that separate nations; those barriers, behind which nestle the feelings of

[10] Hobson, *Cobden*, 166.

pride, revenge, hatred, and jealousy, which every now and then burst their bounds, and deluge whole countries with blood; those feelings which nourish the passion of war and conquest." [11]

From self-interest to class interest; from class interest to national interest; from national interest to universal interest—the transition was natural and plausible. Against the aristocrats, who since the days of Burke had appealed to the wisdom of the past as the great argument against change, Cobden appealed to nature's laws. His appeal involved enormous assumptions: that such laws existed, that they could be discovered, that they were beneficent, and that they could be violated only at the cost of suffering to the whole community. These assumptions he and other liberals of his day unhesitatingly made. Law, at every point, law was the basis of the liberal program, not man-made law, but natural laws for the government of the whole universe. Nature had formed men to operate in obedience to her laws. Ignorance alone was the enemy, ignorance which made men blind to their interests, or impelled men to seek a short-sighted, mistaken interest. In time, if permitted to do so, men would discover their true interest, and act on it. Everyone must be free to think what he would; to say what he believed true; to act as his intelligence dictated—so long as he did not try to oppress others.

A world of individuals, each free to say and do what he thought right and in his own interest; this hurrying, jostling mob guided by the invisible hand of nature into a harmonious procession to a brighter, freer future—a magnificent conception, with magnificent achievements behind it! It is almost impossible to overestimate the weight of cruelty, brutality, and misery lifted from the human race by liberals fighting in the name of scientific self-interest in the early nineteenth century. It is easy to say that this liberalism took its rise in the need of rising industrialism to free itself from the cramping bonds of a state which was the tool of an aristocracy. But men like Cobden did much to universalize their program, to quicken the spirit of the inert mass

[11] *Speeches*, I, 79.

below them. "Have they," he cried, "no Spartacus among them to head a revolt of the slave class against their political tormentors?" [12]

More penetrating criticism of liberalism was levelled by those who argued that the liberal program was too crudely rationalistic and individualistic, who argued that society was not atomic but organic, that a purely negative conception of the state would lead to the oppression of the weak by the strong, that the pursuit of private interest did not necessarily result in the public interest. As early as 1825, when young John Stuart Mill and his friends, staunch Utilitarians, were eagerly debating all opponents, they found it hard to get competent opponents among defenders of the old Tory order, but they found it easy to discover young men who would defend the inchoate socialism of Robert Owen, or the ideal of a society whose interests were different from, and more important than, the interests of the middle classes, the ideal which Coleridge had caught from German thinkers.[13] After contact with these opponents, Mill questioned himself: " 'Suppose that all your objects in life were realized; that all the changes in institutions and opinions which you are looking forward to could be completely effected at this very instant: would this be a great joy and happiness to you?' And an irrepressible self-consciousness distinctly answered, 'No!' " [14] Such questionings drew Mill further and further away from liberal individualism towards socialist beliefs. Simultaneously, another young man, Benjamin Disraeli, was beginning his long effort to inspire new life into the moribund Tories by an incessant barrage of tracts and novels. Through them all ran one message: ruthless individualism was dividing England into two nations, a nation of middle class, money-mad factory owners, and a nation of exploited, depraved workers. From this fatal division England must be rescued by its aristocrats, men filled with the passion to serve the masses of the people. Over and over in

[12] Morley, *Cobden*, II, 365.
[13] Mill, *Autobiography*, 86 *ff*.
[14] *Ibid.*, 94.

his writings the ideal hero recurred. "An indefinite yet strong sympathy with the Peasantry of the realm had been one of the characteristic sensibilities of Lord Henry at Eton. Yet a schoolboy, he had busied himself with their pastimes and the details of their cottage economy. As he advanced in life, the horizon of his views expanded with his intelligence and his experience, and . . . on the very threshold of his career, he devoted his time and thought, labor and life, to one vast and noble purpose, the elevation of the condition of the great body of the people." [15]

The future belonged to Mill and Disraeli, but in the year of the Great Exhibition, the internal economy of England belonged to Cobden. Standing there with the Duke of Wellington, he seemed to symbolize the triumph of middle class England over the eighteenth century. Working class radicalism seemed no less defeated than aristocratic privilege; Chartism was now only an unpleasant memory. Even that natural center of aristocracy, the court, had been made middle class. Gone were days when the court was only the center of the world of fashion. Scholars, scientists, men of affairs, were Albert's friends, and therefore Victoria's; the opening of the Exhibition showed royal concern for commerce and industry.

Art and science, no less than the court, were on the side of liberalism. In 1851 there appeared the first work of the young philosopher, Herbert Spencer. *Social Statics, or The Conditions Essential to Human Happiness Specified, and the First of Them Developed,* is in form as syllogistic as the writings of a medieval scholastic. The scholastic would have been horrified by the exuberant use of the argument from analogy, but Spencer was welcomed by his generation because he drew from the new science of biology seemingly irrefutable proof of the necessity for complete liberty, and the iniquity of any effort to interfere with the free operation of nature's laws. Evolution was already a word to command respect, even though Darwin's great work had not yet appeared. Spencer set out to apply evolutionary principles to the life of man in society. Life in state societies, he de-

[15] *Coningsby,* 2d ed., III, 275, 276.

clared, was the latest phase in the long evolution of man from a solitary creature through the tribe and the manor; beyond, lay the world society of the brotherhood of man, how far in the future no one could say. Man could not hasten his evolution; nature must work out her plan in her own good time. Man could, however, delay evolution by interfering with natural laws, and it was to avert this danger that Spencer was moved to write. He, and students like him, could comprehend the perfection of nature's plan, and he was distressed when he saw "some flippant red-tapist get upon his feet and tell the world how he is going to put a patch upon nature!" The arguments of the red-tapist had a specious logic, because man's mercy could so easily be aroused against nature's edicts. It was hard that a workman should starve because he had not the skill requisite for his trade; it was hard that widows and orphans should want through no fault of their own. Well, then, let the generous feed the hungry out of their charity; charity was ennobling. But let not the gentle intercourse between rich and poor be "superseded by a cold, hard lifeless mechanism, bound together by dry parchment acts and regulations." And let not men think that by their charity they could improve nature. Consider the animal world. Many worthy people were perplexed by the struggle for existence there, but it was best that old, weak, and malformed animals should be destroyed by their fellows. The unfit were thereby saved from pain, room was made for those capable of enjoying life, and "all vitiation of the race through the multiplication of its inferior samples is prevented." In human affairs the same laws were valid, at least until mankind should have become perfect. "Pervading all nature we may see at work a stern discipline, which is a little cruel that it may be very kind. . . . The poverty of the incapable, the distresses that come upon the imprudent, the starvation of the idle, and those shoulderings aside of the weak by the strong, which leave so many in shallows and in miseries, are the decrees of a large, far-seeing benevolence." To try to set aside nature's decrees by state relief was really not benevolence but cruelty, cruelty to those whose misery was prolonged, cruelty to the race, because the strong were kept from breeding by high taxes, while the weak and unfit were encouraged to breed by security.[16]

Whenever he talked of race or society, Spencer's love of analogy threatened to get the better of him, and at the end he did draw out in detail the analogy between society and the individual, the macrocosm and the microcosm. But he was careful to insist that this was only an analogy: to personify society would be to leave the way open for social control over the individual, and that was exactly what he was fighting. Government, he insisted, resulted only from man's imperfect adaptation to social life. It was necessary in this transitional stage to prevent men from injuring one another, but government must not go beyond protection. Life and property must be protected, but protective tariffs were the injury of some for the benefit of others, crutches for industries which should be trained to stand alone, just as poor relief was a crutch. Similarly, education, religion, and the protection of health—except for the suppression of nuisances—were purely private affairs with which the state should not concern itself. The race was to the strong; the strong should not be impeded by restrictions; and the weak should not be saved from the consequences of their weakness. To prevent government from overstepping its protective function, government must de democratic. "If, therefore, class-legislation is the *inevitable* consequence of class-power, there is no escape from the conclusion that the interest of the *whole* society can be secured only by giving power into the hands of the *whole* people." [17]

Spencer's freedom was too virile even for his generation. Many liberals concurred in his dislike of a state church, but few thought of actual disestablishment. On the other hand, many good liberals were distressed by the shocking ignorance of the English people as compared with the people of a country like Prussia, where state education was general; most were, like

[16] *Social Statics*, 294, 321–323.
[17] *Ibid.*, 220.

Cobden, unwilling to see state activities increased by a great educational establishment, but a ferment of discontent was at work which Spencer's syllogisms could not stop. On poor relief, liberals stopped just short of Spencer's heroic prescription: the poor were not allowed to starve, but no Englishman could have been encouraged to idleness by the kind of existence offered in a poor house of that day. In other ways, however, "red-tapists" were slowly making headway. The very efficiency of this state which liberals had created was making it difficult to confine the state to its proper "protective" function. All Englishmen thought knowledge a blessing, but the knowledge which departments of the state were publishing in severely factual and statistical Blue Books was painful to complacency. On sanitation and health; on child and female labor; on conditions in factories and mines; on education, or rather, on ignorance—everywhere, government agents were turning up facts which unpleasantly suggested the necessity of state action. As yet, the advocates of non-intervention had yielded little ground. With slight reservations they subscribed to Herbert Spencer's conviction that in the long run the remedy was not less freedom, but more. "Always towards perfection is the mighty movement—towards a complete development and a more unmixed good; subordinating in its universality all petty irregularities and fallings back, as the curvature of the earth subordinates mountains and valleys. Even in evil, the student learns to recognize only a struggling beneficence. But, above all, he is struck with the inherent sufficingness of things." [18]

The inherent sufficingness of things—that was the remarkable fact upon which Englishmen pondered in the year of the Great Exhibition. What wonders their race had accomplished in the two generations just past! As they looked back, success seemed explained by the reasonableness of Englishmen. They had not reached for the moon, tried to make men over, as Frenchmen had done at the expense of three revolutions. Neither had they

[18] *Ibid.*, 293–294.

dug in, refused to think, as people in central and eastern Europe had done, and were doing. They had been reasonable. They had searched for, and found, the laws governing the life of man in society. They had found that the sum of these laws was to leave men alone, not to interfere with the operation of nature's laws. The economists had shown that the free economic activities of individuals led to the highest possible social good. Bentham and the Utilitarians had riddled the aristocratic, paternalistic conception of the state by pointing out its consequences in terms of human unhappiness. Now Spencer and other scientists were demonstrating that evolution and progress towards the highest good were synonymous. Free instructed men would adapt themselves to their environment; adaptation meant the progressive elimination of evil and approach to perfection.

Liberty had wrought miracles in England. The rest of the world, seeing the results in terms of British wealth, power, and social peace, must in time recognize the inherent sufficingness of things, must in time break the chains which hampered human endeavor. Freedom would spread from England over all the world. The tyranny of kings, aristocrats, and priests would be broken. The oppression of subject peoples would end; every people would have a government of its own choosing, and free peoples would set up free governments. Fetters on economic life would be broken like fetters on political freedom. Every nation would make the goods it was best adapted to make, exchanging its produce for other goods produced under the most favorable possible conditions. Tennyson caught the vision better than economist or statesman:

For I dipped into the future, far as human eye could see,
Saw the Vision of the world, and all the wonder that would be;

Saw the heavens fill with commerce, argosies of magic sails,
Pilot of the purple twilight, dropping down with costly bales; . . .

Till the war-drum throbb'd no longer, and the battle flags were furl'd
In the Parliament of man, the Federation of the world.

There the common sense of most shall hold a fretful realm in awe,
And the kindly earth shall slumber, lapped in universal law. . . .

Not in vain the distance beacons. Forward, forward let us range.
Let the great world spin for ever down the ringing grooves of change.

Through the shadow of the globe we sweep into the younger day:
Better fifty years of Europe than a cycle of Cathay.

CHAPTER II

PALMERSTONIAN ENGLAND

ON THE night of June 25, 1850, the House of Commons was crowded. The occasion was a debate which, from small beginnings, had opened into a consideration of the proper bases of British foreign policy. Don Pacifico, a Portuguese Jew resident in Athens, but a British subject because of his birth in Gibraltar, had filed a claim for damages after his house had been sacked by a Greek mob. The claim was preposterously large, but it was prosecuted energetically by the foreign secretary, Lord Palmerston. Despite protests from the French and Russian governments, Greek commerce was seized and Greek ports blockaded. The House of Lords censured Palmerston's bullying tactics; Palmerston retorted by having a motion introduced in the Commons which was, in effect, an endorsement of his policy, not only in this case, but throughout his long career. Speaking in defence of the motion, Palmerston flatly asserted that Englishmen should not be forced to content themselves with what justice they could procure under the laws of the foreign country in which they might find themselves. "As the Roman, in days of old, held himself free from indignity, when he could say *Civis Romanum sum;* so also a British subject, in whatever land he may be, shall feel confident that the watchful eye and the strong arm of England, will protect him against injustice and wrong."

Britain not only had obligations to her subjects, Palmerston argued, Britain had obligations to the world. Continental Europe was just recovering from the revolutions begun two years earlier; throughout these disturbances, England had been tranquil. "While we have seen thrones shaken, shattered, levelled; institutions overthrown and destroyed—while in almost every country of Europe the conflict of civil war has deluged the land with blood, from the Atlantic to the Black Sea, from the Baltic to the Mediterranean; this country has presented a spectacle honorable to the people of England, and worthy of the admiration of mankind." Palmerston's enemies had tried to lay on him the blame for these upheavals on the Continent. Such suspicions were baseless. Revolution, as such, was repugnant to him; but revolutionists were of two kinds. Far more dangerous than those who sought to overthrow governments were those "blind-minded men, who, animated by antiquated prejudices, and daunted by ignorant apprehensions, dam up the current of human improvement." These were the true makers of revolution, because in the end the dam must break; then the flood "overthrows and levels to the earth, those very institutions which a timely application of renovating means would have rendered strong and lasting." These were the men who called the English revolutionists, and when thus accused, Englishmen could boast of the name. Opposition to reaction was the duty of Britain: duty to herself, because peace, prosperity, and progress abroad were essential if she was to enjoy these blessings herself; duty to the world, because the world could enjoy these blessings only if it followed the example of England. "We have shown that liberty is compatible with order; that individual freedom is reconcilable with obedience to the law. We have shown the example of a nation, in which every class of society accepts with cheerfulness the lot which Providence has assigned to it; while at the same time every individual of each class is constantly striving to raise himself in the social scale—not by injustice and wrong, not by violence and illegality—but by persevering good conduct, and by the steady and energetic exertion of the moral and intellectual faculties with which his Creator has endowed him." [1]

Leaders of all factions in the Commons fought through four nights against Palmerston's contention that it was the right and the duty of England to intervene in the affairs of other countries to protect British citizens and to further British ideals of good

[1] Hansard, 3d Series, CXII, 379–443.

government. Speaker after speaker contended that, in pressing by force the claims of an adventurer against a weak state, Palmerston had earned for England the reputation of a bully and had alienated France and Russia. Similarly, his general arguments for intervention were turned against him. Why was it more right for constitutional England to endeavor to spread her form of government than it was for Russia to intervene in Hungary in the sacred name of autocracy, or for the United States to intervene in Canada in the name of republicanism? Palmerston's opponents accepted as axiomatic the superiority of British institutions to those of other nations; they also assumed that British institutions would spread. But, they contended, the principle of intervention was as dangerous and fallacious in the field of foreign affairs as it was in domestic affairs. Let each nation work out its own interests, just as each Englishman was seeking to further his own interests. Sir Robert Peel, in what proved the last speech of his life, added a warning which was also a prophecy: "Beware that the time does not arrive when, frightened by your own interference, you withdraw your countenance from those whom you have excited, and leave upon their minds the bitter recollection that you have betrayed them." [2] Argument, warning, abuse proved useless; on the division, Palmerston was an easy victor. As Lady Clarendon recorded in her diary: "He has triumphed over a great mass of educated public opinion, over that mighty potentate the *Times*, over two branches of the Legislature, over the Queen and Prince and most of the Cabinet he sits in, besides all foreign nations." [3]

The Don Pacifico case showed Palmerston at his bullying worst, but his defence of himself was a complete and honest statement of his convictions. That these convictions were almost the opposite of Cobden's non-intervention is obvious. That his will, rather than the will of Cobden, directed British policy is shown by a cursory review of Palmerston's career. Born five years before the Estates General met in Paris, he held ministerial

[2] *Ibid.*, 693.
[3] Maxwell, *Clarendon*, I, 312.

posts through most of a parliamentary career of over half a century. In 1830 he abandoned the Tories and became Foreign Secretary in the Whig government. He held this office, except for a five-year interlude, until the end of 1851. Two years later he was back in the Cabinet as Home Secretary. In 1855, when he was seventy, he became Prime Minister. Out of office in 1858, he was back in the year following, not again to be dislodged until his death in October, 1865, two days before his eighty-first birthday. He retained almost to the end the lithe strength, physical and mental, which enabled him to fight through a long night session, and then saunter home in the early morning light looking fresh and free from care. Almost to the end, too, he retained that mastery over English public opinion which enabled him, as Lady Clarendon said, to defy Crown, Cabinet, and Parliament.

How, if an England such as has been described earlier really existed, was it possible to have a Prime Minister like Palmerston? An easy, but inadequate explanation, is the hold which aristocracy still had on popular loyalty. In most branches of the government, family was a valuable supplement to ability; in the foreign service, at least, family was too often a substitute for ability. Queen Victoria's private secretary described the ambassador to Prussia, Lord Augustus Loftus, as a "pompous blockhead," and a study of that gentleman's memoirs tends strongly to confirm the description, but Loftus' career did not suffer from the handicap. Prince Albert pointed out the unsatisfactory results of a diplomatic service thus recruited: "They know, generally speaking, nothing of the countries and the people among whom they live; the *exclusive* system of society, which is the fashion in England they import with them, and instead of mixing in the society of the place where they are, they associate only with one another, and with those of their own countrymen resident where they happen to be." [4] In home as well as foreign affairs, Englishmen still liked to be governed by aristocrats. Palmerston was more than willing to humor this prejudice. His government

[4] *Letters of Lady Augusta Stanley*, 82, 280.

of 1855 was so heavily weighted with titles that it occasioned the following doggerel:

Cease, ye rude and boisterous railers,
Do not dare our crew contemn;
Manned with such patrician sailors,
Our good ship the tide must stem.
A jaunty Viscount is our skipper,
A Duke and Marquis are her mates,
Three Earls do serve on board this clipper,
Four Sirs, and all of them first-rates.
Two Barons and another Viscount,
Duke Bedford's brother, and therewith
One single commoner can I count—
The lord-like looking Mr. Smith.[5]

And even the lord-like looking Mr. Smith in time was transformed into Lord Lyneden. Palmerston had every advantage an aristocrat could have. Money and a charming wife made Cambridge House a place to which most men in public life, and their wives, desired invitations. He was a peer, but an Irish peer, and therefore could sit in the House of Commons, rallying his followers and fighting his opponents, as an English peer could not. Add his love of horses and sports, and his ability to answer hecklers without standing on, or losing, his dignity, and you have an aristocrat such as few Victorian Englishmen could resist.

Closely connected with love of aristocracy, was the Englishman's dread of the logic of his own convictions. Cobden and Spencer had little difficulty demonstrating that liberty and the restricted suffrage established by the Reform Bill of 1832 were incompatible. But the "men of property and intelligence" who had the suffrage believed that security of property was the most important of all liberties. Security would be lost, they feared, if men without property—and therefore presumably without intelligence—had the right to vote. Lord Palmerston was emphatically of this conviction. So long as he held office, radical extension of the suffrage was impossible. Again and again, when

[5] Maxwell, *Smith,* II, 154.

he was attacked by radicals he was saved by conservatives who feared that if he fell, the democratic flood would sweep over England.

On the other hand, when he was attacked by conservatives, he was saved by liberals who refused to listen to Cobden's implacable logic. Peace, free trade, and constitutional government were Palmerston's objectives, and these were all good liberal principles. The difference seemed only one of method. Cobden would teach by example; Palmerston was not of a nature to allow the world to remain in ignorance if he could help it. Instead, he set himself up as the schoolmaster of Europe. In diplomatic dispatches and in public speeches he excoriated bad government and cheered peoples who were seeking to free themselves from despotic rulers. His lectures were not phrased in diplomatic or vague language. They were painfully explicit, citing guilty persons and wrong acts, and they called on public opinion, at home and abroad, to set matters right. Rulers who felt the lash of his tongue hated him; cautious colleagues and the Queen did their best to silence him. Momentarily he could be silenced, but soon he was off again, sure that he would be backed by the generous sympathies of the English people. And usually he was. A strain of missionary fervor which had survived from the Methodist and evangelical movements of the preceding century responded to Palmerston's exhortations, assuring him of a cheering audience when he struck out at despotism and oppression. Much as he hated Palmerston, Cobden was too honest to deny that he represented his countrymen: "The evil has its roots in the pugnacious, energetic, self-sufficient, foreigner-despising and pitying character of that noble insular creature, John Bull. Read Washington Irving's description of him fumbling for his cudgel always the moment he hears of any row taking place on the face of the earth, and bristling up with anger at the very idea of any other people daring to have a quarrel without first asking his consent or inviting him to take a part in it." [6]

[6] Morley, *Cobden*, II, 10.

For long, John Bull refused to see that Palmerston's diplomacy contained elements which, from the outside, seemed far from liberal. There was, first of all, a touch of the bully in Palmerston's crusading, or at least a keen eye for the cost of crusades. Against strong governments he confined himself to words, or to surreptitious encouragement of rebels. Against smaller opponents he was indeed *Jupiter Anglicanus,* as Greece discovered in the controversy over Don Pacifico's claims, as the Chinese discovered whenever trade disputes arose, as all weak countries discovered. Palmerston denied that he was a bully; he was a realist.

Here we meet the most profound difference between Palmerston and more orthodox liberals. Liberalism was a consistent body of doctrine, based on belief in beneficent natural laws which operated universally, if unevenly. In this view, England was merely the furthest advanced along a path in which all nations were walking, the path to free observance of nature's laws. Constitutional government and free trade were part of nature's plan, parts of that emancipation of men from artificial, unnatural regulation. When all peoples had recognized the necessity of submitting to nature's laws of freedom, then the world would receive its crowning boon—peace. To Palmerston, this vision of the world was Utopian. He favored peace, because strife disrupted business. He favored constitutional government, because he thought absolutism oppressive and inclined to strife. He favored free trade, because he thought it made for economic prosperity. But above all he favored vigilant defence of British interests and was sure from experience that those interests clashed with the interests of other governments and other peoples. He was enough of a liberal to believe that when such a clash occurred it originated in the short-sightedness of the opposing government; but he relied on the British fleet to correct the vision of his opponents, not on natural law. He was far from admitting that, even if the liberal program were attained, the necessity for the use of force would be ended. On the contrary, after Cobden had made a free trade treaty with France, Palmerston used the treaty as an argument for increased appropriation for defence. Free trade with England would make France richer; but it would not alter the fact that the French "hate us as a nation from the bottom of their hearts." Increased riches would merely mean more French ironclads; therefore England must be prepared. "Commercial interest is a link that snaps under the pressure of national passion." [7]

What to liberals were universal principles, were for Palmerston merely expedients which usually served the selfish national interests of England. That was the gist of the matter, and the difference explains the hatred which men like Cobden felt for him, a hatred which he reciprocated. Most Englishmen refused to see the difference: they held firmly to their principles, but with equal firmness they held to Palmerston. When foreign rulers resisted the cry for constitutional government, or foreign peoples sought to establish popular government by force; when foreign states disturbed by wars the tranquility so necessary for trade, or refused to join England in the righteous Crimean War, then Englishmen saw Satan at war with God's unalterable law. They believed, with some justice, that in all which made life comfortable, decent, humane, and kindly, they had progressed far beyond the Continent. They saw that political questions which were solved by debate and compromise in England caused violence and bloodshed on the Continent. They saw England trying to train her imperial possessions in the arts of self-government when Continental states were trying to repress their subject peoples, and to make new conquests. They saw British efforts to cut down unproductive expenditures on armaments thwarted by increases in Continental armaments. Not unnaturally they believed that what worked so well for England would work for the world; and their evangelical heritage made it seem right and proper to preach to less advanced peoples the truth England had found. The righteousness of England is easy to understand. But it is equally easy to understand why continental peoples, studying the contrast between liberal principles and

[7] Ashley, *Palmerston*, II, 224.

Palmerstonian diplomacy, should have accused Englishmen of cant.

British policy towards the German states, like British foreign policy in general, was largely a resultant of the shifting, unpredictable interaction of liberal principles and national interests; but to an unusually large extent this part of British policy showed the effects also of ignorance and prejudice. An editorial in "that mighty potentate" the London *Times* on October 20, 1860, is a fair example of the tone used in discussing German affairs. It was occasioned by the rumor that Austria and Prussia had agreed on another effort to wrest Schleswig-Holstein from the King of Denmark. Reasonable men, argued the *Times*, would realize that, now as in the past, Europe would prevent any change in the status of Schleswig-Holstein because Denmark needed these duchies to fulfill her function as guardian of the entrance to the Baltic Sea. But these were not reasonable men, they were German statesmen. "The vagaries of German policy are such that we cannot pretend to follow them. It is useless to look for profundity where, in all likelihood, there is only pedantry, or for a tangible object in what may be only a desire to carry out some dreamy historical notion. Were the ways of Germans like our ways—were they governed by practical statesmen instead of by martinets and sophists—we should fancy that they had some far-seen end in view when they thus propose to create another political complication in Europe. But, knowing what they are, we only see in their conduct another instance of that weakness and perversity which has brought on them so many misfortunes."

Englishmen denied that speech of this sort was indicative of unfriendliness towards Germans. On the contrary, the English press and statesmen like Lord Palmerston were never tired of arguing that their country and the German states were natural allies because they had common rivals in the two really great Continental states, France and Russia. France ceaselessly plotted to push her frontiers up to the Rhine; Russia ceaselessly plotted to extend her control over the Balkan provinces of Turkey. These ambitions ran counter to the interests of England and the

German states, and common interests were the most secure basis for alliance. Other ties between the two peoples were emphasized—their common Teutonic origin; the innumerable connections of Victoria and Albert with German ruling houses, particularly after the marriage between the Queen's eldest daughter, Victoria, and Prince Frederick of Prussia; the common devotion of England and Prussia to Protestantism. Consciousness of common interests seemed to Englishmen sufficient justification for criticism of their German allies. And plenty was found to criticize. Judged by the liberal standards of peace, free trade, and constitutional government, the governments of Prussia and Austria appeared stupidly reactionary, while the quarrelling, selfish, ridiculous princelings of the other German states were either shocking or amusing—here a prince trying to keep his subjects in bestial ignorance because he feared intelligent criticism; there an aging Ludwig of Bavaria causing all Europe to snicker by his amorous adventures with that very lovely, but very frail dancer, Lola Montez. Aside from Lord Palmerston, who understood everything, few Englishmen claimed to understand the vagaries of German political life; but all were appalled by the violence of politics in a region where, according to the English belief, conservatives were black reactionaries, liberals were red republicans, and everyone was more anxious to seize the territory of other countries than to strengthen his own country by constitutional reform. The British tried valiantly to bring the Germans to reason. Through regular diplomatic channels and through the family connections of Queen Victoria, a steady stream of lectures, rebukes, and threats passed from London to the German courts. The English press, particularly the *Times*, unrestrained by the conventions of diplomatic or family correspondence, showed a contempt for things German which was only slightly tempered by the hope that Germany would improve with time.

The case of Captain Macdonald, while insignificant in itself, is valuable as an illustration of the temper in which the discussion of relations with German states was carried on. In 1860 the captain ran afoul of Prussian justice, first by attempting to reserve seats in a railway carriage by placing his luggage on them, and then by resisting the guard—whether forcibly or not was disputed—who demanded that he surrender the seats. At his trial, remarks were made about the intolerable arrogance of British travellers in general, and this one in particular. In the end, the Captain was fined and put in jail for several days. The commotion in England was tremendous. In a series of vigorous leaders, the *Times* passed rapidly from the merits of the Macdonald case to a consideration of the place of Prussia in the world. "Prussia is always leaning on somebody, always getting somebody to help her, never willing to help herself; always ready to deliberate, never to decide; present in Congresses, but absent in battles; speaking and writing, never for or against, but only on, the question; ready to supply any amount of ideals or sentiments, but shy of anything that savors of the real or actual. She has a large army, but notoriously one in no condition for fighting. She is profuse in circulars and notes, but has generally a little to say for both sides. No one counts on her as a friend; no one dreads her as an enemy. How she became a great Power history tells us; why she remains so nobody can tell." England, according to the *Times*, was in a very different position. "We can fight our own battles, whether it is necessary to defend our own shores or to send 100,000 men to the other side of the earth to reconquer an insurgent province. Prussia unaided could not keep the Rhine or the Vistula for a month from her ambitious neighbors. England fought Revolutionary France for twenty years, defeating her enemies continually by land and sea; Prussia was overthrown by a war of three weeks. A good understanding between States so different in vigor and resources must be for the benefit of the weaker."

Soon the foreign office was brought in on the quarrel, and in April, 1861, Lord Robert Cecil asked in Parliament if it would not be well to notify persons contemplating travel in Prussia that "they were liable to dangers to which they were not subject in any other country in Europe." Lord Palmerston, in reply, agreed that the conduct of the Prussian officials merited "the universal indignation with which this proceeding has inspired every Englishman." To be sure, the proceedings against Captain Macdonald had been within the limits of the Prussian law. "One regrets, for the sake of the Prussians, that they should have such a law." The real sufferer was bound to be Prussia, in the end. "It is impossible to cast your eye over the face of Europe and to note the relations of the different Powers to each other without seeing that it is to the interest of Prussia to cultivate, not the friendship of the English Government only, but the good opinion and the goodwill of the English nation; and, therefore, I should say that their conduct in this affair has been that which a distinguished French diplomatist has described—it has been a blunder as well as a crime." [8]

Here again it was obvious that Englishmen felt themselves, like stern parents, harsh that they might bring improvement. Throughout the period from the Revolution of 1848 to the coming of Bismarck, the British maintained this didactic attitude, now preaching, now coercing, but always for the purpose of making good allies of the Germans. When, in 1848, violence swept over Germany, conservatives like Disraeli were horrified by the spectacle of "fifty mad professors at Frankfort" arrogating to themselves the functions of a constitutional assembly and dismissing kings and princes "as we turn away servants, and worse, without a character." Queen Victoria, staunch friend of Germany though she knew herself to be, was "*so* anxious for the fate of the poor smaller sovereigns, which it would be infamous to sacrifice." [9] Palmerston was no friend of revolution, and he was constantly fearful lest the upheavals on the continent should result in a general war, but he was not unwilling to see the rulers of the German states taught the value of timely reform. It gave him real pleasure to see reactionaries like his old enemy Metternich and the Prince of Prussia fleeing for safety to constitutional England. When, however, the professors at Frankfort abandoned

[8] *Times*, Oct. 23, 1860, *et. seq.*, particularly Nov. 1 and Nov. 6; Hansard, 3d Series, CLXII, 1176–1181, 1187–1189.

[9] Monypenny and Buckle, *Disraeli*, I, 994; *Letters of Queen Victoria*, 1st Series, II, 206.

the solid ground of constitutional reform in the German states for visionary plans of uniting these states into an empire, he lost interest: the dream of a united Germany was, he told the Prussian Ambassador, only a plaything. Indifference turned to anger when the Frankfort Parliament commissioned the Prussian army to wrest Schleswig-Holstein from the King of Denmark. Palmerston did not deny that Danish rule in the two duchies had been harsh and unpopular; he would have applauded a rising of the people in the duchies for the purpose of securing popular government; but for badly governed Prussia to invade the duchies in the name of German nationalism seemed to him merely to invent a new name for the old Prussian habit of taking other people's property. The duchies formed a peculiarly important piece of property, situated as they were at the base of the Danish peninsula which controlled the entrance to the Baltic. Free access to the Baltic was, he argued, a vital British interest, and if the duchies were transferred from weak Denmark to strong Prussia, England might some day find the Baltic closed to her ships. Therefore, Palmerston felt justified in intervening with characteristic vigor; after long negotiations, a conference at London confirmed the King of Denmark in his possession of Schleswig and Holstein.

This failure ruined the prestige of the Frankfort Parliament, and German nationalists angrily blamed England for the failure of their plans for a unified empire. "Our only natural friend has acted as an enemy bent upon our destruction," lamented Baron Stockmar, a German liberal and an admirer of England.[10] Victoria was no less vehement in her denunciation of Palmerston's policy, and contrasted his quite unneutral aid to Italians who rebelled against their Austrian ruler with his hostility to German nationalism. Palmerston shrugged these protests aside. He was not, he told the Queen, minister for the Germanic Confederation; he was an English minister, and beyond that he was a liberal. He had been willing to aid Italians who were trying to shake off the incorrigibly bad government of Austria, because he

[10] Gooch, *Russell*, II, 32.

was an enemy of bad government everywhere. In Germany, he argued, the revolutionists had been seeking, not liberal reform, but the phantom of unity, while the governments of Austria and Prussia had been fighting for nothing except ascendancy over the minor states. He would have welcomed "a German Union embracing all the smaller states, with Prussia at its head, and in alliance with Austria as a separate Power." Prussia, however, had let the chance slip and had made opposition from other powers inevitable by trying to steal Schleswig-Holstein. "Her course has been indeed, dishonest, inconsistent, and irresolute and weak." The inevitable result was humiliating failure; if Palmerston had contributed to that failure, he had done so only because British interests dictated opposition to Prussian landgrabbing.[11]

After the Revolution of 1848 the German states became once more, in the English view, minor but unruly actors in the drama of European politics. Wars with China, the Crimean War, the Sepoy Rebellion, the approach of civil war in the United States, the supposed ambition of Napoleon III to emulate the imperial conquests of his great uncle—such topics, and mounting prosperity at home, filled the English horizon. Their minds occupied with more important business, neither journalists nor statesmen had leisure to revise the picture of things German formed before and during the revolutionary years. Monotonously, the old themes were repeated: England needed strong German states as bulwarks against French and Russian aggression; the German states could not be strong until they accepted liberal ideals of government. When Cavour, in alliance with Napoleon III, defeated Austria in 1859 and began the unification of Italy, Palmerston rejoiced that Italy could now have liberal government and that Austria could now devote all her strength to the task of opposing the Russians. When William I of Prussia affirmed at his coronation in 1861 that he held his power by divine right, the *Times* expostulated against this reactionary doctrine so vio-

[11] *Letters of Queen Victoria,* 1st Series, II, 296–298, 328–330; Ashley, *Palmerston,* I, 242–244.

lently that Palmerston, at the Queen's command, was forced to ask the editor to moderate his language. Delane agreed "to give the Prussians a respite from that most cruel of all afflictions—good advice"; but he thought this promise consonant with a warning to King William a few days later that English aid to Prussia against France would not be forthcoming unless the King realized that liberalism was the only form of government compatible with orderly progress.[12] The obstinate refusal of Germans to realize that the Schleswig-Holstein question had been settled once and for all was a perennial source of irritation to Englishmen. In 1863, when discussion of the duchies seemed to portend some sort of action, Lord Palmerston thought a clear warning in order. On July 23 he told Parliament that, in his belief, if any attempt were made to overthrow the rights, or to interfere with the independence of Denmark, "those who made the attempt would find in the result, that it would not be Denmark alone with whom they would have to contend." His warning, apparently, was generally approved; at least there was little dissent.

In July, 1862, the Prussian Ambassador in Paris, Otto von Bismarck, wrote to his friend the Prussian war minister, Albrecht von Roon: "I have just returned from London. There people are very much better informed about China and Turkey than about Prussia. Loftus must write even more foolishness to his minister than I had supposed."[13] Loftus' dispatches were not penetrating, but he cannot be blamed for an ignorance of things German which was almost universal. In part, the ignorance is explained by the apparent weakness of the German states: the Englishman did not feel it worth while to seek to understand a people for whom he had very little respect. The inveterate habit of taking English standards as the norm was also a contributing factor: as the *Times* said over and over, German ways are not our ways; since English ways were good, it followed that Ger-

[12] *Times,* Oct. 22, Nov. 4, 1861; *Letters of Queen Victoria,* 1st Series, III, 588.

[13] Bismarck, *Ges. Werke,* XIV, 599.

man ways could not be good. Dislike of the Prussian government made it natural to ignore the innumerable ways in which the Prussian bureaucracy furthered the welfare of the people. Cobden's appreciation of the superior quality of popular education in Prussia, for instance, was shared only by a few educational reformers; most Englishmen saw only the state interference with the individual which such an educational establishment entailed. Again, Cobden could see that the Prussian customs union, the Zollverein, had immeasurably forwarded the economic life of Germany by sweeping away internal tariff barriers, and would tend to promote political unity under the leadership of Prussia; but Palmerston regarded the Zollverein as evidence of German economic backwardness because its mildly protective duties hampered imports from England. In countless other ways, insular self-satisfaction was a barrier to understanding.

It is significant, however, that insularity was not an insuperable barrier to an understanding of French ways of thought and action, in spite of the tradition of political rivalry, even of hostility, which separated England from France. Beneath the Gallic froth, there was something substantial about the French; but the stolid German seemed nebulous at best, and usually he was simply boring. A few men at the universities and a few writers like Carlyle and John Stuart Mill kept at the task of trying to understand what the Germans were saying; but it is significant that, almost without exception, these were men who were losing, or had never had any confidence in the atomistic individualism and the facile rationalism of the Liberal Economists and Utilitarians. Most Englishmen of the decade after 1851 were far from losing confidence, and although they were willing, as the *Times* did in a gracious mood, to speak of Prussia as "the most active laboratory of thought," they were more likely to characterize that thought as pedantry and sophistry. Palmerston's ridiculing disbelief in German nationalism reflected the Englishman's embarrassment in face of the violent mystical language of thwarted German patriotism. Not only was the Englishman unable to understand these emotional outbursts; he was half-afraid of them. And to hide his embarrassed uneasiness, he took the easy refuge of ridicule.

Such ridicule seemed safe in 1862. Never did the power of England seem more secure. Since the middle of the century, indices of production and trade had mounted. Russian ambitions in the Near East had been thwarted by the Crimean War; bad Austrian rule in Italy had been largely ended with the friendly help of England; across the ocean, the vulgar republicanism of the American Union was meeting its logical nemesis in the dissolution of civil war; imperial France, flushed with victory in Italy, had sought to challenge British sea power by the building of ironclads, but Lord Palmerston had been prompt to meet the challenge by increased appropriations for the navy and for coast defence. Cobden, still fighting valiantly to depose the old Premier, tried arguments calculated to move a nation of business men. He reviewed the bellicose career of this supposedly liberal statesman, and drew up the balance sheet: "Taking into account his Chinese wars, his Afghan, his Persian war; his expeditions here, there, and everywhere; his fortification scheme—which I suppose we must now accept with all the consequences of increased military expenditures—the least I can put down the noble Lord to have cost us is 100,000,000 pounds sterling. Now, with all his merits, I think he is very dear at the price." [14] This argument, like all earlier arguments, was unavailing. No less unavailing was Cobden's truly liberal proposal to avoid a naval race with France by an agreement for the limitation of armaments. With the approbation of the House, Palmerston rebuffed the suggestion. "I think that any British Government would long pause and hesitate before it entered into any agreement with foreign countries for limiting the amount of force, naval or military, which this country ought to maintain. We should judge of that amount according to the circumstances of the moment." [15] Now, as earlier, Englishmen preferred to dilute the wine of liberalism with Palmerstonian concern for national interest.

[14] *Speeches,* II, 262.
[15] *Annual Register,* 1861, p. 94.

CHAPTER III

THE GERMAN SEARCH FOR UNITY

"TO GERMANY!—in science and art, in literature and culture, a star of the first magnitude among the nations of the world. To Germany!—destined to become the richest land on the continent of Europe through its natural resources, the industry of its people, and a wise commercial policy. To Germany!—called to become the foremost guarantor of European peace through unity and internal development. To Germany! To our great and glorious, our common and beloved Fatherland!" A proud toast, but how far from reality it seemed when proposed by the Württemberg economist, Friedrich List, in 1844. He was speaking in Vienna, and, recalling the days of his childhood when Vienna had been the seat of the Holy Roman Emperor, he prophesied that imperial Austria would lead in the national development of Germany. As a prophet of a Germany united under Austrian leadership, he had the map against him: less than a third of the Austrian Empire, in territory and population, was included in the German Confederation, and of the twelve million Austrians in the Confederation, almost a half were Slavs. In these circumstances could Austria hope, or even wish, to take the lead in furthering German nationalism? As a prophet, too, he had the great Austrian statesman, Prince Metternich, against him. Words like common Fatherland and national development left Metternich cold; he was, first of all, the servant of Imperial Austria, and beyond that he was a good European. The Confederation as it stood was close to his ideal of good government. To him, it was the nucleus of a European federation of states, all governed by enlightened aristocrats like himself, all seeing as their greatest task the preservation of European culture against the disruptive forces of revolutionary radicalism, including List's vaunted nationalism. Development was to him a chimera. There was a right order of human relations, aristocratic guidance of the ignorant, heedless masses. The alternative was decay leading to barbarism and chaos. The business men who listened to List might applaud, but all the forces of a state of forty millions were against his vision of the future Germany.

For different reasons, but no less vigorously, the rulers of the other German great power, Prussia, fought against the fatherland of List's dreams. Twelve of the sixteen million inhabitants of Prussia lay within the Confederation, but the fact that East Prussia and parts of Posen were kept outside, was symbolic of Prussia's ambition to be considered one of the great European powers and not merely a German state. This craving for recognition as the equal of states like France and Russia was a weakness upon which Metternich skilfully played to divert Prussian attention from the tempting possibility of replacing Austria as the leading German state. Despite disparity of numbers, and therefore of potential power, Prussia was in a strong position to claim leadership in Germany. When, at the Congress of Vienna, Austria exchanged what was later to become Belgium for control over northern Italy, she implicitly gave up also the claim to be the champion of Germany against French aggression. Prussia had reluctantly stepped into the rôle vacated, taking over provinces on the Rhine as a base for defence against France. Split by these additions into two parts separated by other German states, Prussia of necessity was driven to seek some means of consolidating her domains. A beginning had been made by the Prussian bureaucracy in the Zollverein, a customs union which, beginning with free trade between the various provinces of Prussia, had grown as early as 1834 to include all of southern, and most of northern Germany. Thereafter, the territories within the Zollverein became increasingly an economic unit. Economic unity suggested the possibility of political unity, either by the absorption of the lesser Zollverein states into Prussia, or by a federal union from which Austria would be excluded. King Frederick

William IV of Prussia was not a man to further the realization of either possibility. He believed in German nationalism, but in his mystical imagination, the Germany of the future was a revived Holy Roman Empire, headed by the Habsburgs, with the Hohenzollerns as chief vassals and military commanders, and with the other German princes as lesser satellites around the imperial throne. Furthermore, Frederick William and the men who advised him were no less convinced than Metternich of the necessity of a united conservative front against revolutionary radicalism, although their conservatism was tinged with a romantic religious fervor which Metternich, the cosmopolitan rationalist, was unable to understand.

Conservatism, reverence for the Habsburgs as the traditional rulers of Germany, dependence on Austrian aid to secure recognition as a great power, all were guarantees that "upstart" Prussia would not renew the career of conquest in Germany which had raised her from insignificance. Metternich had one further guarantee against a revival of the expansionist tradition of Frederick the Great: the jealous sensibilities of the smaller German states, the "third Germany." In numbers the smaller states had a larger aggregate population than either Prussia or Austria possessed within the Confederation—something less than twenty million, as against twelve million each for the larger powers—but these numbers were divided among more than thirty states of varying sizes. With a sure instinct, the lesser princes realized that their independence was menaced by traditionally ambitious Prussia rather than by satiated Austria. In any conflict between Vienna and Berlin, Metternich could always count on decisive support in the Diet at Frankfort.

The map, and the statesmen who controlled the map, made the dream of a united Germany seem destined to remain a dream. But almost two score political divisions, including two great powers whose territory and interests lay partly within, partly without the Confederation, did not make up the sum of German disunity. Half of the population of the Confederation was Catholic, half was Protestant, and religious differences were keenly felt in the home land of the Reformation. Economic and social life was likewise full of extremes. Austrian economy was almost completely separated from that of the other states. Outside of the Austrian Empire, three-quarters of the people lived by agriculture, but farming east of the Elbe meant great estates owned by feudal lords, the Junkers, and worked by semi-servile and landless laborers; south and west of the Elbe was a land of independent peasant proprietors where even the farm laborer usually had a small plot of land. Most cities were still small, semi-rural; and most industries were still in the hands of middle class masters who had the technical skill and education combined with the narrowness of aspiration and outlook which characterized guild life in earlier centuries. Along the Baltic and the North Sea, the old Hanse towns preserved the traditions of the age of city states into the age of great commercial states, and struggled vainly to hold their own in competition with commercial cities backed by national power. In the Rhineland, Silesia, and a few scattered cities, the new techniques of large-scale commerce and industry were violently disrupting the old local economy. The coming of the Industrial Revolution in some ways made for greater unity, since the new capitalists were enthusiastic supporters of the Zollverein and of railroad building. By the middle of the century, non-Austrian Germany had a greater railway mileage than France; and as earlier means of transport had been few and bad, the railway was a uniting force no less obviously than the Zollverein. On the other hand, the social tensions which were everywhere the corollary of industrialism, developed more quickly and more acutely than in western Europe. The time element is important. Britain was industrialized slowly, over the course of a century; industry came to Germany in a rush. The painless evolution, the gradual assimilation of new to old, which seemed so natural to the English, was impossible in Germany, where the contrast between the still powerfully entrenched old, and the aggressively new economy was too obvious to be ignored or obscured.

Such was the condition of Germany in the middle of the nineteenth century: interest fought against interest, class against class, state against state, section against section, and Catholic against Protestant. It was obvious that the country could not remain thus distracted. To Englishmen, it seemed that improvement could come only when reaction gave place to liberalism: so long as the pall of repression hung over Germany, so long would Germany continue divided and weak; liberty alone would bring harmony. To Metternich, on the other hand, the failure of aristocratic federalism to bring peace did not suggest the possibility that his principles of government were at fault. Instead, he blamed the depraved nature of man, now, as always, reluctant to see the right. In the resistance to his will he saw at work the forces of revolution which, born in France, had found a new home in England. To the English belief that freedom was the great law of nature, he opposed the principle of order as the only right foundation of government.

Freedom or order, liberalism or conservatism—these seemed the great alternatives between which Germans, like all other men, must choose. Liberals and conservatives were both convinced that there was one fixed, unchanging natural law for mankind: freedom or order, one must triumph over the whole world. Germans themselves thought of the issue in these terms, and those who called themselves conservatives looked to Austria and Russia for support, while those who called themselves liberals hoped for aid from England or France. Increasingly, however, these great battle cries took on a distinctive, peculiarly German meaning, which confused not only those accustomed to the usual connotations of the words, but even Germans themselves. Slowly, haltingly, Germans were developing a common way of thinking.

The process went back at least to the French Revolution. Even before 1789, opposition to bureaucratic government and craving for unity were beginning to appear. With the outbreak of revolution in France, reformers sought to realize their objectives by appealing to the rights of man and of the citizen as established by nature's laws. From the Rhineland, always open to French ideas, the revolutionary enthusiasm spread like a great wave, threatening to engulf privileges, states, and monarchs alike. Conservatives vainly sought to dam the flood by appealing to history and tradition against the levelling arguments of revolutionary natural law—until Napoleon came to their aid. French ideas, like everything French, became odious as the conqueror shuffled and reshuffled the frontiers of central Europe, as he bowled over the armies of Austria and Prussia, and as he herded populations like cattle. From the humiliating impotence of the present, Germans turned to the history of their past for consolation, and for guidance in the task of building a new and greater Germany. Enough of talk about the contractual basis of sovereignty, and about the limitations set by natural law on the power of the state; how, out of anarchy, could the Germans build themselves a state strong enough to confront other states on an equal footing of power? Back into history the Germans probed, seeking to find that which gave them a character distinct from other peoples—the German Volksgeist. Back into history the Germans probed, seeking to find there the pattern for the state which would be the embodiment of the Volksgeist.

History, a willing guide, showed what they sought. History showed that there was indeed a Volksgeist, a peculiar national character for every people, a character stamped indelibly on every individual of each nation, a character basically unchanged throughout history. The concept of humanity receded into relative insignificance; the characteristics of men as members of the human race were overshadowed by the characteristics of men as members of a national group. The individual himself receded into relative insignificance; his peculiarities were overshadowed by the peculiarities stamped on him by the fact that he was part of the group. Ever more portentously, as the pages of history were scrutinized, loomed up the group, marking off the men of one nation from the men of other nations, and uniting the individuals of each nation into a collective personality no less real and living than the individuals who, in the past or present, combined to form the group. Fascinated by their discovery, students pushed on to the analysis of group personality, from the family through all forms of collective activity. Churches, universities, group personalities were seen everywhere, each with its own law of life; but towering above them all was the personality of the nation, the Volksgeist, which included and directed all lesser personalities down to the individual. The failure of Germany to obtain political unity in 1815 merely intensified the search for spiritual unity. Savigny traced the expression which the Volksgeist found in legal institutions; the brothers Grimm searched for the national spirit in folklore and the history of language; Freytag brought the national spirit into tales of domestic life; Stein began the great collection of source material, the *Monumenta Germaniae Historia,* which was to lay bare the greatness of the German spirit in centuries past. To art, to literature, to law, to every part of life was brought the touchstone of the Volksgeist, and there the trouble began. The craze for the pure German spirit repudiated everything foreign, and brought much of the past into violent controversy. Was the Reformation the affirmation or the denial of the German spirit? No matter which way the question was answered, a large part of the German people stood beyond the pale. Was the medieval Empire an expression of the civilizing German spirit, or was it a Latin corruption? Historians battled over the answer. Was Austria a German power, raising Magyar, Slav, and Roumanian to the German level, or was Austria corrupted by her cosmopolitan population?

This question reached to the heart of the problem of the state, the German state of the future. The apologists of the settlement of 1815 tried vainly to demonstrate that the Confederation was the embodiment of the Volksgeist. In increasing numbers, and with increasing vigor, men turned away from the Diet at Frankfort and asked of history: what is the nature of the state in general, and what should be the nature of the German state? Again, history was explicit in furnishing general principles, but gave no one answer regarding the application of these principles. The state, according to the German reading of history, was the personification of the national spirit, catching up and directing the salutary elements of national life, suppressing elements which weakened or polluted the national character. Like all life—and the state was no less alive than the individuals over which it held sway—the state sought to live and to grow. Therefore it must be strong to survive in competition with other states. More and more the power of the state filled the vision of Germans, until in many cases it was hard to discover that the activities of the state had any purpose other than to further the accumulation of physical power for the battle with other states. History became a great battleground whereon states fought for room and for freedom to live and grow, each contestant showing the moral and material power of the community it personified, victory going to that state which personified the highest, strongest national spirit. In their imagination, Germans saw their still unborn state as the leader of the other nations; but when they tried to trace the lineaments of their vision, discord appeared. Was there to be a "great Germany" including Austria, or a "little Germany" linked only by an alliance with the Habsburg empire; was there to be a confederation, a federal state, or a unitary state; if a confederacy or a federal union, would power be divided among Austria, Prussia, and the third Germany of the smaller states; if a unitary state without Austria, would Prussia be absorbed into the rest of Germany, or would Prussia conquer the smaller states?

After a half century of debate the search for the German Volksgeist and the German state seemed merely to have added new occasions for strife. And yet in that search the Germans were developing a common set of values, values very different to those which underlay the political ideals of conservatives like Metternich or liberals like Cobden. Men like Cobden and Metternich differed on most questions, but on one point they agreed: human life was governed by uniform laws which were applicable to all men in all times; it was on the provisions of nature's laws that they disagreed. Germans increasingly turned for guidance, not to natural laws discoverable by human reason, but to history. In history they found no evidence of uniformity; instead, they found clear evidence of infinite variety. No two men were alike; no two groups of men were alike; no two periods of history were alike. Every man, every group, every age had a distinct character and its own conditions of life. Every man should try to understand himself; but he must not think that in doing so he was understanding mankind. The people of every nation should try to understand their own nation; but they must not think that in understanding their own national life they were understanding all nations. To prescribe uniformity of political institutions for all peoples, whether conservative or liberal institutions, was an attempt to put into a strait-jacket the rich and variegated life of spontaneously growing organisms. Political institutions, like all parts of national life, were an expression of the national character, a character produced by the past history and the present environmental circumstances of a people. Proud of their discovery of the teaching of history, Germans tossed aside natural law. Law was a safe guide for the study of science; there was uniformity in the physical world, and therefore fixed laws of causation were operative. But in the infinitely varied, ever-changing world of man there was no uniformity. There history was the only safe guide. Out of a study of the history of a man, an institution, a group personality like the state, might emerge some clues from which future history could be imaginatively and approximately foretold.

History is the traditional ally of conservatives; reverence for the past puts advocates of change on the defensive. It is not strange, therefore, that German conservatives increasingly justified themselves by appealing to history rather than to Metternich's "natural" order of society and government. Around every court clustered historians who, by their learned defence of things as they were, justified Karl Marx's description of the German historical school: "a school which stamps every cry of the serf against the knout as treasonable once the knout is an ancient knout, an indigenous knout, an historical knout; a school to whom history reveals, like the God of Israel to his servant Moses, only its posterior side." [1] Even through the writings of the greatest and most generous of German historians, Leopold von Ranke,

[1] S. Hook, *From Hegel to Marx*, 141.

ran a querulous note of warning against innovation. In his masterly essay on *The Great Powers*, the French Revolution was depicted as a monstrous disturbance of the historical process, an upheaval which had temporarily united the European nations into liberal and conservative alliances; in the end, however, the peculiar needs of each state would reassert their strength, and European history would again become the biography of states, each seeking to live and to grow in accordance with its own law of life.[2] Like a careful gardener, he scrutinized German history, searching for foreign growths which might choke the flowers of native culture. His activities, and those of his colleagues and students, seemed laudatory to the ruling powers, but actually the attempt to use history as a weapon against "the revolution" proved a dangerous expedient. Once the evidence of tradition was accepted, even the most resolute opponents of change were forced to admit that the royal will was restricted by historical precedent. When in 1837 the constitution of Hanover was set aside by royal decree, the "Seven of Göttingen" who preferred exile to silent acquiescence included the historian Dahlmann and the brothers Grimm, whose lives had been devoted to the study of the German spirit in history. It was even possible to argue that if peasant and burgher, as well as prince and bureaucrat, shared in a common tradition, they should also share in the government which protected and furthered this tradition. The demand for popular government, unable to appeal to the natural rights of man, appealed instead to German freedom. German nationalism, also, could appeal to history against the particularist constitution of the Confederation. Except for Austria and Prussia, few of the German states had a past which could hold the loyalty of their subjects. When the German people had turned to the past for consolation during the Napoleonic invasions, what held their imaginations was the glory and the strength of their race—its imperial strength in the age of Charlemagne, its command of the sea in the age of the Hanseatic League, its coloniz-

[2] *Historisch-politische Zeitschrift*, II, 1–52, particularly 43 *ff*.

ing and crusading activities in the age of the Teutonic Knights —and what they looked for in the future was a revival of glory and strength.

The exact nature of the Volksgeist might be disputed, but beyond dispute was a national spirit which animated and united all Germans. The exact nature of the state which would embody the German spirit was a matter of dispute, but the Confederation was not that state. These convictions increasingly pulled German conservatism out of the orbit of Metternich's static, aristocratic, and cosmopolitan conservatism. Frederick William's dream of a revived Holy Roman Empire seemed a crazy whim to the rationalist mind of Metternich. Crazy the dream undoubtedly was, but at least it was an attempt to meet the popular demands. However, to revive an empire which for centuries had been the symbol of German impotence was not the way to placate the demand for a strong state, and to revive the medieval estates was not the way to placate the demand for popular participation in government. All this Frederick William discovered when he tried to create a Prussian diet on medieval lines in 1847: the members of the diet speedily showed that they were not content to be humble petitioners for the favor of a monarch who ruled by divine right. Disillusioned, the King sent them home. His experiment had shown consciousness of the demand for a change in German political life; it seemed to show also that conservatism was unable to satisfy or to control the forces making for change.

Just as German conservatives found it hard to be good conservatives and good Germans, so liberals found it hard to reconcile liberty and nationalism. As liberals, they looked for guidance to France and England. In the Rhineland, where the middle class was numerous and wealthy, the revolutionary program of the rights of man had many adherents. More aristocratic liberals took England as a model, because in England liberalism had proved compatible with aristocracy. Moreover, the English were a Teutonic people, and in British power the greatness of Teutonic genius was demonstrated. The cosmopolitanism which had covered Germany with French châteaux and English gardens in the eighteenth century found expression in plans to import English or French institutions; but now foreign influence had to fight against newly awakened national pride. It was hard to admire French ideas when a French attempt to seize the Rhine was hourly feared. It seemed undignified to glory in racial kinship with the English, when English contempt for German weakness was so obvious. "Whenever I talk with Englishmen about my fatherland," complained Heinrich Heine, "I notice with deep humiliation that the hate which they feel for the French is more honorable to the latter than the impertinent affection which they bestow upon us Germans and for which we must thank some shortcoming in our worldly power or our intelligence. They love us because of our maritime weakness which prevents any fear of commercial rivalry. They love us because of our political *naïveté* which they hope to exploit in the old way in case of a war with France." [3] Alongside the old generous admiration for the power and freedom of England there began a tendency to deprecate, to find fault, to look for some source of weakness. The rather ignoble basis of this abuse was exposed with delightful simplicity by Moritz Arndt, who concluded a tirade against British "jealousy" of Germany with the envious cry: "If only we were, where you are!" [4]

National pride fought against cosmopolitanism, liberal as well as conservative. A more important element in the decline of French and English influence was the fact that western liberalism was hard to adapt to German conditions. Western liberals had only one ambition: to break down the restrictions and the privileges sanctioned by states which were controlled by agrarian aristocrats. This ambition had been realized in France by breaking the power of the aristocracy in the name of human equality, and in England by asserting the right of the individual to freedom from state control. German liberals set themselves a more difficult task. They wished to obtain freedom from the police state,

[3] *Lutezia,* August 20, 1846.
[4] Muncker, p. 160.

but they also wished to create a powerful national state. They were nationalists as well as liberals, and the two parts of their program were hard to reconcile. Englishmen had so far been able to reconcile individual freedom and a powerful state by cheering impartially for Cobden and Palmerston. In Germany the foundation for liberty and power was still to be laid, and whether both could rest on one foundation remained to be proved. In any case, the foundation must be German; of that patriots were convinced.

Of the many ideal plans for a strong and liberal Germany, the most coherent and important was evolved by Friedrich List. Born in 1789 in the south German state of Württemberg, the son of a prosperous tanner, List early imbibed the nationalism of Napoleonic Germany, as well as the principles of constitutional government and of the emancipation of commerce and industry from bureaucratic control which were common to sons of the middle class in all western European countries. When Württemberg experimented briefly with constitutionalism after the fall of Napoleon, List was given a government post and a professorship at Tübingen. Reaction came swiftly, and he fell into disfavor because of his tirades against the Württemberg civil service and his "disloyal" advocacy of a German customs union. He was deprived of his positions, imprisoned, and finally exiled in 1825. After wandering through France and England, he migrated to the United States. There, as throughout his life, he threw himself into political and economic controversies with all the vehement self-assertiveness of the small man. By 1831 he was back in Germany again, protected against disturbance by his title of United States consul at Leipzig, but no less the agitator than before his exile. In 1841 he set down the essence of his voluminous writings in the book which is to German economic history what Adam Smith's *Wealth of Nations* is to England—*The National System of Political Economy*.

List intended the National System to be a refutation of Adam Smith, or rather a demonstration that British advocacy of free trade was a plot to delude other nations. England was, he contended, an example to other less advanced nations, but what should be studied and copied was the process by which she had risen to preëminence, not the false explanation of her greatness given by Smith. "Any nation which by means of protective duties and restrictions on navigation has raised her manufacturing power and her navigation to such a degree of development that no other nation can sustain free competition with her, can do nothing wiser than to throw away these ladders to her greatness, to preach the benefits of free trade, and to declare in penitent tones that she has hitherto wandered in the paths of error, and has now for the first time succeeded in discovering the truth." To such power England had attained: in glowing terms List set forth the evidences of greatness, not merely in finance, commerce, and industry, but in political, moral, and intellectual development. "She has become an example and a pattern to all nations—in internal and in foreign policy, as well as in great inventions and enterprises of every kind; in perfecting industrial processes and means of transport, as well as in the discovery and bringing into cultivation uncultivated lands, especially in the acquisition of the natural riches of tropical countries, and in the civilization of barbarous races or such as have retrograded into barbarism."

The problem of economic science, according to List, was to discover how other nations could be raised to a comparable level of civilization, wealth, and power. Smith had not solved the problem; instead, he had claimed universal applicability for principles which were only adapted to the mature economy of England. If the rest of the world was seduced into accepting the régime of laissez-faire, strong British industries would crush all opposition and turn the whole world into a colonial dependency, a source from which raw materials would be drawn, a market to which manufactures would be sent.[5] The error of the "cosmopolitical" school was to see only the material interests of individuals and of humanity as a whole, forgetting that individuals were united, and humanity was divided, into nations. "Between each individual and entire humanity, however, stands

[5] List, *The National System of Political Economy*, 40, 293–297.

The Nation, with its separate territory; a society which, united by a thousand ties of mind and of interests, combines into one independent whole, which recognizes the law of right for and within itself, and in its united character is still opposed to other societies of a similar kind in their national liberty, and consequently can only under the existing conditions of the world maintain self-existence and independence by its own power and resources. As the individual chiefly obtains by means of the nation and in the nation mental culture, power of production, security, and prosperity, so is the civilization of the human race only conceivable and possible by means of the civilization and development of the individual nation." [6]

Here we have once more the poignant German preoccupation with the national state pushing aside the claims of individualism and cosmopolitanism. Here we have also the German rebellion against natural laws and trust in history as a guide; at every point List buttressed his argument by appealing to the teachings of history. Here, finally, we have the German exaltation of power. Not the wealth of nations, but national power was the object of List's search. "Power is of more importance than wealth because a nation, by means of power, is enabled not only to open up new productive sources, but to maintain itself in possession of former and of recently acquired wealth, and because the reverse of power—namely, feebleness—leads to the relinquishment of all that we possess, not of acquired wealth alone, but of our powers of production, of our civilization, of our freedom, nay, even of our national independence, into the hands of those who surpass us in might, as is abundantly attested by the history of the Italian republics, of the Hanseatic League, of the Belgians, the Dutch, the Spaniards, and the Portuguese." [7]

As a liberal, List was at pains to insist that "history contains no record of a rich, commercial, and industrial community that was not at the same time in the enjoyment of freedom," but to him

[6] *Ibid.,* 141.
[7] *Ibid.,* 37, 38.

freedom was a means, not an end in itself.[8] The end was national power, and power was fed by other means as well, means which an English liberal would have thought incompatible with liberty. It was not merely that List advocated protective tariffs as a means of stimulating commerce and industry; protection was only one of a multitude of ways in which the state must interfere with the individual. Everything in the national society—art, literature, morals, and religion, as well as economic enterprise—had the capacity to strengthen or weaken national power. Therefore, he argued, they must all be guided and controlled, here encouraged, there checked. But was not this the antithesis of freedom? List thought not. In the first place, he believed that state guidance was only a transient phase; when a nation had reached economic, and therefore cultural maturity, when commerce and industry were well established, then free enterprise would best serve the national interest. During the transition from a purely agricultural economy to an economy in which commerce and industry had become firmly rooted, collective action was indeed essential; but the objective was to preserve the greatest of all forms of freedom, national independence. Moreover, List contended, oppression was impossible if social control was exercised by the people as a whole, through a popular government.

Against those who would claim that he had sacrificed liberty on the altar of power, List cited the history of England. In the middle ages, Britain had been little more than a colonial outpost of commercial and industrial states like the Hanseatic League and Venice. Then, beginning with the Tudors, national power had been mobilized and strengthened by regulatory legislation. Finally, in the nineteenth century, England was taking off her protective armor. From insignificance, the island had risen to be the greatest and freest nation in the world. Undoubtedly many elements had brought about the change, but undoubtedly a paternalistic commercial system had been one of

[8] *Ibid.*, 89.

the most important elements. England had shown the way in which the other nations would advance.

Germany, in List's view, was just entering on the stage in which commerce and industry must be fostered by a vigilant state. Potentially, Germany had all the elements necessary to become a leader among the nations of the world: a large, industrious, purposeful, and cultivated population, rich natural resources, and highly developed agriculture. How could these potentialities be realized? List attempted to project the lines of German evolution into the future. The most pressing need was the extension of the Zollverein to its "natural" limits by the inclusion, not only of the north German states, but of Belgium, Holland, Switzerland, and Denmark as well! Defending the inclusion of Holland and Denmark, he argued that Germany would "at once obtain what it is now in need of, namely, fisheries and naval power, maritime commerce and colonies. Besides, both these nations belong, as respects their descent and whole character, to the German nationality. The burden of debt with which they are oppressed is merely a consequence of their unnatural endeavor to maintain themselves as independent nationalities." The next step was to transform the enlarged Zollverein into a political unit, fusing "representative institutions with the existing monarchical, dynastic, and aristocratic interests, so far as these are compatible with one another." [9] Finally, in order to obtain secure access to raw materials, and to find a home under the national flag for the thousands of Germans who emigrated every year, colonies must be obtained. In addition to the Dutch colonies, List cast longing eyes on Central and South America, on the Balkans and Asia Minor, even as far afield as New Zealand and Australia.[10]

In his other writings List showed himself to be fully conscious of the internal obstacles to the realization of his dream of a future Germany. Nationalism would, he felt, overcome these in time. More dangerous was another obstacle which most of his

[9] *Ibid.*, 143, 332.
[10] *Ibid.*, 344–349.

countrymen still failed to take sufficiently into account—the opposition of the other states of Europe. He did not believe Germany could win out against concerted opposition from abroad, and this, it appears, was the fear which finally broke his fighting spirit. In the *National System* he elaborately explored one way of escape, a continental coalition based on the need of a common defence against the overwhelming power of England. "That the idea of this Continental system will ever recur, that the necessity of realizing it will the more powerfully impress itself on the Continental nations in proportion as the preponderance of England in industry, wealth, and power further increases, is already very clear, and will continually become more evident." [11] A Württemberger could not long believe, however, that France would be content to see the mouths of the Rhine in German hands. In 1846, List appeared in London with another solution, an alliance between England and Germany. In a long memorandum which was submitted to Peel and Palmerston, List argued that these two nations of the same race were natural allies. Germany, still far less developed than England, hoped for English guidance and assistance in the development of a national constitutional government. On the other hand, Britain needed German assistance against French and Russian ambitions. The one obstacle to cordial alliance was the unremitting opposition of England to the Zollverein, an opposition which followed from the mistaken belief that all nations should embrace free trade. To overcome this belief, he mobilized the arguments of his *National System*.[12]

How hopefully List advanced his project is a matter of dispute. Certainly, return to London brought back all the admiration, even reverence, for England which slumbered beneath his jealousy of British power. In the House of Lords he witnessed the vote which registered the death of the Corn Laws. As he watched, Cobden and the free traders greeted him cordially, and jestingly asked if he had come over to be converted. Stand-

[11] *Ibid.*, 338.
[12] List, *Werke*, VII, 267 *ff*.

ing there, conversing amiably with his "greatest enemies," he was almost painfully impressed with the greatness of political life in a country where vital issues of world import could be discussed, and settled, with statesmanlike decorum. "Here one sees history growing." [13] Courtesy did not, however, soften the blunt rebuff of his plea for an altered policy towards the Zollverein. Palmerston and Peel were full of fair words about the identity of English and German interests, but fresh from their victory over protection at home, they dismissed his arguments for protection in Germany as "utterly and entirely wrong." [14] The Englishmen were at least willing to reply; King Frederick William's minister, to whom a copy of the memorandum had been sent, was content to go through it and underline List's criticism of German bureaucrats and praise of parliamentary government.[15] Broken by failure, List returned to Germany; within a few months he was dead of his own hand.

Friedrich List was not a representative German in the sense that his views were accepted as commonplace in his day. He foreshadowed and helped to create the future, much more than he reflected the present. During his lifetime, German liberalism was seeking to free itself from dependence on French and English doctrine; List showed the way to emancipation. During his lifetime, German conservatives sought to perpetuate existing conditions by appealing to history and to national traditions; List showed that liberal nationalism could appeal to the same authorities. Tossing aside natural law as a fiction, and denouncing individualism and cosmopolitanism as incompatible with national strength, he built his system on the teachings of history, and on the peculiar needs of each nation as revealed by history, no less confidently than a conservative like Ranke. But while conservatives appealed to the past in order to justify the political and social structure of Germany, List appealed to the past in order to demonstrate the need for a strong national state, and for

[13] *Ibid.*, VII, 627.
[14] *Ibid.*, VII, 525.
[15] *Ibid.*, VII, 679.

constitutional government as one of the necessary elements in national strength. Freedom and power—these Germans had been trying to reconcile. List effected the reconciliation by making freedom contribute to power. Pondering his writings, German liberals came to feel that the riddle had been solved at last.

Slowly, imperceptibly, the German mind was breaking away from older ways of thinking. The kind of conservatism for which Metternich stood was unable to make room for nationalism or for the self-conscious middle and working classes who grew in numbers and power as industrialism grew. The kind of liberalism which flourished in England was ill-adapted to a country where the age of nationalism, science, and the machine had obtruded suddenly on an age of still living feudalism, guild economy, provincialism, and dogmatic Christianity. Not liberty alone, not order alone; some loyalty which would combine liberty and order was needed. Whether they called themselves liberals or conservatives, Germans sought to create that loyalty by appealing to a national spirit which enclosed, subordinated, and harmonized the too-obvious differences between Germans. Gifted with a mind in which daring imagination and sober analysis worked harmoniously, List was able to formulate clearly the aspirations which most of his contemporaries only dimly felt, but these same qualities made him see the formidable barriers to a realization of his hopes.

Other German reformers were just beginning to view the future confidently when List gave up in despair. Unintentionally, Frederick William IV had given the signal for revolt when he called together representatives of the Prussian estates in 1847. To him, the diet was a revival of the old method by which an absolute king discovered the needs of his subjects, and by which the king informed his subjects of his gracious will. The members of the diet, on the other hand, were determined to establish real parliamentary government. In the other German states, the events in Prussia produced an expectant stirring: if absolutism fell in Prussia, it must soon fall in the other states; and once the separate states had constitutions, a national constitution would be easy to secure. So ran the argument of reforming nationalists. Nature itself seemed on the liberal side. Crop failures in 1846 and 1847 caused discontent among the peasants and city workers, inclining them to listen to middle class reformers.

The French revolution of February, 1848, brought a swift change from words to action. Spontaneously, revolt spread through central Europe. Almost without a struggle, the old order collapsed. By the end of March, Metternich was an exile and revolutionists had paralysed Austrian power; in Berlin, Frederick William had agreed to a constitution to save his crown; in Frankfort, liberals from all Germany were drafting plans for a national constituent assembly to be elected by universal suffrage; in Schleswig-Holstein, Germans were fighting to win the duchies from Denmark. Through the spring and summer, hope ran high. In state after state, parliamentary government was established. The Frankfort Parliament met in May and immediately set about the task of defining the rights of Germans and the power of the German national state. The Austrian Empire, beset by nationalist risings among the subject peoples, was powerless to preserve the authority of the old Confederation. The field was open to nationalism and liberalism.

The very fact that public opinion was so faithfully represented at Frankfort proved the undoing of the Parliament. Great Germany and little Germany, monarchism and republicanism, conservatism and democracy—these and many other shades of opinion had advocates who were reluctant to compromise. Weeks passed into months and still the debate continued, while the favorable moment slipped away unused. In September, nationalism lost its rallying point, and the Parliament lost much of its prestige: the powers, led by Russia and England, forced acceptance of the Armistice of Malmo, which affirmed the rights of the king of Denmark in Schleswig-Holstein. Germans had been almost unanimously on the side of the rebels in the duchies; with the failure of the rebellion, Germans suddenly realized that their aspirations had aroused alarm and hostility in the rest of

Europe. Nicholas I of Russia was frankly hostile, and waited only for an opportunity to take up anew the conservative crusade against revolution. French republicans talked of "compensation" on the Rhine if German unity became a reality. England, sceptical of German nationalism and fearful lest the disturbed condition of central Europe give France and Russia an excuse for aggressive action, treated the Frankfort Parliament with annoyed contempt and took the lead in the fight to vindicate Danish rights in Schleswig-Holstein. The German people first became aware of these dangerous cross-currents in the international situation when the Armistice of Malmo was enforced by the powers; humiliated and discouraged, patriotic opinion blamed both England and the delegates at Frankfort for the failure. In this same month of September, the Parliament received another unwarranted blow when conservatives seized on the assassination of two reactionary delegates as evidence that the Parliament was controlled by violent radicals; thereafter, the cleavage between the parties of the left and the right widened rapidly.

By the time that the Parliament had agreed on a draft constitution in October, 1848, enthusiasm had begun to wane, and the princes were recovering from their mood of terrified acquiescence. The constitution set up a strong federal and constitutional monarchy which was to include all of Prussia but only those parts of the Austrian Empire which had been in the old Confederation. The Austrian government refused to consent to this arrangement, and countered with the proposal that the whole of Austria be included, thus forming a great state of seventy millions, with the Austrian ruler as emperor. In German eyes, this looked very much like the annexation of the rest of Germany by Austria. The Frankfort Parliament then turned to Prussia, and offered the imperial crown to Frederick William. Again it was rebuffed: Frederick William refused to accept a crown from a popular assembly. He added, however, that he would be glad to accept the crown of a new federal union of non-Austrian Germany if he was asked to do so by the other princes. Instantly, Austria took alarm at this evidence that Prussia was prepared to make a bid for leadership in Germany. The Frankfort Parliament fell into the background and was soon forgotten. Between hope and fear, Germany watched the battle between Prince Felix Schwarzenberg, the strong-willed mentor of the young Emperor Francis Joseph, and the Hohenzollern king who, belatedly and half-heartedly, took up the traditions of Frederick the Great. Again foreign intervention settled the issue. Nicholas of Russia, as the leader of conservative Europe, forced concessions from both sides. At Olmütz, in 1850, Frederick William agreed to abandon the project for a new federal union led by Prussia; at Dresden, in May, 1851, Prince Schwarzenberg gave up his projected empire of seventy millions, and accepted a revival of the old Confederation as the best available solution.

The month of May, 1851, which saw Englishmen glorying in the strength of their nation, was a month of mourning in Germany. Everything had failed. Liberalism had failed. Prussia had failed. Austria had failed. Unity seemed further away than ever. The fires of revolution had not forged a new Germany; rather, they had hardened the old lines of division. Every state had become more self-conscious, more determined to preserve its identity. Parties, right or left, had become more disciplined and more clearly marked off each from the others. Sectional, cultural, and religious differences had been emphasized. And for the first time, Germans realized the suspicion which their national aspirations aroused in other countries, countries strong enough to impose their will on divided Germany. Hopeless discouragement was reflected in the emigration of more than a million Germans, and these included not only peasants and laborers, but artists and scholars, men of education and substance, men who preferred exile to life in a Germany where nothing had changed.

Actually, much had changed. If the revolutionary tumult had created no new political system, it had killed the system of Metternich both in Germany and in Europe. Metternich had counted on aristocratic and monarchical solidarity to withstand the pressure of revolutionary radicalism and nationalism. As

Schwarzenberg read the lessons of the revolutionary years, aristocracy had proved not only a weak, but a dangerous defence. The old federal structure of Austria and Germany had not been able to resist popular uprisings; worse, aristocrats had in many places shown sympathy with revolution. The leaders of the movement for Hungarian independence had not been plebeians; they were gentlemen. Tempted by Austrian weakness, the King of Prussia had forgotten monarchical solidarity and had tried to use the revolution as a means of uniting Germany under Prussian leadership. Disgusted, Schwarzenberg swept cosmopolitanism aside as outworn rubbish, and set out to build Austrian power on cold, objective self-interest, the interest of Austria and of the other states of Europe. Internally, he transformed the Austrian Empire from a feudal, decentralized state into a highly centralized autocratic state. The change inevitably gave the polyglot empire a common and distinctive character, which seemed increasingly foreign to Germans. That he was thereby accentuating the drift towards a "small Germany" was not an argument calculated to deter Schwarzenberg. Nationalism, like cosmopolitanism, was a word to him. To preserve Austrian influence in the revived Confederation he relied exclusively on the selfish interests of the lesser princes who had learned to fear absorption in Prussia during the revolution. In the Diet at Frankfort he abandoned the old policy of flattering Prussia by conferring with her before taking any action. Instead, the Austrian presiding officer ostentatiously treated the Prussian delegate as an inferior, and openly mobilized the other delegates in opposition to Prussian wishes. The lesser princes were delighted to find so energetic a defender, but Prussian pride was mortally hurt by demotion to the level of a secondary state. When, at Olmütz, Frederick William had given up his plan for a German federal union under his leadership, he had expected a return to the old coöperation between Berlin and Vienna. Soon after 1851 this surrender came to be called "the humiliation of Olmütz," and the Prussian government embarked energetically on military reforms designed to assert equality with Austria in the Confederation. The Prussian representative at Frankfort, Otto von Bismarck, was meditating the possibility of even more daring action, the smashing of the Confederation and the revival of the old open antagonism to Austria which had slumbered since the days of Frederick the Great.

So long as Prussia was isolated she was, from the Austrian point of view, harmless; but what if Austria should herself become isolated? Francis Joseph had been able to weather the revolutionary year only with the help of conservative Russia. The Tsar had forced Prussia to give up her German ambitions; his armies had put down the Hungarians. And yet Prince Schwarzenberg, before his death in 1852, had taught the young Emperor that conservative solidarity was bankrupt in European affairs as well as in Germany and at home. The interests of the Habsburg absolutism alone merited consideration; that lesson Francis Joseph learned from his first minister, and that he made the basis of his policy. The results were ruinous. When, in 1854, Russia became involved in the Crimean War with France and England, Francis Joseph could see only that Austrian interests would be jeopardized if Russia won new territory in the Balkans. Unhesitatingly, he rebuffed the Tsar's appeals for help, and sought to bring the German Confederation into an alliance with the western powers. To his chagrin, not only Prussia, but the lesser princes held back; interest was a weapon which cut both ways, and the German states were not willing to fight over the fate of the Balkans. Afraid to move alone, the Austrians vacillated helplessly, thereby winning the hatred of Russia, and the contempt of France and England. Again in 1859, when herself involved in war with France and Piedmont, Austria found that her "realistic" policy had cost her all support. The Tsar was frankly pleased by the plight of his faithless ally, while Prussia refused to help unless given command over the north German armies, in other words, unless Austria was willing to admit Prussian supremacy in northern Germany. Rather than surrender his leadership in the Confederation, Francis Joseph preferred to accept defeat in Italy, but peace did not save him from the consequences of Schwarzenberg's policy. The success of nationalism in Italy brought to the surface the nationalist aspirations in central Europe which had merely been driven underground by the reaction after 1848. Throughout the Austrian Empire, but especially in Hungary, revolt broke out against centralism and absolutism. Even the Emperor saw that resistance was useless, and set about the painful task of demolishing the unified state structure which had lasted a brief decade.

Isolated and defeated in Europe, weakened by disaffection at home, Austria was forced also to face an upsurge of nationalism in Germany which threatened her age-old supremacy. In 1848, German nationalism had been strongest among the middle classes and a liberal minority of the aristocracy. Despite its failure, the Frankfort Parliament had caught the imagination of the masses. The desire for unity did not die after 1851; rather it was nourished by political reaction and by the feeling that foreign powers had unjustly thwarted German aspirations. Political reaction strengthened the old conviction that liberalism and unity must be won together; one could not be had without the other. The interference of foreign powers in 1848 strengthened the old craving for national power so that Germany might be free to settle her own destinies. A new word, *Realpolitik,* found its way into the language, a word which meant exclusive pursuit of national interests by all available means, and particularly by force. Nationalism was not merely stronger and more wide-spread, however. Increasingly, nationalists looked to Prussia as the natural leader of the movement for unity. Centralization had marked off the German provinces of Austria too obviously from the rest of Germany; Austria was too obviously the ally of the lesser princes against both liberalism and nationalism; Austrian interests were too obviously centering in the Near East rather than in Germany; Austria had too obviously encouraged and supported Catholic fear of the results which the creation of a largely Protestant Germany would have on the Church. On the other hand, Prussia was, except for her Polish minority, a purely German state; Prussia had kept the constitution granted in 1848, although modified so that the upper classes would control both houses of the Landtag; Prussia was a predominately Protestant state; Prussia had already taken the initiative in curbing the particularism of the smaller states through the creation of the Zollverein. It seemed natural, therefore, that when, inspired by the Italian victories of 1859, patriots from all Germany formed a National Association, their program should be a liberal Germany, united under Prussian leadership, with Austria as an ally rather than an integral part of the union.

And so it seemed that List had, after all, been a prophet. Twenty years after his proud toast to the Fatherland of the future, the tide of liberalism and of nationalism was running strong, so strong that even the kings and princes of Germany, even the Emperor of Austria, realized that the national will could not longer be thwarted.

CHAPTER IV

BISMARCK AND GERMAN UNITY

INNUMERABLE ANECDOTES have come down to us about the years from 1851 to 1859 when Bismarck was the Prussian representative at the federal Diet in Frankfort: his inexhaustible strength, whether evidenced in endless verbal duels with other diplomats or in foolhardy tests of physical endurance; his calculated rudeness to opponents and his gentleness with the children who learned prayers at his knee; his drinking bouts, and long evenings with the music of Beethoven. All help us to see this man in whom so many diverse qualities were mixed to make a titanic and harmonious personality. One picture above all others, however, helps us to understand the statesman of the future: Bismarck studying the map of Germany, and of Europe, as it existed in the middle years of the nineteenth century. The hours passed, the blue cigar smoke became ever more dense, the bottle beside him emptied, and still he studied the map. To the left, the island kingdom of Britain and the solid bulk of France; to the right, the great mass of Russia; in the middle, from the Baltic and the North Sea to the Mediterranean, a confused blur of colors with which the cartographer vainly sought to show a multitude of states. Around a part of this central area ran the line which marked the frontiers of the German Confederation, the wavering line which now followed the frontiers of states, and now cut across frontiers. The Netherlands lay outside the line, but Luxemburg was inside, and the King of the Netherlands was also the ruler of Luxemburg. Denmark was without the line, but Holstein was within, and the King of Denmark was the ruler of Holstein, or rather of Schleswig-Holstein, for the duchies were united, although only one was in the Confederation, and neither was a part of Denmark! Most of Prussia was within the line, but East Prussia and Posen were not; and, further to mar the symmetry of the map, the territories of some of the thirty-odd members of the Confederation separated Rhenish Prussia from the rest of the kingdom, while others formed islands entirely enclosed by Prussia. As a final incongruity, most of the Austrian Empire was outside the Confederation, and yet the Austrian delegate presided at Frankfort. That wavering line affirmed the division of Germany; and to one who could, like Bismarck, go back of the map to the land which it represented, political division was only one of many barriers, economic, social, and cultural, which separated German from German.

When Bismarck first came to Frankfort, he was content to leave the map unchanged. He saw then with the eyes of a Prussian Junker who thought God had entrusted to aristocrats like himself the right and the duty to rule. That conception of politics had almost perished in the Revolution of 1848. To Bismarck, the firm reëstablishment of conservative government was the highest duty of statesmanship, calling for a united front of conservative states against the forces of radicalism. He thought the revived Confederation was such a union, and he was eager to coöperate with the other representatives in the great war against revolution. Bismarck was, however, a Prussian as well as a Junker, and he thought Prussian influence in German affairs should be equal to that of Austria. He soon learned that Schwarzenberg and Francis Joseph were determined not to concede equality. Rapidly the Junker fell into the background. The map was no longer seen through the eyes of a conservative European. Emphatically, it was not seen through the eyes of a German nationalist. Bismarck's mind was, to be sure, shaped by the political concepts which through the preceding generations had become the common intellectual heritage of all Germans; but at Frankfort he applied those concepts to Prussia, not to Germany. His contemplation of the map focused on the disjointed, sprawling frontiers of Prussia; other states, whether members of the Confederation or not, entered into the picture because they were potentially useful or dangerous to Prussia.

As the map came to life in his imagination, the words England, France, Austria, and the rest, became symbolical of much more than so many square miles, inhabited by so many people, endowed with certain natural resources. Rather, these became the names of living beings, heroic or contemptible, useful or dangerous, neighbors who were fated to live together, rivals fated to struggle, each for its own interest. This was the world which God had created, the world of states. Through the state, God directed the lives of individual men; through states God accomplished his ever-evolving purposes in the world. As God's will unfolded itself, each state was offered new opportunities and confronted with new dangers—opportunities which might be seized or lost, dangers which might be escaped or realized. The decision lay with the collective wisdom and courage of the community, and with the greatness or meanness of individual statesmen. No statesman, genius though he might be, could mould history to his will; he must mould his will to the opportunities God offered, and make the most of the possible. The sense of dependence on the divine will was ever-present in Bismarck's mind, a divine will which could not be changed or deflected by human prayers or bribes, but which could be recognized, even anticipated. Perception was the first task of statesmanship; equally important was the ability to act. Bismarck was no fatalist: God worked through men, who could be good or bad servants of His will. And there were no limits on action, save the limits of the possible. Action was good or bad, as judgment was keen or faulty. Morals which guided the relations between man and man had no bearing in politics. Success was the only standard of judgment; the will of the statesman must be as strong in execution as was the will of God in creation. The statesman must, as Machiavelli had said, be both lion and fox; but where Machiavelli made princely power an end in itself, Bismarck would be lion and fox so that he might serve his God through the Prussian state.

Therefore he studied the map with one question in his mind: how could Prussia, the weakest of the great powers, broken into two fragments, and shut off from free access to the sea, be made a strong and independent power? The answer early became obvious. If the small states of central and northern Germany could either be absorbed or brought within the Prussian sphere of influence, the two fragments would be united and an outlet would be secured on the North Sea. Naturally, the rulers of the small states would not willingly surrender their independence. Naturally, Austria would not willingly surrender hegemony in so large a part of Germany. Fear alone could compel surrender, fear of German nationalism and of Prussian power. The people of the smaller states must be taught, by propaganda in the press and by the words and actions of the Prussian government, that Prussia alone wished to replace the Confederation by a strong and united Germany. In this way the princes would be isolated from their subjects and, consequently, weakened. At the same time, the other members of the Confederation, particularly Austria, must be made to fear Prussian power and hostility. Alone, Prussia was not strong enough to be feared; therefore alliances must be sought, alliances against the other German states. Loyalty to the Confederation had hitherto prevented such alliances. "All the shades, however, of possibility, probability, or purpose, in the event of war, of concluding this or that alliance, or belonging to this or that group, still form the basis of such influence as a state can at the present day wield in time of peace. Whichever finds itself in the combination that is weaker in the event of war is inclined to be more yielding; whichever completely isolates itself renounces influence, especially if it be the weakest among the Great Powers. Alliances are the expression of common interests and purposes." Yet Prussia persisted in relying on her natural enemies, Austria and the smaller German states. "I ask you whether there is a cabinet in Europe which has a more innate and natural interest than that of Vienna in preventing Prussia from growing stronger and in lessening her influence in Germany?" In his opinion there was none, except the smaller members of the Confederation, who were dominated by fear of Prussian aggression, "and no angel can talk the mistrust out of them so long as there exist maps at which they can cast a glance." Actually, Prussia was isolated, and would remain both isolated and weak until her government awoke to the necessity of safeguarding Prussian interests. The diplomatic situation was propitious. Austria was estranged from both Russia and France; the latter powers were moving towards an alliance against Austria. Let Prussia throw in her lot with the enemies of her enemy. Conservatives said that alliance with France would be a pact with the revolution and with the hereditary foe of Germany. This was pure prejudice. Sympathies and antipathies were out of place in international affairs; interest alone was decisive. "In my opinion, not even the king has the right to subordinate the interests of his country to his own feelings of love or hate towards foreigners." [1]

During his early years at Frankfort, Bismarck veiled his audacious program, fearful of repudiation by his superiors, but after the Crimean War he felt it safe to speak frankly. Not only was the diplomatic map shifting to the disadvantage of Austria; a change of rulers was impending in Berlin. Frederick William was sinking into insanity. His brother and heir, Prince William, was a soldier who had done his best to strengthen the Prussian army. Here, Bismarck felt, was the man to pursue an exclusively Prussian policy. Confidently and clearly, he set forth his views in long argumentative dispatches, not only to the ministry in Berlin, but to the Prince himself. Through all ran the governing conviction that fear alone could force the German states to grant Prussia her rightful influence, fear of a Prussian alliance with France, fear of a Prussian alliance with German nationalism.

William was attracted by the fanatical loyalty to Prussia of his fiery adviser, but he was repelled by the thought of breaking with his fellow princes, and of casting his lot with France. Moreover, he was convinced that his subjects, and the German

[1] *Bismarck, The Man and the Statesman,* I, 171 *ff. Cf.* also *Ges. Werke,* II, 221 *ff.*

people, would not follow him in the path which Bismarck said was the only right one. Undoubtedly William was right. Blinded by the logic of his own arguments and by his devotion to Prussia, Bismarck failed to take account both of the strong popular loyalty to the German princes, including Francis Joseph, and of the hatred for the French despoiler of the fatherland which existed throughout Germany. Above all, he was blind to the alliance between liberalism and nationalism in the German mind. Of this he was unpleasantly reminded when he went to Berlin early in 1858 for the festivities in honor of the marriage between William's oldest son, Frederick, and the English Princess Victoria. Berlin greeted the young couple with tumultuous enthusiasm, and Bismarck's honesty compelled him to see that the enthusiasm was not merely an expression of dynastic loyalty. Rather, he saw that the Prussian people were already looking ahead to the day when Frederick, a liberal prince with a wife from liberal England, would inaugurate an era of reform in Prussia and of nationalism in Germany. Liberalism and nationalism, the two seemed inseparable to Germans.

Bismarck returned to Frankfort much depressed. By temperament and political creed he was debarred from sympathy for liberalism, or for liberal England. Instinctively, his Junker inheritance made him value authority more than freedom, and his own passionate, unruly character made him feel the more keenly the need for some controlling force. The "unseen hand" of the liberals, which made the sum of individual selfishness serve the common good, could not be this controlling force for a man who saw all too keenly the stupidity and short-sighted selfishness of his fellows. Religion alone could force men to work for the common good, religion working, not through an authoritative church, but through the authoritative state. This was not a revival of divine right monarchy, as many of his contemporaries thought; Bismarck's low estimate of humanity would not let him deify his king. Rather, it was the divine right state, the state removed from and above the selfishness, the passions, and the meanness of men. The state was to him a religious union of men through which God curbed the unlovely characteristics of mankind, and in which the interests of individuals and classes were so guided, controlled, and reconciled that every part worked for the good of the whole. Changing parliamentary majorities could not, any more than the whims of an autocrat, direct the destinies of the state: God's will, ceaselessly unfolding itself in history, set the aims and limits of state action. Parliamentary majorities at best reflected a transient popular mood and usually reflected the selfish interests of a coalition; wise statesmanship must take account, not only of the whole contemporary scene, but of the lessons of the past and the needs of the future.

To Bismarck, the practical program of Prussian liberals showed their incapacity to govern. They were more interested in German nationalism than in Prussia; to the servant of Prussia this was treason. They hated force and trusted to the strength of the national ideal to win unity; to a man who saw international relations exclusively in terms of power, this was quixotry. They expected the Emperor of Austria and the lesser princes to surrender peacefully; to Bismarck this demonstrated ignorance of German history and of human nature. They looked to England for support against France and Russia; in this he saw their greatest error. Bismarck loved the England which had produced his heroes Shakespeare and Byron. He admired the England which had fought for, and won, imperial supremacy. But he had no admiration for liberal England, and he feared and mistrusted England as an ally. Since the triumph of liberalism, he argued, English policy had lost its old strength and clarity of purpose. The dangers which he foresaw if popular government prevailed in Prussia were already to be seen operating in England, where newspaper articles were of more importance than the arguments of statesmen, and where fear of the taxpayer triumphed over the needs of national defence. Liberal England was unstable and weak; England under any form of government was a dangerous and treacherous ally. A secure insular position made it possible for Britain to abandon allies when they had served their purpose, without fear of retribution. Bismarck, always the realist, saw nothing immoral in such a breach of faith; but he did see danger for a weak power like Prussia in an alliance which might fail in a crisis. Frederick the Great, he warned, had almost perished during the Seven Years' War when England, her own purposes accomplished, had deserted him. The marriage of Prince Frederick and Princess Victoria seemed to Bismarck a menace to Prussian independence, unless the princess forgot her native land. It rapidly became apparent that she could not and would not forget; "home" to her was always England. Bismarck saw his fears realized. Thereafter he was an implacable enemy of the Princess, seeing in her a means through which liberalism and English political influence entered Prussian life like fatal poisons.

Bismarck's warnings went unheeded. Prince William had no love for liberalism, and he was even more narrowly Prussian in his outlook than Bismarck. But he was unwilling to defy either his subjects or Austria. Doubtfully and hesitantly, he embarked on an attempt to strengthen the position of Prussia by an alliance with nationalism, without breaking with Austria, and without surrendering control over Prussia to the advocates of popular government. When he became regent, a few months after the revealing demonstration in favor of his son and Princess Victoria, he announced that Prussia must make "moral conquests" in Germany. To conciliate the liberals, a "New Era" ministry of moderates was set up in Berlin. To conciliate Austria, Bismarck was recalled from Frankfort and sent into honorable exile as Ambassador to Russia. Bismarck was not deceived by promotion to the status of ambassador. Full of bitterness, he left Frankfort, conscious that his policy had been repudiated. Far from the scene of action, he watched the opportunity to settle accounts with Austria during the Italian war slip away unused. Disgusted, he watched the ministers in Berlin try to win the favor of the liberals without conceding parliamentary supremacy, and the favor of Austria without conceding the supremacy of Austria in the Confederation. Disgust turned to hope as these efforts proved vain. The lower house of the Landtag, encouraged by concessions, pressed for control over finances, in the full realization that financial control once won, parliamentary supremacy would be won. Austria, encouraged by friendliness, pressed for admission to the Zollverein, the one German union from which she had so far been excluded. The Ambassador at St. Petersburg, who had foreseen these results, became once more a personage of importance. When ministry and lower house came to a deadlock over army reforms which William—now king and very sensitive about encroachments on his power—demanded be accepted unaltered by the Landtag, Bismarck's prestige rose higher. He was brought back to Berlin; but the King, fearing a crisis if he gave power to this violent enemy of liberalism, sent him away once more, as Ambassador at Paris. At last, in 1862, the call came. Bismarck was made Minister President of Prussia.

The three years of honorable exile had not changed Bismarck's political views, but they had made him less doctrinaire and more German. He no longer saw the map as something to be manipulated like clay. Now he saw the necessity of winning, first the Prussian people, and then the people of the other German lands; Prussia could win greatness only as a part of Germany. He was still convinced, however, that the key to the problems both of Prussia and of Germany was to be found in the field of foreign affairs, and by the threat or use of power. Therefore he was determined to secure the essential parts of the proposed army reforms, even at the cost of a clear break with the lower house. But first he tried conciliation. The whole question, he told the parliamentary representatives, had been beclouded by the use of precedents drawn from English history. Parliamentary supremacy was something which had evolved slowly in England out of local conditions. It was always a mistake to borrow foreign traditions; Prussia had her own peculiar problems, problems set by her history and by her geographical position. Time and energy should not be exhausted in arguments about the exact distribution of authority between the parts of the government. "Germany has its eyes, not on Prussia's liberalism, but on her power. Bavaria, Württemberg, Baden, may indulge in liberalism, but no one is going to assign Prussia's rôle to them for that reason. Prussia must mobilize and conserve her strength for the favorable moment, which more than once has passed unused. Prussia's frontiers as fixed by the Treaties of Vienna are not favorable to a healthy state life. The great questions of the day will not be decided by speeches and majority votes—that was the great mistake of 1848 and 1849—but through blood and iron." [2]

Bluntly, Bismarck had revealed his mind on the two great problems, the German problem and the liberal problem. He intended to create a united Germany, but that Germany would be a country in which a Prussian would feel at home, not an Austrian dependency, or a copy of liberal England. At home, the liberals took up the challenge; in Vienna, preparations were made for the coming test of strength. The result is too well known to need repetition. The first act was the War of 1864 which wrested Schleswig-Holstein from Denmark. Austria was his unwilling partner in this war, forced to join with him or see Prussia take the lead in Germany by winning the prize which nationalists most coveted. Bismarck was, however, not yet ready to serve German nationalism; Prussia needed the duchies as a window on the sea. Austria, having helped to win the war, was unwilling to allow Prussia to keep all the spoils. Bismarck was quite willing to quarrel, to use the duchies as an occasion for finally settling accounts. In 1866, he goaded Austria and most of the German states into war with Prussia, defeated them in a swift campaign, and proceeded to remake the map of central Europe. Austria was entirely excluded from German affairs; the old Confederation was abolished; most of north Germany was annexed by Prussia and the rest united with her in a North German Confederation; the southern states were linked by close military alliance to the new Confederation. In 1870, Napoleon III, fearful of Prussia's power, and infuriated by Prussian arrogance, declared war. North and south Germany marched with Prussia. Before the war was ended in 1871, Germany was a

[2] *Ges. Werke,* X, 140.

united empire. The Treaty of Frankfort dowered the new empire with a huge money indemnity and the provinces of Alsace and Lorraine.

By the Wars of 1864 and 1866, Bismarck solved the Austrian problem. Austrian influence was shaken off; annexations closed the gaps in the frontiers of Prussia and gave access to the North Sea. Prussia now had the conditions "favorable to a healthy state life." The war of 1870–71 solved the German problem: the loose Confederation gave place to a strong federal state, dominated by Prussia, and ruled by the Prussian king-emperor. It was hard for most Germans to see the immemorial connection with Austria ended, but the prospect of unity soon softened regret. On the other hand, the seizure of Alsace and most of Lorraine seemed a natural consequence, almost a condition, of new-found strength; the intoxication of victory and conquest at the expense of the hereditary enemy, overcame the last reluctance to accept Prussian leadership.

The great ideal issues of the day, no less than the territorial, had been settled by blood and iron. By 1871 the battle cries of liberalism and conservatism had lost their old meaning for Germans; cosmopolitan idealism, like territorial particularism, had been overwhelmed by nationalism. When Bismarck took office in 1862 he was hated by liberals as a reactionary, and mistrusted by his own class as a renegade who was willing to bargain with the revolution. During the years following, the mistrust of conservatives had steadily deepened. Junkers saw their position jeopardized by the territorial acquisitions of 1866, and by the extensive powers delegated, first to the North German Confederation, and then to the Empire; the peoples living south and west of the Elbe far outnumbered the inhabitants of the feudal east. Conservatives were also alarmed by Bismarck's insistence that members of the Reichstag, the lower house of the imperial parliament, be elected by universal manhood suffrage. Was not this the beginning of democratic equalitarianism? Bismarck was angered but unmoved by the reproaches of his old associates. He knew that the day of exclusive aristocratic rule was past and that popular participation in government was inevitable. But he also knew that he had not surrendered to liberalism. He had insisted on universal suffrage, partly to win popularity, partly because he thought the masses more patriotic, less the slaves of class interests, than the middle classes who would profit by a restricted suffrage. After all, the severely restricted suffrage of Prussia had not prevented the election of a liberal majority in 1862. Slowly and reluctantly, conservatives fell into line as they saw that the privileged position of their class in the army and in the higher ranks of the bureaucracy was unimpaired. The old aristocratic cosmopolitanism, the belief in one right, universal ordering of society, largely disappeared, and was replaced by a conservatism which expressed agrarian and aristocratic class interest within an exclusive and self-centered national state.

Liberalism collapsed even more quickly and more completely than conservatism. After the war with Austria, when all could see that German unification was impending, Bismarck called for new elections to the Landtag. His opponents were routed at the polls, and the Landtag hastened to pass a bill of indemnity condoning his actions of the preceding years, or, put more bluntly, giving up the battle for parliamentary control over the state. With equal enthusiasm, the popular representatives accepted the constitution of the North German Confederation even though this document, and the imperial constitution which soon replaced it, affirmed the fact that the state was the master, not the servant, of the popular will. The word liberal, like the word conservative, continued to be used, but as the badge of parties whose real concern was the defense of middle class commercial and industrial interests, not as the symbol of the vision of a perfected world order.

That conservatism could not survive the triumph of nationalism is not strange. In the light of the history of German thought, the capitulation of liberalism is almost as easy to understand. Freedom had been, and continued to be, no less praised in Germany than in England. But freedom to the Englishman meant his right to be himself, uncoerced by other wills, a right derived from laws more binding and more universal than the laws of any state. For the German, freedom had come to mean the right to be a German living in a German state free from coercion by other states, a right derived from the history of his national community. It is, at first sight, paradoxical that a people like the English, so homogeneous and so united, should have been the exponents of extreme individualism and cosmopolitanism, while the Germans, so acutely conscious of the anarchy of their political, social, and economic life, should have affirmed the existence of a national personality to which all Germans owed allegiance and obedience. The paradox cannot be pushed too far; the popularity of Lord Palmerston showed the limits of English cosmopolitanism, and Germans did not cease to revile each other after 1871. Nevertheless it is safe to say that, just as the history of England in the early nineteenth century made Englishmen prize liberty as life's greatest boon, so German history made unity the goal of the German people. Friedrich List was not the first, nor the last, German liberal to make freedom a means by which national power would be strengthened, not an end in itself. After the failure of the Frankfort Parliament it became a commonplace to join liberty and nationalism as cause and effect. British constitutional precedents were used against Bismarck in 1862, not only because England was the home of freedom, but because England possessed the social harmony and the strength which Germans were seeking: liberalism alone could cure the anarchy of German life. When Bismarck showed the error of this reasoning, liberalism withered. The Germans did not really desert liberalism; they discovered that they never had been liberals, as the English understood the word.

The English followed Bismarck's lightning transformation of the map and of the German mind with mixed incredulity and disgust. Invariably, they were still trying to understand the move which he had just completed when his next move confronted them with a new inexplicable situation. Such lack of comprehension was natural. For more than a generation, continental politics had centered around Paris and St. Petersburg, while the German states gravitated uneasily and helplessly between the two centers of power. Napoleon III, to the day when he was a captive of the Prussian army after the battle of Sedan, seemed the man whose ambitions must be watched and curbed. Only after Sedan did the English realize that power had shifted to Berlin. They were blinded, however, not only by the map which had endured so long as to seem changeless; they were blinded also by their inveterate habit of believing British ideals the only right ideals. During the years when Bismarck was crippling German liberalism, the liberal tide was rising to the flood in England. In 1864, Gladstone defied the wrath of Palmerston by affirming in the House of Commons "that every man who is not presumably incapacitated by some consideration of personal unfitness or of political danger is morally entitled to come within the pale of the Constitution." [3] Immediately, reform became a live political word. Palmerston, as if seeing that his day was over, died in 1865. Gladstone stepped into the liberal leadership to find himself opposed by rejuvenated conservatives who, driven on by Disraeli, sought to gain power by even more drastic reforms than Gladstone contemplated. In 1867, Disraeli pushed through a bill which greatly extended the suffrage. In 1868, Gladstone entered on his Great Ministry. During the next three years, the British government finally became the model of a liberal state, an efficient and economical servant of a free people. Once more Britain was giving an example to the world; but now Europe was blind to the example. These were the same years in which the German Empire was being formed by blood and iron. English cosmopolitanism had always assumed that other peoples were somewhat imperfect copies of Englishmen. That assumption was obviously challenged by these Germans who had so long been lectured with impunity, if with slight result.

Slowly, painfully, Englishmen groped to understand a very disheartening situation. They were handicapped at the outset by their low estimate of everything German. To Palmerston, in

[3] Hansard, 3d Series, CLXXV, 324.

1863, Bismarck was "the crazy minister at Berlin"; while German agitation over the Schleswig-Holstein question aroused his amused contempt—"but really it is the Duke of Devonshire's servants' hall assuming to decide who shall be the owner of a Derbyshire country gentleman's estate." [4] Tories were no better informed; in the same year, Disraeli opined that "Prussia, without nationality, the principle of the day, is clearly the subject for partition." [5] The Danish War was the first shock. Palmerston had publicly declared that England must, if necessary, fight to protect Denmark, and his words had been applauded when danger was remote. When Prussia and Austria actually invaded Denmark, however, martial ardor cooled. Palmerston and his Foreign Secretary, Lord John Russell, were still for fighting, but Queen, Cabinet, and Parliament were against them. Peel's fateful warning of 1850 had at last been justified, and the day of "those two dreadful old men" as Victoria called Palmerston and Russell, was over. True liberals rejoiced. John Bright proudly told his constituents that the balance of power, "this foul idol—fouler than any heathen tribe ever worshipped—has at last been thrown down." Cobden prophesied that "non-intervention is the policy of all future governments in this country," and like a true liberal, demonstrated his proposition in terms of economics. British exports were now three times as large as twenty years before; busy, prosperous merchants and shippers wished to be left in peace; their influence had triumphed over the war-mongers. "This is one of the effects which we advocates of Free Trade always predicted and desired as the consequence of extended commercial operations." [6]

In place of the balance of power and intervention, nature's unalterable laws would see that, in the end, justice would prevail. This thesis was argued at length by a well-informed liberal writer, Mountstuart Grant Duff, in a volume of *Studies in European Politics* which appeared in 1866, just before the outbreak of

[4] Bell, *Palmerston*, II, 367.
[5] M. & B., *Disraeli*, II, 75.
[6] Trevelyan, *Bright*, 332; Morley, *Cobden*, II, 450, 453.

the Austro-Prussian War. He admitted that Bismarck's influence had been "simply evil," but argued that it could only be temporary. "When any institutions come directly into contact with the spirit of the time, they may resist for five years, or ten, or twenty, but down they must go in the end." William I was an old man, and "the present Crown Prince has, to say nothing of his English marriage, been brought up under infinitely better influences." English liberals should be patient, and, above all, not encourage the representatives of progress in Germany to resort to force. "We look with absolute confidence to the gradual spread of enlightenment even among the Prussian Junkers, and above all to the increase of the power and position of the middle class. . . . The present situation is only temporary, and a Liberal party, composed of the best of the landowners and the best of the bourgeoisie, will have it all its own way in the end." [7]

Most Englishmen, although they agreed with these arguments, could not suppress their feelings of humiliation and rage in face of Bismarck's confident flouting of British threats. Even Queen Victoria, friend of Germany though she was, was forced to rely on underscoring to convey an intensity of emotion for which she could find no adequate words. "Prussia seems inclined to behave as atrociously as possible, and as she *always has done!* Odious people the Prussians are, *that* I *must say*." [8] The torrent of abuse of "Bismarck, the bold and the bad, with his idiot King in his pocket" was fed by contributions from all classes of society. Probably *Punch* expressed the general opinion most succinctly when, commenting on the fact that a new English minister to Prussia had not been found, it remarked: "We have hanged almost everybody fit to be sent there." [9] Anger was the more acute, because even members of the cabinet could not discover any method in Bismarck's madness. By June, 1866, Russell's successor at the foreign office, Lord Clarendon, could see that war was impending between Austria and Prussia, but why? "Two millions

[7] Grant Duff, *Studies in European Politics*, 234, 245 *ff*.
[8] *Letters of Queen Victoria*, 2d Series, I, 271.
[9] *Punch*, Nov. 25, 1865.

of men armed to the teeth by bankrupt governments, preparing to cut each other's throats and set all Europe in flames, *for nothing*, or rather for the gratification of one man—Bismarck—who says he would rather go down to posterity as Attila than as John Bright." [10]

When Austria had been defeated, and the North German Confederation formed, England took new hope. Perhaps the devil was not as black as he was painted. The new federation, if it could be brought into the liberal camp, would be a better bulwark against France and Russia than the old divided Germany had been; and the grant of universal suffrage encouraged the belief that Bismarck was seeing the light. Furthermore, the wasteful expenditure on armaments was becoming too burdensome, as England had prophesied. In 1869, Napoleon III asked Clarendon to propose to Bismarck a reduction in armaments. After some hesitation, Clarendon agreed. In February, 1870, he addressed a long and eloquent appeal to Berlin, pointing out the innumerable ways in which huge standing armies were injuring the peoples of Europe. "This system is cruel, it is out of harmony with the civilization of our age, and it is pregnant with danger." By taking the lead in reducing this burden, Prussia "would not only earn for herself the gratitude of Europe, but give a great proof of her morality and her power." Bismarck replied in a similar vein. Germany had all she wanted, "there is no object of conquest for her." At the same time, she was surrounded by powerful empires. "He should wish to know what guarantees you could give, or propose should be given, for the maintenance of peace, or the security against danger." Clarendon refused to enter into the question of guarantees; such a discussion would be "endless and dangerous." The best guarantee of peace was the rapid spread of popular government. He denied that Prussia would be exposed to danger by his proposals, and vindicated his belief by an analysis of European politics. Bismarck now answered more frankly. Praise of disarmament, he said, was easy for an island power, immune to attack. On the other hand, England

[10] Maxwell, *Clarendon*, II, 315.

had a navy, a large navy. "What would you say if we were to observe that your navy was too large?" The British minister "saw that it was useless to pursue the question further." [11]

The outbreak of war between France and Prussia in 1870 found the English government and the English people still struggling to come abreast of events. Ignorant of the complex background of the war, the British seized on the French declaration of war as proof that this was merely another example of Napoleonic lust for conquest. Bismarck sought to stimulate anti-French feeling by giving to the editor of the *Times* a draft treaty, written by a French diplomat, which provided that France be given a free hand in Belgium in exchange for permitting Prussia a free hand in Germany. At first, English opinion did regard the draft treaty as conclusive proof of Napoleon's perfidy, but it soon became apparent that Bismarck had overestimated English simplicity. On August 6, *Punch* hit off the revised British estimate with the following doggerel:

> Bismarck *against* Napoleon!—*who the odds will give or take,*
> *Which of the two more lightly his faith will bind or break?*
> *'Arcades ambo—blackguards both!' says John Bull's low'ring eye,*
> *As he 'puts his trust in Providence, and—keeps his powder dry.'*

After Napoleon had been captured at Sedan, and after it was realized that the Germans would make peace only if given Alsace-Lorraine, English opinion turned definitely against Germany. Moreover, when the Russian government took advantage of the preoccupation of Europe with the war in France to denounce those clauses of the Treaty of Paris which prohibited armaments in the Black Sea, opinion turned also against the noninterventionist policy of the liberal government. These clauses were the only tangible gain which England had derived from the Crimean War, and English opinion saw in their denunciation not only a blow to British prestige, but the menace of a Russian naval attack on Constantinople. For a few days there was talk of war; then the London government capitulated. Russia con-

[11] Newton, *Lord Lyons,* I, 251 *ff.;* Morley, *Gladstone,* II, 331–332.

sented to veil the defeat of England by asking for an international conference to ratify her violation of the treaty of 1856, but everyone knew in advance that the conference was only a polite formality.

The moral seemed clear. England was powerless to deflect Bismarck from his determination to dismember France, powerless to force moderation on France, powerless even to enforce respect for treaties which safeguarded British interests. Far from being the moral leader of Europe, the tone of the continental press showed that England was everywhere hated or despised. Shocked and humiliated, Englishmen reëxamined the history of the decade just past, and recognized what Clarendon had privately admitted as early as 1868: "Europe now cares no more about England than she does about Holland." [12]

In October, 1870, when the English people were beginning to mingle abuse of their own government with abuse of Bismarck and the fallen Emperor Napoleon, Gladstone sought to arouse faith in liberal ideals once more by a stirring appeal in the *Edinburgh Review* entitled "Germany, France, and England." The appeal was anonymous, but almost before copies were on the newsstands, it was generally known that the author was the Prime Minister; no one could mistake the long roll of Mr. Gladstone's sentences. His purpose was to show that recent events, far from discrediting British reliance on moral influence, had really vindicated British faith in human progress. "Certain it is that a new law of nations is gradually taking hold of the mind, and coming to sway the practice of the world; a law which recognises independence, which frowns upon aggression, which favors the pacific, not the bloody settlement of disputes, which aims at permanent and not temporary adjustments; above all, which recognises as a tribunal of paramount authority, the general judgment of civilised mankind. It has censured the aggression of France; it will censure, if need arise, the greed of Germany." France had been brought low because her rulers had debauched the national conscience by extravagant display and by

[12] Maxwell, *Clarendon*, II, 343.

schemes of conquest. War had brought down the rotten imperial structure. "The disenchantment may be effectual. Such a state of ideas may come to prevail in France, that the people will not hereafter, even passively or for a time, be led astray by the demon of territorial and military ambition." Germany had seized the primacy which France had thrown away. The demand for Alsace-Lorraine was a disquieting symptom that Germany had fallen victim to the same lust for conquest which had brought low her antagonist. If this was the case, Germany would discover in her turn that the European family was strong enough to correct "the eccentricities of its peccant and obstreperous members." Against the moral deficiencies of her neighbors, Mr. Gladstone placed the virtues of England. At home, liberal government had replaced the old bad rule of privilege; colonial self-government had replaced imperial aggression; moral trusteeship had replaced exploitation in India; Ireland was no longer a reproach. Geographical position "marks out England as the appropriate object of the general confidence, as the sole, comparatively, unsuspected power"; the island realm was immune to attack and incapable of aggression. All in all, Englishmen might take comfort and courage from a study of the world about them. "If we no longer dream of foreign acquisitions, we are content in having treaties of mutual benefit with every nation upon earth; treaties not written on parchment, but based on the permanent wants and interest of man, kept alive and confirmed by the constant play of the motives which govern his daily life, and thus inscribing themselves, in gradually deepening characters, on the fleshly tablets of the heart."

In days not so far gone, Englishmen had thrilled to such self-praise. Somehow, complacency now seemed in bad taste; Mr. Gladstone's appeal met with a cool, even hostile reception. During these months while the Germans sat at the gates of starving Paris, a great debate was going on in the English mind, a debate on the whole liberal vision of Europe and the world. Cobdenite non-intervention and Palmerstonian crusading were alike called into question. Unquestionably, the ringing grooves of change had not followed the course which seemed so certain in the days of the Great Exhibition. Slowly, haltingly, Englishmen groped towards a redefinition of freedom, and a redefinition of the mission of Englishmen. Humiliation by the despised Germans had not alone precipitated the debate; many other experiences, such as the American Civil War, and many changes at home contributed to force a reëxamination of the old liberal premises. But certainly Bismarck could boast that he had taught the English much about themselves and about Germany, although he could not boast that he had won gratitude by his instruction. The humiliation of the years from 1864 to 1871 never ceased to rankle, and Englishmen refused to believe that their own statesmanship had been at fault. Germany, seen through English eyes, was no longer ridiculous; but the new respect which Germany commanded was neither synonymous with admiration nor incompatible with contempt. When the German armies at last entered Paris in triumph, Englishmen turned for a parallel to the Gothic triumph over Rome. It was as the new barbarians that Englishmen greeted the new masters of Europe.

A change no less subtle and far-reaching was taking place in the German view of England. In part, the change was a natural revulsion against earlier adulation, and in part it was the expression of the envy which had so often poisoned admiration. Largely, however, the explanation was wounded pride at the failure of England to appreciate and applaud the miracle of a kindred people achieving the long-sought goal of unity. With monotonous regularity the same complaints recurred until they took on an almost axiomatic quality in the German mind. The British were on the side of Denmark in 1864, and of Austria in 1866; therefore, England was the enemy of German unity. When Bismarck ignored the protests and threats of England, the British gave way with bad grace; therefore, the English were cowards. In 1870, the British, while damning Napoleon III for attacking Prussia, had gladly provided France with ammunition for the ships which were blockading German ports. Profit, that was the Englishman's god, said the Germans; for the sake of profit he would see right betrayed, wrong triumphant. In the days of the first Napoleon, Briton and Prussian had fought shoulder to shoulder against the conqueror. Commercialism had robbed England of her courage and her honor. The England of the centuries from Shakespeare to Byron was dead; on that once glorious island lived a craven race of tradesmen. The leadership of the Germanic peoples had passed from the Anglo-Saxons back to the parent branch on the mainland. Teutonic heroism, forgotten in Britain, was reborn on the battlefields of Königgrätz and Sedan. Isolated voices even proclaimed that as Britain's star was sinking, the star of Germany was only beginning its rise. The descendants of the Hanse sailors would once more take to the sea and complete the saga which England had broken off, half finished.

The shift in German opinion of England was spontaneous. It was encouraged and intensified by Bismarck, although he thought the popular view of England silly, without basis in fact or in logic. Contempt for British statesmen he did feel intensely. For ten years he played on their convictions and aversions, their ignorance and their false assumptions, with uniform success. Each time his trickery became obvious he relied on English military weakness to prevent hostile action, and on the gullibility of the London government for the possibility of renewed deception; each time England acted as he had foretold. He did not even attempt to hide his contempt. To a lieutenant during the Danish War he boasted that when a minatory dispatch arrived from Lord Russell, he tore it up, tossed it in the wastepaper basket; a second dispatch went the way of the first; then Russell said no more.[13] A year later, French ministers were reporting his indiscretions: "The thunders of Albion are no longer backed by lightning charges; even children do not fear them." [14] This was contempt for British statesmen and the British army; but not for the potential power of the British Empire. Bismarck was convinced that so long as the liberalism of "Professor" Gladstone

[13] *Ges. Werke*, VII, 87.
[14] *Origines*, VII, 14.

was dominant, England's army would be weak and her diplomacy impotent. He neither expected nor desired this situation to continue. The British must eventually arouse themselves, if for no higher motive than to avoid endless humiliation. Germany would profit by the change. Success did not intoxicate Bismarck. The Germany he was creating must live between strong and jealous neighbors who were, fortunately, rivals of England. When England recovered from blinding devotion to liberal principles she would recognize a friend in Germany. Bismarck's brutal rudeness and his encouragement of popular attacks on England were partly actuated by a desire to awaken the British to a realization that their interests would best be served by conciliating a rising state which had the power to help or hurt England.

He had another, and more subtle motive. By exposing the weakness of liberal England, he was making more difficult a revival of German liberalism. He had won the German masses from liberalism; he had not won over all the leaders, above all, not the most dangerous leaders, the Prussian Crown Prince Frederick and his English wife. These were foes who could not be converted by military success. In the Prussian camp at Versailles, on the last day of the glorious year 1870, Frederick looked back with horror at the road Germany had travelled. Germany, he wrote, was no longer known as the land of artists, thinkers, and poets; now it was, in the eyes of the world, a land of robbers whose pledge was worthless. "Bismarck has made us great and strong, but he has robbed us of our friends, the sympathies of the world and—our conscience." Unity could have been won without these sacrifices. The damage was done; it was the task of the future to repair the damage.[15] Around the Prince and the Princess stood a small, determined group who received advice and encouragement from English diplomatic representatives at German courts, like Sir Robert Morier at Darmstadt, from Queen Victoria, and even from the British foreign office. The hopes of these liberals were buoyed by the feeling that

[15] *Kriegstagebuch*, 302–303.

time was on their side. "Count Bismarck is not eternal," the Crown Princess wrote hopefully to her mother, Queen Victoria, in 1871.[16] Bismarck was acutely conscious that only the life of a septuagenarian stood between liberalism and the imperial throne. He fought with fury and without scruple to extirpate the last traces of English and liberal influence so that, when the old King died, the new emperor and empress would find no followers. The German press was encouraged, ordered, to attack England with a vehemence which, as the Prussian minister at London warned, jeopardized official relations and provoked counterattacks in English papers. The appointment of Morier to Berlin was blocked, and eventually he was hounded out of Germany. The Crown Princess was subjected to indignities which were known and resented in London. Warnings brought only an occasional lull in the campaign. Bismarck was safeguarding his work from destruction; and in his view of politics the cost seemed slight. He believed that, in the long run, official relations between the two countries would depend on their interests. For public opinion he had only contempt. He had bent it one way; he could bend it another way when occasion arose. Here he erred. He exaggerated his own part in creating the feelings of anger and disdain which dominated the German view of England in 1871; he exaggerated his ability to obliterate these feelings when need arose. Above all, he was blind to the impression of Germany which was taking form in the English mind.

[16] *Letters of the Empress Frederick*, 126.

PART II

NATURAL ALLIES

1871–1894

INTRODUCTION

IN MARCH, 1894, Mr. Gladstone surrendered the premiership to his Liberal Imperialist colleague, Lord Rosebery. An almost incredibly long and brilliant political career, stretching back of Victoria's accession to the year of the First Reform Bill, ended on a note of failure. The occasion for resignation was his refusal to heed the popular clamor for increased naval appropriations. "I admit that I am without support," he explained. "But the world of today is not the world in which I was bred and trained and have principally lived. It is a world which I have had much difficulty in keeping on terms with and those difficulties increase and are not wholly confined to this matter." Very possibly his opponents were right and he was wrong, but he could not take a part "in the controversies of blood which we all fear and seem to see hanging over Europe." [1] In October of the same year, the second German Imperial Chancellor, General von Caprivi, resigned the office which he had held since Bismarck's fall in 1890. Of the two ministerial changes, the substitution of Prince Hohenlohe for Caprivi in Berlin was the more important. Gladstone had long, as he admitted, been struggling vainly against the tide of British opinion; his retirement removed the last impediment to the triumph of imperialism. The retirement of Caprivi, on the other hand, meant the beginning of German imperialism. He had followed the Bismarckian dogma that Germany was a satiated and Continental power; his successor began the period of *Weltpolitik,* of a Germany eager to grow from a Continental to a world power. In broadest outline, then, Anglo-German relations between 1871 and 1894 are the history of relations between a Continental state which asked

[1] Knaplund, *Gladstone's Foreign Policy*, 266, 267.

only to be left alone and an island kingdom which was haltingly moving from liberal idealism towards imperial egoism.

Friendship was impossible between liberal England and Bismarckian Germany. To Gladstone, the Germans were foes of freedom; to Bismarck, Gladstone was a hypocritical demagogue. Imperial Britain and satiated Germany could be very good friends, "on the sound rule that you love those most whom you compete with least," as Lord Salisbury put it in 1880.[2] Germany was afraid of French and Russian ambitions in Europe; England was afraid of French and Russian ambitions in the world outside Europe. Therefore, Salisbury maintained, "Germany is clearly cut out to be our ally." Immediately, however, he hastened to add—for the present. "Matters will, of course, have changed if it should ever enter into Germany's head to desire Copenhagen or Rotterdam." Some such reservation was seldom absent from the mind of the most ardent British imperialist. The memory of Bismarckian aggression before 1871 refused to die; the robber in Berlin had turned policeman, but might not his old habits return? The astute diplomacy or, depending on the point of view, the trickery, of Bismarck in the 'sixties also left its mark. No one wished to be duped again as Palmerston and Russell had been duped; suspicious caution marked every negotiation with Berlin. Conversely, Bismarck found it hard, particularly when Gladstone was in office, to give up the peremptory tone which he had used so successfully in his communications to Lord John Russell. Lord Rosebery, when Foreign Secretary under Gladstone in 1886, found it necessary to give the German Ambassador "a strong hint that they must take care at Berlin of the style of their communications, which is apt to savor distantly of menace." [3] When Bismarck had the whip hand, the menace was undisguised, and Englishmen neither forgave nor forgot, even after threats gave place to flattery. Despite flurries of anger, however, the official relations between the two governments showed a steadily deepening, if always guarded, intimacy.

[2] Cecil, *Salisbury*, II, 273.
[3] Crewe, *Rosebery*, p. 223.

Corresponding intimacy never developed between the two peoples. Barring the way were, first of all, the disappointments of the years preceding 1871. Germany had shown herself not to be what the English believed, a land of professors—the word professor signifying a very learned but slightly ridiculous and completely ineffectual person. Neither had the Germans realized that freedom and force were incompatible. To a large and vocal number of Englishmen, Germany was a poor relation who had suddenly acquired wealth and influence by very shady methods; it was hard to believe the change was permanent, and it was necessary to assert firmly that changed fortunes did not involve changed status. Condescension found fewer opportunities for expression now that Germany was united and strong, but it certainly was not dead among Englishmen. A charitable observer, looking back, may attribute the indignant abuse, with which many Englishmen greeted German economic competition, to the traditional patronizing attitude towards everything German; the unpleasant alternative is to say that competition called forth much unsportsmanlike whining. Ridicule was more noisy than general, but inability to recognize the ascendancy of Germany, or resentment at that ascendancy, were very general in England. Sincere respect, even admiration, were not lacking among more sober men. The Prussian victories of 1866 and 1870 led to a reform of the English army; German industrial advance led to imitation of German technical education and industrial methods; German political and social thought aided in undermining the older liberalism; German cultural achievements were viewed with heightened appreciation after Königgrätz and Sedan.

Nevertheless, the generalization holds: Englishmen, not merely the man on the street, but men of education and position, including statesmen, were rarely able to see Germany with the steady, detached view so many could attain of France or even Russia. Undoubtedly the past was the greatest distorting medium. Until the end of the century English life was dominated by men who had come to maturity before there was a German Empire, and who were never able to adjust their vision to the new map of Europe. No less important was the difference in political outlook. This also was a legacy of the past. Even while German ideas of the state were affecting their own ideas through intermediaries as diverse as Disraeli and the Oxford idealists, most Englishmen were completely at a loss to understand the political structure Bismarck had created. Despotism was the usual word used to describe the German government. Long after Cobdenite liberalism had been discarded by most Englishmen, and long after Metternich's conservatism had been discarded even by most Prussian Junkers, the British were still contrasting English freedom and German despotism.

The past also obscured the German view of England. From the more remote past there lingered admiration and envy of these island kinsfolk, strong even when consciously repudiated. Symptomatic was the difficulty which Bismarck encountered in securing diplomatic representatives who, once placed in London, would not succumb to English influence so completely as to be bad servants of his policy. Just as Bunsen and Bernstorff before 1871 had become more British than Prussian, so Münster and Hatzfeldt in the last quarter of the century were more eager to tell British statesmen what would be pleasant than what Bismarck commanded that they should hear. Many popular movements in Germany, and not least the agitation for colonies and a fleet, arose partly from an effort to acquire what England had. Admiration and envy were old; after 1871 a new note of arrogant defiance was also obvious. The easy victories over Palmerston and Gladstone, the natural exuberance consequent on unification, and initial victories in the field of economic rivalry, all served to encourage the belief that England was no longer the teacher, Germany the pupil. Diplomatic victories at the expense of England were sure of popular support; coöperation with England was viewed suspiciously. If Bismarck had taught the British to fear German trickery, he had also reinforced the old fear of perfidious Albion among his own countrymen.

On one side, condescension and suspicion; on the other, arrogance and suspicion—the popular temper underlying official intimacy was not a secure foundation for permanent good relations. And official intimacy was the expression of a tenuous community of interest. Each government needed the other against France and Russia. As Lord Salisbury said, governments love those best with whom they compete least. When Bismarck reached out for colonies in 1884, intimacy was rudely, if temporarily, interrupted. Simultaneously came the first outcry against German commercial rivalry. All through these years the question loomed in the background—what would happen if competition of interests began?

CHAPTER V

GREATER BRITAIN

THERE IS no worse trade than agitation at this time," Walter Bagehot wrote in 1867. "A man can hardly get an audience if he wishes to complain of anything." Considering the date, Bagehot's remark seems almost ironical. That year saw the passage of the Second Reform Bill, which put England on the road to democracy. The bill was not passed without agitation; and franchise reform was not the only subject being agitated. Lord Palmerston's death ended the quietude which had marked internal politics for two decades. Gladstone and Disraeli were beginning the duel which was to continue through the Midlothian campaign and the elections of 1880, the duel which extended over every aspect of domestic and foreign politics. In 1867, too, appeared Matthew Arnold's *New Poems*, containing that poignant lament on the receding tide of faith,

> *Retreating to the breath*
> *Of the night-wind down the vast edges drear*
> *And naked shingles of the world.*

Surely, the heart-searching precipitated by Darwin's *Origin of Species*, the gulf fixed between father and son by the religious scepticism which Darwin had unconsciously deepened, the debate over evolution and revelation—surely this was agitation. There was another lament in Arnold's slim volume, the elegy for Arthur Hugh Clough, whose short life was filled with complaint. Back in the 'forties, Clough had seemed promising political timber to Gladstone's party managers: "a very favorable specimen of a class, growing in numbers and importance among the younger Oxford men, a friend of Carlyle's, Frank Newman's, and others of that stamp; well read in German literature and an admirer of German intellect, but also a still greater admirer of Dante; just now taking all his opinions to pieces and not beginning to put them together again; but so earnest and good that he might be trusted to work them into something better than his friends inclined to fear."[1] Actually, the worst fears of Clough's friends were realized. Christianity, the creed of liberalism, and what his eyes saw of humanity in Victorian England, these he could not reconcile, and in the *Latest Decalogue* he expressed his disgust at the apparent contradictions—

Thou shalt have one God only; who
Would be at the expense of two? . . .

Thou shalt not covet, but tradition
Approves all forms of competition.

In this same year 1867, another kind of rebel was hard at work on a book which was to be, not only for him but for many others, an escape from the pit of disillusionment into which Clough had fallen. Charles Dilke, like Clough, early lost faith in revealed religion. Unlike Clough, he refused to lose faith in his age. At first he sought refuge in the refined selfishness which earlier radicals had popularized. "My aim in life," he solemnly informed his brother, "is to be of the greatest use I can to the world at large, not because that is my duty, but because that is the course which will make my life happiest—i. e., my motives are selfish in the wide and unusual sense of that word." Meticulously, he had worked out a course of "improvement" for himself, his brother, and the world. Later, coming again on what he had written, Dilke scrawled across the page, "What a prig he was!"[2] Priggish the ascetic liberalism of the early nineteenth century did seem in the opulent 'sixties when all the forts of reaction had been stormed. This prig found emancipation in the new Grand Tour which was just coming into fashion—the tour, not of fashionable Europe, but of the world. Somewhere on that journey, he found a new religion and a new mission. On his

[1] Morley, *Gladstone*, I, 329.
[2] Gwynn and Tuckwell, *Dilke*, 63, 64.

return, he set down his experiences. The result was not a conventional travel book; it was a hymn of praise, to which he gave the pregnant title *Greater Britain*.

> In 1866 and 1867, I followed England round the world: everywhere I was in English-speaking or in English-governed lands. If I remarked that climate, soil, manners of life, that mixture with other peoples, had modified the blood, I saw, too, that in essentials the race was always one. The idea which in all the length of my travels has been at once my fellow and my guide—a key wherewith to unlock the hidden things of strange new lands—is a conception, however imperfect, of the grandeur of our race, already girdling the earth, which it is destined, perhaps, eventually to overspread.[3]

Here was a strange, and as soon appeared, a popular theme: racial pride rising to do battle alike with the cosmopolitanism and the insular patriotism which had hitherto been the only rivals for the loyalty of Englishmen.

Looking back it is easy to see that 1867 marks the time when the age of the Cobdens and the Palmerstons began to give way to a very different age. Such recognition does not deprive Bagehot's testimony of value. No one is better fitted to introduce us to the well-educated, well-bred, prosperous, and tolerant men who ruled England in 1867, and who expected to continue ruling England. That world included not only politicians, but men of commerce, industry, finance, and the professions, and in addition, the recognized leaders of arts and letters. At the center were still the landowners, aristocrats and gentry, old families or families newly emancipated from less exalted activities. "They were educated at the same schools; know one another's family name from boyhood; form a society; are the same kind of men; marry the same kind of women." The English were a deferential people, Bagehot was happy to say, and they preferred to be represented by one of their betters. "If he was rich, they respected him much; if he was a lord, they liked him the better." Bagehot realized the disadvantages of deference. Inevitably, landowners favored their own class, and this was bad in a

[3] Dilke, *Greater Britain*, Introduction, v, vi.

country where commerce and industry were the chief occupations. Inevitably, where birth counted more than ability, inefficiency resulted. Still he feared rather than hoped that the enlarged franchise might alter this situation materially. What were the alternatives? France was more democratic, and every interest could press directly on the French parliament; but the oscillation between anarchy and despotism which had marked the political life of that volatile people during the past century did not encourage imitation. Prussia was more efficient, and many Englishmen, awed by the recent victories of Moltke's arms, would copy the Prussian bureaucracy. "But it is quite certain that the Prussian bureaucracy, though we, for a moment, half admire it at a distance, does not permanently please the most intelligent and liberal Prussians at home." Bureaucracy inevitably hardened into routine. The Prussian bureaucracy had so hardened after the death of Frederick the Great; the result was collapse in face of Napoleon. Then had come violent reform, with results apparent in the work of Bismarck. After this spasm of activity, a new hardening and decline to routine was inevitable. Efficiency was temporary; and at what a cost such efficiency was purchased! Red-tape, regulations, restrictions on every detail of life—would Englishmen long tolerate such regimentation? Englishmen had won their freedom by resisting authority, and the tradition of resistance lingered on, even too strongly for the national good. "We look on State action, not as our own action, but as alien action; as an imposed tyranny from without, not as the consummated result of our organized wishes." For such a people, bureaucratic rule would be intolerable. On the whole, observing the excesses of their neighbors, Englishmen might glory in their deference to men of superior position, in spite of the disadvantages such deference entailed. "Sensible men of substantial means are what we wish to be ruled by." With loving care, he dissected the interlocking of the "dignified" and the "effective" parts of English government, from the squire up to the Queen and the Prince of Wales—"it is nice to trace how the actions of a retired widow and an unemployed youth become of such importance."[4]

Deference, Bagehot thought, was such a settled attitude among the middle classes that its indefinite continuance might be hoped for. In 1867, however, the vote had been given to the city workmen. Would these men also be content to follow their betters? The answer to that question, he maintained, was in the hands of the upper classes themselves. If the Liberal and Conservative parties continued, as in the past, to debate great questions of national interest on their merits, the old order would continue; if the parties competed for the workers' favor, all would be lost. "I can conceive of nothing more corrupting or worse for a set of poor ignorant people than that two combinations of well-taught and rich men should constantly offer to defer to their decision, and compete for the office of executing it. *Vox populi* will be *Vox diaboli* if it is worked in that manner." Confident as he was of the solid good sense of the upper classes, Bagehot saw these dangers only as remote and improbable.

Even as late as 1894, most well-taught and rich men still thought the danger possible to avoid, but others could see that the old harmony was disappearing. When, in that year, Sir William Harcourt proposed to tax landed estates as other estates were taxed, Lord Rosebery warned him of the danger of arousing class conflict. Harcourt bluntly replied that the conflict was already going on, and that it was stimulated rather than checked by aristocratic privilege. "You desire to avert the 'cleavage of classes,'" Harcourt wrote. "The hope on your part is natural, but you are too late. The horizontal division of parties was certain to come as a consequence of household suffrage. The thin edge of the wedge was inserted, and the cleavage is expanding more and more every day. I do not wonder at your casting a longing lingering look on the 'variety and richness and intellectual forces' which have passed away, but these are not the appanage of democracy."[5] Harcourt was a wise old man, but

[4] "The English Constitution," *Works,* V, 116 *ff.*
[5] Gardiner, *Harcourt,* II, 284–285.

he was anticipating a future which had not arrived in 1894. Deference was losing ground, but it still sufficed to keep believers in the old system at the top: Rosebery was rich and well-born, and he was Prime Minister. Bagehot's analysis of English constitutional life was almost as close to actual practice as it had been a generation before, so close that only an alert observer could see that the foundations of the old system were slipping. To most Englishmen, stability rather than change, security rather than experiment, seemed the characteristics of the generation following the Second Reform Bill.

The intellectual and spiritual controversies precipitated by the theories of Darwin are no less muffled than political debates when they are reported by Bagehot. The misery and the blind anger caused by the *Origin of Species* are known to all; but most Englishmen did not go through the anguish of soul described, for instance, in Edmund Gosse's *Father and Son*. That religious faith declined, needs no demonstration. That the decline had effects in every part of the national life is equally obvious. Finally, it is obvious that a large part of the emotional force which formerly found an outlet in religion, now was poured into steadily heightened nationalism and its offspring, imperialism. But for most men these changes went on quietly, unmarked by acute spiritual crisis, almost unobserved. Here again Bagehot may be taken as a guide. As always, he was representative of the temper, rather than the expressed convictions, of Englishmen. Few could approach him either in knowledge or in felicity of expression; but out of an alert and informed mind he spoke for his less articulate countrymen.

Bagehot, writing his *Physics and Politics* in the years following 1867, was aware that "a new world of ideas was in the air and affects us, though we see it not," a new world of science dominated by the concept of evolution. He refused to be terrified by this new world; indeed, he argued that most men had lost their first horror of expressions like natural selection. "The new principle is more and more seen to be fatal to mere outworks of religion, not to religion itself;" like himself, most men found their faith as secure as ever. The real significance of evolution, apart from its strictly scientific uses, was not to be obscured by controversies about apes and angels; it was to the student of man as a political animal, that the new ideas had revolutionary import. No longer was it possible for an educated man to talk about uniform natural laws, about human equality, about individualism, even about the human reason, as theorists had talked earlier in the century. On all these subjects it was necessary to generalize, not from abstract reason, but from history. Looking back, ages could be found when none of the laws of political economy were valid, and ages when individualism would have meant weakness and death. On the other hand, looking at history it became evident that human equality was a myth, and that the human reason had always, for the good of the race, been held fast in a "cake of custom." Finally, and most important, on looking back it became evident that everywhere and at all times men were organized into coöperative groups. It was not enough to study the individual; he was formed by the group. It was not enough to study mankind; common human characteristics were twisted into as many different forms as there were political societies. Individuals were important, because great, creative individuals "set the tone which others take, and the fashions which others use"; but a man was great or infamous because he improved or corrupted his countrymen. Human nature was important because it set the purpose and the limits of group action; but within this general frame each group lived its peculiar existence. Therefore, the object of the student of politics should be to discover the laws of group action by a scrutiny of political societies past and present.

Bagehot stated his own conclusion at the outset: "In every particular state of the world, those nations which are strongest tend to be the best." Roughly, he believed, human societies fell into three categories or levels. In the first stage, the lower side of man was most nearly dominant, that part which was lazy, quarrelsome, selfish, and short-sighted. Even then, men realized the necessity for some group action; the rudest form of cooperative society could better preserve life than could the strongest individual. Among these rude societies, those possessing the greatest solidarity conquered those with less. In other words, he argued, social cohesion and discipline, were the "best" qualities at this stage, because they enabled men to survive. When a group had attained to relatively complete internal harmony, it had reached the second stage of evolution, the age of stability. The ascent, even to this elevation, was arduous and painful, entailing as it did the imposition of rigid conformity on all members of the community. Here was no place for rebels or innovators. Intolerance was a social necessity; man must learn to bend his unruly will to the common will. The process was aided by the imitative nature of man—"unbelief far oftener needs a reason and requires an effort than belief." It was aided also by the process of natural selection, which operated within tribes as well as between tribes—"the child most fit to be a good Spartan is most likely to survive a Spartan childhood." The result of this combination of imitation and persecution was a national character, a disciplined, orderly, coherent group consciousness. Now, "best" included not only the power to fight other tribes, but the ability of members of the group to think, act, and work harmoniously together.

Finally, there was possible a third stage, the age of discussion. When coöperation had become habitual, when the national character was formed, intolerance and monotony could be discarded. The danger of discussion was obvious. "Once effectually submit a subject to that ordeal, and you can never withdraw it again; you can never again clothe it with mystery, or fence it by consecration; it remains for ever open to free choice and exposed to profane deliberation." If the danger was great, however, the rewards were even greater. Gone were the brakes on intelligence; everyone might hope for a hearing, if not for acceptance of his ideas. Gone was bigotry; the nation was sure enough of itself to tolerate dissent. Above all, now it was possible to have rapid progress. The word "progress," Bagehot admitted, was hard to define, but it could be understood at least by contrast. Consider the Australian bushman confronted by the English immigrant. Obviously, the colonist was superior in the art of killing. More than that, he was superior in his ability to control nature, not only because he could make better machines, but because he was himself a better machine. Finally, he was better equipped to use the forces of nature for his own comfort and pleasure. "Beyond particular invention, there is a general strength which is capable of being used in conquering a thousand difficulties, and is an abiding source of happiness, because those who possess it always feel that they can use it." So much could be said with confidence, and it was enough to demonstrate that there was a "verifiable progress." Thus defined, progress might be seen in every stage of the slow ascent of man from relative anarchy through the ages when coöperation was being learned, to the summit of free government by discussion. Only in the final stage, however, could progress be quick and limitless.

Few nations in the long record of history had been able to ascend even from loose tribalism to a stable national life; still fewer had been able to break the cake of custom so laboriously formed, and emerge into the free air of government by discussion. Among the favored few, England possessed beyond all others the "animated moderation," the energy and balance of mind, which was the secret of progress. England had her faults, as critics both at home and abroad were constantly demonstrating, but on the whole her career had been successful and admirable, and all because her people possessed animated moderation. Her business men knew when to forge ahead, and when to pull up short. Her statesmen knew when to be daring, when to be cautious. The electorate had repeatedly shown ability to steer a safe course between extremes. In science, other nations might have greater and more diffused knowledge, but Englishmen could show as many, if not more, important discoveries. Even the workman, "though so much less sober, less instructed, and less refined than the artisans of some other countries, is yet more inventive than any other artisan." More generally, England had freely entered the commerce of the world; when custom ruled, international commerce was avoided lest it weaken, dilute the national character. Colonies, for a country sure of national solidarity, were a stimulus to progress; a nation unsure of itself could not risk the contact with other countries which colonization entailed. The English had broken the cake of custom, they had released the inventiveness of man, the taste and judgment of man. They had reached the age of government by discussion, the age of limitless progress, progress transcending the bounds of verification. "Then, for the first time, almost every part of human nature begins to spring forward, and begins to contribute its quota even to the narrowest, even to 'verifiable' progress. And this is the true reason of all those panegyrics on liberty which are often so [un]measured in expression but are in essence so true to life and nature. Liberty is the strengthening and developing power—the light and heat of political nature; and when some 'Caesarism' exhibits as it sometimes will an originality of mind, it is only because it has managed to make its own the products of past free times or neighboring free countries; and even that originality is only brief and frail, and after a little while, when tested by a generation or two, in time of need it falls away." [6]

While claiming much for his own country, Bagehot was careful in his *Physics and Politics* not to disparage other countries. Evidently, from scattered references, he considered France and the United States to be nations in the final stage of evolution; on Germany he was silent, unless the reference to Cæsarism may be considered a veiled allusion. In an editorial written for *The Economist* in May, 1875, he spoke more freely. Bismarck was then doing battle with the Roman Catholic Church; many Protestants in England were disposed to applaud. Bagehot reminded his countrymen that they should be proudest of their tolerance, their success in reconciling theological controversy with the order of a civilized state. "In Germany at the present moment this solution is being treated as if it were the mere invention of cowardice and weakness." Englishmen had learned otherwise

[6] "Physics and Politics," *Works*, VIII, 1–145.

from experience; bigotry was symptomatic of a stage in history they had long passed through. "Germany is going through a sort of epidemic of blind and frantic nationalism, a sort of political measles to which great nations in the infancy of their conscious unity and power are very liable." Prince Bismarck was encouraging these passions, partly to win popularity, partly "from real inability to measure moral influences as he measures material forces." Evidently, for Bagehot, Germany was a nation which had only incompletely entered the age of stability; the age of discussion lay far in the future. Other Englishmen might use other expressions, but most agreed that Germany was not mature, as Britain was mature.

Reading Bagehot, the world of Cobden seems far away. The whole accent had changed. The individual and humanity had receded to the background; the national community and national power were to the fore. "The characters which do win in war are the characters which we should wish to win in war." [7] This was not the language which Englishmen had earlier liked to hear; but it was the language which many wished to hear in 1872, when *Physics and Politics* was published. Within the space of a few years the current of English thought was changing.

The change can be seen dramatically in the field of practical politics. There, after the death of Palmerston, Gladstone and Disraeli battled for power. Gladstone was close to the liberal ideal. His moral earnestness and his faith in freedom; his conviction that Englishmen should be allowed to run their own lives, and that England should influence the affairs of other countries only by example; his middle class origin and his Oxford training—all these were calculated to make him the hero of liberalism. Opposed to him was Disraeli, a man who in his own words, had climbed the greased pole burdened with every possible handicap. A Jew, derided even by members of his own party as a fop and a society novelist who described society from hearsay, he had slowly fought his way to leadership over the Tory party in the House of Commons. For long, the conquest

[7] Bagehot, *Works*, VIII, 139.

of leadership had seemed an empty victory, made possible by the defection of the best Tory minds, and many Tory votes, to the ascendant Whigs. Through a quarter of a century he had struggled to give his party cohesion and meaning, years of toil rewarded only by fugitive holds on office. During this long apprenticeship, the lineaments of his vision of England's future shifted so often that it might seem to have had the unsubstantiality of a dream. Beneath all changes, however, there remained one conviction which never changed, the conviction that national character was the most real and most important fact in the world. At the outset of his career he had seen clearly the gulf which separated his mind from liberal ways of thinking, and characteristically he took the offensive. "The schoolmen are revived in the nineteenth century, and are going to settle the State with their withering disquisitions, their fruitless logomachies, and barren dialectics." The liberal mind could see only the individual and humanity, but between these extremes was the nation. "Nations have characters as well as individuals, and national character is precisely the quality which the new set of statesmen and speculations either deny or overlook."[8] Liberalism, he was convinced, was a creed for merchants, men who set their profit above the common good; the common man, like the gentry who were removed from the temptations of greed, could see that individual gain was not the same as the common good. Sure that the masses would follow him, he pushed through the Reform Bill of 1867, extending the franchise far beyond the demands of the moderate Gladstone, and infinitely beyond the limits which frightened Tories thought safe. Like Bismarck, Disraeli would destroy liberalism by pushing it to its logical conclusion, democracy. Descriptions of him in 1867 show him confident of the outcome. "And the potent wizard himself, with his olive complexion and coal-black eyes, and the mighty dome of his forehead (no Christian temple, be sure), is unlike any living creature one has met." Men said truly that he was an actor, but he was more than that. "This mightier Venice—this

[8] *Whigs and Whiggism,* 119, 120.

Imperial Republic on which the sun never sets—that vision fascinates him, or I am much mistaken. England is the Israel of his imagination, and he will be the Imperial Minister before he dies—if he gets the chance." [9]

The elections of 1868, however, showed the liberal tide running strong, and Gladstone's "Great Ministry" began with the overwhelming backing of the newly enfranchised democracy. During the next four years one emancipating reform after another was pushed through Parliament. Commissions in the army were put on the basis of merit, religious tests for university posts abolished, the Irish Church disestablished, education reformed, the civil service put on a competitive basis, the last vestiges of protective tariff removed—the list could be greatly extended. And yet by 1872, Disraeli was again moving confidently to the assault. "As I sit opposite the treasury bench, the ministers remind me of one of those marine landscapes not very unusual on the coasts of South America. You behold a range of exhausted volcanoes. Not a flame flickers upon a single pallid crest. But the situation is still dangerous. There are occasional earthquakes, and ever and anon dark rumblings of the sea." In the Crystal Palace, that symbol of liberal England, he set forth his program: "The maintenance of our institutions, the preservation of our empire, and the improvement of the condition of the people." He would stop the dismantling of the state, the stripping away of one function, then another. Instead he would strengthen, mobilize the power of the state at home and abroad. At home, he would heal the cleavage between Englishmen, the two nations of the rich and the poor who had drifted apart through liberal indifference and selfishness. The state would step into its rightful place as regulator, take the lead in housing, in the protection of health, in all social questions. Abroad, he would end the sterile rule of non-intervention, restore the depleted prestige of Britain, give her a voice in the settlement of world affairs commensurate with her greatness. The Empire would be for him a precious trust to be guarded and

[9] M. & B., II, 292–293.

strengthened as the great source of British power, not treated as a necessary, temporary nuisance. Against liberal logic, liberal cosmopolitanism, liberal individualism, he appealed to "the sublime instinct of an ancient people," asking Englishmen to recognize that they were a people, a people not only marked off from other nations, but a people with duties towards each other and the rest of the world—a nation and an empire. "The issue is not a mean one. It is whether you will be content to be a comfortable England, modelled and moulded upon Continental principles and meeting in due course an inevitable fate, or whether you will be a great country, an Imperial country, a country where your sons, when they rise, rise to paramount positions, and obtain not merely the esteem of their countrymen, but command the respect of the world." Against such emotional appeals, Gladstone appealed to his record of emancipating reform, to trade figures mounting above all earlier records, to a full treasury, to the hope that under an economical administration the income tax might be abolished. But when the poll was taken in 1874, Disraeli's followers were the ones elected; the Liberal ranks were decimated.[10]

The shift from Gladstone to Disraeli was no less a contrast than the change which Bagehot showed when compared with Cobden. In politics and thought alike there was the same break. Undoubtedly a host of minor causes contributed to the change, but singly or together they do not suffice. It is much too simple to attribute decisive importance to a single book, like Darwin's *Origin of Species*. Darwin's theory of the survival of the fittest was applied to social groups by Bagehot and his successors, but Darwin himself refused to make this application. Moreover, Herbert Spencer had shown in *Social Statics*, and was continuing to show in successive volumes of his *Synthetic Philosophy*, that the struggle for existence could be made to justify complete individualism and a policy of laissez-faire. English thought was increasingly preoccupied with questions of national solidarity and national power; other writers were quick to follow Bagehot's

[10] Morley, *Gladstone*, II, 290, 291; M. & B., II, 536.

lead in depicting the history of political societies in terms of the survival of the fittest; but it would be presumptuous to make Darwin more than an ally of the forces making for change.

The same may be said of the influence of German thought and action in producing a climate of opinion in so many ways like that which had long prevailed in Germany. Since the days of Coleridge, German ideas of the state had been finding their way into the minds of English philosophers, poets, novelists, and even statesmen. The very fact that these ideas had been current so long, however, deprives them of more than suggestive import. A more tangible influence was the military success of Germany. Englishmen were humiliated, but they were also impressed, by Bismarck's military victories over Austria and France, and by his diplomatic success over British statesmen. It is possible to trace the change in individuals like Sir Robert Morier. Morier had long hoped for a liberal, that is a peaceful and democratic, solution of the problem of German unity. He was quick to see that Bismarck stood for everything most detested by liberals and he continued to feel only implacable hatred for "the chauvinist Baal enthroned at Berlin." The iron had entered his own heart, however, and when Benjamin Jowett wrote him, after the Franco-Prussian war, that peace should be the one object of British policy, Morier challenged the great Oxford scholar. "Would you restore the Pope his temporalities, dismember Italy, and return Lombardy and Venetia to Austria, if by so doing you could call the dead of Solferino and Magenta to life?" There were things worse than war, and one of these was the national habit of looking at war as the worst of all evils. As for him, he was possessed by "a frantic desire to restore the international prestige of England, not for the good of England only, but for the good of the human race, because it so happens that England is about the only great Power which can really in pushing forward her own ends at the same time further those of the rest of the world." For him, the Franco-Prussian war had changed the whole course of history. "There was a stream of international comity which by proper direction might have been made to take the whole human race a long way towards a better future. But that infernal war has destroyed all this for our generation at least, and a political state of things has remained as the outcome in which it seems to me of the greatest importance that we should strengthen and evoke all the Nationalism and Imperialism left within us." [11] The stimulus of Königgrätz and Sedan could be seen in other ways, large and small—in the sensational sale of *The Battle of Dorking*, an anonymous description of an imaginary German invasion of England which appeared in 1871, as well as in the sweeping reform of the English army pushed through by Cardwell, Gladstone's Secretary for War. Within a few years after 1868, troops were brought home from the self-governing colonies, the size of the regular army increased, a new rifle introduced, the purchase of commissions abolished, the whole military structure remade, and—crowning heresy from the liberal point of view—military appropriations raised by almost a third. All this indicates that the stirring events on the Continent during the years preceding 1871 helped to precipitate a reëxamination of the liberal creed, but it is very doubtful if they did much more than hasten an impending change which must have come.

A very usual way of disposing of the problem is to explain it away. It can be argued that Disraeli's program was not very new. After all, the electorate had thrilled to Palmerston's buoyant patriotism; was Disraeli so different? Again, was Disraeli's social reform program so new; if a date is wanted for the change from laissez-faire to what may be called the social service state, might not the Factory Act of 1847 be chosen as the turning point? There is point to these arguments, but they cannot be carried very far. Violent patriotism had been known in England long before the word jingo came into use during Disraeli's administration. Palmerston's pride, however, had been based on the belief that the English were further advanced along the path in which other peoples were also advancing. The exponents of the new nationalism gloried in the belief that the English were

[11] Morier, II, 291–293, 298, 299.

different from other peoples, were a chosen race with a peculiar mission. As for social reform, undoubtedly one exception after another had earlier been made in the rule of freedom, but these had always been admittedly exceptions, defended as such. Disraeli's "Tory Democracy" was the first official defence of state interference as a good in itself since the collapse of the old Toryism early in the century. Equally important, state interference with natural law was playing havoc even with the Liberal party by 1874. Earlier, a radical had been an extreme individualist; now a radical was coming to mean an advocate of what Gladstone contemptuously called "construction." Finally, it must be remembered that in the new ways of thought, social reform and nationalism were not separate programs. They were fused into a coherent whole by concern for national power. Reform, spirited foreign policy, protection and tightening of the imperial bond—all served the needs of the group. Britons were no longer atoms whose activities centered in certain geographical areas; they were parts of a living body.

If this be true, a contrary objection falls to the ground, the argument that the victory of 1874 meant little. The Great Ministry was, to be sure, only the first of four Gladstone governments. Disraeli's imperialism was denounced at the time as a "policy of Bounce and Bluster," as a romantic oriental drama which almost completely disregarded the self-governing colonies and concentrated itself exclusively around India as the real empire; did not the electorate register its disapproval of this adventurer in 1880? Should not imperialism be dated much later, in the middle 'nineties, and its vogue then be interpreted as an expression of the need of capital for new outlets and for some means of distracting attention from the demand for social reform? Even before 1880, the Tories had lost their enthusiasm for social reform, and they never regained it; may not Tory Democracy be dismissed as a fraud? Something can be said for all these contentions. Individualist liberalism was long in dying, and it retained much strength so long as it was personified in the revered Gladstone. Conversely, the strength of imperialism and social reform had no steady rise, and the two did not grow in unison; sometimes they seemed rivals rather than allies. But the trend was clear, as Gladstone himself admitted. He fought hard and long, but he knew it was a losing fight. Increasingly, men of his own party insisted on "taking into the hands of the state the business of the individual man"; increasingly, men bearing the strange label of Liberal Imperialist came to the fore, and to one such he finally surrendered his power.

The new nationalism did not take hold in a day, but it did rise to prominence in the years of *Greater Britain*, *Physics and Politics* and Disraeli's Crystal Palace speech. It cannot be explained in terms of Hegel, or Bismarck, or Darwin alone. Possibly it cannot be explained. Undoubtedly emotional needs contributed greatly. The decline of religion can be measured statistically by such symptoms as church attendance, which was falling rapidly; it can be measured by the alarm of discerning observers like Gladstone. "I am convinced," he wrote in 1874, "that the welfare of mankind does not now depend on the state or the world of politics; the real battle is being fought in the world of thought, where a deadly attack is made with great tenacity of purpose and over a wide field, upon the greatest treasure of mankind, the belief in God and the gospel of Christ." [12] How much of the fervor which was formerly poured into religion found an outlet in nationalism, and more particularly in the missionary zeal of imperialism? Here there can be no clear evidence, but it can be said with safety that the decline of religion and the rise of nationalism were intimately connected.

Simultaneously, it was becoming more difficult to cleave to that other English religion, liberalism. While there was oppressive privilege to be fought, the liberal battle could be absorbing. It had seemed almost incidental to Gladstone that by "the fixed laws of Providence"—that is, the laws of economics—"the mass of mankind is composed of men, women, and children who can but just ward off hunger, cold, and nakedness; whose whole ideas of Mammon-worship are compromised in the search for their

[12] Morley, *Gladstone*, II, 500.

daily food, clothing, shelter, fuel; whom any casualty reduces to positive want." [13] But now the forts of privilege had fallen, freedom had been won. In the reaction of victory, the crusaders could count the cost. Looking at life in factories and factory towns, it was hard to believe that this was the best of all possible worlds. Particularly, it was hard for the workmen enfranchised in 1867 to hold this belief. The very success of liberalism was its nemesis. The state had been changed from an inefficient and corrupt tool of a minority into a perfected instrument capable of doing almost any task which was humanly possible. It seemed more natural to trust than to mistrust the reformed state, to use it, rather than to hedge its use. The crusading zeal once turned against the oligarchical state was now directed to the task of correcting the defects of industrial civilization through the state. Young Sir Charles Dilke had sought refuge from religious scepticism in the enlightened self-interest of the older liberalism; very soon he fled this austere shelter for the warmth and purpose of the new nationalism. He still called himself a liberal, but that word was slowly changing its meaning out of recognition. Again, how many prigs were emancipated in these years by the new Grand Tour, taken actually like Dilke's, or vicariously through his writings, and the books of others like him? The life, like the creed, of liberalism had been devised for an ascetic generation. Life, in years when the curve of trade was rising, demanded an escape from the narrow round of duty, as duty had earlier been defined. This world whose distances were shrinking before the telegraph, compound engines, and slim steel ships, offered an escape and a wider duty. By the time Kipling came, he found an audience waiting.

All this is far from Marxian economics, because Marxian economics does not go far to explain the popularity of Dilke, Bagehot or Disraeli. In the years from 1870 to 1874 the index of imports and exports was pointed sharply upward as the boom following war in Europe and America reached and passed its peak. Goods were not begging for a market, nor capital for

[13] *Ibid.*, III, 548.

virgin areas to exploit. Economics, more broadly defined, does help to explain the change. Labor was more articulate and self-conscious than formerly. Trade was pushing out to every corner of the globe. Science was panting to keep communications and means of transport abreast of the possibilities of trade. But it is hard to see how the shift of loyalties from the individual to the community, from insularity to imperialism in the days when Disraeli was appealing to "the sublime instinct of an ancient people" can be reduced to terms which a Lenin could consider valid.

In the transition to the new nationalism, Disraeli proved himself a better stage director than playwright (the man was so consciously an actor that it is impossible to speak of him in other than theatrical terms). He did replace the simple stage on which the Englishman and his family had played out the drama of political freedom and religious duty, by an opulent and spacious set, fit for the drama of a chosen race. His imperial stage was not the world; it was the great triangle between England, the Cape of Good Hope, and India. To every people and every land along the bounds of the triangle, the director assigned a rôle, with the leading parts reserved for the ruling English and their Indian wards. This work consumed the first two years of his administration, and it was his most permanent work. The English government never lost again the aura of exalted purpose, purpose towards Englishmen and towards people ruled by the crown. In 1878, the boys of the Eton Literary Society were filled with a sense of their mission as they listened to Sir James Stephen talk about India. "There is on the Asian continent an empire more populous, more amazing, and more beneficent than that of Rome. The rulers of that great dominion are drawn from the men of our own people." Twenty years later Lord Curzon, who had been one of the listening boys and who was now viceroy of India, recalled the effect of Stephen's words. "Ever since that day, the fascination and *sacredness* of India have grown upon me." [14] This lift to the imagination of a whole

[14] Ronaldshay, *Curzon,* I, 309; Nicolson, *Curzon,* 12.

generation was Disraeli's greatest achievement. As the play unfolded after 1876, however, it cannot be said to have been a success. It was too ambitious in conception, and very faulty in execution. Some of the actors were unequal to their parts; others refused to act as they were told. Disraeli was conscious of his inadequacy to complete what he had projected. Already past seventy, tortured by gout and asthma, deprived of a strong support by the death of his wife in 1872, he saw his infirmities as part of the play. "Power! it has come to me too late. There were days when, on waking, I felt I could move dynasties and governments, but that has passed away." [15] And yet, although the British electorate repudiated the director in 1880, they never succeeded in repudiating his ambitious dream.

At home, the action was largely played out before the first two years had passed. During the parliamentary session of 1875, Tory Democracy advanced with a rush. State supervision was tightened over public health, food and drugs, and safety at sea. Farm tenants were given greater rights in the lands they worked, with corresponding curtailment of the rights of landlords. The formation of trade unions was facilitated, although unions curtailed the power of capital. A beginning was made towards better housing for the poor, despite the rights of property. In this year, Disraeli's enthusiasm even outran his judgment when he tried to enlist Queen Victoria as a patron of an artisans' building association. She refused on the ground that it was dangerous to lend her name where she could not supervise financial management. Her caution was later vindicated by the defalcation of the director, a Mr. Swindlehurst. The legislation of 1875 was impressive as a beginning, but the years following showed that Tory zeal was exhausted by these first efforts. Succeeding sessions were barren of important reforms. Through half a century Disraeli had lamented liberal blindness to social injustice; in the light of his past hopes, the achievements of 1875 seemed almost an anticlimax. It was easy to argue that foreign affairs consumed all his energies; but it would be more accurate to say that foreign

[15] M. & B., II, 639.

affairs provided an escape. The plain fact was that Disraeli had succeeded in drawing a large part of the wealth of England into his party, and social reforms cost money and hedged the freedom of property. Social idealism fought an uphill fight against immediate interest. Here, as in so much else, Disraeli's influence was to be measured in terms of the future rather than the present. If he had not inaugurated an age of social harmony, he had at least broken through the barriers which made the state a passive spectator of the struggles of rival groups.

Possibly his greatest achievement made little mark on the statute book—his refurbishing of the crown. Bagehot had indicated the importance of the crown as a symbol of unity, but when Disraeli took office it could not be said that Victoria held any great place in the affections of her subjects. For more than a decade she had been living remote and inaccessible, brooding on the death of her beloved Albert. Disraeli, with the curious mixture of sentiment and calculation which marked all his actions, set out to win her as an ally. In a cynical mood he could jest that he applied flattery to most women with a camel's hair brush; to the queen, he laid it on with a trowel. The technique was often shockingly crude, but he was not entirely insincere, and she was not entirely a dupe. In some ways she was as good an actor as her minister. She had solaced herself by creating the part of a mother of sorrows which she played to the exasperation of a people who were tired of laments for a half-forgotten foreigner. Disraeli merely created a new and more useful rôle for her—the weak and womanly but heroic and prescient protector of a nation and an empire. The "faery" learned her part and played it to her death. Liberals of the old school were disgusted and appalled by the change. Conservatives were delighted by the slightly unconstitutional grief with which thereafter the Queen saw Conservative ministers replaced by Liberals. As early as 1875, Victoria was the loyal supporter of Disraeli, "who has *very large ideas*, and *very lofty views* of the position this country should hold. His mind is so much greater, larger, and his apprehension of things great and small so much quicker than that of

Mr. Gladstone."[16] The English people were slower to admire his handiwork. Only reluctantly would Parliament consent in 1876 to the addition of "Empress of India" to the royal title; the transformed Queen was reverenced only when the magic of Disraeli's imperialism had done its work. Victoria did her best to hasten the change. When she assumed the imperial title on New Year's Day, 1877, she appeared at dinner loaded like some Indian idol with enormous uncut precious stones and pearls. She did, indeed, find it easier to play the Empress than the reformer; as with all Disraeli's creations, she was more Tory than democrat.

In foreign affairs, unlike domestic reforms, neither party nor Queen was a brake on Disraeli's exuberant imagination during his first two years in office. He had come into office pledged to restore British prestige, and at first his policy showed no higher objective than prestige. Bismarck had hurt British pride, and like most of his countrymen, Disraeli was convinced that the record of German aggression was not yet ended. Even Gladstone, in 1874, had prompted Queen Victoria to write to Emperor William, warning him that a new attack on France would imperil relations with England. Despite the Emperor's disclaimer of aggressive intent, fear did not subside. In May, 1875, fear was intensified almost to panic by the threats of a "preventive" war which appeared in German newspapers and were echoed by responsible German statesmen. The British ambassador at Berlin, Lord Odo Russell, who had earlier refused to believe in the danger of war, now was alarmed by Bismarck's ominous silence. Disraeli was easily convinced of the necessity for action: "Bismarck is really another old Bonaparte again, and he must be bridled."[17] Russell was instructed to impress on the German government the fact that Britain saw no justification for hostile action against France. More important, efforts were made to induce Italy and Austria to speak in the same sense. The Tsar, who was about to visit the Emperor William, had already signi-

[16] *Letters of Queen Victoria*, 2, II, 428.
[17] M. & B., II, 761.

fied his intention of urging the necessity of peace. Italy and Austria refused to intervene, but they were careful to inform Bismarck that common action had been proposed. No sooner had representation been made in Berlin than the war scare subsided almost as rapidly as it had arisen. "Although Bismarck is as civil, confidential, and amiable to me as ever," Russell reported, "I fancy that he must be frantic at our combined action with Russia in favor of peace, which took him by surprise."[18] Disraeli exuded satisfaction, and congratulated his Foreign Secretary, Lord Derby, on a victory which in retrospect seemed easily won: "We must not be afraid of saying 'Bo to a goose.'" The old spacious days when Britain commanded and the world obeyed had returned once more. "I believe, since Pam, we have never been so energetic, and in a year's time we shall be more."[19] Derby's defence of his policy in the House of Lords was frank, almost boasting, in its insistence that danger of war had been real. The German Emperor vainly protested to Victoria against the insinuation that his government had planned a war; the Queen energetically defended her ministers. She was more blunt in writing her daughter, the German Crown Princess. "Bismarck is so over-bearing, violent, grasping, and unprincipled that *no one* can stand it, and *all* agreed that he was becoming like the first Napoleon whom Europe had to join in PUTTING down."[20]

In the summer of 1875, the British enjoyed the comfortable feeling that the years of inaction, almost of impotence, in foreign affairs were over. Disraeli had shown that the master diplomat in Berlin could be put in his place by a united Europe led by Britain. That Bismarck himself was showing anxiety for friendship, did not disarm suspicion, but was welcomed as a recognition of newly aroused strength by a man who respected force alone.

While the English scene, domestic and foreign, was being rapidly shifted, the setting for the new imperialism was being

[18] Newton, *Lyons*, II, 79

[19] M. & B., II, 764.

[20] *Letters of Queen Victoria*, 2, II, 402–409.

prepared. Along the frontiers of India, the prevailing policy of inactivity was abruptly abandoned. For years, the Russians had been quietly pushing south towards India, annexing one buffer state after another. In 1875, a Russian mission appeared in Kabul, raising the fear that Afghanistan would be the next victim; then the enemy would be planted on the northwest frontier, through which invaders had entered India in ages past. Disraeli ordered an offensive against Russian influence in Kabul; when the Indian Viceroy held back, he was replaced by Lord Lytton, a man who possessed the requisite "imagination." In 1876, the British counterattack began with the strengthening of military control over Baluchistan, a good jumping-off place for an advance on Kabul from the south.

Along the road to India, also, the new active spirit took hold. Back of the self-governing Cape colony, South Africa was in the hands either of unreliable natives, or of the unreliable Boers who had established two sparsely settled republics with nebulous frontiers, the Transvaal and the Orange Free State. Disraeli aspired to unite all this territory south of the Portuguese colonies into a federation under British rule, and thus obviate any chance that a rival power would be in a position to cut the long route to India. Friction between Boers and natives made possible the first and most important step; in April, 1877, the Transvaal was annexed. The way to a British federation seemed open.

The short route to India was of even more pressing concern, now that the Suez Canal had been built with French capital, and projects for a railroad through the Euphrates valley to the Persian Gulf were being seriously discussed. Here again fortune favored Disraeli. In November, 1875, he learned that the bankrupt Khedive of Egypt must sell his shares in the Suez Canal. Within ten days, Disraeli closed the deal, borrowing the money from his Rothschild friends, and forcing acceptance on his bewildered cabinet. The shares gave Britain effectual control over the canal; but the canal raised a new problem of defence. Earlier, when France had been the great rival, Gibraltar and Malta had guarded the western Mediterranean. Now the eastern Mediterranean, and particularly the canal, called for protection against a possible Russian attack. To many Englishmen, the logical base for operations was Egypt; consequently, the logical result of the purchase of the Khedive's shares seemed the seizure of his territory. Disraeli, however, hung back. For one thing, France claimed a voice in Egyptian affairs. For another, Bismarck indiscreetly suggested the taking of Egypt, and Englishmen suspected a trap in every proposal from Berlin. When the German Crown Princess wrote her mother in support of Bismarck's suggestion, Victoria and Disraeli concerted a crushing reply. "It is not *our* custom to *annex countries* (as it is in *some others*) unless we are obliged, and forced to do so, as in the case of the Transvaal Republic." No doubt Bismarck would like to see England estranged from France by such a greedy action, but fortunately Bismarck was not in control of British policy. "Buying the Suez shares is quite another thing. That was *more or less a commercial transaction*. How can *we* protest against *Russia's* doings, if *we* do the same ourselves?" [21] Disraeli's calculations were also influenced by another and less noble conviction. The defence of the Suez, he maintained, was a military rather than a naval problem. "If the Russians had Constantinople, they could at any time march their Army through Syria to the mouth of the Nile, and then what would be the use of our holding Egypt?" [22] The ignorance of geography shown by this question was astounding; the author of *Tancred*, if not a British premier, might be expected to imagine the horrors of such a military expedition. Given his ignorance, however, it was inevitable that Disraeli should seek to protect the Suez at the one point where the British fleet could operate, Constantinople. In the Near East, as in the Middle East, the defence of India involved resolute opposition to the southward push of Russia.

By 1876 the consequences of imperialism could already be seen dimly in a succession of adventurous prospects. An "active" policy in India meant pushing out to meet the advancing Rus-

[21] *Letters of the Empress Frederick*, 153.
[22] M. & B., II, 956.

sians, with the possibility of an armed collision at the end. An "active" policy in South Africa meant the extension of sovereignty over thousands of miles of territory claimed by warlike natives and hostile Boers. An "active" policy in the eastern Mediterranean meant support of the crumbling Turkish Empire. In the summer of 1875, revolt against the Turks had begun in Bosnia, and as the year drew to a close, the revolt showed signs of spreading over the Balkan peninsula. In the autumn, the rickety structure of Turkish finance collapsed; interest payments on foreign loans went into default. In Russia, the Pan Slav press was demanding that the Tsar march his armies to the assistance of the Slav brothers in the Balkans. It was a bad time to undertake the defence of Turkey, and Disraeli's two most influential advisers on questions of foreign policy were inclined to seek safety by abandoning the Palmerstonian tradition that Turkey must be held intact. Lord Derby, the Foreign Secretary, hesitantly suggested freeing the Balkans from Turkish rule. Lord Salisbury, the Indian Secretary, urged with increasing boldness the advisability of agreeing with Russia on a policy of partition. Austria, he argued, would be the only loser if the Balkan states were freed. "Her existence would be menaced if she were hedged on the south by a line of Russian satellites. But her existence is no longer of the importance to us that it was in former times. Her vocation in Europe has gone. She was a counterpoise to France and a barrier against Russia: but France is gone and the development of Russia is chiefly in regions where Austria could not, and if she could, would not help to check it." Why not use this opportunity to lift the weight of Russian hostility which hung over the British Empire, not only in the Near East, but on the frontiers of India? [23]

Disraeli's imagination, however, was stimulated by the approach of the risks implicit in his imperialism. In the same month which brought him the Suez shares, he was dreaming of future glories. "I really believe 'the Eastern Question,' that has haunted Europe for a century, and wh. I thought the Crimean

[23] Cecil, *Salisbury*, II, 85–86.

War had adjourned for half another, will fall to my lot to encounter—dare I say to settle?" [24] Settling the Near Eastern question did not mean that he was prepared to follow the advice of Salisbury and Derby. Quite the contrary. Despite the persistence of revolt in the Balkans, and despite Turkish financial difficulties, he was convinced that the Turk could reëstablish order, if given time to do so. He was aware that nationalism was taking hold of the Turks as it had earlier grown among the Italians and the Germans, and he was confident that nationalism would bring about a renaissance of Turkish power. On the other hand, he saw only Russian plots in the continued resistance of the rebels, ignoring the fact that nationalism was spurring on the Balkan peoples as well as their Turkish masters. Seeing only one half of the situation, he played for time, seeking to prevent foreign intervention until the Turk was strong enough to stand alone.

It was a hazardous game, but he was confident of victory if he could once manœuvre the Tsar into an isolated position. That was the real difficulty. For years, the Emperors of Russia, Austria, and Germany had been bound together by some sort of alliance. The logic of such an alliance of reactionary rulers was obvious, so long as no issue cut across common opposition to enlightened government. The Near East, Disraeli hoped, would furnish just the needed sundering force. Austria was obviously fearful of Russian supremacy in the Balkans, but Austria was too weak to risk the united hostility of Russia and Germany. If, however, Germany could be pulled out of the league, Austria would gladly follow, and the Dreikaiserbund would be ended. Once ended, the Russians could easily be restrained; the eastern question would then soon settle itself. Such was the strategic problem as Disraeli saw it. He knew it could not be easily solved, but until it was solved he saw no chance of a successful British foreign policy, in the Near East or anywhere else. So long as the Dreikaiserbund endured, England must face unaided the solid block of the three really important Continental powers.

[24] M. & B., II, 886.

France and Italy were useless as allies; they would not stand up against the new Holy Alliance. "There is no balance, and unless we go out of our way to act with the three Northern Powers, they can act without us." [25] More, then, than the fate of Turkey was involved; the whole future of British power demanded that coöperation between the strongest continental powers be replaced by salutary rivalry, salutary from the British point of view.

Just when Disraeli worked out his policy, it is impossible to say. Very soon after castigating Bismarck as a new Napoleon, however, a marked change appeared in his references to the German Chancellor, and by the opening days of 1876 he was expatiating on the straightforwardness of the man who so recently had seemed the incarnation of wickedness. Meanwhile, he played the waiting game. When confronted, in December, 1875, by a joint proposal of the three imperial governments to enforce reforms in the Turkish administration, the "Andrássy Note," he at first refused to concur; but when the Turks, sure that the Emperors would proceed with or without England, begged him to accept, he did so. With the new year, the awaited soundings from Berlin arrived. Bismarck complained to the British Ambassador that the sphinx-like silence of England made any settlement of the Turkish question impossible; Germany would gladly further English wishes, if he knew what they were. In succeeding weeks, Bismarck's requests for an exchange of views became more pressing, so pressing that Disraeli concluded that Germany was ready to abandon the Russian alliance for one with England. "If the practical good understanding with Germany be accomplished," he assured the Queen, "it will place our external relations on a rock, and England will again exercise that influence which, of late years, has so painfully and mysteriously disappeared." [26] Derby found it harder to forget the Bismarck of earlier years; there might be some trap in this sudden intimacy. He preferred to feel out the ground carefully, and instructed Russell to stress the fact that England had only

[25] M. & B., II, 885.
[26] *Letters of Queen Victoria,* 2, II, 444.

one objective, to preserve the peace and existing treaties; had Bismarck any proposals for insuring these objectives? Bismarck amiably replied that he had none. There the matter rested, but Disraeli was confident that the Continental alliance was now practically ended. When a new proposal of the imperial governments—the Berlin Memorandum of May, 1876—setting forth new and more stringent demands on the Turks was presented for his concurrence, he flatly refused. This time the cards seemed to break right. In the same month, a palace revolution brought in a new Sultan who promised all the reforms anyone could wish. The Berlin Memorandum was withdrawn by its authors and, favorable sign, Bismarck seemed very pleased that it had not been accepted.

Disraeli was weary and sick, but he was sure that his strategy was working. All, of course, was not as he might have wished. At home, both industry and agriculture were depressed, but that would pass. The opposition press was making a great fuss about supposed massacres by Turkish troops in Bulgaria, but the dispatches from the Near East did not bear out the atrocity stories. The important thing was that the Dreikaiserbund was broken, and England had gained the freedom of action so necessary for the success of an imperial policy. "All the Great Powers, Russia included, seem anxious to defer to England," he boasted in July, 1876, "and something like the old days of our authority appear to have returned." In the following month, he rose in the House of Commons to answer those who denounced his support of Turkey as an alliance with the murderers of Christians. He did not deny that there had been some atrocities, and he did not condone them. But he did deny that his policy should be determined by sentimental considerations. He had but one duty, "to maintain the Empire of England." When the debate ended, he slowly surveyed every part of this House, familiar to him through a generation, and slowly walked out, for the last time. The next day, his elevation to the peerage as Earl of Beaconsfield was announced. Among the tributes which this event evoked, none would have pleased him more than the unheard execration of those who realized the break he had helped to make in British tradition: "I can remember nothing more humiliating than the chorus of adulation with which the Press has greeted his elevation to what I trust will prove his political extinction." [27] The hope was a vain one, but it was true that Disraeli's great work was done before his name was hidden by the title, irreparably done. After these two years, empire was inseparably linked with liberty in the dominant tradition of British thought.

[27] Russell, *MacColl*, 46.

CHAPTER VI

BISMARCK'S SEARCH FOR ORDER

TO *US* and to many quiet and reflecting Germans it is *very sad*, and appears *very* hard—to be made an object of universal distrust and suspicion, which we *naturally* are as long as Prince Bismarck remains the *sole* and *omnipotent* ruler of our destinies. His will alone is law here, and on his good or bad humor depend our chances of safety and peace. To the great majority of Germans and to *most* Prussians, this is a satisfactory state! He possesses a prestige unequalled by anything and is *all powerful!* To me this state is simply *intolerable* and seems *very dangerous!* Germany wants rest, peace, and quiet—her commerce and the development of her inner resources are *not* progressing as they should! Our riches do not increase and we are in a most uncomfortable and crippled state which will so remain as long as the sword of war hangs over our head." [1] Thus the German Crown Princess to Queen Victoria in 1875. The ethics of writing in this way to the ruler of a neighboring power might be questioned. Certainly, such letters helped to explain the fact that, for all her beauty and charm, the princess was an object of suspicion, even hatred, to many Germans. Certainly also, such letters, dropped into the center of a country like England where the governing group was small and discussion was free, were calculated to heighten English fear of Germany. Ethics aside, the letter did reflect the judgment of a shrewd if biased observer who was placed where observation was widest. Abroad, Germany an object of universal mistrust; at home, Germany uncomfortable and crippled. So far, the Princess was right. Economic conditions were very bad. Catholic Ger-

[1] *Letters of the Empress Frederick,* 138.

mans, one third of the population, looked on the imperial government as their enemy. Bismarck's own class, the landowners of the feudal east, was mutinous. In the French war scare of 1875, most of Europe showed suspicion of Germany.

The Princess erred, however, in ascribing omnipotence to Bismarck. It would be more accurate to say that events culminating in 1875 helped to show Bismarck the limits of his powers, power over himself, over the German people, and over Europe. As she wrote, he was preparing to leave Berlin for the estate at Varzin which a grateful nation had given him after the war with Austria. It was not a retreat which an Englishman would have chosen. Lord Dufferin, who, like all wise diplomats, made the pilgrimage to this "rambling unpretending house of no style," was distinctly unimpressed. "What induced him to pitch his tent in such a God-forsaken district of Pomerania I cannot conceive. It possesses a Russian climate, and is destitute of any picturesque feature to relieve its barren expanses and monotonous pine forests; but its owner is evidently very proud of his possessions, and is perpetually planting trees, and taking his guests to see them grow." [2] In this wilderness, Bismarck buried himself during the next three years, returning to Berlin as rarely as possible. Varzin meant more than planting trees, however. It meant living, living among farming gentlemen who had as little use for cities and ceremonies as he had, living with crops and trees, dogs and family, all of whom could be trusted to give loyalty in exchange only for affectionate care. It meant the opportunity to rebuild, or at least repair, a body which was in perpetual rebellion against the superhuman tasks he had laid on it during the years following 1862. Many actions could be blamed on the overwrought nerves of the man who took refuge at Varzin in 1875. For it must be admitted that the master's touch had been very rough, even bungling, during the four preceding years, showing a strange combination of overconfidence and panic which only taut nerves could explain. The damage, much of it irreparable, which resulted from this brief loss of control, testifies to the

[2] Lyall, *Dufferin,* I, 306, 307.

intricacy of the forces which Bismarck usually manipulated with such deceptive ease. At Varzin he could think himself out of the impasse into which he had wandered because he had ignored the limits of force.

The irascible temper of a sick man was only one of the handicaps under which Bismarck was laboring. His past was also a burden. Europe, including the German people, was slow to realize that his objectives had shifted. Before 1871, his objective was to win power for Germany; after 1871, his objective was to consolidate German power. The change in purpose necessitated a change in strategy: before 1871, war was essential; after 1871, peace was essential. It was not strange that Europe was blind to the shift in policy. Few precedents warranted men in trusting a conqueror who suddenly professed horror of war. Moreover, there was the memory of that blunt speech of 1862 prescribing blood and iron as the one remedy for German ills; might he not use the same remedy again to escape domestic discontents? Suspicion received apparent confirmation from the fact that Bismarck's peace tactics were identical with those of war. Where formerly he had manœuvred his enemies into an isolated position for the purpose of overwhelming them with superior force, he now used the same tactics to prevent them from fighting. Pacific militarism was new to Europe, and easily mistaken for aggressive militarism.

Bismarck could justly complain that he was suspected because he was misunderstood. In one vital sense, however, he was suspected because he was understood. Lord Clarendon had understood him when, at a conference on the Schleswig-Holstein question in 1864, the British statesman had left the room overcome with an almost physical nausea, and vowed he could not remain in the presence of this man without faith and without morals. Crown Prince Frederick had understood him when he lamented that Bismarck had deprived the German people of their conscience. Queen Victoria's hysterical fears showed an understanding which, for all her underscoring, she could not adequately express. Monstrous Bismarck, she called him, and monstrous he not only seemed but was, in his generation. He was one of the first great European statesmen of the nineteenth century who consciously and deliberately subordinated every ideal to the needs of the state. More than that, he was convinced that a statesman who spoke of any other political purpose was either a fool or a hypocrite. Europe, he said, was a purely geographic expression; anyone who spoke of Europe as more than that—as a cultural community, for instance—was trying to get something he was afraid to ask for. Humanity, truth, and justice were words which the statesman must use on occasion as a concession to the proprieties, but not words to guide action. Interest alone, reason of state, had meaning for the statesman. If statesmen of a rival country were gullible, they must be tricked to the limit set by state interest. If weak, they must be coerced to the limit set by state interest. Chivalry and honor had no place in international politics, or domestic politics either. When old Emperor William was shot by a socialist, Bismarck's first thought was not of his master's life, but of the political advantages which might be wrung from the act. When William opposed an alliance with Austria, Bismarck mobilized every possible ally against the Emperor, leaving him the alternatives of isolation or surrender. Subordinates and political parties were petted or persecuted with deadly impersonality. Public opinion was won indifferently by truth or falsehood. Constitution or treaties, emperor or prince, parliament or the wishes of the people—these were not Bismarck's master; reason of state was his master, to be served with all his powers, by fair means or foul. Right and wrong, in the sense that these words were used in dealings between men, were meaningless in politics. Political action might be wise or foolish, successful or unsuccessful. Morality was irrelevant.

Bismarck maintained that he differed from other statesmen only in his greater frankness, and his contention was a hard one to meet. Was not Disraeli a good Bismarckian when he boasted that his one duty was to maintain the Empire of England? Was not Victoria's defence of the annexation of the Transvaal based on Bismarckian principles? Such queries could be levelled at every page of British imperial history. Germans, seeing the ruthlessness with which the English pursued their own interests when ruthlessness was advantageous, and seeing evident examples of hypocrisy, smiled with contempt at British professions of righteousness. Ironically admitting the deficiencies of the German language, they borrowed the word *cant* from the English language, and used it to describe British political moralizing. For their own part, the Germans preferred to learn how to face without flinching the necessary consequences of the pursuit of national interest, under the guidance of the master realist, Bismarck. Harsh realism, they argued, deprived Germany of the satisfaction which resulted from the identification of one's own interests with the good of mankind, but realism did permit clarity of thought and action. The English were always exposed to the danger of choosing a leader like Gladstone who, desperately attempting to reconcile morality and interest, in the end sacrificed both. In the German view, international relations would become more stable, more predictable, when every nation avowed its egoism; and though the weak must then go under, just as they had always done, it was surely better to be overcome in a frank conflict of interest, than to be conquered ostensibly because morality demanded conquest. As Germans delighted to point out, it was the Englishman George Canning who had most clearly formulated the principles of Bismarckian diplomacy: "Things are getting back to a wholesome state again; every nation for itself and God for us all."

Undoubtedly, some of the anger which Bismarck's principles, or lack of principles aroused among Englishmen, was anger at hearing unpleasant truths. It was hard to cheer Disraeli's foreign policy and at the same time be shocked by Bismarck. The feat was possible, but only for one who could, like Queen Victoria, instinctively and immediately identify every British interest with God's will. It was easier, and more usual to evade the truth in the German indictment by loss of temper, by insisting with obstinate vehemence on German immorality. There are few more dreary occupations than to read what Englishmen had to say about Bismarck's faithlessness—except to read what Germans said about British hypocrisy. It is significant, however, that penetrating thought about the nature of the state glimmers faintly through the most blind German invective, while the most pharisaical British homily is partially redeemed by recognition of the anarchical consequences of a policy frankly based on reason of state. Faith in dogmatic religious truth was declining in England; faith in the capacity of the human reason to discover the natural and eternal laws governing man's life in society was fading as evolution became a commonplace. Conversely, with the heightening of nationalism in the age of Disraeli, national interest was coming to be a more nakedly avowed concern. Yet Englishmen, with a few conspicuous exceptions, refused to admit a complete divorce between public and private morality, or to accept the state as the highest good. Jeremy Bentham's Utilitarianism seemed outmoded in its specific precepts, but Bentham's injunction that every political act must be judged in terms of its consequences still swayed English minds.

The consequences of Bismarck's realism, seen from England, were despotism in Germany, and a dangerously uneasy Europe. The British had seen Bismarck twist the hostility of the German people into almost idolatrous loyalty by war. They had seen him move the Prussian King like a puppet. They saw the cold hatred with which he destroyed rival German statesmen who defied his will. In particular, they saw his power coil around Prince Frederick and his English princess, isolating them from all influence, slowly breaking the Prince's power of resistance. Emperor, Parliament, public opinion—he dominated them all, ceaselessly playing off individuals and parties against each other so that effective opposition was impossible. In short, "reason of state" meant whatever Bismarck willed. The German people were ruled by an uncrowned despot. And this despotism was far more dangerous than the irresponsible absolutism of the eastern empires. The Tsar was a despot, but he ruled a ramshackle empire, inefficient and corrupt; German efficiency was a recent and painful memory.

This despot also possessed intelligence, a rare quality in autocrats. His skill had been shown when he twice fought a rival great power without precipitating a general European war; not even Frederick the Great had been able to do that. The strongest continental state in the hands of a skilful despot who frankly admitted he respected power alone—it was not a comfortable situation, for other European countries. The Germans did find their situation to their liking, but would they be content if, as seemed likely, the fumes of success went to Bismarck's head and he made a single serious misstep? Or, as also seemed possible, if Bismarck's health broke under the strain and this mighty machine fell to less competent hands? That Bismarck was unwell, everyone knew after 1871; Englishmen scarcely knew whether to pray for his recovery or for his complete breakdown. In any case, what they saw of the consequences of a "realistic" policy based on state interests, rapidly discouraged the impulsive admiration for Prussian ideas which Bagehot had deprecated. For all their growing racial pride and their craving for national solidarity, Englishmen refused to bow down before the state; the German example made individualism and freedom seem only the more precious. For all their newly awakened imperialism, they refused to admit the crude operation of the rule of the survival of the fittest; like Bagehot they insisted that "the best" was synonymous with brute strength only in the more primitive stages of history. Faith in a natural moral law binding on individuals and states was fading; but, making all allowance for exceptions and even for hypocrisy, it is safe to say that the identification of morality and expediency still seemed monstrous.

Hence it was that the growth of a national spirit in England which was closely akin to German nationalism did not lead to better understanding between the two peoples. The English saw more or less clearly that to make reason of state the final test meant the grant of limitless discretion to the man or men who operated the mechanism of state power, with consequent loss of individual freedom at home, and anarchy in the relations between states. Therefore, as their loyalties became increasingly centered in the national state, they insisted the more vehemently on the rights of the individual and of humanity. The Germans, studying what British imperialists said, and what British statesmen did, concluded that their cousins were illogical at best, and hypocrites at worst: the only way Englishmen avoided a choice between values was to make the interests of individual and humanity identical with national interests, a false reconciliation which could be succinctly described as cant. And so the argument went, around and around.

Bismarck was no metaphysician. For him, a policy based on interest and supported by power seemed so obviously right that he could not conceive of a sensible man assuming any other basis. The debates in the press of the two countries had neither interest nor importance for him: "My respect for so-called public opinion—or, in other words, the clamor of orators and newspapers—has never been very great." [3] He made no effort to check the clamor, probably because he was not sorry to weaken the "English party" of the Crown Prince. References to Bismarck's desire to neutralize the Anglophile sympathies of Frederick in anticipation of his accession are naturally scanty, but there are enough to indicate that this was a settled objective. Fear of possible future English influence over German policy did not, however, indicate a desire to quarrel. England and Germany, he thought, were natural friends; their interests as satisfied states were identical. The British would recognize this fact when they ceased to listen to the doctrinaire Gladstone. He was glad when Disraeli won in 1874, because anyone was better than Gladstone; but since he thought Disraeli only an actor, he expected little gain from the change. Under such misguided leadership, he thought England was of minor importance. Until non-intervention ceased to be a fetish, he must confine his calculations to the continent.

There he found plenty to occupy his attention after 1871. Consolidation, no less than achievement of power called for keen eyes to see every opportunity and every danger, and his somewhat fevered imagination made him exaggerate both opportunity and

[3] *Bismarck, The Man and the Statesman*, II, 14.

danger. He had succeeded in effecting the political unity of Germany without calling into existence a hostile coalition. Would he now be able to prevent the other continental states from uniting out of fear or jealousy of German strength? That was the question which haunted him, and it was a vital question for a state in the middle of Europe, open to invasion from east, south, and west. It was a question which could never obtain a final answer. The geographical situation of Germany would forever tempt her neighbors to crush her by invasion from two or even three sides—unless they were afraid, or unless they needed German help against each other.

Bismarck's policy, given his pacific purpose, was set by circumstance: he must create fear or dependence, or both. To create a sense of dependence, he fell back on the old watchword of conservatism, monarchical solidarity against the revolution. Monarchy, like everything else, was a question of utility to him, not an ideal. The emperor was a useful symbol of unity and a useful focus for popular loyalty. In that sense, Bismarck was a royalist, but he certainly did not believe monarchy was the one right and divinely ordained form of government. Alexander of Russia, Francis Joseph of Austria, and William of Germany did take their divine function seriously, and did regard "the revolution" as blasphemy. Bismarck was very willing to encourage these, to him, delusions; monarchical solidarity helped to draw Russia and Austria towards Germany, and away from republican France. In 1872 the three emperors met at Berlin. In the year following they drew up a formal bond of union, "an understanding direct and personal between the Sovereigns, an understanding independent of changes which may take place in Their administrations." They promised, in case of disagreement on any question, to find a basis of agreement "so that these divergences may not prevail over considerations of a more elevated order which preoccupy Them." They promised also to consult for the purpose of adopting a common line of action in case one of their number should be forced to meet the attack of an outside power.[4] For

[4] G.P., I, 206, 207.

Bismarck, this understanding meant that fear of a hostile coalition was partially and temporarily banished. He was too sceptical of monarchical solidarity to believe the league would survive a severe conflict of interest or even a tempting opportunity to win an advantage from one of the royal "brothers"; but he was also too much of a realist to expect either perfection or permanence. The Dreikaiserbund gave him time, and time was what he needed in order to perfect the real bulwark of German safety, the national strength which would discourage the greed of neighbors, monarchical or republican.

In theory, the German Empire was a limited monarchy. The constitution limited the power of the Emperor and his Chancellor, first of all, by delegating certain functions of government to the states and others to the Reich. However, as Bismarck had seen to it that all questions of power were entrusted to the Reich, and as power was what preoccupied him, this limitation seemed unimportant. More vital was the requirement that new legislation received the consent both of the popularly elected Reichstag and of the state delegations in the Bundesrath. Bismarck not only acknowledged but welcomed this limitation, provided that Reichstag and Bundesrath stayed within their function of limiting the monarchical power, and did not try to destroy it. By a limited monarchy, he was far from meaning a monarchy like the English, retaining only the shadow and the tinsel of power; he meant by that ambiguous expression a monarchy whose power was real, even dominant, within the limits set by the constitution, the popular will, and the will of the separate states. The constitution was a skilful effort to give effect to this conception. The Emperor and his Chancellor were in complete control over executive functions. They could also propose new policies and institutions, but they could not make laws or prevent the making of laws. The states could successfully resist an extension of imperial powers, as they did when Bismarck proposed an imperial railroad system. The popular representatives could set limits on freedom of action, as they did in refusing to vote a permanent military budget. The states and the popular representatives might modify or reject proposals; they could also initiate legislation. The Emperor had no veto power, except his power as King of Prussia to block constitutional amendments. Theoretically, the legislative and executive powers were almost distinct. Almost, but not quite. The Emperor could, if the Bundesrath consented, dissolve the Reichstag and call for new elections. This exception—necessary if a deadlock was to be avoided—Bismarck exploited with unforeseen consequences. From the first he influenced opinion by pressure on the newspapers through his press bureau, and the work of the bureau was facilitated by a secret fund, the so-called "reptile fund," whose use is still obscure. Later, he forced the civil service to act as electoral propagandists for the government program, a practice which his opponents denounced as not only unscrupulous but demoralizing to the integrity of the civil service.

In the first years of the Empire, however, such a measure was unneeded, and the press bureau found it very easy to secure a good press in all but a few papers. Parliamentary opposition was too rarely effective to call for strong pressure. The enthusiasm for unity was still running strong, and under its impetus the relics of the old particularism were swept away by laws establishing or authorizing a national currency, a national banking and postal system, a national legal code and supreme court, and a national army—all within relatively unimportant limitations set by the constitution. Throughout this legislation there ran one aspiration: to create, by common institutions, a common loyalty to Germany, to make unity a more than formal reality.

The staunchest allies of Bismarck in pushing through his program were—the liberals. Occasionally the liberal parties showed some trace of their old enthusiasm for popular government, but these few feeble gestures were easily controlled by the firm hand of the Chancellor. Except for an intransigent but powerless minority, the liberal members of the Reichstag were now concerned with unity; liberty was a lost cause, a cause whose defeat was scarcely noticed. This became obvious when the liberals followed Bismarck enthusiastically into a campaign of persecution against the Catholic Church. It was a liberal who gave this campaign the name by which it became known in history, the *Kulturkampf*, the struggle for German culture against the alien culture of Rome. It was the liberals who called for new restrictions on religious freedom when old ones were found ineffective, who plunged ahead even faster than their leader wished to move. And in the end, when the failure of the Kulturkampf became obvious, it was the liberals who were discredited, repudiated by the German people because they had so obviously impaired the unity for which they had sacrificed their own earlier ideals.

Liberals, thinking in terms of the German spirit, the Volksgeist, called the campaign against the Catholic Church a Kulturkampf. Bismarck, thinking in terms of the German state, regarded the campaign as a fight against enemies of the state. He had no quarrel with Catholicism as a religion; all religions were equally welcome to him so long as they enjoined Christian obedience to the state. His fear was purely political, fear of the power of the papacy, in Germany and in Europe. He did, to be sure, speak movingly of his desire to vindicate Protestant liberty against the bondage of Rome, but he often professed boundless loyalty to causes which actually meant nothing to him. His appeals to religious prejudice were designed partly to mobilize opinion at home, but chiefly to win support in countries like Russia and England where prejudice against Catholicism was strong. This indifference to Catholicism as an ideal was, indeed, the secret of his failure. He greatly overestimated the political strength of Catholicism; he fatally underestimated its spiritual strength. Not only was he unable, as Bagehot suggested, "to measure moral influences as he measures material forces"; he showed inability to measure either moral or material forces. The double error is understandable only in the light of his over-fearful and over-confident temper. Everywhere his fevered imagination saw enemies ready to wreck his handiwork.

In part his fears were justified. In an age of nationalism the map had become a living thing, and three times he had violently operated on the structure of the map. Each operation left bleeding frontiers which time alone could heal, frontiers within as well as along the borders of the new Germany. France and Austria were unreconciled to defeat; England was suspicious; Russian friendship depended on the unstable will of an autocrat. Would some or all these neighbors unite to restore the old map? At home, there were many unhappy subjects—Poles, the Danes of Schleswig, Alsatians and Lorrainers, Hanoverians and other north Germans who had forcibly been made Prussians. At home and abroad, Bismarck believed that he must keep his opponents divided; without leadership, the malcontents would dissipate their strength in temporary and harmless gestures. He feared, however, that the Catholic Church would provide the leadership for his enemies in Germany and in Europe. Most German Catholics had naturally supported Austria against Prussia during the years of conflict; and although loyalty had shifted after 1866, particularly among laymen, the hierarchy was uneasy for the future of Catholicism in a predominantly Protestant empire. The Church sought protection by emphasizing the federal structure of the empire, hoping thus to preserve independence at least in the south German states, and by furthering the growth of the Catholic or Center party in the Reichstag. Bismarck was alarmed by these tactics. In Catholic federalism he saw an obstacle to the completion of national unity; and undoubtedly many Catholics hoped this would be the result. In the Center party he saw the leader for disloyal minorities; again, he was partly right. In the background he saw the papacy as an absolute monarchy without territory but with millions of obedient subjects in all the great continental states. France and Austria were Catholic countries; Russia had a large Catholic minority. A hostile coalition was his greatest fear. He believed that the Pope, through his Jesuit emissaries, was plotting such a coalition. Through these supposed designs of the papacy, the problem of domestic Catholic opposition became a problem of foreign policy.

Convinced of Catholic enmity, he did not wait to be attacked; he began the battle, with all his strength, and on all fronts. He was confident of success, because the chances of dividing the enemy seemed good. Catholicism was passing through an acute internal crisis, the result of the decree of papal infallibility promulgated at the Vatican Council in 1871. The decree had aroused the fears and prejudices of Protestants and rationalists; more important, it had caused dissension among Catholics both on political and spiritual grounds. With one hand, Bismarck supported the so-called Old Catholics in Germany who refused to accept the new doctrine; with the other, he struck at the privileges of the Church. Since the German constitution reserved cultural questions for the state governments, most of the restrictive legislation was adopted by the Prussian diet, but the parliaments of the other states adopted some or all of the Prussian laws. Systematically, one right after another was abrogated: the church courts, the training and appointment of priests, church schools, all were placed under state control; civil marriage was instituted, and the dropping of church membership facilitated; religious orders were proscribed; state financial grants were abolished in districts where obedience to the new laws was refused; fines, imprisonment, or exile were the lot of rebels. Step by step the state moved to complete control over religion. Each step provoked resistance which was interpreted as proof of the treasonable designs of the hierarchy.

Simultaneously, the campaign was carried abroad, in an effort to build up a united front of governments supposedly menaced by papal political aggression. The Dreikaiserbund seemed to guarantee at least the friendly neutrality of Russia and Austria; Italy, fearing a move to restore the papal states, was sympathetic; in England, mass-meetings and even the speeches of leaders like Disraeli promised coöperation. Only France and Belgium were recalcitrant. So long as the anti-clerical Thiers held power in France all had gone well, but in May, 1873, a royalist and clerical government was formed and MacMahon made president. Bismarck had tried vainly to save Thiers by dire threats of the effects which his fall would have on relations with Germany; repeatedly he had threatened that, if convinced of French aggressive designs, Germany would attack. The fall of Thiers filled the Chancellor with alarm, it meant to him the change from "a weak, civilian, anticlerical, isolated France, to a strong, militaristic, ultramontane France which can easily secure alliances." He had no doubt that the new government would pursue the policy "which undoubtedly is dictated by a cold calculation of French interests—to go hand in hand with Rome and, through Rome, with our most active and dangerous internal enemies." [5] Again he saw the omnipresent papacy plotting the destruction of Germany. Again he took the initiative. He demanded that the French government silence bishops who preached against the Kulturkampf. He spoke ambiguously of influential elements in Germany who wished a preventive war, and he made ostentatious military preparations. Similar demands and threats were addressed to the Belgian government. In April, 1875, rumors of impending war began to appear in the German press. "Is War in Sight?" the Berlin *Post* asked, and proceeded to analyse the dangers which French military preparations entailed for Germany. Other papers took up the cry. Military men expatiated on the advantages of a preventive war. Then old Emperor William intervened, demanding that war talk cease. It did cease publicly, but the discussion went on privately. The French Foreign Secretary, Decazes, viewing the situation with cool scepticism, decided that the Chancellor had overreached himself with the Emperor and with foreign governments; the time was ripe for a counterattack. From the French foreign office went up a piteous cry for help addressed to the newspapers and the governments of England and Russia. The cry was thought sincere and it was heeded. Urgent warnings against an attack on defenceless France were given in Berlin. The Emperor not only promised peace, he showed clearly that he blamed Bismarck for the uproar, and that he was much displeased. Precipitously, Bismarck's offensive against the imaginary papal coalition collapsed. There had been no coalition, but now a coalition to restrain German will to war seemed possible. At least Germany was suspect and isolated.

Never had Bismarck miscalculated so badly. Although he set

[5] G.P., I, 189.

up interest as his own political guide, he had expected England and Russia to act on the basis of religious prejudice; in this he was disillusioned. Confident that his skill had isolated France, he had tried to bully her into submission; the steady hand of Decazes had ended French isolation, and isolated Germany. He had permitted his press bureau to whip up German opinion to a fury of passion and fear; in his defeat, the press turned on him, angry at being duped. The press bureau tried to avert popular anger by blaming the whole scare on English meddlesomeness and jealousy of Germany; but only those papers most dependent on the government were deceived by this ruse. Naturally, left wing liberal papers like the *Vossische Zeitung*, which had always refused to follow Bismarck's lead, were delighted. On May 12, this journal ridiculed the efforts of the "official" press to put all the blame on the alarmist articles in the London *Times*. The *Times* had said that the thought of a "preventive" war was popular in Germany; well, so it had been, until the last few days. Army officers and newspapers had talked of nothing else; over their beer mugs or in society, men had gravely nodded their heads and said a preventive war was the height of political wisdom. Now that an English paper had reported these sentiments, and pointed out the danger of such a war—in much milder language than a German paper would have thought proper under similar circumstances—there were cries of injured innocence, and the *Times* was denounced as the mortal enemy of Germany. Four days later the *Vossische Zeitung* used the events just past as an opportunity to attack the whole "official" press system, blaming the press bureau for the scare, and public opinion for believing whatever the government said about foreign affairs. "The reptile fund is a misfortune, a cancerous sore for Germany. It is gradually bringing the whole German press into discredit abroad, and it brings only shame to the reputation and honor of the German Empire." It was not surprising that opposition papers should take this tone, although these papers were usually sparing in their criticism of Bismarck's foreign policy. Even papers close to the government rebelled, however, at the effort to push the blame off on "irresponsible" newspapers and on English "arrogance." The *Kölnische Zeitung* had been one of the first important journals to stress the danger of war, but after the crisis was over it turned on the government. The press had not started the alarm, it maintained on June 2; "during the weeks just past our official circles have denied that the sky was blue." Neither had the English acted officiously. The past policy of England was certainly open to criticism (as the *Kölnische Zeitung* had been pointing out very frequently in the past decade); but England had in this case acted from real alarm which was not unjustified. Coming from one of the most persistent critics of England, this was strong language.

Since Bismarck's internal policy derived much of its prestige from his successes abroad, the open check administered by England and Russia was a bad omen. There were other omens equally bad. The campaign against Catholicism was proving a costly failure at home. It had not broken the Center party; both in popular vote and in deputies elected, the party showed a gain in the elections of 1874. Under persecution, Catholicism was becoming what Bismarck wrongly thought it in 1871, a state within the state. Furthermore, non-Catholics were becoming restive. Protestants slowly recognized that religion in general was being weakened by the abuse of one denomination. Civil marriage and facilities for surrendering church membership hurt Protestantism rather more than Catholicism. Advocates of states' rights were also becoming afraid; they suspected that Bismarck's real objective was to replace federalism by a unitary empire.

By 1875 these malcontents had an unexpected and unwelcome, but very powerful ally—acute business depression. In 1871, the economic energies of the German people, long checked by political unrest and disunity, were suddenly released. Expansion was accelerated by the removal of most restrictions on the formation of corporations and by the huge indemnity received from France. The result was a wild boom, an industrial boom, a housing boom, and, above all, a stock market boom. The crisis came at the end of 1873 when a world-wide depression fell with crushing force on German finance. The collapse was as violent as the expansion had been. Companies, sound and unsound, were ruined. Ugly stories of fraudulent financing in the boom years were first whispered and then shouted. Many of those incriminated were Jews, and anti-Semitism rose as the stock market fell. Other culprits, however, were highly placed gentiles, even aristocrats and bureaucrats. Since integrity had always been the proudest virtue of those who ruled in Germany through birth or official position, the shock of these disclosures could scarcely be exaggerated. Coming soon after the spiritual exhilaration which accompanied the achievement of unity, they cast a pall of disillusionment over the German people. During 1875 and 1876 the economic stagnation intensified to almost complete paralysis, and its effects were made more disastrous by a series of poor harvests culminating in the crop failure of 1876. As the economic indices fell, disillusionment was replaced by a variety of moods, all equally dangerous—cynical contempt for all virtue, public or private; anger with a government which claimed great power over its citizens, but which could not avert disaster; hatred of the hungry for the well-fed.

It was a dismal scene which Bismarck contemplated in the solitude of long nights at Varzin, a scene which was a sad contrast to the future he had envisaged in 1871. Then he had been confident that, once Germany was placed in the saddle of political unity, she would soon learn to ride; unruly party passions gave the lie to that hope. Then he had been confident that he could manipulate the states of Europe as he had done in the past; the war scare showed that he was no longer invincible. Then he had been confident that the state could allow free play to economic forces; free enterprise had brought the evils both of a wild boom and a sickening depression. And the one danger which he had really feared, the Catholic menace, had become a reality only through his efforts to combat it.

Slowly the conviction grew that he must begin over again, must work out a new plan of campaign, as he had once planned at Frankfort. Beginning anew did not mean a change either in objective or in strategy. Now as before his purpose was to make Germany secure by making her strong. He did not abandon his old conviction regarding the springs of action, whether in individuals or in states: men acted from fear or hope. Consequently, success followed from strength, strength to punish or reward. The big battalions must be on his side, drawn there by hope or fear. Opponents must be isolated; he must not be isolated. These maxims had brought success too often to be discarded. If he had not succeeded after 1871, it was because he had either misinterpreted the hopes and fears of others, or had failed to judge correctly the drift of history, had not given due consideration to what he called the "imponderables." The loyalty of Catholics to their faith was one such imponderable, so was the play of economic forces which had produced both boom and collapse, and so was an unexpectedly astute rival like Decazes. It did no good to lament the appearance of such weights in the balance; the statesman must take account of imponderables, must make them fall on his side of the scale. The mistakes of the years just past had been errors of judgment; the old bases and methods of action remained valid. There could be no others. The problem now was to see more clearly, to play the game better, not to change the game or the rules. At Varzin he could stand aloof from the distracting eddies and surface disturbances of day-today events. There he could come to see the deeper current of history, could understand the relative importance of the forces at home and abroad which affected that current, and, with this knowledge, could steer Germany safely into calmer waters. Whatever else might be said of the man, his tenacious courage could not be questioned.

In foreign affairs, Bismarck feared that the other powers might be encouraged to attempt a hostile coalition by the isolation which the French war scare of 1875 had brought upon Germany. The fear of coalition was a nightmare which never left him. England and France might ally, and draw Austria into their union. More dangerous would be an alliance between Russia, Austria, and France; even if two of these powers drew together, the third would be in a position to put serious pressure on Germany by threatening to join the others. Such perils were the inevitable consequence of Germany's central position in Europe, and of the jealousy aroused abroad by German strength. Both position and strength might, however, be converted into assets, given luck and skilful guidance. The problem was to separate the powers from one another, and to make them dependent on German aid for the realization of their ambitions.

The rebellion against Turkey which began in the summer of 1875 seemed the opportunity Bismarck needed. The eastern Mediterranean was a region where Germany had no vital interests to protect, and where every other great power did have vital interests. Russia aspired to the rôle of protector over the Balkan Christians, and dreamed of turning the Black Sea into a Russian lake by securing Constantinople. Austria, cut off from the west by the loss of Italy and Germany, likewise regarded the Balkans as a field for expansion, although her ambitions were primarily economic rather than political. Britain feared any spread of Russian power as a menace to the Suez route to India. France hoped to regain in the Mediterranean the prestige lost at Sedan. Even Italy was remembering that the Mediterranean had once been a Roman lake. Here was discord enough, not merely to estrange the powers, but to plunge them into war! That was the danger. Wars between great powers were likely to spread, to become European wars. If Germany remained neutral in a general war, she would be hated by all the belligerents; if she was drawn in, the choice of the right side would be a ticklish task, and the sacrifice of men and money would be sheer waste—Germany wanted no more conquests, in Europe or overseas. Friction was desirable; war was evil, from the point of view of German interests. Therefore, in the crisis which dragged on through three nerve-wracking years, Bismarck was the most loyal and most effective friend of peace in Europe. The peace he sought was, to be sure, not based on abstract justice or on harmonious coöperation. It was a peace produced and maintained by a balance of conflicting forces. Early in the crisis he outlined the settlement he desired. If Russia established herself in the eastern half of the Balkans, Austria should seize territory in the western half. Egypt would go to England; Syria, to France. Italy he apparently thought unworthy of consideration. The result would be a balance of forces: Austria and Russia balanced in the Balkans; England in Egypt balanced Russia in the Balkans and France in Syria; Constantinople and the Straits would be guarded by a Turkey strengthened by the loss of rebellious subjects. Everyone would have something, no one would have everything, and peace would be preserved. "This is, to be sure, only a fantasy of my imagination, but if I had a commanding voice in the situation, I would try to preserve peace between the European powers—certainly a desirable objective—at the expense of Turkey, which cannot be preserved intact in any case."[6] Not only peace, tension also would be preserved. Once established in their new possessions, the powers would be ambitious of further gain, fearful of each other, and, whether from ambition or fear, eager to win German aid. By throwing his influence, now to one side, now to another, Bismarck could maintain the balance of power necessary for continued peace and for German security.

Bismarck had a plan, but he knew there was little chance that the other powers would willingly follow his lead. He was not ignorant of the suspicion, the fear of being duped, and the jealousy which his name aroused in Europe. The memory of the war scare of 1875 was still fresh; statesmen feared that while attention was focused on the Near East, Germany might either crush France once and for all, or buy French friendship by giving her Belgium, Germany taking Holland. The persistent fear, particularly in England, that Germany wished to seize Holland, or the German provinces of Austria, or some other territory, was unfounded; but given Bismarck's past it was natural. On the other hand, the suspicion that he might attack France, if sure there would be no interference, was not only natural but well-founded; at least he spoke longingly of the possibility to his intimates. Founded or unfounded, however, suspicion was too

[6] G.P., II, 69–72.

strong to permit trust in Bismarck's counsels. Moreover, the two really important contestants, England and Russia, had not yet learned the necessity of listening to his advice. The statesmen of both countries saw clearly that the central position of Germany invited the formation of hostile coalitions; they did not see the uses to which that position could be put. London and St. Petersburg seemed the rival centers of power; Germany must follow one or the other. Time was needed to shatter this illusion.

Time was also needed to clarify the policy of the contestants. In the summer of 1876, after a year of discussion between the powers, and after unlimited bloodshed in the Balkans, the revolt smouldered on, and the outcome remained obscure. In England, Disraeli saw only that it was politically desirable to keep Turkey intact; he refused to see that the rise of nationalism in the Balkans made change inevitable. Gladstone saw so clearly that Turkey could rule her rebellious subjects only by brutal coercion, rising at times to wholesale slaughter, that he was blind to the political consequences of territorial changes. Salisbury was at heart very close to the "immoral" Bismarck, but he was discouraged by the fact that his party, and particularly Disraeli, were still dominated by the Crimean War tradition. Derby saw all possibilities and dangers so clearly that his will was paralysed; amid the tumult of conflicting counsels the Foreign Secretary did nothing. Some day England would do something, but it was impossible to say which line of policy would win. Vienna also drifted, sure that any change would be for the worse, conscious that, in the end, the decisive voice would be that of some power stronger than Austria. The highest aspiration of Andrássy, the chief Austrian minister, was to emerge from the crisis with as little loss as possible. He was convinced that losses could be held to a minimum by coöperation with England and, if possible, Germany, but at any moment he might be swept aside by those Austrians who still hoped to reverse the verdict of 1866 through a coalition with Russia against Germany. Finally, there were the Russians, pushed towards action by the clamor of the Pan Slavs and by fear of terrorist bombs, afraid to act lest a too-powerful coalition bring defeat and consequent internal convulsions, convinced that the dilemma in which they were caught was the result of German refusal to promise unquestioned support. Here again, inaction might suddenly be replaced by blind action; but action might be directed against Turkey, against Austria, or it might even be a crusade against Germany, with the support of Austria and France.

While counsels were thus confused, and while the English and Russians were willing to have him for an ally, but not for an arbiter, Bismarck could only bide his time. He explained his plans for a partition of Turkey to all who would listen to him, but always as a personal expression of opinion, never as a policy backed by German power. Germany, he blandly explained, had no policy except the preservation of peace; any solution which promised peace had his support. Above all, he refused to commit Germany to action in case of war. His calculated reticence infuriated other statesmen. "And now about Germany?" Lord Beaconsfield angrily asked Lord Derby in September, 1876. "When I am told its Prime Minister is in solitude and cannot be disturbed, and that the Queen's Ambassador is here because it is of no use being at his post, I listen to eccentricities, which must not be permitted to regulate events affecting the destiny of generations and Empires." [7] Beaconsfield had reason to be angry. The Bulgarian atrocities which he had airily dismissed a few months earlier as insignificant and irrelevant were now obviously neither. English opinion, under the passionate lead of Gladstone, was cursing the massacring Turks with the fervor formerly expended on the Russians. His whole policy threatened with ruin, Beaconsfield tried to revive Bismarck's proposals for Anglo-German coöperation, which Derby's suspicions had blocked at the beginning of the year. Beaconsfield would go beyond intimacy; he suggested alliance between the two countries guaranteeing the territorial status quo in Europe. "This wd. make us easy about Constantinople, and relieve Bismarck of his real bugbear, the eventual alliance of England and France, and the loss of his two

[7] M. & B., II, 925.

captured provinces."[8] The "fox at Varzin" refused to be smoked out; nothing, Bismarck insisted, would be more pleasing to him than a rapprochement between England and France. Courtesy did not quite permit him to say that he had no intention of taking on the responsibility for Turkish territorial integrity which even the English people were finding onerous. So died another of the frequent but unsubstantial proposals for an Anglo-German alliance which were so common in these years, killed by the lack of mutual trust or common interests.

Russia was harder to put off. Bismarck ceaselessly intoned his loyalty to the Dreikaiserbund, which still existed in form; whatever was desired by both Russia and Austria, he would support. But Russia and Austria were finding it hard to agree on anything. How could determination to preserve the status quo be reconciled with determination to alter the status quo? That, Bismarck replied, was up to Vienna and St. Petersburg. When they were agreed, he would throw the weight of Germany behind the agreement. So long as possible, he pretended not to understand that Russia wanted aid against Austria. At last the Tsar put the question bluntly: what course would Germany pursue if Russia and Austria were at war? Bismarck turned and twisted, but Alexander insisted on an answer. The German answer was ambiguous in form. Germany would not take part in such a war unless the position of one or the other antagonist as a great power was imperilled.[9] Actually, this meant German assistance to Austria, the weaker power. The Russians, fearful of driving Germany further into the enemy camp, restrained their anger at this "ingratitude" for earlier service; but from October, 1876, Bismarck realized that the Russian alliance, upon which he had leaned so heavily since the day he first took power, had lost its efficacy.

The situation was dangerous. The other powers were quarrelling, and that was good; but they were more ready to abuse Germany for refusing to promise support, than they were to accept Bismarck as arbiter of their disputes, and that was bad. Eu-

[8] *Ibid.*, II, 953.
[9] G.P., II, 72–79.

rope was drifting. The end might be war, it might be an agreement made without consulting Germany, and at her expense. Bismarck tried to escape, on his own terms. He offered a mutual guarantee of territory to Russia. The Russians declined. What Russia wanted was more territory, and fear of losing Alsace-Lorraine was the best means of forcing Germany to support Russian ambitions; a mutual guarantee of territory would relieve Bismarck from his fear of a Franco-Russian alliance, and would bring Russia no conquests. He offered to conclude an alliance with England against France. Again he was rebuffed. The English, like the Russians, hoped to use fear of French revenge as a lever to win German support.

The drift continued. Projects for reform of Turkish rule in the Balkans were launched by one statesman or another; all foundered on the suspicions of the powers or on the determination of the Turks to maintain their empire intact. At last, terrified of revolution if he continued to disregard the Pan Slavs, the Tsar declared war on Turkey, in April, 1877. Bismarck immured himself more closely than ever at Varzin. "Prince Bismarck has become a *myth*," the German Crown Princess reported at the end of 1877; "He is neither seen nor heard of." [10] Now that the Tsar was in the hands of the Pan Slavs, German talk of compromise would be interpreted as enmity, and complete the breach between Germany and Russia; if Russia was to be restrained England must take the blame. Beaconsfield was quite willing to act, to fight if necessary, and public opinion was moving steadily to his side, away from Gladstone. The poor Bulgarian and the Terrible Turk were forgotten; now, the gallant struggle of the weak Turks against England's ancient enemy aroused the cherished British sporting instinct. In the music-halls, crowds wildly sang the song which was to survive as a symbol of hysterical lust for war:

We don't want to fight,
But, by Jingo! if we do,

[10] *Letters of the Empress Frederick*, 157.

We've got the ships,
We've got the men,
We've got the money, too!

If the determination of Beaconsfield had been more evident the Russians might have been terrified into moderation, but Derby was still Foreign Secretary, and he was still a passive barrier to strong action. For months, British policy followed a zigzag course, pulled towards war by the Prime Minister, pulled towards peace by the Foreign Secretary. Deceived by this indecision, the Russians concluded that no effective opposition was to be feared. Rashly, they brushed aside all warnings to keep their troops back from Constantinople, and to remember that Turkish territorial integrity was guaranteed by treaties. The collapse of Turkish resistance made an attack on Constantinople unnecessary, but the Treaty of San Stefano, which brought the war to a close in March, 1878, embodied the most extreme Pan Slav hopes: a large, autonomous Bulgaria, stretching from the Danube to the Ægean, and from the Black Sea to Albania, including most of Macedonia and Thrace, and splitting European Turkey into two insignificant fragments.

Long before the Treaty of San Stefano was signed, Bismarck realized that war between Russia and England was certain if the Tsar insisted on setting his own terms. Forced to choose between the certainty of antagonizing Russia and the incalculable risks of a European war, the Chancellor decided for peace. Emerging from his long retirement in February, 1878, he dramatically told the Reichstag that Germany must be an "honest broker" for Europe, an honest broker who, asking nothing for himself, sought to harmonize the interests of his quarrelling clients. The Reichstag, and Germany, were enormously impressed by this evidence that their Chancellor was the arbiter of Europe; here was a tribute to the new strength of Germany such as patriots loved. For Bismarck, however, the self-confident oration was really a confession of defeat. Turkey would be partitioned, as he had advocated. He would be outwardly the arbiter between all the powers of Europe. But actually the settlement would be dictated by England, because England was prepared to fight for the terms she demanded; after Salisbury replaced Derby as Foreign Secretary there was no room for doubt on that score. The honest broker would win only the hatred of the disappointed Russians. Beaconsfield would see his hope of smashing the Dreikaiserbund realized; Bismarck's hope of binding every power to Germany would be blasted, at least temporarily. All that was obvious. Nevertheless, he preferred defeat to a European war. War no longer served German interests. Germany had everything she needed, except security.

In June, the representatives of the powers met at Berlin, under Bismarck's presidency, to tear up the Treaty of San Stefano. The German people joyously contrasted their position in Europe now, with their position a quarter of a century before, when the powers had met in Paris to end the Crimean War by a congress to which Prussia had been invited only as a contemptuous afterthought. In 1878, the chief statesmen of Europe—Beaconsfield from England, Gorchakov from Russia, Andrássy from Austria, and a host of others—were meeting in the German capital, under a German chairman. The Congress of Berlin did at least give Bismarck needed prestige at home which would be valuable in securing acceptance of his new internal policies. More than that, the Congress permitted him to give a spectacular demonstration of his lack of territorial ambition, spectacular because unique in that assemblage. With strange lack of humor, Beaconsfield reported the Chancellor's comment on hearing that Britain intended to take the island of Cyprus as her share of the spoils: "You have done a wise thing. This is progress. It will be popular; a nation likes progress." His idea of progress, Beaconsfield concluded, "was evidently seizing something." [11] It would be more precise to say that Bismarck alone did not have this idea. In addition to Cyprus, England secured a treaty with Turkey which, had not Gladstone abandoned it, might have made the whole Turkish Empire a British sphere of influence. Austria occupied Bosnia and Herzegovina, and obtained vague rights over

[11] M. & B., II, 1204.

the neck of territory between Serbia and Montenegro, the Sanjak of Novibazar. France was privately assured by the English and the Germans that she might take Tunis, a Turkish dependency, when she wished. Other fragments of Turkey went to the Balkan states. Italy got nothing, because no one thought her hunger worth satisfying. The Russians got Bessarabia and parts of Turkish Armenia, but they saw half of Bulgaria handed back outright to Turkey, and the other half divided into autonomous provinces called Bulgaria and Eastern Rumelia. Amid this land-grabbing, Bismarck sat tossing morsels to others, but asking nothing for Germany. It would have been impossible to devise a more effective method of disarming the general suspicion of German aggression. His generosity with Turkish territory also served to prepare the way for that state of tension between the powers, and of dependence on Germany, which he had sought to create during the crisis just past. Although Russian ambitions in the Balkans had been checked, they had not been killed; England from Cyprus, and Austria from Bosnia would always be watching for a new Russian advance. By directing French aspirations towards Tunis, Bismarck was increasing the probability of an Anglo-French contest for Mediterranean supremacy; in any case, it was good to have France thinking of something other than Alsace-Lorraine. With dogged patience, he began anew the contest for control over the European balance of power.

He had to do so. As things stood, Germany had a hostile France on one flank and a hostile Russia on the other. Among the many anecdotes which Beaconsfield reported to his feminine friends back home, one had symbolical significance. On the morning the Congress opened, he wrote, "P. Gortchakoff, a shrivelled old man, was leaning on the arm of his gigantic rival, and, P. Bismarck being seized with a sudden fit of rheumatism, both fell to the ground. Unhappily, P. Bismarck's dog, seeing his master apparently struggling with an opponent, sprang to the rescue. It is said that P. Gortchakoff was not maimed or bitten thro' the energetic efforts of his companion." [12] In the Balkan crisis, Rus-

[12] M. & B., II, 1190.

sia had advanced in the confident expectation of support from Berlin; that support had failed, and the Russians blamed their defeat on Germany. If Russia avenged her defeat by an alliance with France, the nightmare of coalition would be a reality. At the Congress, Bismarck tried to avert disaster by securing as favorable terms for Russia as Beaconsfield would permit, and by turning French attention to the Mediterranean; but he also prepared for the worst. England was, at least for the moment, the dominant power in Europe, and Beaconsfield was in control of England. "The old Jew, there is the man!" Bismarck admiringly exclaimed; and he set out to win the protection of the old Jew, who described the campaign, and inferentially its success, for his friend Lady Bradford.

> Bismarck soars above all: he is six feet four I shd. think, proportionately stout; with a sweet and gentle voice, and with a peculiarly refined enunciation, wh. singularly and strangely contrasts with the awful things he says: appalling from their frankness and their audacity. He is a complete despot here, and from the highest to the lowest of the Prussians, and all the permanent foreign diplomacy, tremble at his frown and court most sedulously his smile. He loads me with kindnesses, and, tho' often preoccupied, with an immediate dissolution of Parliament on his hands, an internecine war with the Socialists, 100's of whom he puts daily into prison in defiance of all law, he yesterday exacted from me a promise that, before I depart, I will once more dine with him quite alone.[13]

On his return from Berlin, Beaconsfield received a tumultuous welcome. "I bring you Peace with Honour," he told his countrymen. In many ways this was not the peace he had envisaged three years earlier. He had not by any means settled the Near Eastern question; that question was to plague Europe until it precipitated war in 1914. He had not preserved the territorial integrity of Turkey; in the end he had accepted the policy of partition which, when proposed first by Salisbury, he had denounced as immoral. But he had smashed the Dreikaiserbund: "Next to making a tolerable settlement for the Porte, our great object was to break up, and permanently prevent, the alliance of

[13] *Ibid.*, II, 1200–1201.

the three Empires, and I maintain that there never was a general diplomatic result more completely effected."[14] Now that rivalry had replaced coöperation between the most important continental states, Britain could play them off, one against the other, and thereby force acquiescence in her imperial program—if the English people continued to wish imperial growth. In 1878, there seemed no reason for making this reservation; confidently, he continued to preach his old program, *Imperium et Libertas.*

Bismarck, also, was cheered by his countrymen, but the end of the Congress meant no break in his labors. Vigilantly, he studied the diplomatic reports from Russia, and those reports became steadily more ominous. Humiliation at Berlin turned the Russians against their own government; terrorists became increasingly active. Angry and frightened, the Tsar sought a scape-goat to blame for his own errors of judgment. He called the Congress of Berlin a "European coalition against Russia under the leadership of Prince Bismarck." He contrasted Russian services in preventing the formation of a coalition during the wars of 1866 and 1870, with German refusal to silence Austria and England in 1878. His complaints gradually changed to threats as Russian wishes were disregarded by the commissions appointed to execute the Treaty of Berlin: "*cela finira d'une manière très sérieuse.*"[15] Old Emperor William was sure that his Russian nephew would soon become reasonable, but Bismarck was oppressed by a sense of isolation. The Pan Slavs had forced the Tsar's hand in 1877; they might do so again. As he explained to the Russian envoy later, he knew that Alexander's angry words were written by a nephew to an uncle; "but it is a nephew whose every gesture represents a force of two million bayonets!"[16] Rumors of alliance negotiations between Paris and St. Petersburg became more persistent. In Vienna, Andrássy was about to resign; his successor might be sympathetic to a coalition against

[14] *Ibid.*, II, 1239.
[15] G.P., III, 3, 10.
[16] Saburov, 73.

Germany. Evidently, Bismarck feared encirclement rather than immediate attack, because Russia was in no condition to fight a first-class antagonist so soon after the war with Turkey. Evidently also, he was genuinely alarmed, because for a brief interval he was ready to discard the policy of balancing between the powers, to which he had consistently adhered for years.

In August, 1879, he met Andrássy at Gastein, and proposed a defensive alliance. Such an alliance might not of itself complete the breach with Russia, if the Tsar could be convinced that "defensive" was a word to be taken literally; it might even end Russian threats by convincing the Tsar that an attack would surely mean defeat, and that the encirclement of Germany was no longer possible. Bismarck did not stop with this proposal, however. Finding Andrássy and Francis Joseph more than willing to discuss an alliance, he directed the German Ambassador in London, Count Münster, "to find out from Lord Beaconsfield, what the policy of England would be if Germany came into conflict with Russia by continuing to refuse Russian demands. No German interest would be injured if we agreed to the Russian wishes. We only refrain from doing so out of our friendship for Austria and England. Therefore, we must know what England would do, if our present policy involves us in a conflict." [17] Stripped of diplomatic reticence, Bismarck proposed a coalition against Russia. He must indeed have been desperate. If Germany allied with both England and Austria, the Russians would see their worst suspicions justified; they would justly see Germany as the barrier to their expansionist ambitions, not only in the Near East, but in Asia. Implacable Russian hatred would be the inevitable result, and Russian hatred was far more dangerous for a power in the center of Europe than for an island power like England. Disraeli was quick to see that this was an opportunity to transfer the burden of Russian hostility to German shoulders. He saw only one danger—that Bismarck would try to turn the edge of the alliance against France—but he had confidence enough in his own skill to feel that he could avert the danger.

[17] G.P., IV, 3, 4.

Victoria and Salisbury were even more suspicious of a trap, and they doubted the ability of an Englishman to escape from a Bismarckian trap. Nevertheless, Salisbury was ready to negotiate, and he readily promised that, if Russia attacked Germany and Austria, England would fight. This was the promise Bismarck had sought.

Münster was instructed to sound Beaconsfield on September 14, 1879. A month passed before he was able to report Salisbury's encouraging reply. In that short interval Bismarck drew back from his momentous proposal. The alliance with Austria was signed on October 7. It provided that if either power was attacked by Russia, or if Russia joined forces with any other great power which one ally was fighting, the other ally must give armed aid. Austria proposed to invite England to join the alliance. Bismarck refused. Clearly and at great length, he pointed out the dangers of a coalition against Russia! Meanwhile, British statesmen vainly waited for a resumption of negotiations. The conclusion of the Austro-German alliance was known in London, and welcomed; but it was Andrássy, not Bismarck, who gave news of the alliance. Berlin was silent. In November, Beaconsfield informed Victoria that the project was obviously dead. He seemed half relieved, half disappointed. The Queen, as usual, knew her own mind: "We are well out of it." With a daughter in Berlin, she knew better than to trust Bismarck.

Actually, there was no reason for doubting that Bismarck had proposed the coalition in good faith. The real problem is to decide whether the proposal was more than a desperate measure, conceived in a moment of panic, and discarded when the danger of immediate Russian action receded. Undoubtedly, he always thought of England, Austria, and Germany as "natural" allies. That is, all three had common interests. From this premise, many scholars conclude that it was his settled policy to unite the three powers in one general defensive alliance; the offer of 1879 is the chief evidence for the conclusion. The quick withdrawal of the offer is explained by the resistance of Emperor William: it required a stiff battle, culminating in a threat of resignation, to make the Kaiser agree to the treaty with Austria; a coalition against Russia would provoke even stiffer resistance, probably an adamant refusal; therefore Bismarck gave way. So runs the argument. It may be correct. The Chancellor had too little respect for the opinion of either colleagues or future historians to feel that an explanation of his actions was necessary. The difficulty is that this conclusion cannot be reconciled with so many of his statements and actions, after 1879 as well as before.

The opposing evidence suggests that his objective, except on this occasion, was not a general defensive alliance, but a series of alliances for special purposes. Germany made a defensive alliance with Austria to avert encirclement, and because Russia must not be permitted to crush the only other great continental power which desired to preserve the status quo; Austria allied with Germany as insurance against a Russian attack. The basis of this union was purely defensive, but defence is a slippery word. Germany, as the stronger partner, could define the word as she would, could restrain or encourage, could even desert if her interests required desertion. Therefore, while the alliance held Austria away from Russia, and acted as a salutary check on Pan Slav recklessness, it did not necessarily alienate Russia from Germany. Rather, it made Bismarck the mediator between his two eastern neighbors. An Anglo-Austrian alliance would be no less advantageous for Germany. Austria wished more than protection against attack; she also wished to increase her influence in the Balkans, and to prevent Russian expansion in the Near East. Bismarck refused to support these objectives. He did not care what happened in the Balkans, or at least he would like the world to believe he did not. Britain did care, greatly. Well then, he argued repeatedly, let Austria and England make an alliance for the protection of their common interests. If a crisis arose, he would be glad to seek a compromise satisfactory to his good friends the Russians and to his good friends in Vienna and London; in other words, he would be the arbiter. Finally, an Anglo-German alliance was suggested by common rivalry with France. Germany feared a war of revenge; England feared French imperialism. Why not agree to hold their restless neighbor in check? Here again he would be the arbiter. Germany asked only that France leave her alone. England and France were engaged in active and growing rivalry for specific imperial prizes. German influence, thrown on either side in any dispute, would be decisive.

These three alliances—Anglo-German, Anglo-Austrian, and Austro-German—Bismarck sought repeatedly. The reason seems obvious: he could dominate each, and the total result would be German mastery in Europe. A general alliance between the three powers, he openly sought only once, and he quickly abandoned that attempt. Again, the reason seems obvious. A general alliance would turn French and Russian anger at thwarted ambitions full against Germany, and would force them to unite for the destruction of Germany, the most vulnerable member of the union. Fearful of an attack on two fronts, Germany must follow her allies, no matter where they led. A general alliance meant German servitude.

This analysis is consistent with Bismarck's words and actions throughout his career, except for a few weeks in the autumn of 1879. While English statesmen were still waiting for a clearer statement of his purpose, he was rebuffing with unusual vehemence the repeated suggestions of Vienna that Britain be invited to join the Austro-German alliance. Possibly he drew back so quickly because he feared the Emperor would not follow him; but this would not have prevented him from returning to his original position later. He was not a man to abandon lightly a settled conviction. Rather, it may be said with reasonable assurance that he drew back from the abyss into which he had momentarily been willing to jump, because his position was no longer desperate. Russian threats ceased abruptly with the first rumors of negotiation between Berlin and Vienna, and even after the conclusion of the alliance became a certainty, the Tsar continued to assert his desire for improved relations. Alexander was no less afraid than Bismarck of isolation in face of a coalition. Probably the Chancellor's fears had never had much foundation; possibly, as he preferred to believe, the Austro-German alliance ruined the Russian designs.

No matter what the real explanation, it was soon evident that Bismarck had reverted to the old line of action, seeking patiently to gather into his own hands the control over European international action which Beaconsfield had thought safely in English possession. And this time he was successful. Discussions for a revival of the Dreikaiserbund were begun before the year was ended. The negotiations were long and difficult. Russia would much have preferred an agreement with Germany alone to one including the hated Austrians. This Bismarck refused, foreseeing a ceaseless struggle between his two allies for German favor. When the Tsar saw that he must choose between an agreement with both his neighbors, or none at all, he gave way. Chastened by defeat at the Congress of Berlin, the Russians were willing to leave things as they were in the Near East, and to seek satisfaction for their insatiable lust for conquest in central Asia, where England alone would oppose them. Bismarck, while not suggesting this shift of activity, naturally saw no reason to regret it.

He had a harder time with the Austrians, who, already having an alliance with Germany and still hoping for English entrance into that alliance, saw no reason for making terms with Russia. An astoundingly maladroit election speech by Gladstone opportunely frightened the Austrians into a more accommodating mood. The speech was an indictment of Conservative foreign policy, and one count in the indictment was the coöperation of Beaconsfield with that "unflinching foe of freedom," Austria: "There is not one instance, there is not a spot upon the whole map, where you can lay your finger and say, there Austria did good." As the Austrian Ambassador complained in his inevitable protest against the speech, "I cannot imagine a more sweeping condemnation of the whole history and policy of a country." [18] When Gladstone emerged victorious from the campaign, in April, 1880, he apologized, but on the ground that a prospective prime minister should not say such things, not because those

[18] B.D., IX, part 1, 773.

things were untrue. The Austrians sadly recognized the moral—Germany was their only friend, and they must follow where Bismarck led. It took another year to agree on terms, but in the end a common need for peace and common hatred for radicalism brought the three empires into alliance once more. The treaty signed in 1881 repeated the promise of the earlier agreement that neutrality would be observed by the other contracting parties if one "should find itself at war with a fourth Great Power." The effect of the Balkan crisis was seen in the modifications and additions to this central clause. The promise of neutrality was not to apply to a war with Turkey unless "a previous agreement shall have been reached between the three Courts as to the results of this war." No changes were to be permitted in the territorial status quo in Turkey unless all three had agreed on a division of the spoils. Two exceptions were permitted: Austria might annex Bosnia when she chose, and no opposition was to be made to the union of Bulgaria and Eastern Rumelia. Implicitly, these exceptions were an acceptance of Bismarck's plan to make the western Balkans an Austrian, and the eastern Balkans a Russian, sphere of influence. More explicitly, the requirement that all three powers must agree on any future territorial changes in the Balkans, made him the arbiter in future Austro-Russian disputes.[19]

Inadvertently, Gladstone had helped Bismarck to obtain security by a new and much more advantageous League of the Three Emperors, the league which Beaconsfield had thought permanently ended. Inadvertently, Gladstone made Bismarck's task easier in other ways. France and Italy had come away from the Congress of Berlin empty-handed. Neither country concealed its chagrin at this result, and the statesmen of both countries eagerly sought a means of placating popular discontent. France hoped to win Tunis and, if possible, Egypt. Italy also eyed Tunis covetously. Gladstone's hatred of imperialism was too great for him to do more than decry such ambitions. When France, undeterred by the disapproval of the Liberal ministers, obtained a protectorate over Tunis in 1881, the British were pre-

[19] Pribram, *Secret Treaties,* I, 36 *ff.*

pared to object, but they were silenced by Bismarck's energetic support of the French action. That the French should feel more kindly towards Germany, was to be expected. More surprising was the action of the chagrined Italians. Recognizing their impotence to conduct an imperial policy unaided, and impressed by the strength of the central empires, the Italians sought admission into the Austro-German alliance. The result was the Triple Alliance of 1882, a defensive union against France and Russia. In the same year, Gladstone, by a series of missteps, blundered into the occupation of Egypt. Undoubtedly he was sincere in maintaining that British troops had been landed only to suppress revolutionary disorders; undoubtedly he sincerely believed the occupation would be brief. But the French could not be blamed for feeling that they had been cheated.

With the British occupation of Egypt, Bismarck's control over the European balance of power was completed and made secure. Russia had tried vainly to dominate the Continent by exploiting German fear of encirclement. Disraeli, with temporary success, had exploited the insular advantages of England to win control. With unfailing tenacity, and with only one brief loss of nerve, Bismarck had patiently worked to attain the hegemony which, he believed, would alone make Germany safe. By 1882 he had succeeded. Austria and Russia had been taught to look to Berlin for the settlement of their perennial quarrels. Italy had been forced to silence her longing for the Italian provinces of Austria, and to place herself under the protection and direction of Berlin. France had been forced to postpone hopes of revenge because Bismarck's aid was needed in her imperial strife with Britain. Even England, her work in Egypt impeded at every step by the treaty rights of other powers, recognized that the occupation would be a failure without German goodwill.

Not even Metternich had commanded such respect, such deference. Undoubtedly, Bismarck had been aided by many lucky breaks of the game; but he had known how to minimize the effect of bad breaks as well as how to make the most of every favorable turn of fortune. His genius cannot be doubted. There were moments when Disraeli could equal his uncanny ability to understand the strength and weakness of an opponent's position. Other rivals, he had none, in these years. Without minimizing the importance of sheer intellect, however, his success may in great part be explained by the policy for which he stood. He asked nothing for Germany except the right to be left alone, at peace with her neighbors. Since he feared that Germany might be drawn into a war between other great powers, he tried to keep the peace in Europe. By 1878, the sincerity of his pacific professions was beginning to obtain general recognition, and his victories after the Congress of Berlin resulted partly from that recognition. He actually was an honest broker, anxious to satisfy his neighbors' craving for prestige and territory, demanding only that his clients not go to war with each other, or blame him for their losses in the market.

Luck, genius, and a defensive policy had brought success after years of effort, years in which failure had sometimes seemed imminent. By 1882 the question was pressing for an answer: could this hard-won supremacy be maintained if the last element was changed, if Germany changed again from a satiated to a hungry power? Bismarck himself was unconsciously raising the question by the changes in domestic policy which he worked out at the same time that he was moulding the international situation to his liking.

Were such a presentation not fatal to clarity, it would be best to discuss his activities at home and abroad simultaneously. Then it could be seen that they were inseparably connected, not only in time, but in purpose and method. The purpose was to make Germany strong, immune to coercion or attack. The method was to play off opponents, one against the other, to create a balance of forces which he could control. Then also it could be seen that the numerous efforts to label him as an imperialist or anti-imperialist, social reformer or reactionary, as any one type of statesman, have little meaning. The power of the state was his one concern, all else was secondary, means to an end. Undoubtedly his domestic policy was sometimes influenced by other loyalties. As an aristocrat, he was suspicious of efforts to alter the existing social structure. As a Christian, he was suspicious of men who did not cherish existing moral relationships. These loyalties are, however, a tricky guide to an understanding of the man. They help to explain his feeling towards socialists and Jews; but he hated socialists and he was only mildly anti-Semitic. He could, as he said, distinguish between Jew and Jew. "Those who have become rich are not dangerous. They will not put up barricades, and they pay their taxes punctually. It is the enterprising ones who have nothing, particularly those on the press." [20] As the saying goes, some of his best friends were Jews, or at least his most useful friends, like the banker Bleichroeder. On the other hand, he would not admit the existence of a harmless socialist, that is, Marxian socialist. In the 'sixties he had been quite willing to bargain with Ferdinand Lassalle, a Jew as well as a socialist. But Lassalle had preached a social revolution through state action, state financed socialism. Marxian socialists urged revolt against the state. When the disciples of Karl Marx won the leadership of German socialism from the disciples of Lassalle at Gotha in 1875, Bismarck recognized an enemy and prepared to attack.

At every point, the Chancellor's loyalty to aristocracy and Christianity may be dismissed as a minor factor. In the early years of the Empire, he had leaned for support on the middle class National Liberals because they were the largest political party and were willing to work for greater internal unity. With the growth of socialism at one extreme, and of big business at the other, the middle classes were weakened, and frightened. Finding them less useful as allies, and less dangerous as opponents, he broke the alliance when the National Liberals ventured to oppose him. Similarly, the Kulturkampf was abandoned, not because it was obviously weakening all religious faith, but because it was a failure, and unnecessary. When victory was more than dubious, and when he realized that Catholicism at home and abroad was willing to accept the Empire, he

[20] Busch, *Bismarck*, II, 260.

sought an alliance with his late enemies. Even his own junker class was fought until an alliance was obtained on his own terms. Again the conclusion becomes apparent: ideals other than state power had little hold on Bismarck; this was his strength, and his weakness.

When, at Varzin after 1875, Bismarck minutely scrutinized the internal situation, he was studying what was to him a relatively unknown political field. Hitherto, he had concentrated on foreign affairs, relying on victories abroad to win him support at home. He had taken support where he found it, and the easiest allies had been the middle classes who had so willingly subordinated liberalism to nationalism. The middle classes had, however, preserved a belief in free enterprise, laissez-faire, from the wreckage of their hopes; they worshipped nationalism, but they feared the state. Bismarck's sceptical mind was disturbed by talk of the Volksgeist, and while he did not worship the state, he did think it by far the most important human institution. A break between such allies was inevitable. They could work together in building a uniform legal framework for the Reich; they could coöperate in the Kulturkampf. Even in this work they were seeking different objectives, Bismarck to make the position of the new state secure, the liberals to strengthen and purify the national spirit. The break came when Bismarck decided that the state must do more than impose common institutions on Germany; to be strong, it must guide and control the lives of the German people, here restricting or suppressing, there encouraging or aiding. The economic crisis which had begun in 1873 forced him to this decision. The depression sent hungry workers flocking to socialism: between 1871 and 1874 the votes received by the Social Democrats jumped from slightly more than a hundred thousand to almost a half million. The depression sent business men and agriculturists flocking to Berlin for legislative aid. And, the depression created a deficit in the imperial budget. Under the constitution, the Reich must be supported by indirect taxes or by levies on the states; the states alone could levy direct taxes. If he was to avoid emphasizing the federal structure of the Empire by asking for money from the states, Bismarck must get the Reichstag to levy new indirect taxes.

An unbalanced budget, industry and agriculture prostrate, a rapidly growing revolutionary party—these were facts. The National Liberals maintained that they had been produced by economic depression, and would disappear with economic revival. The resignation of the Minister of Finance, an ardent advocate of laissez-faire, indicated as early as 1876 that Bismarck did not agree with this analysis. In the same year he tried to pass a law withdrawing freedom of speech and publication from the socialists; the National Liberals refused to vote for this dangerous precedent. Attempts to secure new taxes also failed; the National Liberals feared that secure and permanent revenues would completely emancipate the government from parliamentary control. Unable to control his old supporters, Bismarck looked about for new allies. The conservative parties, representatives primarily of agriculture, were quite willing to promise support. Their earlier fears that the Reich would be dominated by liberalism had proved groundless, and the collapse of farm prices under an avalanche of Russian grain made them eager for government protection against foreign competition. Conservative backing alone would not insure a majority. The Chancellor next sought to split the National Liberals. As he could see, the party was already falling to pieces. The right wing, discouraged by inability to meet English industrial competition, wished to forsake free trade; the left wing not only clung to free trade, but fretted at the party's subservience to government instructions; the center, which included the party leader Bennigsen, was primarily concerned to prevent the impending split. Bismarck, by the offer of a cabinet post to Bennigsen, tried to win the right and center. Bennigsen was tempted, but when the National Liberals defeated a new anti-socialist bill in 1878, it became obvious that the manœuvre had failed. There was only one alternative, to abandon the Kulturkampf and to win the Catholic Center party. Surrender was humiliating, but the new pope, Leo XIII, was willing to be a generous victor, and the Center was willing to persecute socialists.

Like a skilful chess player who sees how the game will turn out, Bismarck swept the pieces from the board and prepared to start anew. In June, 1878, Emperor William was shot by a socialist. On hearing that his master had been wounded, the Chancellor exclaimed, "Now we will dissolve the Reichstag!" New elections were ordered, and an angry campaign began in which the National Liberals were denounced as allies of assassins. To make the alliance obvious to untutored minds, the Jewish origin of many liberal and socialist leaders was stressed, and the Jew was depicted as the enemy of Germany, the cause of all the distress of the years just past. The campaign was a success, in that the parties of the left were weakened. Like many of Bismarck's appeals to the masses, anti-Semitism proved easier to arouse than to silence after its usefulness was exhausted; as in other cases, he disregarded the popular tumult as harmless.

Despite the fact that it had been formulated with one eye on the party line-up, the program which Bismarck presented piecemeal to the Reichstag from 1878 to 1881 formed a coherent whole. Its total effect was to strengthen the state, by lessening the possibility of effective opposition in the Reichstag or through the states, by arming the government against revolutionary agitation, and by teaching both industry and agriculture to hope for governmental aid. A law of 1879 prohibited agitation against the existing social and political order, in language so loose that any reformer might be silenced by fear of prosecution. In the same year, a protective tariff on industrial and agricultural products was passed; thereby the government obtained a source of revenue which almost certainly would be permanent. Having won the producing classes by these favors, Bismarck set out to win the workers from socialism by outlining an ambitious program of social reform. Insurance against sickness, accident, unemployment, and old age, against all these dangers the worker was promised security. The program was revolutionary for the Europe of 1881, but it was significant for what it omitted as well as for what it promised. Employers need worry only about expense, not about the rights of property. Hours and wages were carefully left untouched; Bismarck even frowned on the efforts of trade unions to win concessions on these questions. Conditions of work were only slightly regulated. Farm labor was given practically nothing; ignorant and isolated, the rural worker was almost immune to socialist infection.

The break with laissez-faire was complete. Between 1879 and 1881, Germany turned her back conclusively on natural law as a guide to economic practice, and on free discussion as the means of discovering truth. It was an easy break for Germans to make. For generations their leading thinkers had been urging that truth was not absolute, but relative to time and place, that natural law was an invention of shallow rationalism, that national institutions should express and protect the national character. Friedrich List was quoted in support of the tariff of 1879; defence of the national spirit was a potent argument both for social legislation and for outlawing socialism. And yet these laws represented the final defeat of nationalist aspirations as personified in men of the middle classes, men like List. The state was now very largely freed from parliamentary control. So long as the National Liberals had been a strong popular party, the Reichstag had at least partly controlled the government. But the National Liberals split, as Bismarck had prophesied, the right wing joining with the conservative parties, the left joining the noisy but ineffectual radicals. Only a remnant remained with Bennigsen. Of the parties in the new government majority, all except the Center represented some group or class interest, and were content so long as their interest received favors. The Center was a mass party, and it never became completely subservient to the government. Bismarck, resenting this independence, accused the Catholic leaders of disloyalty, but they could now afford to smile ironically at his jibe.

The old German curse of disunity survived into the age of political unity; and unless it blundered badly, the government could exploit factional strife to prevent effective, coherent opposition. In this sense, 1879 may be taken as a turning point in German history no less than 1871, or rather as the completion of the work of 1871. The middle classes, the proudly self-confident Protestant burghers of the old cities, the leaders in German thought and life, the men who had first fought Bismarck and then tried to save some part of their hopes by alliance with him, now saw themselves pushed aside. Threatened from below by the workers, pushed down by the growth of big business, mistrusted by the Catholics whom they had wronged, no longer heeded by their rulers, the middle classes were happy to become suppliants for governmental protection against their enemies, and to solace themselves with the thought that the real rulers of Germany, the civil servants, were members of their class. This was true; but it meant nothing. Teachers and professors, judges and administrators, most of the highly respected *beamte* were sons of the middle class. They did not, however, serve their class. They served the government, and the government favored those it needed or feared, the capitalists and aristocrats above, and the workers below. Empty also was the boast that Germany was a democracy in the sense that behind the government stood law, law which was supreme and impartial. Bismarck knew how to get laws on the statute books, and how to prevent their enactment. The middle class had lost, largely through circumstances beyond its control, but partly because it had been content to accept half of its ideal, sacrificing the free citizen to win the free state.

The state alone was free, the military and bureaucratic state which Bismarck had at last brought to perfection. New revenues lessened dependence on the Bundesrath and the Reichstag; the princes were content to preserve their positions under imperial guardianship, and the Reichstag so quickly showed its weakness that able men scorned a political career. Through every part of German life, the bureaucracy was at work, conscious of its obligation to further the government program; even scholars in the universities found orthodoxy the surest road to promotion. Every year, young men were drawn into the army, where they were trained to good citizenship as well as to arms. Jackals wrote to Bismarck's order for the press, and the press printed official news, not from fear, but because readers wanted to know the official point of view. This great machine, controlling the lives of forty-five million people, was Bismarck's to manipulate. In freeing the state of control, he had freed himself. Above him stood only the Emperor, too feeble now to offer effective resistance. Bismarck ruled, as Germany and the world knew.

In Machiavelli's phrase, all power was his, within the limits set by nature on all power. These limits were as yet scarcely perceptible, but they must inevitably grow. To strengthen Germany, he had set out to protect both industry and agriculture by tariffs and subsidies, by railroads and canals, by subventions to technical education, by innumerable governmental favors. Would it always be possible to play off industry and agriculture against each other and thus to master both? More vitally, could this domestic program be harmonized with his foreign policy? A tariff on grain hit Russian agriculture hard, and invited reprisals, political as well as economic. Aids to industrial exports meant competition with other countries, particularly England, and this competition would obviously be more than economic. Already German business men were quarrelling with English traders in the weak countries of Africa, Asia, and the South Seas. It was impossible for the home government to remain entirely aloof from these quarrels; but when the demand for protection had been heeded, the "logical" next step would be the establishment of colonies. Bismarck recognized that overseas trade might lead to colonization. He did not shrink from the possibility, if colonies could be got without disturbing the international position he had won. That was an essential condition. It seemed a safe reservation; German industry was young, and he was strong. Just here, however, was one weak point in his control over Germany, and Europe.

There was another, and more obvious, menace to his power. The Emperor was old, past fourscore. Would Bismarck, Bismarck's state, Bismarck's policy, would any of these survive when death claimed William?

CHAPTER VII

THE REVOLT AGAINST LIBERALISM

IN 1925 Lord Balfour was discussing the failure of representative government in so many parts of the world. The trouble was, he said, that the true basis of representative government was not to be discovered by studying constitutional law. "The whole essence of British Parliamentary government lies in the *intention to make the thing work.*" Less experienced nations had not learned that. "They learn about our Parliamentary methods of obstruction, but nobody explains to them that when it comes to the point all our Parliamentary parties are determined that the machinery shan't stop. 'The King's government must go on,' as the Duke of Wellington said. But their idea is that the function of opposition is to stop the machine. Nothing easier, of course, but hopeless." [1]

Possibly the decade following 1877 was the exception which proves the rule. Certainly during that decade repeated efforts were made to stop the machinery of government. The traditional feeling of almost friendly rivalry between Liberals and Conservatives was replaced by an angry and not too scrupulous struggle for supremacy. Within each party, rival factions fought for control. Even the Queen forgot that her chief duty was to keep down the spirit of faction; like everyone else, she attacked her enemies and protected her friends with any weapon which came to hand. The genius for obstruction shown by the Irish members led by Parnell was quickly imitated by other factions. In 1880, a handful of Conservatives so completely snarled the work of the House of Commons that a member of the Liberal

[1] Dugdale, *Balfour*, II, 269.

majority lamented, "our free institutions are choked and neutralized by the forces intended to protect them." [2]

To most Englishmen at the time, Gladstone was the center of the storm, the protector or the destroyer of Britain's greatness. In 1876, already in his sixty-seventh year, he emerged from retirement, goaded into action by the conviction that Disraeli's policy was both immoral and ruinous. The old Liberal hated Tory Democracy at home, but his attack was directed even more fiercely against the new imperialism. He denounced the "forward" policy along the frontiers of India as extravagant, and as heedless of the right of border states like Afghanistan to independence; in 1879 his warnings seemed justified by the massacre of Englishmen who had been sent on an armed mission to Kabul. He denounced the dream of a British federation of South Africa as a needless extension of obligations, and as unfair to the Boers; again his warnings seemed justified by Boer protests against the annexation of the Transvaal. Above all, he denounced Disraeli's Near Eastern policy. That policy was immoral, because it made Britain an ally of corrupt despotisms like Austria and Turkey, and an enemy of Christianity and freedom in the Balkans. The policy was also foolish. It did not prevent the partition of Turkey. It ignored the fact that, as Gladstone had said decades before, there was no barrier like the breasts of freemen against Russian expansion. The acquisition of Cyprus and the promise to supervise the strengthening of Asiatic Turkey burdened England with new and useless imperial responsibilities. In opposition to Disraelian Jingoism, Gladstone proposed a return to the true bases of British policy. The strength of the empire should be fostered by "just legislation and economy." International peace should be fostered, not by entangling alliances, but by coöperation with the other great powers through the Concert of Europe. The equality of every nation, great or small, must be admitted and respected. Love of freedom must inspire the work of the foreign office no less than the home departments. In short, the old liberal program, the program set

[2] Garvin, *Chamberlain*, I, 317.

by the laws of nature and nature's God. "There is going on a profound mysterious movement, that, whether we will or not, is bringing the nations of the civilized world, as well as the uncivilized, morally as well as physically nearer to one another, and making them more and more responsible before God for one another's welfare." The program was the same, and the enemies and allies were the same. "We cannot reckon on the wealth of the country, nor upon the rank of the country, nor upon the influence which rank and wealth usually bring. In the main these powers are against us, for wherever there is a close corporation, wherever there is a spirit of organized monopoly, wherever there is a narrow and sectional interest apart from that of the country, desiring to be set up above the interest of the public, there, gentlemen, we, the liberal party, have no friendship and no tolerance to expect. Above all these, and behind all these, there is something greater than these—there is the nation itself. This great trial is now proceeding before the nation. The nation is a power hard to rouse, but when roused, harder still and more hopeless to resist." [3]

Through the last years of the Disraeli ministry, "The People's William" campaigned incessantly. When the verdict of the nation was taken in 1880, he was returned triumphantly to office. To office, but not to power. The Queen did not conceal her displeasure at his return. In the House of Lords, the Liberal peers moved in increasing numbers to the Conservative side. In the Commons, the opposition resorted to obstructive tactics which almost paralysed legislative processes. Even the Liberal party in the lower house was soon disrupted by factional strife. Abroad, one dangerous crisis followed another. Disgusted, Gladstone resigned in 1885. Elections early in 1886 returned him to office, but he had a majority only if the Irish voted with the Liberals. New elections in the summer brought decisive defeat. In the event, the victory of 1880 proved to be the last time the Liberals obtained an English majority for twenty-five years; and the Liberals of 1905 had abandoned the principles which Gladstone

[3] Morley, *Gladstone*, II, 595–610.

thought eternal. It is easy to blame, as many members of the party did, the accident of Gladstone's longevity for the débâcle. Possibly if he had died at threescore and ten, and if the partnership of Chamberlain and Dilke had not been wrecked by the successful determination of a jealous woman to make Dilke a moral and political outcast, and if—if many things had been different—then the Liberals might have been able to lead England as they had done in the preceding half century. Possibly, but not probably. Beneath the violent swings of public opinion there seemed a deep desire for safety and security, a reluctance to strike out in new paths, a half-conscious recognition that England was passing through one of the great crises of her history. This may merely be reading into the past what is obvious today, and it is certainly true that no one saw clearly the perils of the dozen years between Disraeli's victory of 1874 and the beginning of the Conservative ascendancy in 1886. The remarkable fact is that, seeing so little, the English managed to avoid so many pitfalls.

One aspect of the crisis was obvious enough, the transition from suffrage based on property to at least approximate manhood suffrage, through the Reform Bills of 1867 and 1884. The difficulty was to estimate the necessary consequences of this transition in social and economic life as well as politics. Would the masses continue to show the deference, and would all classes continue to show the animated moderation, which Bagehot had thought the secret of British greatness? The chances seemed good that they would not. A ferment of social unrest was at work. Henry George, the single taxer, received a warm welcome when he toured England in 1881. Landlords were denounced as a parasitic class; and the "New Domesday Book" of 1874—a blue book which revealed the concentration of land ownership in a few thousand families—made agitation for wider ownership seem socially desirable and politically profitable. Trade unions were growing in self-confidence as they grew in membership; between the 'sixties and the 'eighties their members swelled from a quarter of a million past the million mark. Although socialism was still largely a fad of well-to-do men and women, able and ambitious young statesmen on the left wing of both parties were outbidding each other in efforts to win the newly enfranchised masses. Lord Randolph Churchill, apparently destined for Conservative leadership, was reviving and extending Disraeli's Tory Democracy, despite the frightened warnings of his political superiors against the danger of arousing class feeling. Joseph Chamberlain, fresh from a successful experiment in social reform as Mayor of Birmingham, was not to be deterred by the threats of the Whig element among the Liberals, or even by Gladstone, from putting political questions in the form of a choice "between the Peers and the People, between the privileges of the few and the rights of the many." Gladstone could rail on occasion against the "Upper Ten Thousand," but he railed against their selfish blindness, not against the iniquity of permitting them to exist. Joseph Chamberlain, at least in words, struck at the very foundation of their power. "Lord Salisbury constitutes himself the spokesman of a class—of the class to which he himself belongs, who toil not neither do they spin (great cheering), whose fortunes, as in his case, have originated by grants made in times gone by for the services which courtiers rendered kings (renewed cheers), and have since grown and increased while they have slept by levying an increased share on all that other men have done by toil and labor to add to the general welfare and prosperity of the country." [4] This was not the old Liberal cry against privilege; it was an indictment of property itself.

While the social harmony which had earlier been one source of British strength seemed to be disintegrating, England was also forced to adjust herself to changes abroad. The task was painful, because the world which was vanishing had been so close to ideal. In the days of Palmerston, Britain had, for all practical purposes, been the only great industrial and imperial power; at the same time, agriculture had been flourishing and progressive, the most important single British industry. The world had begged for British machines and for the products of machines;

[4] Garvin, *Chamberlain*, I, 392, 402.

out of soaring profits, British finance had been able to make loans to the world, loans which were largely used for further purchases of manufactures, creating new profits which made possible new loans. So it went, a spiral whose rapid ascent was interrupted only briefly by financial panics and industrial depressions. England was the world's banker as well as the world's work shop, and she could, if the improbable necessity had arisen, keep her population from starving by the produce of her farms. It was a loose and easy time which bred loose and easy habits. It developed the habit of command, exercised not only by Palmerston as the collective voice of England, but by business men and bankers in their dealings with customers. It developed a craving for the time and accomplishments necessary to enjoy increasing wealth—not laziness, rather a feeling that work was merely a necessary means to the good life. It developed a feeling of relative indifference to those imperial possessions not immediately vital for industrial or commercial expansion. The new nationalism of Disraeli's day had partially overcome this indifference, had stimulated racial pride for colonies where Englishmen had settled, and the pride of responsibility for India. But there was little desire to expand the empire, unless new acquisitions were necessary for the defence of existing possessions. Finally, the habit of success developed the conviction that this desirable world not only would, but should, continue unchanged.

It was bound to change. In terms of human intercourse, the world was shrinking rapidly. New marine engines had cut fuel consumption and increased speed; ocean freight rates fell fast. Railroads were opening the American west and the interior of Russia to markets. What this meant to England was shown when the wet years of the late 'seventies ruined crops. In the past, short crops had meant high prices. Not now. Cheap grain from America and Russia poured in, and prices remained low. The ruin of Britain's first industry had begun. Slowly at first, then rapidly, farmers gave up, turned grain land into pasture; slowly at first, then rapidly, laborers gave up, left the countryside for the towns. At the time, few realized what was happening. Agriculture was depressed, men said; it would revive with good crops. Only the immediate effects were seen, and these were grave enough. The welcome accorded Henry George was a reflection of the resentment against landlords whose rent rolls were out of all proportion to the return received from crops. In Ireland, where the landlord was likely to be an Englishman, high rents and nationalism combined to precipitate a land war: a landlord's agent, Captain Boycott, added a word to the English language when he attempted to collect rents legally due.

A new noun also entered the language, "the unemployed." The farm laborer who came to the city for work found things had changed there. An industrial depression began even before agriculture was hit, and it was intensified and prolonged by the shrunken buying power of the farmer. In 1879, Beaconsfield was able to hail the first signs of recovery, but the rise proved both slow and short. In 1883 a new decline began to a new low, reached three years later. By 1887 times were better, but after almost a decade and a half of stagnant business conditions, Englishmen had lost their first easy confidence in a resumption of the old easy conditions. Sadly, they were forced to admit that the day of their industrial monopoly was over. The machine had found new homes in other countries; the machine which Britain had developed, very frequently the very machines which Britain had made, now turned out the goods formerly bought in England. From a monopolist, England had become only the largest of many competitors. That was discouraging, but more terrifying was the possibility that the island industries might not be able to face competition any better than the island agriculture. The "condition of England" once more became a subject of anxious debate.

Even this was not the end of troubles. In the colonial field as well, the monopoly of England was being challenged. Here the blow came without warning, or at least without any warning seen by the government in London. Disraeli had, to be sure, been alarmed by the expansionist ambitions of Russia in the Near and Middle East, but even many members of his own cabinet had thought his fears exaggerated, and the elections of 1880 showed that a majority of Englishmen believed, with Gladstone, that goodwill alone was needed to end the Anglo-Russian quarrel. Similarly, Queen Victoria's secretary had informed her as early as 1875, that "there is great jealousy in this country, and in the Colonies, of the Germans, and the desire of the Australians to annex New Guinea is not to colonize it, but to prevent the Germans from taking possession of it. The German houses in the Australian cities are increasing, and hence the alarm of their rising power." The Disraeli government refused to take action; and eight years later the Gladstone cabinet was equally sceptical when the Australians requested the annexation of all important territory in the Pacific, south of the equator. "I asked them whether they did not want another planet all to themselves," the Colonial Secretary reported, "and they seemed to think it would be a desirable arrangement, if only feasible. The magnitude of their ideas is appalling to the English mind." [5] A few months after this flippant retort, the Secretary was taking very seriously the fate of New Guinea, and of much else besides. The scramble for Africa and for the islands of the south Pacific had begun. England found herself involved in apparently endless quarrels with France and Germany over territory which she had earlier refused to annex. Simultaneously the Russians began to move once more in Central Asia. Moral suasion proved a totally useless deterrent; by the spring of 1885 even Gladstone was becoming reconciled to the thought of war with Russia. As Lord Salisbury ironically said, the Liberal ministers "have at last achieved their long-desired 'Concert of Europe': they have succeeded in uniting the continent of Europe—against England." [6]

The shift to democracy, the collapse of agriculture, industrial stagnation, the first clash of rival imperialisms—all pressed for attention in the years following 1880. It is not strange that tension within and between parties reached the breaking point.

[5] *Letters of Queen Victoria*, 2, II, 414; III, 432–433.
[6] Cecil, *Salisbury*, III, 136.

Neither is it strange that, in this crisis of their country's fortunes, most Englishmen refused to trust the operation of beneficent natural laws for a solution. To counteract social strife at home, and to resist the economic and political competition of other countries, they turned with a new eagerness to the nationalism and imperialism which Gladstone had thought conquered when the electorate repudiated Disraeli. In the popular mind, Ireland became the test of Liberal capacity to bring England through unscathed. Gladstone's efforts to secure social justice for Ireland by putting the rights of native tenants above the rights of English landlords, inevitably antagonized all those Englishmen who feared the radicalism of men like Chamberlain and Churchill. Conversely, his efforts to secure political justice for Ireland by permitting the Irish people to have their own legislature inevitably antagonized men like Chamberlain who were imperialists as well as social reformers. In 1886, when the House of Commons defeated the bill by which Ireland was to be given home rule, Gladstone appealed to the people in the name of freedom, the old liberal war cry. His opponents appealed to nationalism, and won decisively.

The defeat of liberalism in the field of foreign affairs came even earlier, and was more humiliating. On the Irish question, Gladstone at least had shown loyalty to his ideals, and it will always remain debatable whether he was defeated in a fair battle of principles or whether the issue was decided by irrelevant elements like class interest and contempt for the Irish. In his dealings with other nations, Gladstone was forced tacitly to admit, after innumerable compromises with conviction, that liberalism no longer worked, because men no longer thought or acted as liberals expected.

Compromise began almost as soon as the Gladstone government took office in 1880. In campaign speeches, the acquisition of Cyprus had been denounced as a corrupt bargain by which England secured an unneeded island in exchange for a promise to bolster up the corrupt Turkish despotism. In office, the Liberals repudiated one half of the bargain, but not the other. They took the lead in enforcing every clause of the Treaty of Berlin favorable to the Balkan states, and they tried to compel Turkey, by the united pressure of the great powers, to grant reforms favorable to the subject people of the Ottoman Empire. They were not, however, prepared to surrender Cyprus, even when the surrender was a way of insuring gains for the Balkan states. The reform program came to nothing because the eastern empires, anxious to revive the Dreikaiserbund and realizing that new disturbances in the Balkans might mean an Austro-Russian quarrel, refused to coöperate. Although the Turks escaped, they were naturally angered by the defection of their historic protector, particularly since the English retained the territory given in payment for protection. Thereafter Britain ceased to enjoy the privileged position in Turkey, economic as well as political, which had been so profitable since the Crimean War. Furthermore, the mixture of idealism and interest in Gladstone's actions led the continental powers to conclude that even his sincere efforts to improve the lot of Turkish subject nationalities were really inspired by desire to keep the three emperors fighting; ironically enough, he seemed a trouble-maker, not a peace-maker.

The same confusion marked the settlement of two other problems inherited from Disraeli. The Boers in South Africa objected to their incorporation in the British Empire; Gladstone—before he took office—protested against the annexation of the Transvaal. In office, he recalled the advantages to all concerned, and particularly to the native tribesmen, of a single, and British, political union of South Africa. The Boers asked for the redemption of his campaign pledges. Gladstone hesitated. The Boers took to arms and defeated a British detachment at Majuba Hill, in February, 1881. Gladstone then gave way, but not entirely. He agreed to independence, but the treaty signed in 1881 and modified in 1884 was vaguely worded: the Transvaal agreed not to make treaties with other nations without British consent. The Boers, already feeling self-confident because they had won at Majuba Hill, thought their independence complete save for an unimportant detail; the British continued to think of the

Transvaal as a protectorate. Many years later the ambiguity was to have serious consequences.

Ambiguity at the other end of Africa had more immediately serious results. In bankrupt Egypt, a tug of war was going on between a nationalist party led by an army officer, Arabi, and agents of European bondholders, whose position was guaranteed by a close network of treaty rights granted by the desperate Khedive. Under Disraeli, the British and the French had co-operated in the task of protecting the foreign interests. In 1882, nationalist riots broke out. The French and the English could not agree on a program of action, and efforts to turn the problem over to the concert of the powers came to nothing. Gladstone did not want to take Egypt. Neither did he want to see disorder spread. He insisted that Arabi was merely an adventurer, not the leader of an oppressed nationality. To chasten the adventurer, British warships bombarded the fortifications being built by Arabi at Alexandria. Promptly, anti-foreign riots swept through Egypt. To put down the riots, troops were landed. Arabi was decisively defeated at Tel-el-Kebir in September, but his removal settled nothing. Rather, the Khedive's government was completely demoralized, unable to preserve order in lower Egypt, and faced with a revolt in the Sudan led by the Mahdi, a religious fanatic. The London Cabinet decided that evacuation was impossible until stable government had been restored. In September, 1883, Evelyn Baring, the later Lord Cromer, was sent out to perform this task. Then the real trouble began. Gladstone knew that at every step he had been guided by the highest motives, by a desire to further the interests of the Egyptian people and of Europe. He had not realized how far the bombardment of Alexandria would take him, but once started he could not in justice retreat until stability had been achieved. He was sure that Baring's work would soon be done. Then England would leave Egypt for the Egyptians to rule. Possibly he would have been proved right if anyone had believed him; but possibly he might have been believed if he had been willing to promise to get out, and stay out, at some specific date. He refused to make the promise before the end of his task was in sight; in Europe, his refusal was taken as conclusive proof of insincerity. The opinion was general that England would not go out unless forced out. The French were the only people who cared, but their attitude was decisive. Feeling themselves tricked, they determined on revenge. For twenty years they fought the British occupation, and although they did not compel evacuation, they did cause plenty of trouble. Their most effective weapon was finance. By international agreement, the revenues of Egypt were pledged to the European bondholders; without revenue, Baring was powerless to effect the reforms necessary to put Egypt on her feet. When a majority of the powers voted with England, Baring got the money he needed; when they voted with France, he did not.

Actually, the success or failure of the British occupation of Egypt could be decided less from London and Paris than—from Berlin. In every one of the votes on vital financial issues, Germany, the leading member of the Triple Alliance, would determine the result. How would Bismarck use his power? Both antagonists early began to bid for his support; even Gladstone's hatred for the "foes of freedom" was subordinated to political necessity. In September, 1882, before the battle of Tel-el-Kebir, the Prince of Wales told his German brother-in-law that all parties in England realized the necessity for more intimate relations with Germany, not only out of selfish interest, but to further the cause of world peace. Prince Frederick even felt justified in concluding from this conversation that a general defensive alliance with Germany and Austria would be welcomed. Bismarck's reply, after perfunctorily explaining the difficulty of alliance with a parliamentary state, went straight to the problem which weighed on the English mind: his policy in Egypt had been to support England so far as was possible without giving France and Russia the impression that the British were directing German policy. *Had been,* there was the catch. Throughout, he spoke of the past and of the present. Of the future, not a word, except the assurance that he recognized the necessity of maintaining good relations with English public opinion. The conclusion was plain. Egypt was one more means by which the ideal of which he had dreamed for years might be realized and maintained: "a political situation in which all the powers except France would need us, and would be deprived of the possibility of coalition against us by their relations to each other." [7] The reality of 1882 was actually an improvement on the dreams of 1877. Even France now needed German aid. In the center of Europe he had the solid block of the Triple Alliance. The Dreikaiserbund meant peace in the east. On the west, French desire for revenge seemed submerged by hatred of England and by enthusiasm for imperial expansion. England was a suppliant for German favor. The lesser states, straws in the wind, were moving into his "League of Peace"—Spain, Serbia, Roumania, all were more or less formally joined to the Triple Alliance. As he said, foreign affairs no longer gave him an anxious moment; they ran themselves.

By backing into Egypt, Gladstone had broken the entente with France, which had endured for half a century; by his Near Eastern policy he had won a reputation for incompetent duplicity; in South Africa his half measures had prepared future trouble. Failure, failure everywhere, so complete that the Queen was driven to contrast her present prime minister unfavorably with Lord Palmerston, "who with all his many faults, had the honor and power of his country strongly at heart." [8] The failure of Gladstone has often been used to show the futility of idealism as a guide to policy. A more just criticism would be that, caught between the new nationalism at home and the new imperialism abroad, he became tangled in compromises and inconsistencies which were fatal to success. Even in Palmerston's day, when England had been dominant and the Continent had been weak and divided, compromises between liberal cosmopolitanism and narrow national egoism had been common enough. Now, pressed on all sides, disillusioned with "the inherent sufficingness of

[7] G.P., IV, 31–36; III, 154.
[8] *Letters of Queen Victoria,* 2, III, 447.

things," the English people were still able to thrill to Gladstone's prophecies of the impending world commonwealth, but like the Queen, they had the power of their country most strongly at heart. That power, they were coming to feel in these years of crisis, could not be based so completely in the home country as in the past. Disraeli had taught them that India was the complement of England, and though they repudiated him in 1880, they could not shake off his teaching. Other prophets seized on Dilke's catch-word, Greater Britain, and looked to the dominions for the needed strength.

The most impressive and popular plea for a wider interpretation of what was Britain, appeared in 1883—John Seeley's *Expansion of England.* If imperialism implies the desire for new territorial conquests, Seeley was not an imperialist; throughout, he took it for granted that the age of territorial conquest was past. Neither did he believe that England had won so vast a share of the earth's surface through any peculiar virtue or through any God-given mission. The empire had been acquired without plan, "in a fit of absence of mind"; it had been retained through the accidents of European political evolution. Finally, subject peoples played little part in his imperialism. Unlike Disraeli, he regarded the possession of India as a very mixed blessing; for the present, he saw some advantages and disadvantages in the connection, both for the English and for the natives. Whether the union would prove mutually profitable in the long run, he felt unable to decide, but he thought separation possible, and he did not lament the possibility. Greater Britain to him meant that land which was under the Queen's sovereignty and which was inhabited by people of British stock.

There was the opportunity. Though acquired and peopled by chance, this territory was now the one means by which the power of Britain, relative to the rest of the world, could be safeguarded. The islands of the United Kingdom were too small a base upon which to build, too small even to hold a rapidly multiplying population. This was an age of giant states. "If the United States and Russia hold together for another half century, they will at the end of that time completely dwarf such old European States as France and Germany, and depress them into a second class. They will do the same to England, if at the end of that time England still thinks of herself as simply a European State, as the old United Kingdom of Great Britain and Ireland, such as Pitt left her." Science had made possible the growth of these giants. "Science has given to the political organism a new circulation, which is steam, and a new nervous system, which is electricity." A state on the scale of the United States would have been inconceivable before transportation and communication had been transformed by invention; these same inventions "tend to make states which are on the old scale of magnitude unsafe, insignificant, second-rate." Britain, like America, must use science, or drop behind. The territories were there; the population was there, or could be provided out of the surplus millions which were a dead weight on the economy of the mother country. No other nation, with the possible exception of the United States, was so advantageously placed for competition in the new age. Russia had the land, but it was inhabited by a great conglomeration of races and religions. Germany had the people, but not the land. "We see a constant stream of emigration from Germany to America, but no Greater Germany comes into existence, because these emigrants, though they carry with them and may perhaps not altogether lose their language and their ideas, do not carry with them their State. This is the case with Germany because its emigration has happened too late." The land of the world was already divided.

According to Seeley, British thought had not yet adjusted itself to the age of invention. That was the trouble. Australia was not seen to be as real a part of England as Devonshire, because in the eighteenth century it had not been. Then the English state had only a tenuous connection with its outlying parts. Now, jurisdiction over the dominions could be exercised as easily as California was governed from Washington. Only a recognition of its existence was needed to make Greater Britain not only a reality but a robust reality. Britain was not a country of 120,000 crowded square miles. Its extent was limitless. "If there is pauperism in Wiltshire and Dorsetshire, this is but complementary to unowned wealth in Australia; on the one side there are men without property, on the other there is property waiting for men." When reality was recognized, when the government of Greater Britain was knit as closely as the government of the United Kingdom—by means which Seeley felt unable to describe precisely—then the power of Britain would be equalled perhaps by the United States, but by no other state in the world.[9]

Seeley's ideas were not new; they had been discussed ever since the days when Bismarck's career had awakened misgivings about British strength. The *Expansion of England* was read, discussed, praised, partly because Seeley's gift for the felicitous phrase and his severely matter-of-fact approach made the ideas seem more convincing, almost like scientifically demonstrated propositions. More important, the appearance of the book was well timed. The very fact that Gladstone was known to oppose imperialism is all its forms, made imperialists redouble their efforts to win public opinion. Significantly, Seeley was applauded by many Liberal leaders, almost all young men. Disliking the jingo and "oriental" character of Disraeli's imperialism, but sharing the heightened national feeling which he had utilized and increased, they welcomed an imperial program which called neither for aggression nor for exploitation, but only for the preservation and strengthening of the English state. The Imperial Federation League, founded in the year after the *Expansion of England* appeared, was dominated by Liberals, and devoted to the task of strengthening the ties between the parts of Greater Britain. Conservatives also, however, were willing to build on Seeley's work. The depression of industry and agriculture, and the levying of protective tariffs by the United States and by Continental states, had led to an agitation against free trade in England during the late 'seventies. As protection had an evil sound to Englishmen, the rebels called themselves Fair Traders. It was unfair, they argued, that English industry

[9] Seeley, 10, 18–19, 50, 69–72, 87–89.

should be exposed to competition at home, and debarred from competing in protected markets. Seeley's arguments for a more solid connection between the mother country and the dominions were easily adapted to the purposes of the Fair Traders. Why not secure solidarity by making the British Empire a great free trade area within which agricultural and industrial products would be freely exchanged, but cut off from the unfair competition of protected producers by an equalizing tariff duty? The argument was attractive, and many Conservative leaders, including Salisbury and Churchill, made gestures of sympathy, although they were too conscious of the fighting strength which free trade still possessed to commit themselves completely until the drift of opinion became obvious.

Gladstone had shown that Disraeli's exuberant imperialism could be successfully attacked; he would have welcomed a fight against the imperialism of the Fair Traders, but the Conservatives warily refused to accept the challenge. Against an imperialism which ostensibly argued merely that colonials were Englishmen, he could not fight openly, although he showed an uneasy consciousness of the political dynamite concealed in the concept of Greater Britain. It was not merely that a believer in cosmopolitanism was repelled by the growing cult of exclusive nationalism, or that a liberal trained to regard the state as a necessary nuisance, could not understand the increasing disposition to glorify the state. A real Greater Britain would not be at all analogous to land masses like Russia or the United States; territories scattered over the world presented colossal problems of government even in the age of steam and electricity. Men like Seeley were at a loss to describe the processes of administration. Defence and communications were important questions, and these the imperialists scarcely touched. After all, control over New Guinea and the other islands of the south Pacific was strategically as vital to Australia as control over Ireland was to England. The territory along the flanks of South Africa seemed no less important to South Africans than Belgium did to Englishmen. The oceans of the world were the highways of

Greater Britain. They must be policed, and, more difficult, strategic points along their shores must be kept out of the hands of potential enemies. For all his sobriety of expression, Seeley had described a project so daring and hazardous, that Disraeli's visions seemed prosaic by comparison. And yet Greater Britain was a catchword which had undoubtedly caught the English imagination. Gladstone did not dare deny that colonial interests were identical with British interests; to do so would have created indignation both at home and in the colonies. To act on the supposition that they were identical, however, would not only have run counter to his convictions; it would have aroused the wrath of the whole non-British world. Torn between fear of the electorate, of the other great powers, and of his conscience, Gladstone floundered, with results which have been seen in South Africa, Egypt, and the Near East. The effect of these maladroit attempts to reconcile irreconcilables was fatal. Englishmen, knowing his aversion to imperialism, complained that he was betraying national interests; concessions which an avowed imperialist might readily have made, seemed almost treasonable when he made them. The Continental peoples, studying his words and his actions, set him down as Machiavellian, a sanctimonious hypocrite who hoped to increase the British Empire without cost by keeping the Continental nations too busy fighting each other to interfere with his plans. His unhappy plight was not an inevitable result of the effort to apply idealism to international relations; rather it resulted from the effort to save some part of an ideal which now commanded only wavering allegiance in England, and almost none in the rest of Europe.

As the fourth year of the Gladstone ministry drew to a close, the British public was dissatisfied with the "weakness" of Liberal foreign policy, but there was no realization of the serious position into which the country had drifted. France seemed a troublemaker, and not in Egypt alone. A strange mania for colonial expansion had seized the French, who were trying to gain a foothold on the strategically important island of Madagascar off the east coast of Africa, in addition to expanding the frontiers of their colonies in northern Africa and, at the other end of the world, in Indo-China. How much further the French would go before awakening to the fact that colonization was an expensive and exhausting luxury, no one in England could say, but it appeared wise to guard against new attempts to seize areas where British interests were important. The mouth of the Congo River was one such region. Portugal had earlier tried to claim the territory, but England had insisted on preserving the independence of the natives. Now, it was better that an old and weak ally should control the Congo than that France should step in. In February, 1884, therefore, an Anglo-Portuguese treaty recognized the Portuguese claims. The prompt protest of France against the treaty was interpreted as proof that action had been taken just in time.

Russia also was thought a trouble-maker. The Near East was relatively quiet, but, despite many assurances to the contrary, Russian troops were busy north of Afghanistan. Steadily, the wall of buffer states crumbled, and with the occupation of Merv early in 1884, Russia had reached the Afghan frontier. Whether the advance would now stop was more than dubious; whether England had the military force to compel a halt was equally dubious. But Afghanistan was a wild, inhospitable country inhabited by wild, hard-fighting tribesmen. Probably some compromise would be reached; it was fashionable in London to jeer at "Mervousness." Russia, like France, was irritating, not really dangerous. Neither power would dare go too far, because both realized that a war with England would make the supremacy of Germany in Europe complete and permanent. French ambitions in Alsace-Lorraine, and Russian ambitions in the Balkans were Britain's best insurance against a war over Africa or Asia. If the hope of stable peace through the coöperation of all powers in a Concert of Europe had not materialized, at least the conflicting fears and aspirations of the Continental states prevented any of them from defying England. So the British public thought in the opening months of 1884, and they grumbled because Gladstone did not exploit the advantageous situation to the utmost.

The facts were very different. They were analysed with admirable clarity in a dispatch which Bismarck sent to his Ambassador in London, Count Münster, on May 5, 1884. German friendship was very useful to England, he pointed out; fear of German intervention was an effective check on any warlike ambitions which France or Russia might have. So far, no one in England would have disputed him. He went on, however, to maintain that there was nothing to compel Germany to support British policy. Germany would never, of course, be an active enemy, but she could make herself very unpleasant by supporting France and Russia in their quarrels with England. Apparently the British were not conscious of the value of German friendship; they seemed to feel that fine words were sufficient to hold Germany in line. Words were not enough. Some sacrifices must be made, though small ones. For instance, greater consideration must be shown for German interests in Africa and in the South Seas. Again, it must be recognized that agreements such as the Anglo-Portuguese treaty were not sufficient to determine the ownership of colonial territory. Finally, there was the island of Helgoland off the German coast. England did not need the island; Germany did. By ceding it, England would conciliate German public opinion, and make it easy for Bismarck to continue his support of British policy. These considerations were to be suggested to the Foreign Secretary, Lord Granville, if Münster thought it advisable to do so. "I regard them more as an *offer* on our part than as a request; the support which we can, and would, give to England, is actually worth more than Helgoland, Fiji, and Little Popo put together." [10]

Bismarck believed the English to be in a tight place. He was willing to help them out—for a price. In fact he had already begun to take his price, although the English did not know it. In November of the preceding year, he had begun, very in-

[10] G.P., IV, 50–52.

directly, by asking if the British possessed any claim to Angra Pequena, a port in southwest Africa; if they had, he wished to know the nature of the claims. The reply was ambiguous: although sovereignty had not formally been proclaimed, legitimate British rights would be infringed by "any claims or jurisdiction by a foreign power" in the region between Portuguese Angola and Cape Colony. On December 31, the German request for information was renewed. Had Britain any rightful claims to the region? If she claimed the territory, what protection might foreigners trading with the natives expect? This time the Foreign Office turned the request over to the Colonial Office, and the Colonial Office sent it on to the Cape Government. There it remained unanswered. Obviously, neither the home government nor the Cape wanted to take on the expense of governing this barren waste; obviously also they did not want anyone else to take the land. Four months later, on April 25, 1884, Germany announced that the trading settlements of Herr Lüderitz, in and around Angra Pequena, had been taken under the protection of the Imperial Government. And on May 5, Bismarck confidently outlined the other items in the bill for services rendered and services to come: further colonial concessions, and Helgoland.

Münster, who did not believe in colonies, and who was very much of a gentleman, executed his instructions badly. According to Granville's report of the conversation, colonies were not mentioned, while no one could guess from Münster's gentlemanly remarks just why Bismarck felt entitled to demand Helgoland. The Ambassador did say that the German people would like England better if given the island, but Granville promptly replied that he "supposed the cession of Gibraltar would strengthen our good relations with Spain." Might not people suspect, Granville asked, that England wished to buy German assistance "on another matter"?—obviously a reference to Egypt. "Count Münster strongly disclaimed any such idea"—disclaimed the very basis of Bismarck's argument.[11] This was

[11] Fitzmaurice, *Granville,* II, 351.

a bad beginning, but worse followed. Questions were asked in Parliament about Angra Pequena. The Colonial Secretary implied that England was not prepared to recognize the German protectorate. The Cape Government, suddenly coming to life, asked that all land between the Cape and Angola be annexed. The Colonial Secretary seemed prepared to consider the request. Furious, Bismarck ordered Münster to say nothing more about Helgoland; there, German wishes had no legal basis. Africa was different. England could not promulgate a new Monroe Doctrine, say that she could take colonies but not Germany! "This naïve egoism is an insult to our national feeling." The German public would be told the facts, without consideration for the explosion of wrath which would follow. The effects of a complete shift in German policy should be weighed in London, and a complete shift would come if friendship with England meant sacrificing German national interests—on and on rushed the torrent of very undiplomatic words. The Chancellor was not content with words, however. A conference on Egyptian finance was to meet at the end of June, and in the preliminary discussion Germany sided with France. Tardily recognizing that the Chancellor was in earnest, the Gladstone ministry tried to escape by surrender. Adjudication of old German property claims in the Fiji Islands was promised. The Anglo-Portuguese treaty was abandoned. The German protectorate over Angra Pequena was recognized. Despite surrender, however, the German vote went to France at the conference, and the British efforts to release Egyptian revenues for use in rebuilding the country were blocked.

The English searched for an explanation of Bismarck's actions. Their Ambassador in Berlin was sure that the Chancellor was merely trying "to increase his popularity before the general election by taking up an anti-English attitude. Compelled by the colonial mania, which has gradually come to the surface in Germany, to act contrary to his better convictions in the Angra Pequena question, he has discovered an unexplored mine of popularity in starting a colonial policy, which public opinion persuades itself to be anti-English; and the slumbering theoretical envy of the Germans at our wealth and our freedom has awakened and taken the form of abuse of everything English in the press." Münster encouraged this interpretation by remarking privately, "all will change after the elections: thunderbolts come and go." The British Foreign Secretary was half-inclined to agree. He also suspected that Bismarck meant to force the cession of Helgoland by making himself disagreeable. The price might be worth paying to secure an end to "the Egyptian financial mess," except that public opinion would interpret the cession as a new sign of Liberal weakness.[12] As the year wore on, these explanations became increasingly untenable. On the one hand, the scope of German colonial demands widened. The claim to Angra Pequena was broadened until all of Southwest Africa, except the British port of Walfish Bay, was included in the German protectorate. German agents appeared in other parts of Africa—in Togo and Kamerun on the west, around St. Lucia Bay in the southeast, in the continental possessions of the Sultan of Zanzibar on the east coast—and in South Sea islands as far apart as Samoa and New Guinea. In the face of this activity, it was hard to believe that Bismarck was merely playing at colonization. Furthermore, the colonial issue played only a minor part in the German elections held in the autumn of 1884; almost all political parties joined the clamor for colonies. And after the elections, the tone of the German press and of official communications became even more harsh. An attempt to buy peace in January, 1885, by holding out the possibility that Helgoland might, after all, be given up, met with no response.

What then did the Germans want? Tentatively at first, then more distinctly, the fear was expressed in England that Bismarck's objective was nothing less than a Continental coalition against the British Empire. Such a design seemed preposterous —how could France forget Alsace-Lorraine, or Russia forget her conflict with Austria in the Balkans? And yet the suspicion grew, despite repeated assurances in the German press that if

[12] Fitzmaurice, *Granville*, II, 358–362.

Germany got the colonies she wanted, England would get the support she needed. Were the Germans only trying to cover their tracks until their horrid plot was completed? The past record of German diplomacy seemed consistent with such tactics. Even a close reading of the "official" press seemed to warrant the question. The *Kölnische Zeitung* was then the generally accepted mouthpiece of the press bureau of the Berlin foreign office. Almost daily this journal was attacking England as the opponent of German expansion. Usually these attacks were directed at Gladstone for refusing to recognize the fact that Germany was really England's best friend; and usually they ended with the assurance that when the right of Germany to acquire colonies was admitted, when "that Quaker" was out of office, the natural friendship would revive. Occasionally, however, there were complacent references to the decline, the "Hollandization," of Britain. "England is going the same inexorable way that Phœnicia went against the Greeks, the Carthaginians against the Romans, the later Venetians and Dutch in their contest with the national strength of modern peoples. It seems to be a law of world history that the commercial spirit and the manly fighting spirit cannot long be united in one people, and that unscrupulous diplomacy is substituted, diplomacy which can postpone the national decline for a time, but only for a time. Defy England, and England will astound the world by her cowardice!" [13] To be sure, every such attack was followed by a swift retreat, a hurt protest against being thought anti-English, an explanation that the only purpose was to warn Britain of dangers which would come if present policies continued. Englishmen feared the retreat was only tactical, and looked to their defences. A wave of alarm rolled up slowly in the closing months of 1884, forcing even the economical Gladstone to consent to naval increases at the end of the year.

Aside from concern over means of defence, however, the British government and press kept its head remarkably well in face of the insults and threats which were daily shouted across

[13] K.Z. Jan. 21, 1885.

the North Sea. Isolated voices did demand that German presumption be punished. There were complaints that the "unfair" competition of German industry was the real cause of economic depression in England. There was some speculation on the possibility of creating a new triple alliance between England, France and Russia, for the purpose of putting the upstart Germans in their place. There were assertions that British honor would be tarnished by surrender in face of German threats. A formidable collection of such writings could be made; but they would not be representative of the prevailing opinion. On the whole, Englishmen recognized that the Germans did, as they maintained, hold all the trumps of the game. It was easy to talk about an understanding with France and Russia; it was another matter to make the arrangement. Off in the Middle East, British agents had been waiting for months to discuss the exact location of the Russo-Afghan frontier; the Russian agents, despite repeated promises, did not even appear, and, in the meantime, Russian armies were occupying the very regions whose ownership was to be decided. Again, France could be conciliated only by evacuating Egypt and by colonial bribes more exorbitant than those demanded by Germany. According to more sober British judgment, a Continental coalition did not exist; but some sort of tacit understanding did exist. Germany was obviously pleased by the Russian advance in Central Asia, even if she was not encouraging it. In the colonial field, at least an informal agreement existed between France and Germany. That became obvious when a conference was held in Berlin at the end of 1884 to settle the status of the Congo basin. Under the leadership of France and Germany, the powers turned the whole Congo basin over to King Leopold of Belgium. Under the same sponsorship, it was decided that effective occupation was the only legitimate basis for claiming colonial territory—a thrust at English efforts to keep foreign powers out of regions close to British possessions.

Isolation was a fact, and a fact which could not be escaped either by sneering at Bismarck's determination to squeeze bribes out of a helpless victim, or by threats of revenge which could not be carried out. The only thing to do was to buy him off. It was not an escape comforting to pride, but a scapegoat was found in the Liberal ministry. The Gladstone government was already on its last legs. The final blow to popularity was the death of General Gordon, killed with nearly all his men by the forces of the Mahdi at Khartum in January, 1885. English opinion was quite willing to lay new sins at Gladstone's door. The Conservatives pointed out that when Beaconsfield left office, Anglo-German relations had been intimate; now they were strained. Liberal blunders had made the change, a change so disastrous to British interests everywhere.

Stung to desperation by one such righteous contrast between Conservative and Liberal relations with the mighty Chancellor, Lord Granville committed a blazing indiscretion. Perhaps, he said with angry irony, the Liberal error had been to disregard the advice of Bismarck with regard to Egypt which was—"take it." But in that case, Beaconsfield had been equally wrong, because he also had been told to take it. If Granville had been a more clever diplomat, it might be suspected that this outburst in the House of Lords on February 27, 1885, was carefully calculated. For it cleared the air in wondrous fashion. To be sure, Bismarck publicly denied that he had ever given such advice, and he whipped the Reichstag into a fury by an unsparing denunciation of English policy towards German expansion; but privately he showed that he was frightened. Within a week, the Chancellor's oldest son, Herbert Bismarck, was in London, conferring "in a modest and thoroughly friendly manner" with Gladstone. "We are the youngest of the Great Powers," he explained, "and we wish to undertake this function of colonization, which belongs to a Great Power. But we only hope to do it in a very small and humble manner, and we are in doing it giving to you the strongest proof of confidence in the future friendship of the two countries. For we know that if a Continental Power were to attack our little colonies, we could invade them in return. But we also know that you can assail our colonies with effect; and that we cannot get at you in return, as you are masters of the sea."[14] Encouraged, Gladstone urged the foreign office to "wind up at once these small colonial controversies" while the favorable mood lasted. "It is really impossible to exaggerate the importance of *getting out of the way the bar to the Egyptian settlement.*"

With the British willing to give, and the Germans to take colonial bribes, terms were soon arranged. Germany got part of New Guinea and some other islands in the south Pacific, England keeping the part of New Guinea adjacent to Australia. In Africa, Germany added Togo, Kamerun, and an indefinite share of Zanzibar's territory on the east coast; her title to Southwest Africa had already been recognized. Southeast Africa and the island of Zanzibar were conceded to England. More important, the long delayed settlement of Egyptian finance, though not mentioned in the Anglo-German agreement, was now assured. By March 12, Gladstone could publicly welcome Germany to the ranks of the colonizing powers: "She becomes our ally and partner in the execution of the great purposes of Providence for the advantage of mankind." On the day following, Bismarck less exuberantly told the Reichstag that the battle was over.

It is hard to say what the battle had really been about. Many circumstances of this first direct clash between England and Germany remain obscure; any interpretation can claim only tentative validity. It is fairly clear that British policy was poorly directed, and it is possible to describe the nature and the sources of error with some confidence. The real difficulty is with Bismarck. His objectives and his methods confused Englishmen at the time, and they are still confusing, particularly in the later phases of the contest. Probably the English could have retained German support by relatively slight concessions in the spring of 1884; then Bismarck apparently hoped only to win much popular acclaim at home and some solid political advantage abroad by exploiting the isolation of England. Possibly his objective re-

[14] Fitzmaurice, *Granville*, II, 431.

mained unchanged after his offer was rejected. But it is also possible that he was testing out the possibility of a Continental coalition against England.

By 1884, colonization had rather suddenly become a live political issue in Germany. The groundwork had been laid earlier in the century by men like Friedrich List. While national energies were concentrated on the problem of unification, their teachings had little visible effect, but actually the search for unity was making imperialism seem a natural extension of nationalism. In the course of that search, national aspirations had subtly changed. National freedom came to mean national power, and national power came to mean the power of the state. Nation and state became almost interchangable words; for many Germans, the state actually was the living embodiment of all the national hopes. Once state and nation had become identified in men's imaginations, a momentous conclusion followed naturally: the more powerful the state, the freer the nation. Germany was not, of course, the only country in which the search for freedom was changing into a search for power. In England, Cobden gave way to Bagehot, and Bagehot to Seeley; and the argument which Seeley was popularizing in England was the argument which Continental imperialists were propagating: in an age of great states, a merely European state was doomed to fall behind in the struggle for power. Seeley, judging the future by the present, thought of Great Britain as the only imperial state, but even as he wrote the Continental peoples were awakening to the possibility of building new imperial states. Explorers were bringing home reports of infinite wealth, real and imaginary, to be found in Africa and in the South Seas. Here was room enough for a Greater Germany, a Greater France—even a Greater Belgium, in the opinion of King Leopold. Here was a new outlet for national aspirations which had changed into craving for power.

In Germany, small but very articulate colonial societies pointed out the new opportunities and the new dangers which lay just ahead. Germany, they argued, had set out to achieve economic independence by imposing protective tariffs. Full independence could be achieved only by securing territory from which raw materials could be drawn, and to which the surplus products of industry could be sent. Economic independence required therefore, that claims be staked out in the unowned lands beyond the seas. Again, man power was the most precious resource of the state. Year after year, thousands of Germans left their fatherland, and were lost, became a part of the strength of rival states. Continental Germany was too crowded. A new Germany must be built in these newly discovered lands where people were few. Then the emigrant would be an asset, not a tragic loss. Finally—and this was the most pressing argument—Germany must make haste, or the opportunity would be lost. Other states with greater foresight would seize this last chance to widen the national base. Germany would wake up to find the world already divided, would find herself too weak to hold her own in the race against imperial giants. The old days of despised weakness would return, and the achievements of the years of unification would be lost. The quest for freedom had only just begun; won in Europe, freedom must be won once more in the great world outside the Continent, won quickly, before it was too late.

Bismarck certainly never subscribed to the doctrines of the "colonial jingoes." As always, his actions are a better guide than his words. The eagerness with which he sought to involve the other powers in imperial adventures showed clearly that he regarded imperialism as incompatible with a strong Continental policy—and he knew Germany needed all her strength to protect her Continental position. His actions also showed that he was not impressed by the theatrical "now or never" outcry; colonies, if taken at all, must be secured when things were quiet in Europe, and when some specific German interest needed imperial protection. His colonial policy was really an incidental consequence of his newly adopted protectionist system. He had concluded that the state must stand behind private economic enterprise, lending a helping hand wherever possible. Assistance to German overseas commerce might take one of many forms: insistence on the opportunity to trade, the building of the Kiel

Canal, or the declaration of a protectorate. In his first overture to England in May, 1884, he had shown what was in his mind. He had objected to the Anglo-Portuguese treaty, partly because the mouth of the Congo had been turned over to Portugal without any guarantee that the freedom of Germans to trade on the river would be respected. He had asked for a re-examination of German claims in the Fiji Islands, which England had recently annexed. He had asserted the right of Germany to establish a protectorate over regions where German traders were already established and where there was no stable government to provide protection against the natives. Above all, he had asked for Helgoland, a vital link in the defence of the projected Kiel Canal. It was a closely circumscribed and closely integrated program, put forth at a time when the Continent was quiet and when England might be expected to be anxious to conciliate Germany. It was also designed to win applause at home. The Reichstag was in one of its rebellious moods; as in the past, success abroad might be counted on to impress internal critics. Bismarck was not a colonial jingo himself, but he would be glad to harness the new movement to his governmental chariot.

Almost certainly, the English would have done well to pay at least a good part of what Bismarck asked. Granville's later efforts to defend himself against the accusation that he had lost an opportunity to win German support were not very convincing, although they did convince many Englishmen. On the one hand, he claimed that he did not know Bismarck wanted colonies. Münster and the British ambassador in Berlin had both dismissed the whole matter as an election manœuvre; how was the Foreign Secretary to know they were wrong? But when accused of weakness because he allowed the Germans to take Southwest Africa, he said Bismarck had played him false by concealing his intention to take the territory. Ignorance is at best a lame defence for a statesman, and Granville was here pleading ignorance as an excuse both for his refusal to support German colonization and for his failure to thwart German colonization. Furthermore, English resistance did not stop even when it had become clear that Bismarck did want colonies. Shifting his ground, Granville now argued that the Liberal government feared repudiation by public opinion at home and in the dominions if too great complaisance was shown to the German demands. The logical corollary would seem to be, although he naturally did not say so, that the Liberals abandoned resistance when they became more afraid of Germany than they were of public opinion.

This explanation comes nearest to fitting the words and actions of the English. Put crudely, they at first did not understand why the Germans wanted colonies, or why Germany should be given colonies. By March, 1885, they saw, at least for a time, the necessity of permitting German colonization, but they remained incapable of seeing any justification for a German overseas empire. That expatriate Englishwoman, the German Crown Princess, expressed the general feeling perfectly in a few sentences of a letter written to Queen Victoria in May, 1884. "If I may say, the Germans are of an *arrogance* that one *longs* to see put down, especially their tone towards England. Their ideas of Colonies I think very foolish and I do not fancy they will succeed, but are as *jealous* of England as they possibly can be. . . . How I wish, dear Mama, you would read that *admirable* little book, *The Expansion of England*, by Prof. Seeley!! It is wonderful and so statesmanlike, so farsighted, clear, and fair. . . ."[15] It did not occur to her, or to most Englishmen, that Prof. Seeley's arguments were perfectly calculated to turn Germans into enthusiasts for colonial expansion. To her, to the Seeleys, to everyone, Britain was the one imperial power. Germany was a land power, and a land power in a particularly uncomfortable position, sandwiched between France and Russia. The thought of Germany seriously contemplating an imperial policy was too ridiculous to be taken seriously by more than a few unheeded alarmists. In 1885, one of the most respected British diplomats could still write of Bismarck's "childish colonial

[15] *Letters of Queen Victoria*, 2, III, 505–506.

schemes, which I cannot help suspecting are founded as much on what, for want of a better word, I must call spite against us, as on any real expectation of advantage to Germany."[16] Amused or angry scepticism was, of course, a perfectly natural reaction. Judging the present and the future by the past, and seeing in the record of history no great imperial achievements of Germany, it seemed rather more strange to believe that such achievements were beginning, than it would have been to expect a resurgence of Spanish imperialism, far more strange than the resurgence of French colonial enthusiasm, which was inexplicable enough to the English. In addition, it seemed madness that the Germans, with jealous rivals on the east and the west, should take on the added burden of rivalry with England.

The experiences of 1884 and 1885 did not destroy these settled convictions. In the English view, a transient political difficulty had enabled Bismarck to take a mean advantage of Britain for the attainment of a foolhardy ambition. German imperialism remained something exotic, unnatural; Germany remained a continental power dependent on British friendship for aid against France and Russia. The only impression which remained after the tension eased was one of irritation with a political friend who, when aid was needed, turned extortionist. This was not a hopeful augury for the future.

English policy, while blind and inconsistent, was at least understandable; Bismarck's actions, after his first proposals were disregarded by Granville in the summer of 1884, were hard to reconcile with the policy which he professed to be following. It was not merely that his budget of colonial claims grew, or that his press jackals worked overtime concocting new attacks on England. The real puzzle was his ardent wooing of France. Earlier he had encouraged French colonial aspirations, partly to distract attention from Alsace-Lorraine, partly to create tension between the western powers. Now he repeatedly tempted France to forget the past by holding out the prospect of limitless gains at British expense. If his words meant anything, he hoped

[16] Newton, *Lyons,* II, 342.

to make a close understanding, possibly an actual alliance, for common action against England. The advantages of such an alliance for Germany were obvious enough: it would end for the indefinite future Bismarck's nightmare of hostile coalitions. The Continent was tranquil since Russian energies had been diverted to central Asia, and since France had become absorbed in colonial rivalry with England. The Dreikaiserbund was giving Russia the courage to disregard English commands that the advance on Afghanistan be halted. France would be more likely to become irrevocably committed to rivalry with England if sure that Germany would be at least benevolently neutral and possibly an ally. The advantages were obvious, but the risks were equally obvious, and more certain. Although Bismarck did sometimes show a blindness to the strength of national passions which was strange in a man who had risen to greatness through his services to nationalism, it is hard to believe that he thought France would so quickly forget Alsace-Lorraine, or Russia ever forget the Balkan Slavs. Some day European problems would once more take the center of the stage, and the position of Germany would then be serious indeed if England had been made an enemy. So clear does this seem, that it would be unnecessary even to discuss the possibility that Bismarck contemplated a Continental alliance, if every other explanation of his actions did not seem even more improbable. Certainly he did not risk alienating England merely to win a few pieces of territory which, by his own admission, were of dubious value. Possibly he was merely giving rein to his hatred for Gladstone, or, as his son later asserted, trying to make it more difficult for Prince Frederick to accept English guidance when he ascended the throne. These were not motives worthy of Bismarck's genius. Neither can he have been driven on by the desire to win applause at home, although that was an incidental result. It was symptomatic of the temper of German opinion that even many opposition papers thought his conduct towards England moderate and cautious; so quickly had the colonial movement become a part of German national life.

Whatever hopes Bismarck may have built upon the isolation of England, they were wrecked by a sudden upsurge of *revanche* sentiment in France during the spring of 1885. An undercurrent of resentment at coöperation with the hereditary enemy had been apparent, even when France was obviously profiting by the partnership. As the costs of imperialism in terms of soldiers and money became apparent, the current of opposition ran stronger; men said that Bismarck had lured France into a policy which was dissipating her strength, strength needed to prepare for the day when the verdict of 1871 would be reversed. Vigilantly, the old Chancellor watched the conflict of opinion across the Rhine, ready to change his course at the first sign of danger. Granville gave the signal, probably without intention, when he asserted that Bismarck had repeatedly urged England to take Egypt. Here was evidence of German perfidy which would be used with effect in France. Without stopping to see if the effect would be decisive, Bismarck picked up what colonial gains the British were willing to concede, and stood aside, watching. By the end of summer, he had become convinced that Frenchmen of all parties, "no matter how they may differ, are one in the determination to use the first favorable opportunity to break with Germany. Fifteen years of friendly coöperation on *every* political problem with the *single* exception of Alsace-Lorraine have not sufficed to change or even to moderate this determination." [17] He made no effort to conceal his failure from English statesmen. His recent unfriendliness to England, he explained, had originated in his hope of effecting a reconciliation with France. The hope had proved illusory. "He washed his hands of France." Now England and Germany could be friends again. So far, he was speaking with the disarming frankness which contemporaries found hard to reconcile with other facets of his personality. He went further, however—and whether he was still speaking frankly is hard to say: "As far as colonies went, he had got all he wanted, and already more, he believed, than Germany could digest." [18] If this was

[17] G.P., III, 452.
[18] Cecil, *Salisbury,* III, 257.

an honest statement of his belief, and the balance of evidence suggests that it was, he had partially lost control over German imperialism. Even the newspapers closest to him were using different language. The *Kölnische Zeitung* reflected the official swing away from France and towards England, but it insisted that the English must continue to recognize the maritime and colonial aspirations of Germany. "If England is now prepared to accept Germany as a competitor, friendship is possible and desirable, but it must be on the new basis." [19] This proved a more accurate forecast than Bismarck's nonchalant assurance that "there remained now no grounds for difference." Colonial disputes continued to arise, and Egypt continued to be the means by which Germany forced grudging concessions from the British. Bismarck ridiculed the colonial jingoes, pungently in private, decorously in public; but he did his best to placate them.

The events of 1884 and 1885 are of decisive importance in German history, marking the beginning of overseas expansion, and the beginning of the half hurt, half angry conviction that the British were jealous of the efforts of their German cousins to become an imperial people. In England, the colonial quarrel momentarily conjured up the spectre of a hostile Continental coalition, and left a disagreeable impression of German loyalty; but on the whole the dispute was overshadowed by more pressing concerns. Gladstone and Granville, according to the dominant feeling, had been weak in their dealings with Germany as they had been weak in every part of their foreign policy. Afghanistan and Egypt were more important counts in the indictment of Liberal diplomacy than Angra Pequena or New Guinea; they involved the risk of war with Russia, the loss of the entente with France, and the tragedy of Gordon's death at Khartum. Germany would not have dared to slip into regions where British influence had long been dominant, if there had not been so much bungling in the Mediterranean and the Middle East. Comparing the position of their country in 1885 with the promises which Gladstone had made before he took office in 1880,

[19] K.Z. June 22, 1885.

Englishmen were disillusioned with love of freedom as a guide to policy; and they could not see that other nations were coming nearer to England, or were showing solicitude for English welfare. The hope of a rebirth of the liberal spirit in world affairs, which Gladstone had foretold when Disraeli was overthrown, now seemed fatuous. While the issues of domestic policy were still under debate, the fate of Gladstonian foreign policy was decided. The ministry which Lord Salisbury formed in the summer of 1885 was popularly known as "the caretakers' government" because it had no majority in the Commons, and held office only on sufferance until new elections could be held. During the interval, domestic politics drifted, but in foreign affairs a clean break was made with the past. The brief and troubled Liberal ministry of 1886, revolutionary in Irish affairs, made no attempt to form a distinctive foreign policy; Granville was pushed aside, and the foreign office was given to Lord Rosebery, a Liberal Imperialist who promised to continue the policy inaugurated by Salisbury. The Conservative victory of 1886 ended any hope that the break would be temporary.

Lord Salisbury's name, even in his own day, could never arouse the love or the hate which sprang up instantly at the mention of Palmerston or Disraeli or Gladstone. Today the name is a dim memory, suggesting to some, the chill white mist of an unheroic age, to others, the warm sunlight of past security. Either impression may be fitted to the facts. When he took office in 1885, England was debating domestic and imperial issues more profound than those fought to a decision two generations before, in the days of the great Reform Bill. Within a few years, the debate had become muffled and the issues blunted. Again at the end of his years of power, the old questions came up, argued in subdued voices until he resigned in 1902, then breaking all restraint until they were hushed once more, this time by war. Possibly he cured the symptoms but drove in the disease, thereby making certain its virulent recurrence. Possibly if the Irish problem, the social problem, the industrial and commercial problem, the imperial problem—possibly if all had been grasped firmly, all might have been solved. But there is another possibility, that rash action might have so weakened Britain as to insure her downfall. For in 1886, as in 1914, social tension seemed too great for endurance, and it may be that in effecting a temporary relaxation, the necessity of a break was ended, and time was gained in the race against imperial rivals.

No matter what the right interpretation of the years when, in or out of office, he unobtrusively dominated the English scene, Salisbury would have disclaimed a decisive part in determining the outcome: in his opinion, the long drift of opinion was too strong for any man to direct or thwart. The statesman did not lead; it was not his function to ride ahead bearing the standard of some high ideal. Judgment was the test of statesmanship, the ability to see the real drift of national purpose, and the ability to see how much of that purpose was possible of attainment. Politics could not be an exact science, because the movement of history could never be accurately foretold, but the ideal should be to see with the scientist's impartial eye— "Do look at the question chemically!" Pondering the injunction, think chemically! the line separating Salisbury from Bismarck narrows. Both were possessed by a passionate love of country, and both put service to country above all else. The line was thin; but it was all-important. It was not merely set by temperament, although the Englishman did have a more modest estimate of his ability to see, and to manipulate, the flow of historical necessity than did the Prussian; the gambler's daring, natural to the creator of a new state, could not be anticipated in the ruler of a people more conscious of what might be lost than eager to make new gains. In other ways they were divided by the traditions of the two nations. A minister of the English state, no matter how convinced in his own mind that his devotion was unselfish, could not aspire to enforce his will as Bismarck did. Compared to the freedom from popular control enjoyed by the German state, the English state remained more servant than master. The consequences in home affairs were obviously far-reaching. Only a despised and rebellious province like Ireland could be treated as Bismarck treated socialists and other dissenters; the "reptile fund" and much else that only mildly shocked German opinion could not exist where opinion made government. Possibly because "reason of state" was an argument of limited effectiveness at home, Salisbury found it impossible to apply with cold logic abroad. He did not, like Gladstone, believe that the interests of humanity and the interests of Britain coincided, or that the moral standards of private life should govern the relations between states. But try as he would to think chemically, he could not quite believe that the defence of national interests justified the use of any necessary means. He could not act on that belief himself, and he could not admire others who, like Bismarck, were severely logical. This failing, or remnant of virtue, was shared by Salisbury's countrymen. Like him, they were very conscious of the line separating the conduct of British and German diplomacy, and thought the line broader than it was. Germans, recognizing a kindred spirit in Salisbury, failed utterly to understand that the short distance he refused to go, might rightly justify a claim to greater rectitude. Here, as in so many other ways, the two peoples found it harder to understand each other as their ways of thinking and acting became more alike.

Whether, in choosing safety as the highest ambition to which Britain could aspire, Salisbury was merely choosing a course suited to his own temperament, or whether no other goal was possible, is debatable; but certainly he did eschew adventure, seek to conserve, not to make a new start; and certainly his caution was approved by the dominant elements of English opinion, though often without enthusiasm. Much of his effort was expended on the task of smothering controversy over domestic problems. One of these controversies had more than domestic importance, the debate over free trade and protection. The Fair Trade agitation had won many Conservative converts, and although Salisbury had concluded that free trade still held popular loyalty, he did not want to divide his party. The usual expedient of a Royal Commission was adopted to gain time and to test opinion. The Fair Traders were represented on the commission, but as they constituted a small minority, they could only hope for success if the representatives of commerce and industry summoned as witnesses proved overwhelmingly dissatisfied with the workings of free trade. That hope proved unfounded. The witnesses agreed on only one thing, that there was, and had long been, a most disheartening depression of British trade and industry. On the causes, the nature, and the remedies, there was complete disagreement. The conflict of testimony chilled popular interest, and enabled the commissioners to end their examination with the same convictions they had at the outset. When the reports were published in 1887, the fact that a majority favored continued free trade and a minority favored protection was duly noted and briefly commented upon in the press; but it was evident that the Fair Traders were no longer politically important. As so often in these years, a movement which seemed formidable at the outset was in the end halted by cautious reluctance to abandon old traditions. In this case, caution was made easier by a revival of domestic and foreign trade during 1887.

Although the volumes published by the Commission sank out of public sight, leaving scarcely a ripple behind, they are valuable. In them can be studied the first shocked realization that an epoch in English economic history had closed. The committee as a whole agreed that the total production of goods was increasing in proportion to the growth of population; profits, not production, were depressed. They also were in general agreement on the causes of decreased profits: the agricultural crisis had decreased buying power in rural areas; prices were falling all over the world; the distribution of the aggregate wealth of the country was shifting to the disadvantage of industrial producers; sales abroad were hampered by tariff barriers; foreign competition was driving down profits both at home and abroad.

The majority was confident that the fall in prices and the agricultural crisis were temporary, and would soon end; the "more equal distribution" of wealth was socially desirable. The growth of competition was more serious. The competition of German industrialists and traders was especially severe. "In the actual production of commodities we have now few, if any, advantages over them; and in a knowledge of the markets of the world, a desire to accommodate themselves to local tastes or idiosyncrasies, a determination to obtain a footing wherever they can, and a tenacity in maintaining it, they appear to be gaining ground upon us." Monopoly had dulled the edge of British enterprise. "Less trouble appears to be taken to discover new markets for our produce, and to maintain a hold upon those which we already possess. . . . The reputation of our workmanship does not stand as high as it formerly did." In other ways, notably in technical and commercial education, the Englishman was ill-prepared to meet the test of a competitive world. Only if these defects were overcome could Britain expect to hold her own in the race, and they were defects which business men themselves, not the government, must rectify. So far, the majority believed competition to be natural, and even salutary. Other forms of rivalry were, however, thought definitely unfair. Minor unfairness, such as the practice of stamping "Sheffield" on German cutlery, could be checked by requiring that wares imported into England bear the name of the producing countries. Tariffs were equally unfair, and far more damaging. Behind a tariff wall, industries could grow artificially, protected from competition on equal terms with British wares, and able to dump their surplus production on the English or other markets at a price which unprotected manufacturers could not meet. Time alone could cure this evil. In time, protective tariffs would defeat their own ends by raising the cost of production above the tariff level, even if consumers did not rebel against the necessity of paying high prices. For England to retaliate by adopting protection herself would be suicidal; unless she bought from others, and unless her costs of production were kept low, she could not sell. The folly of protection had been exposed in Cobden's day. Even if the world persisted in folly, England would remain sane.[20]

The Fair Trade minority stressed unfair competition almost

[20] *House of Commons Sessional Papers,* 1886, XXIII, 30 *ff.*, 48.

exclusively; economic ruin faced England "unless the nation shall determine to counterwork by active measures the disturbing influences which are artificially produced by foreign legislation." The only escape was to make the British Empire a great free trade area in a protectionist world, protected against bounty-fed competition by a tariff. Everyone would gain by the change —the mother country and the colonies, capital and labor, producers and consumers, industry and agriculture. Somehow, industrialists were to make higher profits, but consumers were not to pay more; somehow, farming was to become profitable, but food was not to cost more. It was a silly argument, beginning with the false premise that the depressed condition of British economic life was "artificially produced by foreign legislation," and ending with the false conclusion that everyone would profit economically from an imperial protectionist system.[21] The *Times* thought it scarcely worth while to expose the fallacies; it was enough for readers to know that "the fair-traders have stuck to their pop-guns." [22] Yet these were not foolish men, and they were urging a course of action which had won in many other countries after exhaustive debate, notably in Germany. Some protectionist arguments, such as the defence of infant industries, were not applicable to English conditions, but others were. Friedrich List's *National System of Political Economy* was translated as an aid to Fair Trade propaganda, and List had urged protection chiefly because he wished to promote national strength and solidarity. English protectionists, by constantly speaking of their objective as an imperial Zollverein, sought to popularize the belief that a customs union would unite the Empire politically, as the Zollverein had helped to unite Germany. They did not, however, develop the concept of a Zollverein as the Germans did. Little was said about the need for each nation to develop its own complete and autonomous economic life; instead, lip service was paid to cosmopolitanism by the assertion that disturbing influences were artificially produced. Nothing was

[21] *Ibid.*, 94 *ff.*, 137.
[22] *Times*, Jan. 17, 1887.

said about the necessity of sacrificing the economic welfare of individuals or groups in the interest of national strength; instead, the untenable contention that everyone would profit was advanced. The very weakness of the Fair Trade position was a tribute to the still powerful hold of cosmopolitanism and individualism on the English mind, despite the growth of imperial nationalism, and despite discontent with the workings of the liberal program.

Undoubtedly, the failure of protection in England, like its success in Germany, resulted partly from purely economic forces. The agricultural interest in Germany was united and vigilant; farming land in England was largely in the hands of men who had become allied with trade and finance through investments, at home and overseas. Similarly, English importers and exporters, industrialists and financiers, had divergent interests, some looking primarily to the home market, others thinking primarily of the shippers and the investors in foreign securities who would be hurt by a protective tariff. Where interests so sharply conflicted, the advocates of change had a harder task than those who asked only that nothing be done. It was also true, however, that Germans found it easy to believe in protection because they already believed the interests of their state were likely to conflict with the interests of the world outside, and might conflict with the interests of many individuals in Germany. Although Englishmen were learning to think as Germans thought, they still liked to assume an identity of interest between individual, nation, and humanity. In the effort to flatter that assumption the Fair Traders fell into error and inconsistency. The effort was unsuccessful, but it is noteworthy that popular repudiation of protection as the remedy for depression was more general than popular recognition that "unfair" foreign, and particularly German, competition was not the cause of depression. Even the free traders were disposed to attribute a considerable part of German success to sharp practice, including tariffs and bounties as well as pirated trademarks and false marks of origin under that head.

How far German competition had succeeded in displacing

English commerce and industry is still debatable, despite investigations at the time and since. An official report of 1888 concluded that "Germany has not been gaining in common markets in late years at the expense of English trade. Its gains have been special and in certain directions. Our preponderance remains substantially what it was ten years ago." [23] Probably the conclusion erred on the side of optimism, but not grossly. Ground was being lost in some foreign markets, and in the home markets for some products. The opening of the Suez Canal had somewhat hurt the position of England as the center of trans-shipment; trade between foreign ports now tended to be direct, rather than through English ports. On the other hand, as the Royal Commission pointed out, if allowance was made for falling prices, it could be shown that "the actual products of British labor and capital have largely increased." [24] The British were, on the whole, holding their own against foreign competition, though with increasing difficulty. Why, then, was the air filled with lamentation? Partly because individual firms or trades which were unable to compete successfully thought England was ruined because they were ruined, while successful firms said nothing because they had no complaint to make. Even more important, the long fall of prices which began in the 'seventies and was to continue until the end of the century, made the pulse of commerce slow and labored. The cause of the fall baffled economic experts. Some blamed it on the spread of industrialism to new countries, and on cheaper costs of production and distribution; others complained of a gold shortage. Whatever the cause, the slackened pace of business was disheartening. In the testimony before the Royal Commission, one note recurred: "Our attention was again directed to the maintenance and even increase of the volume of trade accompanied by the diminution of profit and growth of foreign competition." Whether or not a cause and effect relationship actually existed, it was natural to conclude that decreased profits were the result of foreign competition. And pride would not permit the

[23] *H.C. Sessional Papers*, 1888, XCIII, 10.
[24] *H.C. Sessional Papers*, 1886, XXIII, 31.

admission that foreigners could compete successfully with representatives of the pioneer industrial nation of the world, except by using unethical methods. The foreigner's goods must be shoddy and adulterated, his business methods must be unscrupulous, his government must give him tariffs, bounties, and other favors—in some way the competition was unfair. The Royal Commission might contrast English business men unfavorably with Germans. English consuls, accused of falling behind their German colleagues in assistance to traders, might angrily retort that it was the English trader who was falling behind: "The average English commercial man of the present day is unfit to compete with the thrifty and industrious Germans. The former is bent on the pursuit of pleasure, whilst the latter gives himself no leisure until his future is assured." [25] Clear-sighted men in all walks of life might realize that the complaint of unfair competition was largely unfounded, and certainly was a poor substitute for effort to meet competition. Still the complaint was made. For the unthinking, the "duplicity" of German diplomacy from Schleswig-Holstein to Angra Pequena, was now matched by the "unfairness" of German economic competition.

Lord Salisbury could not be characterized as unthinking, but he sympathized with those who held a low opinion of German morality, particularly as personified in Bismarck. In 1864, he had described Bismarck as the heir of Frederick the Great, the heir "of his unblushing perfidy, of his cynical contempt for pledges given and treaties signed." [26] In 1870 he had been on the side of France. As a member of Disraeli's cabinet he had been unable to share his chief's enthusiasm for an alliance with Germany. Now, as prime minister, his aversion for Bismarck was unabated: "I believe he is still true to the main principle of his policy—employing his neighbors to pull out each other's teeth." Egypt was the instrument by which colonial teeth were extracted from England. "He is perpetually telling us of the offers France is making of reconciliation on the basis of an attack upon England

[25] *H.C. Sessional Papers*, 1888, LX, Commercial No. 16.
[26] Salisbury, *Essays, Foreign Politics*, 138.

in Egypt, and of the sacrifices which Germany makes by refusing these proposals; sacrifices for which, he adds, England must make some return, and then he demands this and that." Salisbury thought such tactics could be described by only one word—blackmail—and he writhed under the necessity of submitting to extortion. This humiliation was, however, merely a minor manifestation of Britain's helplessness. The Chancellor's really dangerous designs involved the fate of all Europe. "He would like to see Russia at Constantinople, for he believes that Turkey, England, and Austria would then be forced into war, while he maintained a benevolent neutrality, or, if the occasion should arise, struck another blow at France." [27]

Undoubtedly Salisbury's prejudices made him put the worst possible construction on Bismarck's motives. What seemed blackmail in London, was reciprocity in Berlin: if England wanted support in Egypt, she must not stand in the way of German colonial expansion. Similarly, war in the Near East and war with France were disagreeable, rather than attractive prospects to Bismarck. But, though biased, Salisbury's opinions were held honestly and firmly, and they were also held by other Englishmen. The close coöperation between England and Germany which began when he took office in 1885 was not based on conscious similarity of purpose, or mutual trust. On the English side, it was based on disagreeable necessity, on the fact that no other course was possible. All Salisbury's sympathies made him desire as ardently as any Liberal to coöperate with France, but Egypt barred the way. English opinion prohibited, and French opinion demanded, the evacuation of Egypt. Salisbury's efforts to find some compromise satisfactory to both countries failed. The failure meant helplessness in face of German colonial demands, and enmity between England and France. There was little chance now that England would help France if Germany attacked. Rather, as Salisbury said, it was hard not to wish for another Franco-German war, to put a stop to incessant wrangles over Egypt and other colonial questions. Even if the Germans

[27] Cecil, *Salisbury,* IV, 26, 41–42, 9.

went through Belgium, English opinion would probably not tolerate intervention.[28]

In the light of his feelings towards the two countries, it is safe to say that Salisbury dreaded an increase of German strength at French expense; but he saw no prospect of successful opposition from England if the Germans chose to move, as he feared they might. Worse, he found himself driven towards action which might encourage the Germans. In the Mediterranean, France was at odds with Italy as well as England. The ministers at Rome maintained with desperate sincerity that if, after taking Tunis, France took either Tripoli or Morocco, the Italian government must declare war even though defeat was almost certain; the alternative was a revolution in Italy. Salisbury was in a quandary. England could not permit France to conquer the only other important Mediterranean power. An Anglo-Italian agreement to preserve the status quo would probably keep France quiet; but it might also encourage Italy to start a war herself, with German connivance. The same dilemma appeared in the Near East. There, Russia was trying to reëstablish her control over Bulgaria, while Austria was threatening to fight if Russian troops entered the Balkans. Publicly, Bismarck was on the side of Russia; privately, he told Salisbury that the Tsar would not dare move if England promised to support Austria. Salisbury was inclined to make the promise. British opinion still insisted that Russia be kept away from Constantinople, and Austrian aid was almost essential to that task. But he feared a trap. Once Britain was committed to action, Bismarck might push his "friends" into war. "It is very necessary under these circumstances," Salisbury warned Queen Victoria, "to pick our steps very carefully, so that we should neither, on the one side, pull Bismarck's chestnuts out of the fire, nor, on the other, from fear of that mishap, neglect to defend our own general interests."[29]

Slowly, fear of isolation overcame fear of being used as a cat's paw. It was impossible to seize control over the international

[28] B.D., VIII, 374, 375. Cecil, *Salisbury*, IV, 55–62

[29] Cecil, *Salisbury*, IV, 9.

situation and guide it as Palmerston might have done. Public opinion at home was too completely absorbed in the controversy over home rule for Ireland to be mobilized behind a decided policy. Abroad, statesmen were too awed by Bismarck to accept other leadership. Isolation meant impotence, and it might prove dangerous, Salisbury feared. "If, in the present grouping of nations, which Prince Bismarck tells us is now taking place, England was left out in isolation, it might well happen that the adversaries, who are coming against each other on the Continent, might treat the English Empire as divisible booty, by which their differences might be adjusted; and, though England could defend herself, it would be at fearful risk and cost." Although Bismarck's League of Peace was anything but pacific as seen from London, it was too strong for Britain to oppose. The safest course was to make terms. The Italian Ambassador had been proposing an Anglo-Italian alliance against France. Salisbury could not go that far. He was willing to state privately his belief that "very probably" England would fight if France attacked Italy, but he would not make an alliance and he believed English assistance would be very unlikely if Italy took the offensive even "to anticipate a certain attack from France." Eventually, an exchange of secret notes was agreed upon. The Italian note of February 12, 1887, was still too ambitious for the British Cabinet, which would promise only to coöperate with Italy in the task of preserving the status quo in the Mediterranean, Ægean, and Black Seas. "The character of that coöperation must be decided by them, when the occasion for it arises, according to the circumstances of the case." This was less than the Italians, and their German mentor, had hoped for, but it was, as Salisbury said, "as close an alliance as the Parliamentary character of our institutions will permit." Jubilant, the German government informed Austria that "we have succeeded in bringing about a written agreement between England and Italy"; Austria should join as soon as invited. The Austrian adherence followed in March.[30]

[30] *Letters of Queen Victoria,* 3, I, 272, 269. G.P., IV, 315, 316. Pribram, *Secret Treaties,* I, 96.

England had taken her place in the League of Peace, assigned the duty of restraining France in the Mediterranean and Russia in the Balkans. Fearfully, Salisbury watched to see if peace had been strengthened or war made certain. After weeks of waiting he could not be sure, though he still suspected that Bismarck would plunge all Europe in war if given the opportunity. He could see, however, that he had not won a respite from "black-mail." The old "very inconvenient and somewhat humiliating relation" between Egypt and German colonial demands continued. As the summer of 1887 approached, he looked into the future no less despondently than at the beginning of the year. "The prospect is very gloomy abroad; but England cannot brighten it. Torn in two by a controversy which almost threatens her existence, she cannot, in the present state of public opinion, interfere with any decided action abroad." [31]

The Prime Minister was certainly more sceptical than his countrymen. Indeed, it can be argued that Englishmen showed no scepticism in this summer of the Queen's Golden Jubilee when the whole world, in honoring an old lady, honored the empire she ruled. In England, the jubilee evoked an emotional response, half personal devotion, and half national pride, which spread from the massed crowds along the route to the Abbey, out through the island, to the furthest ends of the Empire. In this age of electricity, beacon lights flared on the Malvern Hills. In this age of emptying churches, rectories were crowded for teas in honor of the Queen. In this age of failing agriculture, country homes became once more the center of a patriarchal society. In this age when stock companies were separating industrial ownership and management, that sense of intimacy natural when the master's home had stood under the shadow of the works, was briefly recaptured. In speeches, in pictures, and in leading articles, men relived the past. They turned back a generation to the Great Exhibition, to the hope of peace and progress through the machine. They turned back a half century to the Queen's accession, to the beginning of the age of reform. They turned

[31] Cecil, *Salisbury,* IV, 43. *Letters of Queen Victoria,* 3, I, 263.

back three centuries to the procession of thanksgiving after the Armada, when England was ruled by another queen with another Cecil as her first minister, when the empire of England was beginning its long proud growth. They turned back from the warships assembled for review, to recall the great names and great actions in British naval history. And they returned always to survey the present with an emphatic affirmation: It is the same old England. England's navy and merchant marine, England's trade and industry, England's domestic institutions and imperial power, all were still the first in the world.

It was perhaps natural that the jubilee should turn thoughts to the past; but in their fathers' generation, Englishmen had looked back only to see how far they had climbed and to gather courage for further ascent. It was new to seek assurance, to conclude that all was well because today was in essentials like yesterday. Less consciously and for less clearly seen reasons, the nation shared Lord Salisbury's apprehensions. Like him, they were willing to put aside for a time their dreams of a new and greater Britain. Joseph Chamberlain and Lord Randolph Churchill, with their programs of sweeping social and imperial reforms, had been pushed aside by both the major parties. The colonial ministers came to London for an imperial conference during the jubilee full of confidence that they could demonstrate the necessity for a firm stand against the colonial pretensions of other European powers. Salisbury patiently explained the relation between diplomacy and force. If the colonies wished to contribute to the military and naval power of the mother country, the foreign office could do more; as things stood, the arm of England was not long enough, or strong enough, to hold back all Europe. The colonial ministers departed, now conscious of changes which were ignored in panegyrics upon England's greatness. Even though it might be the same old England, it was not the same world. Competition had appeared to challenge the monopoly which had endured so long as to seem part of the natural order.

It was somewhat later that Mr. Gladstone was walking with

his disciple, John Morley, along the shore at Biarritz, watching the masses of water shatter themselves among the rocks. "For myself," said Gladstone, "I think I can truly put up all the change that has come into my politics into a sentence; I was brought up to distrust and dislike liberty, I learned to believe in it." Morley saw a different change in men of his own generation. "They have ceased either to trust or to distrust liberty, and have come to the mind that it matters little either way. Men are disenchanted. They have got what they wanted in the days of their youth, yet what of it, they ask?" [32] Doubtless much of the contrast of generations was compressed into these words shouted above the roar of the sea. The world was not what it had promised to be when belief in freedom was young. It was not even what it had seemed when Disraeli joined faith in empire to faith in freedom. For the present, the best to be hoped for was the strength to hold on, to conserve the legacy of the past. But this was not really disillusionment. Confidence in the imperial and emancipating mission of Britain was checked, not destroyed. Even Salisbury, for all his scepticism, believed England could win, though all Europe united against her. Continental peoples might jeer at decadent England, but the islanders knew better. When faction had been conquered at home, when bearings had been taken in this strange and hostile world, then the advance begun under that earlier great queen would be irresistibly resumed.

[32] Morley, *Gladstone*, III, 475.

CHAPTER VIII

THE REVOLT AGAINST BISMARCK

IN THE years preceding Queen Victoria's jubilee, Germans had watched the efforts of Englishmen to adjust the individualist and cosmopolitan tenets of liberalism to an age of democracy at home and competition abroad. As observers, the Germans showed neither sympathy nor understanding. Their belief that the laws of political evolution were to be discovered through a study of the past made them search for historical parallels as an aid to understanding events in England; their envy of the British world empire and their resentment of British condescension, made them choose historical parallels comforting to German pride. Now Venice, now Holland, was chosen, but always some commercial empire which, rising to greatness from small beginnings, declined rapidly. The moral, sometimes explicitly drawn, sometimes left to the reader's imagination, was always the same: England was decaying as earlier commercial states had decayed. For a time, guile and the prestige of the past would conceal the rotting foundations of English power, but only for a time. Germany must, therefore, beware of being used as a prop for the tottering edifice, beware of risking her young strength to save an empire doomed by the inexorable laws of historical evolution.

Beginning in 1887 it was the turn of England to stare, without sympathy or understanding, at an equally painful crisis in German national life. The scrutiny was obvious at Victoria's jubilee, where the Queen's son-in-law, the German Crown Prince Frederick, was an honored guest. For a generation he had been an object of affectionate interest to Englishmen as the husband of Victoria's favorite daughter. More important, since Bismarck first awakened mingled horror and admiration, Englishmen had looked to Frederick to preserve the good in the Chancellor's work and to undo the evil. Not that it was expected or desired that the Prince would take orders from London. Men who were in a position to know the facts were alarmed by the indiscreet fervor with which the Crown Princess preached the superiority of everything British to everything German. Inevitably, Germans must resent efforts to remake their country in the image of England. But Frederick was known to be a liberal; he was known to have opposed the policy of blood and iron, both at home and abroad, in the 'sixties; he was known to consort with Germans who desired parliamentary government and who opposed a foreign policy based on force. He would not ape England. He would replace the "medieval" German government by a "progressive" government based on right principles, principles England had already discovered and put into operation.

Of late, such relatively disinterested motives had been reinforced by more immediately important considerations. Germany and England were coming to be regarded as natural allies, united by common fear of French and Russian aggression. Intimacy was barred by British aversion to Bismarckian oppression of dissenters within Germany, and by fear of Bismarckian treachery and brutality in foreign affairs. When Frederick ruled, these barriers would fall; and he would soon rule. Kaiser William's ninetieth birthday was celebrated in the year of Victoria's jubilee; since 1885 the old man's strength had been ebbing. The auspicious change, so long deferred by the accident of an iron frame which would not yield to death, must be imminent. So it was not merely the son-in-law of their Queen that Englishmen cheered when they saw the heroic figure of Frederick, this new crusader whose bearded face, in its awe-inspiring simplicity and nobility, seemed an augury of all the good expected from the Prince. There was also a note of relief in the cheering. Earlier in the year there had been rumors that the hoarseness with which the Prince was afflicted resulted from a cancerous growth in his throat; fate had seemed about to cheat Germany, and England, of Frederick's cleansing rule. These fears had now been set at rest by an English physician, Dr. Mackenzie. The Prince was still almost voiceless, but a period of rest in England was expected to restore his health.

In the autumn, a new diagnosis showed, almost beyond doubt, that the growth was cancerous. Hope, so recently revived, disappeared, was replaced by confusion and fear. Would death first claim William or Frederick? If the father went first, would the son have time enough or strength enough to effect the regeneration of German political life? If the crown passed to the old Emperor's grandson, what kind of Germany must England reckon with?

Back of these anxious questions was a momentous assumption: the destiny of Germany and, to a great extent, of Europe, depended on the fortunes of four men, one a senile nonagenerian, one ailing, one an untried youngster, and one the statesman who had stood for Germany in the minds of Europeans through a quarter of a century, but who tomorrow might be thrust into oblivion. The wishes of forty-five million Germans, the economic or cultural forces at work within Germany, everything might be ignored except the autocratic will at the top. Whether he be an autocratic minister like Bismarck, or an autocratic emperor, one man was Germany, capable of using or abusing people and army, capable of affecting all Europe. It was an astounding, and fallacious, assumption. But it was believed by high and low alike in England, and it was fortified with every passing year. Disgusted, Englishmen observed what they thought the apathy of the German people in face of the struggle around the imperial throne during the years after 1885. There seemed no recognition of the importance of the struggle; instead, there was all the pettiness and irrelevance of a squabble between village politicians over the election of a vestryman. The old Emperor died in March, 1888; in June, Frederick followed him to the grave; in March, 1890, Bismarck was forced to resign; in October, 1894, Bismarck's successor Caprivi resigned, and tired old Prince Hohenlohe accepted the Chancellorship which now seemed emptied of importance.

Through it all, the German people looked on, gossiping maliciously about the men and women who were elevated or toppled over by the turn of fortune's wheel. Could there be more decisive proof of the fact which Englishmen had long suspected: politically, the German people were children, helpless children?

Such, roughly and approximately, was the English view of Germany. Judging everything by English practice, and seeing that those instruments of popular control most trusted in England—a free press, parliamentary government, and ministerial responsibility—either did not exist, or existed imperfectly in Germany, it was natural to conclude that the popular will was of negligible importance in Germany. Prizing freedom, and realizing that the word freedom had not the English meaning when used by Germans, it was natural to conclude that Germans were slaves. Clinging to the view that the state was a passive mechanism which obeyed the men in control of the mechanism, and believing that the checks on imperial power in Germany were few and ineffective, it was natural to conclude that Germany was an autocracy. In short, Englishmen continued to apply the political theories of natural law liberalism when studying and judging other nations, long after their own political life had been altered by more organic views of the state and the nation. They continued to believe Germans were much like Englishmen, except that Germans had, after 1862, made the mistake of surrendering political control to one man. Since the mistake had been made, it was not necessary to study the needs and purposes of the German people; it was enough to study the man in control. While Bismarck was in control, this conclusion meant that Englishmen respected the sagacity and feared the duplicity of German policy. After Bismarck left, respect rapidly gave place to contempt; fear, however, remained and was strengthened.

Even today it is hard not to explain the relative passivity of the German people when faced by an event like the dismissal of Bismarck in terms very close to the contemporary English judgment, to lay everything to the fact that the German people lacked political education. Undoubtedly Bismarck's craving for power had made him seek to crush all opposition, and undoubtedly he had succeeded to a very large extent. He had strengthened the power of the chancellor, not reflecting that the chancellor held office only on sufferance; above him was the emperor. When the imperial office fell to a man who aspired to rule, a conflict was inevitable, and the chancellor was bound to lose. As Lord Rosebery told Bismarck with the cruelty of a sympathetic friend: "You are overthrown, Prince, with the power you created—hoist with your own petard as Shakespeare says." And the fallen Chancellor could only reply, "Quite true." [1]

The difficulty with the explanation is that Bismarck was not overthrown against the will of a helpless people. No sooner did an early change of rulers appear likely in 1885 than opposition to the Chancellor appeared. Rebellion against his will flared up repeatedly thereafter, and when he fell the dominant popular mood was not anger, but relief. It is this relief which requires explanation. Consciously, there was no rebellion against the objectives of Bismarck's domestic and foreign policy. With insignificant exceptions, his opponents accepted his ideal: stability and security within the geographical limits established by the wars of the 'sixties. The fight was over the best method of achieving those objectives.

The only peace Bismarck thought possible in this world of fallen men was a peace of balanced tensions. He took for granted the clash of rival economic, political, social, and religious groups within Germany; division and strife always had existed and always would exist. The function of the state was to make the energy of competing groups serve the national interest and increase the national strength, by neutralizing the thrust of divergent interests. Like the arches of a cathedral, interest must balance interest, with the state as the keystone of the arch. The architect could, however, work out the problem of balance once and for all. The statesman must expect a constant shifting of the balance of forces, and must always be prepared to shift the alignment of forces so that equilibrium would never be violently disturbed. In

[1] Crewe, *Rosebery*, 555.

the constitution of the Empire, Bismarck had worked out a balance between the people, represented in the Reichstag, the states, represented in the Bundesrath, and the Emperor. He did not think the constitution ideal; he was prepared to change it, violently if necessary, when balance was destroyed. Similarly, he played the parties in the Reichstag against each other, always seeking a temporary equilibrium. Forces he could not neutralize peacefully, he was willing to fight actively, as he had fought the Catholic Church, and as he was fighting the socialists.

In foreign affairs he saw the same problem of balance, with tensions so nicely neutralized, thrust and counter-thrust, that stability resulted, precarious and temporary, but the only possible stability. Here again, he was ready to use force if necessary. Security, not peace, was his ideal purpose. He dreaded war, not because it was immoral, but because it was a dangerously unreliable weapon. If, however, war was the only means of securing or maintaining stability, it must be used. With steadfast eye he measured the risks and advantages of the many possible wars. If words mean anything, he would have seen a maritime war between England and France, or a war in central Asia between England and Russia without regret. These wars would relax the pressure on the frontiers of Germany; they would almost certainly not hurt England vitally, and he had too much need of England's weight in the European balance to wish her seriously weakened. It is possible that he would have taken Germany into some wars without regret—a war against France, with Italy as an ally and England as a benevolent neutral, apparently seemed an attractive prospect. This may be reading too much into his casual remark that an Italian attack on France "would be very delightful, but unfortunately hardly to be hoped for." [2] But a study of his words and actions warrants the conclusion that he at no time made peace his ideal. His ideal was stability, to be achieved through the ceaseless search for a controllable balance; to achieve stability he would stop at nothing.

After 1885, in Bismarck's view, changes in one part of the

[2] G.P., IV, 211–213, marginal comment no. 5.

state, the crown, threatened to destroy the whole delicate mechanism. Every rumor concerning the health, either of William I or of Prince Frederick, sent a tremor through the German people. Until 1887, the liberal opposition were heartened by the impending change of rulers. Although Frederick had lapsed into silence after his early protests against Bismarck's methods, the advocates of parliamentary government were certain that the Prince was still their ally. This confidence sufficed to bring about a liberal revival within a few years after the crushing defeat of 1878. Conversely, when Frederick's throat ailment was first diagnosed as cancer in the spring of 1887, gloom fell on the liberal camp; conservatives were overjoyed, particularly the military leaders who had long resented the Chancellor's refusal to grant them complete power, and who had looked forward with horror to rule by "English" Frederick. "Naturally there is general excitement," General Waldersee wrote in his diary. "The Chancellor is confronted with an entirely new situation." For years Bismarck had been trying to make terms with the Crown Prince. "Now he must prepare to go along with Prince William. In my opinion that cannot be done. The energetic, ambitious 28 year old prince, and the 72 year old chancellor!" [3] Then Dr. Mackenzie denied that the growth was malignant. Liberals regained their courage; conservatives were discomfited. The definitive diagnosis brought a new shift. Rival groups formed around the Crown Prince and Prince William; time-servers fearfully sought to discover the stronger pack; the Chancellor was increasingly isolated. Capital and labor, industry and agriculture, Catholics and Protestants, bureaucracy and army, Jews and anti-Semites, each hoped for an end of the system of checks and balances. Individuals who had silently submitted when the Chancellor's will was unchallenged, because they knew they must be "assimilated or annihilated" by the master, now stirred hopefully, ready to rebel when the Emperor, the master's master, gave the signal. Abroad, too, there was an expectant stirring, though it was compounded of fear as well as hope. In Paris, in

[3] Waldersee, *Denkwürdigkeiten,* I, 327.

St. Petersburg, in every capital, the memory of the fate of governments which had defied Bismarck in the 'sixties, and even later, had made statesmen afraid to risk his wrath; now they saw the prospect of relief from restraint, but they also feared what would happen to Europe when the Continent lost its greatest diplomat.

The princes around whom the rebels against Bismarck were gathering had, so far as can be seen, no quarrel with Bismarck's policy of security and stability. No less than the creator of the German state, they prized his ideal of the state. The quarrel, insofar as it was not a personal struggle for power, was over tactics. The Princes, Frederick and William alike, took a more kindly view of human nature than the Chancellor. They dreamed of peace achieved, not by neutralizing conflicts, but by the harmonious coöperation of likeminded men and nations. They were repelled by the tortuousness, the frank acceptance of that old evil proverb, divide and conquer, which obviously characterized Bismarck's methods. They would make an end of ambiguity and deceit, acknowledge their policy and their ideal, seek peace at home and abroad through harmony; if harmony proved impossible they would fight, openly and frankly, loyally shielding allies, loyally combating foes. Frederick and William differed as only father and son can quarrel, but in their attitude to Bismarck they were at bottom agreed: they hated his methods. Like Bismarck they were fighting for power as well as principle, but the conflict of principle was there.

Bismarck saw further. He knew that the choice of tactics, methods, was inseparably linked to the choice of policy, and even to the nature of the German state. Abandon the ceaseless search for a balance, he argued, and all was lost. If Germany "simplified" her foreign policy by breaking any part of the complicated network of agreements binding the other powers to Berlin, skilfully woven out of hope and fear, the result would not be harmonious coöperation, but the formation of hostile coalitions, the loss of German freedom of action and, ultimately, war. Allow free rein to the conflict of parties, classes, and creeds within Germany: the result would not be harmony. The immediate result would be strife, strife which would dissipate German strength and encourage the rivals of Germany in Europe. Very quickly, out of that strife would come a preponderance of some one interest or combination of interests which would wreck the policy of stability. In the end, the German state would serve the needs, not of the nation, but of temporarily dominant groups. Men would scramble for political power and use it for their selfish purposes as in parliamentary democracies, but in Germany the struggle for power would not be tempered by respect for traditional forms as in England; it would be naked, unashamed and unrestrained. The ideal of a state above party and faction would be lost.

All this seems so obviously true now that it is hard to understand that it was so little realized at the time. It was inevitable that a young, self-confident emperor should rebel against Bismarck's despotic will. But why did the German people not only acquiesce, but approve, when they saw the old hero challenged? No doubt, their reverence for the state made them minimize the importance of the individual statesman. Because Englishmen regarded the state as a mere mechanical contrivance, the men who controlled the mechanism seemed all-important. Because Germans believed the state to be a living personality with a will shaped by the history of the nation, the statesman seemed relatively unimportant. This would explain acquiescence, but not the feeling of release. To explain that, it is necessary to resort to conjecture. In the light of what happened after he was gone, it seems probable that the German people were unconsciously in rebellion, less against Bismarck's repressive tactics, than against his policy of security. The sacrifices he demanded of individuals and groups in the name of national necessity were too great to be borne if security alone was to be the reward; a more positive and attractive prize must be offered. After the policy of "simplicity" proved an egregious failure, the advisers of William II reverted to Bismarckian tactics. But they made the return to the old methods tolerable by setting as their goal, not stability, but growth. The tension which had seemed intolerable when demanded by Bismarck as the price of security, was easily sustained by the thought that Germany, as in the years before 1871, was once more moving forward.

Whether or not there was unconscious rebellion against the objectives of German policy in the years just before Bismarck's fall is debatable. Undoubtedly William II and his advisers did not, at the outset, intend to change these objectives; they intended only to change the methods by which the old policy was pursued. Stability, security, was the highest purpose of the German government throughout the years from 1885 to 1894. Throughout these years, also, the rulers of Germany believed that friendship with England was essential to the success of their policy; here again 1890 marked a shift of method but not of purpose. By a study of these years when direct conflict of interests seemed slight, and when the recognition of common interests was most complete, an understanding of the barriers to Anglo-German coöperation may be attained.

In 1882 Bismarck had, through the Triple Alliance and the revived Dreikaiserbund, regained the control over the European balance of power which Disraeli had tried to seize during the Near Eastern crisis. Simultaneously, the Chancellor had created a new internal balance of political forces; protective tariffs, war on the socialists, and social reform had built up a government majority in the Reichstag and in the country as a whole. For a time all went well. Then, in 1885, the equilibrium was again jeopardized, at home most obviously by the impending change of rulers, abroad most obviously by a new crisis in the Balkans and by a revival of the spirit of revenge in France. As in the 'seventies, the internal and foreign difficulties developed simultaneously and in close relation to each other. As before, success abroad made success at home easier; but this time the imperial will prevented the Chancellor from consolidating his victories.

That events look different seen from different vantage points, is a commonplace, but the commonplace is very pertinent to an understanding of British and German policy during the second half of the 'eighties. The international scene as observed from London has already been described. There, the rise of French passion for revenge was half welcomed, because it relieved the strain of imperial controversy, and half feared, because Germany might at any moment resort to war as a means of silencing the unruly French. Similarly, the efforts of Russia to regain control over Bulgaria relieved strain in the Middle East; but there was danger that Bismarck might try to push England and Austria into a war with Russia. As a horrible solution of Continental quarrels there was the remote but dangerous possibility of a union of the Continent against England; the British Empire was big enough to satisfy the appetite of all the other powers. To Lord Salisbury, the least risky policy seemed a carefully hedged union with Italy and Austria, the so-called Mediterranean Entente made in 1887. It was a policy adopted with little enthusiasm and much misgiving. Salisbury feared he was merely pulling Bismarck's chestnuts out of the fire.

The two wars which Salisbury saw lowering over Europe were seen no less clearly in Berlin, in fact Bismarck's perspective was undoubtedly closer to the real shape of things. Salisbury, knowing Germany was far stronger than France, thought German alarm over the rise of General Boulanger on the tide of *revanche* was only assumed; the Germans were looking for an excuse to begin war. Bismarck, although he did not say so publicly, was conscious of the disparity between the forces which would meet along the Rhine; if it had been a question of France alone he would not have lost any sleep. He knew, however, that the followers of Boulanger were hopeful because they expected Russian aid, and he knew that there was a good chance that their hopes would prove justified. The course of events in the Balkans was making Russia ever more resigned to the thought of war with Germany. The Tsar was determined to establish in Bulgaria a government amenable to "advice" from St. Petersburg. The Bulgarians, led by their ruler, Prince Alexander of Battenberg, were determined to emancipate themselves from Russian control. In September, 1886, Prince Alexander was terrified into submission;

he abdicated and departed from Bulgaria. His former subjects, however, refused more vehemently than ever to acknowledge their dependence on Russia. Obviously, their submission could be obtained only by force. The Tsar claimed that the terms of the Dreikaiserbund justified the dispatch of an army of occupation; Austria flatly asserted that she would not tolerate a Russian army in the Balkan peninsula. As a decade before, the Tsar was not terrified by Austrian threats, but he was afraid of Germany. Why not hold Germany in check by an alliance with France? The question was asked with increasing frequency and openness in Pan Slav circles. If the Tsar listened to the Pan Slavs, it would not matter whether war began in the east or in the west. Germany must fight on two fronts. As Bismarck said in April, 1887, "the decision for war or peace depends almost entirely on the will and temper of the Russian emperor." [4]

The most obvious escape for Germany was to form a solid alliance between all the great powers menaced by France or Russia, in other words, to bring England into the Triple Alliance. Probably France and Russia would be frightened into silence by such a coalition; certainly they would be defeated if they insisted on war. Italy and Austria were anxious to seek peace by this road. If newspaper opinion is any guide, most of the German people would have applauded. Prince Alexander was popular, not only because he was a German, but because he had refused to accept Russian dictation. When he was forced to abdicate, a wave of hostility to Russia swept over the German press. Momentarily, the humanitarian cosmopolitanism of early nineteenth century nationalism returned to life. The feeling that Germany had not only selfish interests, but interests as a member of the European family of nations, found vehement expression. Germany was once more described as the defender of European culture against Russian barbarism; like the Teutonic Knights of the middle ages, modern Germany must hold the eastern frontiers of Europe.

Even the conservative aristocracy would not have presented a

[4] Schweinitz, *Denkwürdigkeiten,* II, 339.

united front against the new international alignment. Military men were weary of the incessant effort to balance between the powers. They demanded action, and whether they marched east or west seemed a matter of indifference. The great landowners of the feudal east, traditionally in sympathy with Russian political ideals, were now troubled by doubts. Pan Slavism recognized no class loyalties. When Bismarck sought to end the Polish problem in East Prussia by evicting Poles and planting Germans in the frontier lands, Russia retaliated by dispossessing the Germans in her Baltic provinces. If the Tsar intended to take up the cause of the Poles, there could be no peace between Germany and Russia. Economic interests were also in conflict with loyalty to conservatism: grain was becoming a political force. German landowners resented the competition of Russian agriculture; Russians were angered by the high tariffs which kept their grain out of German markets. Finally, alliance with England would have had support from the princes waiting on the steps of the throne. Prince Frederick had long dreamed of this union; Prince William, although the outside world was still ignorant of the change, had lost his earlier devotion to the Tsar, and was now willing to contemplate even war with Russia.

There is some evidence that Bismarck would have been willing to shift his tactics, had he thought coalition with England possible of attainment. In 1889 he told Francis Joseph that "the whole purpose of German policy during the last ten years had been to win England for the Triple Alliance." In 1888, the German Ambassador, in explaining to Lord Salisbury why William II had been unwilling to come to Vienna while the Prince of Wales was in that city, made what Salisbury thought a "curious" remark. "If there had been that real defensive alliance between England and the two Empires which the presence of the Prince of Wales on such an occasion between the two Emperors would have seemed to announce to the world, Germany would willingly have accepted any risk of displeasing Russia which such a spectacle might have caused." [5] Other similar "curious" hints

[5] Lucius, *Bismarck-Erinnerungen*, 500; Cecil, *Salisbury*, IV, 112.

might be cited. They suggest that the Chancellor would have been willing to revert to the proposal of coalition made momentarily in 1879, had he felt there was a real chance that the proposal would have been accepted. Salisbury, and English opinion, undoubtedly were not prepared to give a clear promise of armed support; Bismarck undoubtedly did not feel it safe to accept anything less. As later, it was a case of the whole, or nothing. William II and his advisers have often been censured because, in 1901, they refused to consider an informal understanding with England. By insisting on the entrance of England into the Triple Alliance, it is argued, they sacrificed all hope of any understanding. The censure may be warranted, but it should be remembered that Bismarck, no less than the men who came after him, believed that only a solemn written promise would insure British loyalty, if indeed even that would suffice.

In the 'eighties, as at the turn of the century, mistrust and misunderstanding prevented real intimacy between England and Germany. Salisbury was afraid of pulling Bismarck's chestnuts out of the fire. Bismarck used exactly the same figure of speech: unless the Triple Alliance watched vigilantly, it would be used as a cat's paw. England, he argued, wished to see the Continent paralysed by war. To bring on war, England would make vague promises of assistance to the Triple Alliance; but when war came, England would draw back and watch, rejoicing, while the Continental powers ruined themselves. Certainly there was little trust between these "natural allies," England and Germany!

Since coalition between England and the Triple Alliance was out of the question, if indeed he wanted coalition, Bismarck was forced back on the old delicate process of immobilizing all of the powers by balancing them against each other. A difficult game at best, the difficulties were now greater than earlier. Year by year, the other powers, even Germany's partners in the Triple Alliance, were becoming more rebellious against his will. At home, too, there was rebellion. The popular outburst of sympathy for Alexander of Battenberg showed how deep was the longing to end this perpetual doubt and uncertainty, to find a clear, direct line of action. A reckless temper was evident in every Continental country, a feeling that war must come some time and that, since it must come, better now than after a few months more of suspense. Although guessing what might have happened is a futile exercise, it is almost impossible to evade the conclusion that from 1886 to 1888 Bismarck prevented war, singlehanded. The cost was, to be sure, heavy. Germany never lost the reputation for duplicity earned during these years. Whether the reputation was deserved, may be considered when the record has been examined.

The problem, as he saw it, was first to separate the two wars which threatened; next, if possible, to prevent either from breaking out; finally, to make sure that if either did come, Germany would be sure to win. The key to the problem was the Tsar; he must be convinced that alliance with Germany was more advantageous, or less dangerous, than alliance with France. Hope and fear, the old controlling emotions, must keep Russia from trying to secure her Balkan objectives by the threat of a war on the Rhine.

The tactical objective was first clearly shown in home politics. The popular sympathy for Prince Alexander was dangerous, because the Tsar might conclude that Germany intended to support the rebellious Bulgarians. Unable to control opinion by the direct pressure of his press bureau, Bismarck attacked indirectly. Newspapers amenable to foreign office inspiration developed an ingenious thesis: Prince Alexander had lost his throne, not because of Russia, but because of England. The Tsar had given the Prince his crown; seduced by promises of English help, the Prince had turned against his protector; when danger appeared, the British drew back and let him fall, unaided. The old English trick, the trick played on great powers as well as small, the trick England was now seeking to play on Germany! The London press was full of sympathy for the fallen Prince, full of threats that he would be brought back to power by the united efforts of England and the Triple Alliance. What would happen if the Triple Alliance, led on by natural sympathy and the hope of

British support, took up the cause of Prince Alexander? Russia would stand firm, the Continent would be ravaged by the flames of war—and England would stand by, saying virtuously: "I promised nothing." The misguided Prince had fallen through trust in faithless England; was Germany to be involved in war through the same misplaced trust? Day after day in the "official" press, the same assertions were made, and the same questions asked. Before long, the newspapers which boasted loudest of their freedom from official control began to waver; soon their readers could scarcely have told which was the real villain, Russia or England. So easy was it to arouse the fear that England would never be loyal.

Having disarmed the Tsar's fears that German opinion would compel the adoption of a policy hostile to Russia, Bismarck set out to create the kind of fear he thought necessary. In the autumn of 1886 he introduced a bill in the Reichstag authorizing an increase in the size of the army. By this action he broke a tacit agreement with the Reichstag which had endured since the founding of the Empire, an agreement that army appropriations were to be voted every seven years and that the size of the army would be based on the preceding imperial census of population. Although the septennate had not expired, he asked that increases be made on the basis of the population in 1885. Since he had broken his part of the bargain, the Reichstag attempted to gain more complete control over the military budget by granting the proposed increases for three years only. Bismarck insisted that the grant be for seven years. In view of the popular temper, he could almost certainly have forced the parties into line if he had been willing to say that the bill was needed for protection against Russia. Instead, he argued that more troops were needed to hold France in check; there was, he stated repeatedly, no danger of war with Russia. It was not a convincing argument. The party leaders scoffed. Statesmen abroad concluded that he wanted the increases because he intended to attack France. Undeterred, he refused to change his tactics. At all costs, the Tsar must not be persuaded that war on Russia was contemplated, although it was well that the Tsar should be impressed by the striking force of the German army if war did come.

The prospect of defeat in the Reichstag was rather welcomed than feared by Bismarck. He was irked by the attempt of party leaders to win greater parliamentary control over the government. He feared that, when Frederick ruled, the pretensions of the Reichstag would receive imperial support. If there was a head-on collision with Parliament now, and over a question of national defence, he believed that the Reichstag could be permanently curbed by a constitutional change restricting its powers and altering its composition. History had not vindicated the prophecies he had made when the constitution was formed. Then he had feared the advocates of states' rights and the middle class liberals, and he had believed the masses to be both nationalist and respectful of authority. Therefore he had insisted that the Reichstag be elected by universal suffrage. Time had shown his fears and his hopes to be exaggerated. A growing segment of the lower classes, the urban proletariat, had fallen under the sway of anti-national and anti-authoritarian socialism. The Bundesrath, representing the states, had proved easy to control. The most influential members of the middle class, the capitalists, were zealous advocates of an authoritarian imperial government. If the Bundesrath could be given more power, and if the middle and upper classes could be given greater representation in the Reichstag by altering the franchise, then affairs would run more smoothly, and then the accession of a liberal emperor would not be such a fearful possibility.

Almost provocatively, the Chancellor invited defeat in the Reichstag by using only those arguments for the army bill which would not jeopardize relations with Russia. The bill was defeated. New elections were ordered. Fear of France, the France of General Boulanger, was assiduously preached. The elections held early in 1887 returned a majority favorable to the bill, which was speedily passed. Since the rebels in the Reichstag had been chastened, the thought of constitutional change was discarded. Domestic war, like foreign war, was an expedient to be used only when necessary.

The military increases would make the Tsar more reluctant to risk war with Germany. Simultaneously, Bismarck was manipulating the European alliance system with the delicate precision learned by long practice. Two wars threatened, on the Rhine and in the Balkans. Since all wars were full of unpredictable risks, he wished to make sure that if either of the threatened wars came, Germany would be immune from the risk of defeat, so far as it was humanly possible to secure immunity. Above all, he wished the two wars to be fought separately; in a general European war, Germany would be exposed to attack by France and Russia, would bear the brunt of the fighting. As he diagnosed the situation, only fear of an overwhelmingly powerful coalition would deter France from intervening if Germany was at war with Russia. Therefore he must build up such a coalition. Russian action in case of a Franco-German war was harder to predict, but he thought it might be possible to keep Russia neutral, if a judicious combination of fear and hope could be created in the Tsar's mind. If Alexander III became convinced that Germany would support Austria in the Balkans, he would, in desperation, seek an alliance with France. If Alexander III became convinced that Austria alone barred the way to Russian ambitions in the Balkans, then he might recklessly precipitate war. The problem was to create in the Russian mind fear, but not desperation, and hope, but not recklessness. The answer, as Bismarck saw it, was to create a coalition which would restrain Russia; but Germany must not be a member of that coalition. Instead, the Tsar must continue to hope for German aid in securing some part of his Balkan ambitions.

Three agreements resulted from Bismarck's efforts: the Mediterranean Entente between England, Italy, and Austria, concluded in February, 1887; the renewed and revised Triple Alliance between Germany, Italy, and Austria of the same month; and the Reinsurance Treaty between Germany and Russia, signed in June. Each of these agreements contributed something to the solution of the problems raised by the fact that war threatened in the east and the west.

Since he believed fear alone would restrain France, the Chancellor made the coalition against France rigid and complete. By the Mediterranean Entente, England and Italy were obliged to oppose French expansion in the Mediterranean; how the opposition was to be made effective, England refused to say. By the revised Triple Alliance, Germany was obliged to go to war, not only if France attacked Italy, but to oppose French expansion in the Mediterranean if Italy demanded war. France, therefore, must reckon on a war on two fronts, and probably a naval war with England as well.

The ring around Russia had one conspicuous gap. By the Mediterranean Entente, England, Austria, and Italy promised to oppose Russian expansion in the Balkans, at the Straits, and in the region of the Black Sea. By the Triple Alliance, Germany promised to fight if Russia attacked Austria. But Germany did not promise to fight to prevent Russian expansion in the Near East, or even to oppose such expansion. On the contrary, Bismarck stated publicly that he would not help to restrain Russia from forcibly seizing control over Bulgaria.

The Mediterranean Entente and the Triple Alliance were both secret, but their general purposes, if not their exact provisions, were speedily known. The Reinsurance Treaty was secret, and the very fact of its existence was kept a secret. Bismarck maintained, however, that his treaty with Russia merely put on paper what he had frequently stated in speeches which all the world could read. By the Reinsurance Treaty Germany and Russia promised that if one party was at war with a third power or powers, the other party was to remain neutral—except in two cases. Russia need not remain neutral if Germany attacked France, and Germany need not remain neutral if Russia attacked Austria. In other words, in case of a Russian attack on Austria, Germany was free to fulfil her obligations under the Austro-German alliance, which was shown to the Tsar and, in 1888, published. The

Reinsurance Treaty did, to be sure, contain other clauses requiring German support of Russian efforts to regain control over Bulgaria and to keep the Straits closed to the battleships of other powers; but here again Bismarck could say that he had warned Vienna not to count on German assistance in any case except a Russian attack.

It was Bismarck's contention that these three agreements reduced the possibility of war to the minimum possible in a world where chance could upset the nicest calculations. France would be afraid to move, either in the Mediterranean or on the Rhine; movement either way would bring at least two powers into the field against her. Russia would be afraid to strike either west or south; a thrust in either direction would be countered by at least two, and probably by three or four powers. A Franco-Russian alliance was made improbable, because if such an alliance was made, Germany would certainly join the Mediterranean Entente; the Tsar could hope that, if he did not join with France, Russia would receive some German assistance in the Near East, and, no matter how slight this assistance, it would be better than German opposition.

At the time and since, Bismarck's new demonstration of the mechanics of balance was criticized as dishonest and ineffectual. Whether or not the criticisms are justified depends on the way in which the words in the indictment are defined. Was it not hypocritical to promise German help in the achievement of Russia's Near Eastern ambitions, and at the same time to bring into existence the Mediterranean Entente, a combination based on common determination to thwart Russian ambitions? Certainly, most European statesmen did think this a double game. In March, 1888, Lord Salisbury briefly reported to the Queen a long interview with Herbert Bismarck, "in which Count Bismarck spoke the whole time. He was principally engaged in showing that Prince Bismarck's policy of advising his allies to support the Russian proposals at Constantinople, while secretly encouraging them to take the opposite course, was not open to the charge of duplicity."[6] Similarly, in the year following, a German dispatch from St. Petersburg cited, as proof of Russian disillusionment, the Tsar's lament that, aside from the Prince of tiny Montenegro, he had not a sincere friend in the world. To which Bismarck made the no less disillusioned comment: "Who really has one?"[7] Monarchs and ruling statesmen, in his view, should not hope for the joys of ordinary mortals in addition to the joys of power. The statesman must mould his own character to the character of the state, and in the world of states there was no room for loyalty and self-sacrifice, there was room only for the relentless pursuit of interest. Words like ally and friend, words suffused with emotional warmth, must be used, but they must not delude those whose task was the jealous protection of state interest.

What Bismarck claimed he had done by his alliance system was to make clear in time of peace the conflicts of interest which might otherwise have become obvious only after someone had decided on war. He had forced Europe to see the real lines of political force; seeing what war would entail, no one dared to move. Away with talk of friendship and duplicity; these were the facts, unpleasant perhaps, but facts nonetheless! This was an argument proper to one who had, like the old Chancellor, worked out all the implications of the theory of sovereign states. It was an argument incomprehensible to Englishmen, who were still trying to remain loyal to the belief that concern for the individual at the one extreme, and mankind at the other should put moral restraints on state action. Such men could see only the undoubted hypocrisy with which Bismarck played on the moral ideals of his fellow men, whether Germans or the statesmen of other countries; they could not see, or would not see, that his precepts did coincide with a goodly part of the practice of every state and statesman, did even, sometimes, serve the cause of peace which they also sought to serve.

Bismarck's interpretation of his own policy is most clearly re-

[6] Cecil, *Salisbury*, IV, 83.
[7] G.P., VI, 354–355.

vealed in a letter which he wrote to Lord Salisbury in November, 1887. During the preceding months, the governments of Austria and Italy had repeatedly asked that the Mediterranean Entente be made more precise. Salisbury had no objection to this proposal in itself, although he did, as usual, suspect that Bismarck was setting a trap. "If he can get up a nice little fight between Russia and the three Powers, he will have leisure to make France a harmless neighbor for some time to come." Bismarck was not to be trusted, Salisbury argued, but at least it was possible to estimate the risks attendant on dealings with him. He might start a war in the east as the prelude to an attack on France; but neither of these wars would jeopardize the position of England in the world, and possibly that was not his game. If Bismarck fell, however, the risks became incalculable, and the chances were great that he would fall. "Between us and Prince William's perhaps unchecked rule," Salisbury pointed out, "there only stand now three lives—one of ninety-one, one of seventy-three, and one menaced by a disease 'that does not pardon.'" [8] Prince William was thought to be a partisan of a Russo-German alliance. If he came to power during a war in which England, Italy, and Austria were fighting Russia, he might bring Germany into the war on the side of Russia. To avert this possibility, Salisbury refused to reaffirm the Mediterranean Entente until Germany had officially and irrevocably committed herself by approving the proposed understanding. The young autocrat must find his hands bound when, through a great historical accident, irresponsible power became his to use or abuse.

When Salisbury made it clear, naturally without a complete statement of his motives, that he would not accept the Austrian and Italian proposals until they had been approved by Germany, Bismarck was perplexed. Although he did not say so, he was obviously puzzled by the belief that, in relations between states, a written promise was a guarantee of performance. More important, he was perplexed by English notions concerning the German government. His reply took the form of a treatise on Ger-

[8] Cecil, *Salisbury,* IV, 71, 72.

man politics. The day when wars were made by individuals was gone, he argued. Certainly no one, whether he be emperor or minister, could dictate the foreign policy of Germany; the real determinant was national interest as interpreted by the popular will. The German army was actually the armed nation. It was a splendid fighting instrument—if fighting for a cause which was known to be a national cause. If the will of the whole people was not aroused, concentrated, determined, that army would be useless, would turn against the rulers who demanded needless sacrifices.

The German people, Bismarck reasoned, asked nothing from their neighbors except the right to live in peace. This did not mean that Germans would fight only to resist invasion. For a country with three great powers for neighbors, and frontiers which could easily be crossed, a hostile coalition was a constant danger, a danger to be averted by vigilance and by coöperation with other powers who were menaced by the same potential enemies. "Austria, like contemporary Germany and England, belongs to the class of satisfied nations, 'saturated,' as the late Prince Metternich expressed it, and is therefore pacific and anxious to keep things as they are. Austria and England have loyally accepted the existing status of the German Empire, and have no interest in seeing her weakened. France and Russia, on the contrary seem to menace us." To protect herself, Germany must protect other nations with similar interests. "If Austria is beaten, weakened, or converted into our enemy, we would be isolated on the continent of Europe, faced by Russia and France, and faced with the possibility of a coalition of these two powers. It is to our interest to prevent this state of affairs from arising, even by force of arms. The existence of Austria as a great power, strong and independent, is a necessity for Germany which the personal sympathies of a sovereign cannot change in the slightest." Germany would not fight to further the interests of Austria or England in the Near East. Germany would, however, welcome a union of these friendly powers for the purpose of restraining Russia from war, a union which would give them victory in case war did come. "So long as no German interest was involved, we would remain neutral; but it is impossible to conceive that any German emperor would lend the *aid* of his armies to Russia to help her overthrow or weaken one of the powers whose support we count on, either to prevent a war with Russia or to assist us in such a war. From this point of view, German policy will *always* be obliged to fight if the independence of Austria is menaced by Russian aggression, or if England or Italy should be in danger of being overwhelmed by the armies of France. German policy moves, therefore, along a path prescribed with compelling force by the political conditions of Europe, a path from which neither the aversions nor the sympathies of a monarch or a directing minister could make that policy deviate." [9]

In a postscript, Bismarck stated that his outline of German policy had the "full approbation" of Prince William; and it may safely be surmised that this information, rather than the Chancellor's exposition of the logic of German policy, was decisive for Salisbury. In December, the earlier exchange of notes between England, Austria, and Italy was strengthened by a detailed statement, defining "their common interest to uphold the existing state of things upon the shores of the Mediterranean and the adjoining seas."

Undoubtedly if Bismarck had been writing to a Russian statesman, the lights and shades of his analysis of German policy would have been different, but in essentials there would have been no difference. Whether these shades of expression justify a charge of duplicity is dubious. In any case, no one was deceived. Every European chancellery rang with denunciations of Bismarckian perfidy. The really significant fact is that no government dared to demand that Germany take an unequivocal stand. The prestige accumulated over a quarter of a century, not skill in the arts of dissimulation, permitted him to balance precariously, but safely, between the powers. No other statesman of his day, it is safe to say, could have performed the feat.

Duplicity was, then, a matter of definition. Success or failure

[9] G.P., IV, 376–380.

was also a matter of definition. From one point of view, the success of Bismarck's tactics was incontestable. In 1886 and 1887 two wars seemed imminent; neither materialized. Possibly, though this is hard to believe, they would not have come had Bismarck not been in power. Certainly, however, a policy cannot be said to have failed when the stated objective of that policy was attained, and peace was what Bismarck wanted. Possibly, as Prince William argued in 1888 and as some Germans have argued ever since, it would have been better to allow war to come, because success would have been easier then than later; but this is a criticism of the Chancellor's objectives, not a demonstration that the objectives were unattained. A better case can be made if it be recalled that peace was only the immediate aim. The deeper purpose was security, and it can be argued that, in internal and foreign affairs, Bismarck won immediate safety, but impaired German security. The part of this argument which is usually most stressed is really the weakest link. It can easily be demonstrated that by 1888 France and Russia were moving towards that intimacy which Bismarck had always dreaded. He had been forced to accelerate the movement in 1887 when, as a final means of holding the Tsar from war, he had practically closed the German capital market to Russian government bonds. In desperate need of funds, the Russians turned to Paris, where every facility for flotation was gladly given. The financial bond between Russia and France rapidly became stronger and more obvious; must not financial ties soon become political ties, men asked? In 1889 a clear indication of political intimacy was perceived in the announcement that the Russians would be permitted to copy the new French army rifle. Possibly the countries were by then moving irresistibly towards an alliance. The alliance had not, however, come into existence by 1890 and the Russians were prepared to continue the Reinsurance Treaty when Bismarck fell. It cannot be demonstrated that the Franco-Russian alliance would have come into being if he had continued in power. More important, it cannot be demonstrated that tactics other than those he used in 1886 and 1887 would have kept his neighbors further apart. Such purely speculative criticisms on the basis of what might have happened, had everything been different, are possibly interesting but certainly fruitless. The incontestable facts were, that a crisis had been tided over, and that after 1887 France and Russia were coming closer. Criticism must, to be of value, be confined to Bismarck's attempts to counteract the latter fact.

One escape he was determined should not be chosen, war with Russia. Military men argued that this was the only way out. Prince William apparently thought it the only way out. Bismarck refused to heed their arguments. He pointed out that war with Russia meant, first of all, a war with France as well, the incalculable war on two fronts. It meant war with a country which could not be decisively beaten, a country of limitless distances, without any vulnerable vital point. It meant, finally, another neighbor obsessed by the desire for revenge. Napoleon's disastrous invasion of Russia at the beginning of the century showed the impossibility of decisive victory; the Franco-Prussian war showed the impossibility of securing permanent acquiescence in defeat. At the end of 1887, the military men in Berlin and Vienna, encouraged by the attitude of Prince William, sought to broaden the provisions of the Austro-German alliance to include a "preventive" war against Russia. Bismarck threatened to resign, and had his way. Later, in August, 1889, when the Prince had become Emperor William II, the question came up again in a discussion between William and Francis Joseph. William swept caution aside. "No matter what the cause of your mobilization," he declared, "whether it be Bulgaria or anything else, the day you mobilize is also the mobilization day for my army—and then let the chancellors say what they want to." [10] This was all the army chiefs could ask, if Bismarck was really as unimportant as the Emperor's words implied; as yet no one could be sure.

Only in the west, according to Bismarck's calculations, was greater security obtainable. France might be frightened away from Russia; he had long since abandoned the belief that France could be won by the hope of reward. Russia might be convinced

[10] Glaise-Horstenau, *Beck,* 338.

that the French alliance was a liability, rather than a means of coercing Germany. At the end of the 'eighties, as at the beginning of the 'seventies, exorcising the nightmare of hostile coalitions meant keeping France "in quarantine." Earlier, this task had been made easy by French weakness and Russian hatred of radicalism. Now, France was strong, and Pan Slavism was undermining Russian loyalty to conservatism. To keep France isolated, he had increased German military power, created the Mediterranean Entente, and given the Triple Alliance a potentially offensive character. These measures had temporarily sufficed. The failure and ignominious flight of General Boulanger in 1889 did not, however, mean French acquiescence in isolation. Indications of Franco-Russian intimacy multiplied. To bring Italy to terms, France was resorting to financial reprisals similar to those Bismarck was using against Russia. Further pressure was needed to silence the French.

That pressure could come only from England. If it was known that, in the event of a Franco-German war, the British fleet would be at the service of Germany, France would realize the futility of war, and Russia would not think the French alliance a better bargain than German friendship. An Anglo-German alliance against France would also serve as a guarantee against the remote but terrifying possibility of a reconciliation between England and France, or even between England, France, and Russia. Not the least important element in Bismarck's long success was his ability to envisage every possible contingency, and among the contingencies which he kept before him was a sudden swing of England from the side of the Triple Alliance to the side of France and Russia. It is hard for a later generation to realize how impossible such a diplomatic revolution seemed in the late 'eighties, when Egypt was a guarantee of Anglo-French hostility, and when Anglo-Russian enmity was guaranteed by every mile of land from the Adriatic Sea to the frontiers of India. As always, men concluded that what was, would be. Some men dreamed of a diplomatic revolution, but they were usually men like Gladstone who refused to see that the existing alignment of the powers was the result of basic conflicts of interest; and they had few supporters. In England, Lord Salisbury's foreign policy commanded more general support than his domestic policy, even though the foreign policy was based on the necessity of coöperation with the Triple Alliance.

Bismarck was one of the few men, even among statesmen, who saw the possibility of a complete reversal of British policy, and Salisbury was another. Salisbury hated dependence on Germany, partly because he disliked German eagerness to exact "blackmail," partly because he disliked dependence on anyone. If he could have made terms with France and Russia, even by considerable sacrifices in Egypt and the Near East, he would have made the sacrifices. Since any concessions would be resented by English opinion, and since there seemed no chance that concessions would bring lasting agreement, his hands were tied; but he did not think his policy was ideal or eternal, and he was determined not to bind England inextricably to the Triple Alliance. Naturally, he did not wish his doubts and antipathies to be seen in Berlin. When he resisted suggestions for more sweeping commitments, it was ostensibly because of parliamentary or ministerial difficulties; when he refused to concur in a proposed course of action, it was because public opinion was so preoccupied with the Irish and other internal problems that a strong foreign policy was out of the question; when he explored the possibility of a settlement with France and Russia, it was because some of his colleagues or the Liberal opposition insisted on these gestures. Apparently the Germans accepted these excuses and believed Salisbury lacked the courage, rather than the desire, to challenge France or Russia; at least they sought assiduously to demonstrate that a courageous foreign policy was the best antidote for domestic strife. Herbert Bismarck, at his father's request, assured the Prime Minister in August, 1887, that his battle against internal faction was watched with sympathy and anxiety in Berlin. "It did not appear impossible to the Chancellor that the increasingly obvious disintegration of the English empire, and the irresponsibility of the political parties, might be ended by some, possibly only diplomatic, action abroad." With a heavy sigh and a sorrowful shake of the head, Salisbury asked that the Chancellor be thanked for his advice; unfortunately, "lack of conviction and selfish opportunism" had grown to such frightful proportions in English political life that no one could compel unity of action.[11]

While Bismarck exaggerated Salisbury's goodwill, he did not minimize the possibility that England might some day desert the Triple Alliance. While he also exaggerated the extent to which internal strife lessened the striking power of England, he did not minimize the importance of England as a means of insuring French isolation. Therefore he wanted an Anglo-German alliance against France. He also had hopes of securing the alliance. To obtain his objective he counted on Salisbury's support, and on the panic which the growth of French sea power was causing in England; the German army was no less useful to the English as protection against France than the British fleet was to Germany.

Here is where Bismarck's policy in his last years is open to criticism, to the same criticism which may be levelled at his whole career: he was persistently indifferent to the sympathies and antipathies of public opinion, when he believed those passions ran counter to national interest. He feared Pan Slavism and French revenge, because these emotional loyalties might harmonize with Russian or French national interest. English opinion of Germany, or German opinion of England, he thought unimportant, because the interests of the two countries were harmonious. Repeatedly after 1887 it suited his purpose to encourage popular outbursts against England; without hesitation, he gave the needed encouragement. At the same time he was working to secure an alliance. It is true that Salisbury almost certainly would not have agreed to the alliance under any circumstances. Nevertheless it is true that Bismarck's press campaigns against England ruined

[11] G.P., IV, 348–349.

whatever chance there was of a binding union and, more important, jeopardized even the informal coöperation which the ruling statesmen of both countries thought essential.

In whipping up German feeling against England, Bismarck was practicing the precept he had given to Salisbury: domestic enemies might be silenced, and national unity promoted, by creating a diversion in foreign affairs. At the end of 1887 it was evident that William I and Prince Frederick were both dying. Even if he outlived his father, Frederick could not hope for a long reign; so far, those who had feared the accession of a liberal emperor had occasion to rejoice, and they did rejoice. But the very gravity of his condition made it more possible that Frederick's reign, no matter how brief, would see a violent overturn of traditional practices. The Crown Prince had, with the passing of years, come to realize that the foundations of Bismarckian Germany had been in place too long to be easily altered; his wife, the Princess Victoria, had kept intact her hatred for everything the Chancellor stood for, and her determination to end his rule. Illness had brought the Prince once more under her influence. Speechless, consumed with pain, surrounded by the Chancellor's spies, Frederick allowed her to stand before him, to shield him, to fight his battle. Fight she did, with her mother's implacable will, but without her mother's shrewd common sense; with her father's intelligence, but without his judgment. Still incapable of admitting that the disease was cancer, she was determined that Frederick's reign should create "that which Germany lacks and which it thirsts for, and that is peace among its classes, races, religions and parties, good and friendly relations with its neighbors, liberty and the respect of right instead of force, and the protection of the weak against the oppression of the strong." [12] She and Frederick had waited and planned through a generation. They had been calumniated by the ruling powers of Germany. They had seen their sons won over to their opponents. Through it all, they kept their courage, sure that one day they would be able to right everything. Now, with victory

[12] *Letters of the Empress Frederick,* 272.

near, it was to be snatched away. History knows few more poignant episodes, few more impressive demonstrations of the power of chance.

The tragedy of the Empress Frederick evokes sympathy which sweeps over all criticism. But the facts must be stated, and in fact she was a very foolish woman: in her vain struggles against fate, she marred or destroyed much that she valued. Like her mother, she drove her son to revolt by seeking to bind his will to hers; some share of the blame for the instability of William II must be put on his parents. Alliance between England and Germany was her highest aim; but she had helped in some small measure to prevent good relations by her lack of tact or discretion, and now she was unwittingly to be the occasion for a more significant phase in the estrangement of the two peoples.

It is not possible to feel sympathy for her enemies, among whom were included Bismarck and her son William. Their methods were unspeakably vile. Their fears, however, were understandable. Whether as princess, empress, or widow, Victoria demanded to be treated chivalrously; but she sought unconsciously to exploit her sex and her sorrows to further a political program which her enemies thought dangerous for Germany. To avert danger, they not only denied her claim to chivalric consideration; they fought her with despicable weapons. Since she had made herself the champion of the liberal opposition, it was not strange that those who hated liberalism hated her. Neither was it strange that they should strike at liberalism through her. A direct attack on Frederick would have broken on popular dynastic loyalty; liberal political organizations could not be persecuted without raising fears of despotism. The Princess, "the Englishwoman," was vulnerable; through her, liberalism could be dealt a death blow.

The campaign began with hints that when Frederick reigned, the real ruler would be his wife. This thesis was supported by the undeniable fact that she made everyone, even the highest political authorities, approach the Crown Prince through her. She could protest that her only purpose was to conserve Frederick's strength; but it was easy to argue that a man who saw only what his wife wished him to see, was under her complete control. The next step was to show that when the Princess became the real and unconstitutional ruler, Germany would be little more than an English colony. All her indiscreet and disparaging comments on German ways of life were recalled. She was blamed for calling in the English doctor who had denied Frederick was afflicted with cancer. It was hinted that, if German science had been heeded, an operation would have saved him but ruined her design to control him, and Germany, for English purposes. It is unnecessary to elaborate on the unsavory details of the indictment. The purpose, and in large part the result, was to create a belief in the German mind that any changes Frederick might seek to effect after his accession would be inspired from England and would be for the purpose of making Germany an appendage of the British crown.

In this poisoned atmosphere, William I fought his last and losing battle. Around his narrow camp-bed, his family waited through the bleak March nights, all except Frederick, still at warm San Remo. The wavering mind of the incredibly old man lived over the events he had seen, the decisions he had made. At first he spoke of France, his fears of another war, his efforts to remain loyal to his fellow emperors. Then he turned back, back to the already legendary days of his youth, to his heroic mother, Queen Louise, to the officers who had been his companions in arms during the war of liberation against Napoleon, officers whose names came more readily to his lips than the names of a later generation. On March 9, 1888, he died.

Everywhere there was uneasy waiting. What now? Queen Victoria—like the dying Emperor more preoccupied with the past than with the future—wrote in her diary: "Poor old Emperor, he was always very kind to me, but for some years, alas! he was made a tool of for no good!" Lord Salisbury peered ahead. "The ship is leaving harbor . . . this is the crossing of the bar . . . I can see the sea covered with white horses." To avert, if possible, the coming storm, he told his ambassador to keep in the background. The new Empress was to be discouraged from "any leaning to English notions of policy." Politically and personally, she would be safest if she appeared "mildly Bismarckian and intensely German." It would be impossible, even if desirable, to give a permanently anti-Bismarckian direction to German policy during the two or three months at her disposal. Above all, it must not be possible to accuse England of meddling.[13]

His precautions were vain. On his journey to Berlin, the Emperor Frederick issued a proclamation to "My People," full of promises of an age of concord. The people were stirred, but hesitant. Who was speaking, the German Frederick or the Englishwoman? Almost immediately, the Empress played into the hands of her enemies. For long she had hoped to consummate a marriage between one of her daughters and the former prince of Bulgaria, Alexander of Battenberg. Bismarck, through William I, had prevented the marriage on the ground that Russia would be offended if Alexander was honored by union with a Hohenzollern. Now, before March had ended, Alexander was invited to visit the German Imperial family, almost an announcement of the betrothal. Here was the opportunity Bismarck had awaited, a crisis, not over domestic policy where his enemies might unite against him, but over foreign policy where he could create a union against the Empress. The inspired press saw the subtle hand of England, working through Queen Victoria and the Empress, to create enmity between Germany and Russia. With some difficulty Bismarck induced the Tsar to protest against the match. He demanded that the English government intervene. Salisbury was furious at this new example of "diplomatic blackmail," even inclined to believe that "friendship with Germany is a more uncertain staff to lean upon than friendship with France," but there was no escape. The demanded expression of disapproval was secured from the Queen, and, "with regret," conveyed to the German foreign office. Thus fortified at home and abroad, Bismarck threatened to resign if the engagement was announced. The Empress surrendered. Her help-

[13] *Letters of Queen Victoria*, 3, I, 389; Cecil, *Salisbury*, IV, 96–97.

lessness, and her husband's, to change the course of German history had been demonstrated. To keep the realization of helplessness sharp, the campaign continued. The announcement that Queen Victoria was to visit Berlin was followed by a new outburst of hysterical warnings against foreign meddling, although when the Queen arrived Bismarck was, in private, most charming and affable.

In June, 1888, the sordid tragedy seemed played out when Frederick died, but his Empress was still thought a potentially dangerous center for liberal agitation. Promptly on his death, the royal palace was surrounded to prevent the escape of dangerous documents. That the fears were justified is attested by the fact that the Empress did later succeed in smuggling to England her private correspondence, filled with denunciations of Bismarck and of her own son, the young Emperor William II. Despite all possible excuse, however, it was not a pretty sight to see the Empress practically a prisoner on the day she became a widow. Neither did there seem much filial loyalty in the way William II ostentatiously passed over his father's reign as an interlude between the truly German reigns of the first and second Williams, or in his obvious determination to exclude his mother from all influence over himself, over German politics, even over such apparently harmless things as charitable organizations. Here again, liberalism was being struck through her. Scenting the kill, the opponents of liberalism pressed on, led by Bismarck. An indiscreet professor published fragments of the diary kept by Frederick during the Franco-Prussian war, fragments which made clear Frederick's moral rage against Bismarck. The professor was prosecuted, but the courts refused to convict. The papers of other liberals were ransacked for incriminating documents. Sir Robert Morier, now the British Ambassador in St. Petersburg, was falsely accused of using his position as the confidant of Frederick during the Franco-Prussian war to gain information regarding the Prussian plan of campaign, and of giving this information to the French. Indiscreet remarks of the Prince of Wales were twisted into an assertion that England wished, and Frederick had been prepared to sanction, the return of Schleswig to Denmark, and of Alsace-Lorraine to France. In every way, the specious syllogism was pounded home: liberals were followers of Frederick, who was ruled by his wife, who was an English agent; therefore, liberals were English agents, enemies of Germany.

Whether it was cold calculation or vindictive passion which was driving Bismarck on, cannot be determined; but undoubtedly he was injuring himself, the new Emperor, and Germany. At home, even though liberalism was further discredited, every thinking German was nauseated by the scandalous processes used to attain this purpose; the feeling grew that Bismarck was an irascible old man whose loss would be, in some ways, a boon.

Abroad, William II seemed merely an erratic tool of the Chancellor. His embittered mother did her best to create this impression in England by her letters to Queen Victoria. Meticulously, and with endless repetition, she set forth the insults which were heaped on her. Without reserve, she damned every action of her son and his advisers. Consider the effect of her words: "All that is foreign, especially all that is English, is hated. . . . Caprice, tyranny and despotism are rampant. . . . William allows his father and me to be insulted and attacked, and sanctions it! . . . He has had a long and careful training and preparation in the Bismarck atmosphere, so that his sense of right and wrong, of gratitude, chivalry, respect, affection for his parents and pity for those who are so stricken has been thoroughly destroyed! . . . Bismarck could not have a better tool than William. . . . W. reads only the papers prepared for him, does not understand or care for all the difficult and intricate questions of internal Government and is utterly ignorant of social, industrial, agricultural, commercial and financial questions, etc., only occupied with military things, with a little smattering of foreign affairs, and constantly being fêted, travelling about, having dinners, receptions, etc. Bismarck wishes his head to be thoroughly turned. . . . I think William is totally blind and that the Government makes one mistake after another. . . .

Prince Bismarck is anxious now [April, 1889] for England's friendship, as well he may . . . in view of European complications which he is anxious to avoid, but which I fancy are beyond his control. He has made a fatal mistake with Austria! He has so weakened her that she becomes almost useless as an ally. . . . When I think of the first year of the new reign!! mistake after mistake—blunder after blunder!" [14]

The effect on the British royal family of events in Germany, and of the Empress Frederick's comments on these events, was immediate and violent. For the Queen to speak of Bismarck as "untrue and heartless" merely meant the reopening of old wounds. Soon, however, she was referring to her grandson, William II, as "a hot-headed, conceited and wrongheaded young man, devoid of any feeling." In her rage at the way "poor darling Vicky is being persecuted," she even sought, with some success, to arouse public opinion, relating the secret details of the campaign of persecution to members of her court. A supposed slight to the Prince of Wales led to an open break between the Kaiser and his English relations, a break which was plastered over on the insistence of Lord Salisbury that political considerations required at least the appearance of intimacy; personal relations between the dynasties, he argued, must not obscure the fact that the countries needed each other. But what were personal relations? Germany to him meant first of all, Bismarck, and the Chancellor's temper had, he thought, "become more than usually unbearable." Beyond Bismarck, he saw only the incalculable Emperor, and in the autumn of 1888, Salisbury pronounced a judgment on William which was, with greater or less intensity, to be held thereafter: "I think that the Emperor William must be a little off his head." [15]

In January, 1889, German newspapers were saying that the Emperor Frederick had been made into a British agent by the daughter of Queen Victoria, and that the British Ambassador in

[14] *Letters of the Empress Frederick*, 330, 351, 352, 358, 372, 373, 378.

[15] *Letters of Queen Victoria*, 3, I, 421, 441, 442, 447; Cecil, *Salisbury*, IV, 112.

St. Petersburg had been a French spy in 1870. In January, 1889, English papers were commenting on German hatred of England, and on the degradation of German political life. In January, 1889, Bismarck, after many hints had been disregarded, made a direct proposal for an Anglo-German alliance against France! Evidently, he thought the moment auspicious; he would not have made a definite offer had he thought a rebuff certain. Evidently he thought the angry mood of the two peoples irrelevant; his contempt for public opinion was notorious. The relevant facts were German need to keep France isolated, and British fear of French naval construction.

The proposal was rejected. When the German Ambassador outlined the projected alliance, Salisbury promised to consult his colleagues, and expressed his pleasure at this new evidence of confidence and community of interest between England and Germany; he would reply later. Weeks passed and nothing was said. At the end of March, Herbert Bismarck went to London and revived the subject. Salisbury again expressed his personal approval. He regretted, however, that his colleagues in the government feared public opinion would not understand the necessity for abandoning isolation; this was one of the unfortunate results of democratic government. He hoped some day opinion would change. "Meanwhile, we leave it on the table, without saying yes or no: that is unfortunately all I can do at present." [16]

So ended the hope of encircling France. It cannot be said that the ugly temper of British opinion prevented the alliance. We cannot say definitely why Salisbury rejected the proposal for the good reason that he apparently did not write or say a word about it to anyone. All our information comes from German sources. Salisbury's whole public life shows, however, an aversion to binding agreements involving military obligations; his career also shows an almost Bismarckian indifference to popular sympathies and antipathies. Therefore it is safe to say that his decision was not determined by Bismarck's press campaign against

[16] G.P., IV, 400–406.

English influence. So far as the hope of securing an alliance was concerned, Bismarck's error was to underestimate the strength of British fear of entanglement in Continental politics, and especially Salisbury's fear of such entanglement.

In a more general way, however, it may be said that Bismarck was destroying his own policy. He always believed England and Germany were natural allies, whether the bond of union was written or tacit. Yet from 1887 to 1889, as in many earlier years, he was intensifying the old mistrust between the two peoples, encouraging German belief in English perfidy, and English belief in German brutality. While the interests of the two countries were so obviously identical, the popular temper was of importance because it was an obstacle to political intimacy. After interests diverged, suspicion and ill will showed their real strength, hastening and magnifying conflicts of interest, thwarting all efforts to compromise differences. English critics of Bismarck could not see that his political philosophy found a place for many aspects of a nationalist world; but Bismarck was no less blind. He could not see that national passions were an effective force, even when they jeopardized national interests. It was Bagehot, the English liberal, who diagnosed the weakness of Bismarck's political philosophy: "inability to measure moral influences as he measures material forces."

How the Chancellor proposed to meet the failure of his hope to encircle France is uncertain. There are indications that he hoped to remove the supposed obstacle to the English alliance by an agreement on colonial affairs: Germany would make concessions in Africa in return for Helgoland. Other evidence suggests that he contemplated greater intimacy with Russia, even at the risk of alarming England and Austria. More probably, he felt compelled to relax his grip on European politics in order to reserve all his strength for battles at home. That his position as chancellor was menaced, he was slow to see, or at least to admit. What he did see was a revolt, spontaneous and general, against his determination to eliminate, once and for all, the radical and socialist elements in German life. Specifically, he proposed two changes in the laws against subversive activities: the laws were to be made permanent, where formerly they had been passed only for a few years; and the government was to be permitted to deport radical agitators. Only in this way, he maintained, could the socialists be convinced of the futility and the danger of their activities. The prospects for success at first were good. The liberals were demoralized by the abuse heaped on them during and after Frederick's brief reign; the middle and upper classes were frightened by the violent strikes which were accompanying a slow economic revival. Then opposition appeared. The parties of the left were encouraged when, in the spring of 1889, William II intervened in a coal strike and forced the owners to heed the workers' demands. The hope took root that the new Kaiser would be, like his father, a friend of the lower classes; the demoralized left opposition began to fight with more vigor and confidence. Simultaneously, the parties of the right began to waver. They had looked on William II as their champion, not only against Frederick, but against the eternal shifts and turns of Bismarck's policy. They had no love of socialism, but they would be glad to see the Chancellor lose his reputation for omnipotence, and they did not want to risk angering the Emperor.

Over and above these specific motives for opposition, there was a widespread, though half-conscious, craving for release from long subjection to Bismarck's will. The very fact that William's views were unknown, or dimly guessed, made all groups see him as a possible champion of their interests; and William's ignorance made him see in this spontaneous revolt the possibility of establishing real harmony in Germany. Like his father, he had neither sympathy nor understanding for Bismarck's tactics. He knew these tactics were based on the premise that Germans were divided against each other and could be ruled only by setting one group against another. It was that premise he detested. Was this strife necessary? Was it not true that the fact of a common nationality, a common devotion to country, provided the foundation for coöperation? Did not Bismarck's tactics produce the tension which they were designed to neutralize? In the international field, William made the same criticism of the Chancellor. Why this incessant strain, this fear of war which might come any day? Would not simple honesty, the determination to coöperate, accomplish more than trickery and manipulation? These were doubts which troubled, not only the Emperor, but many another German. There was a craving for peace, at home and abroad, a real peace, not this struggle which was as tiring as war, without war's exaltation.

When it was all over, Bismarck summed up the issues briefly: "75 and 30 do not go together; that is the whole story." It was a large part of the story. Some sort of quarrel, and break, was inevitable. But the break was made more easy for the Kaiser and the German people by the conviction that, when the old despot who had so long broken every opposing will was himself broken, Germany would have peace. Quite naturally, everyone thought of that peace as the embodiment of his own interests and purposes. So events moved slowly to a crisis. The socialist law was not passed. Instead, William issued a call for an international conference on conditions of labor; a congress which, it may be added, accomplished very little except the passage of noble resolutions. New elections in February, 1890, saw a violent swing to the left. The socialist vote mounted almost to a million and a half. The government majority was destroyed. Bismarck returned to the possibility of constitutional changes, which he had contemplated three years earlier. The Kaiser refused; he wanted harmony, not new friction. In March, 1890, there was an explosive conflict of wills. The Chancellor's resignation was demanded; at first he refused, then yielded. Loaded with honors, a dukedom, a portrait of William, he was hustled out of the Chancellor's palace, so long his home. There was a round of farewell visits, stiff, constrained. Humbly, he visited the Empress Frederick, searching for that sympathy in affliction which, like all human frailties, he had thought unbecoming a statesman; and he received perhaps more than he had a right to expect.

After a moment of suspense, the swift current of German life ran on, unheeding. The impossible had happened. Bismarck was ousted, and so easily, with so little stir. "The aspen leaves of the Bourse never so much as quivered at the Prince's fall."

CHAPTER IX

A NEW COURSE AND AN OLD POLICY

WHEN BISMARCK fell, something snapped, in Germany and in Europe. The break was quickly seen abroad; more slowly it became apparent at home. Prince Hohenlohe, visiting Berlin in June, 1890, sensed the change in Germany. "Individuals seem to have grown larger," he noted in his diary. "Each separate personality is now conscious of his own value. Formerly the individual was oppressed and restricted by the dominant influence of Prince Bismarck, but now they have all swelled out like sponges placed in water. This has its advantages but also its dangers. There is no unity of will." [1] What he noted of individuals was soon true of factions, parties, and classes; they also became self-conscious and self-assertive. The internal harmony of which William II had dreamed was not achieved. Instead, by 1894 the Emperor was contemplating a coup d'état to enforce his authority. The change in the international situation was sensed by German diplomats. At first, foreign statesmen were uneasy lest the changes in Berlin meant that Germany would be more bellicose; when reassured on this score, they showed an increasing disposition to ignore Berlin. Soon it was obvious that the German capital was no longer, as in Bismarck's day, the capital of European diplomacy. By 1894, the traditional friends and allies of Germany were wavering in their allegiance, while France and Russia had become allies. When the second imperial Chancellor, General Caprivi, slipped almost unnoticed out of office in 1894, the international position of Germany was less secure, and the internal situation less stable than when he had taken Bismarck's place. The attempt to follow

[1] Hohenlohe, *Memoirs,* II, 416.

the Bismarckian policy of stability and security under new leadership and by new means had failed. After Caprivi was gone, the Emperor and his advisers groped for a new means of winning peace at home and prestige abroad; very quickly they concluded that a policy of imperial expansion, Weltpolitik, was the proper means. Weltpolitik, however, was the antithesis of security and stability.

In the history of Germany, Caprivi's chancellorship is at once the conclusion of the age of stability and the prelude to the age of expansion. In the history of Anglo-German relations also, these years gather up the threads of the past and bring in new threads, to weave a pattern which is reminiscent of the days of Richard Cobden and Friedrich List, but which also suggests the days of Admiral Tirpitz and Winston Churchill. It is possible to argue that the impasse into which the German government had drifted by 1894, and from which an escape was found in the glamorous word Weltpolitik, was the result of bad statesmanship. According to this line of reasoning, the difference between the Bismarckian Old Course and the New Course of William II, was the difference between government by a genius and government by fools. Undoubtedly, the statesmanship of the New Course showed few traces of genius, and more than a trace of foolishness. Nevertheless, it may be doubted whether poor statesmanship was the sole, or even the chief, cause of the insecurity and instability of 1894. It may be argued, instead, that the fall of Bismarck released forces in Europe, in German national life, and in German relations with England, which had been long in preparation and which the old Chancellor had controlled with increasing difficulty—indeed, that Bismarck's fall was one evidence of the strength of these forces. Which argument has the greater validity must be judged in the light of events.

In March, 1890, the Emperor and his new Chancellor were forced to deal promptly with two pieces of unfinished business. On the day before Bismarck left office, the Russian ambassador had returned to Berlin with instructions to renew the secret neutrality agreement of 1887, the Reinsurance Treaty. The English and German foreign offices had for several months been cautiously exploring the possibility of an agreement on the African claims of the two countries. William was anxious to demonstrate that the change of chancellors did not foreshadow a change in German foreign policy. Unhesitatingly, he intervened in both negotiations. At a hastily arranged conference on the morning of March 21, he assured the Russian Ambassador of his determination to continue the Reinsurance Treaty. On the evening of the same day he appeared at a banquet in honor of the Prince of Wales attired in the uniform of a British admiral, and, recalling Anglo-German comradeship in the battle of Waterloo, expressed the hope that coöperation between the British fleet and the German army would insure European peace.

The new Chancellor, with greater deliberation and caution, explored the relationship of the two projected agreements to the policy of simplicity, honesty, and harmony which he and the Kaiser agreed was the only right policy. A conference of foreign office officials considered whether or not the Reinsurance Treaty was compatible with other German treaty obligations. A conspicuous absentee was the Foreign Secretary, Herbert Bismarck, who was preparing to follow his father into retirement; a conspicuous participant was Baron von Holstein, a bureaucrat with long experience, great knowledge and, it was believed, sound judgment. Following Holstein's lead, the foreign office officials argued that the Reinsurance Treaty was not compatible with either simplicity or honesty. By this treaty Germany promised neutrality in all wars except a war forced on Austria by Russian aggression; but Germany also had a treaty promising aid to Roumania in case of a Russian attack. Even if the Roumanian treaty could be dismissed as of minor importance, Holstein believed there remained serious discrepancies between the obligations, expressed or implied, which Germany had assumed. By the Reinsurance Treaty, Germany promised to support the Near Eastern policy of Russia. But Germany had helped to create the Mediterranean Entente between England, Austria, and Italy, and so far as the Near East was concerned, the one purpose of the Mediterranean Entente was to thwart Russian policy. The real friends of Germany—Austria, Italy, and England—would regard the Reinsurance Treaty as sheer duplicity if they learned of its existence. Russia had only to reveal its existence to jeopardize the Mediterranean Entente and the Triple Alliance. Safety as well as honesty demanded that the treaty be ended. Such was the foreign office argument. Caprivi was impressed. He consulted the German Ambassadors to St. Petersburg and Vienna. They also advised that the treaty be ended. Convinced, Caprivi informed the Emperor that further negotiations were impossible. Although it meant breaking his word, the Emperor concurred. On March 29, the Russians were informed that Germany was not prepared to renew the treaty.

Alarmed by this sudden change of mind and fearing it presaged an anti-Russian orientation of German policy, the Russians sought to salvage at least the neutrality provision of the treaty, and offered to drop the clauses relating to German support of Russian policy in the Near East. After some hesitation, Caprivi rejected this proposal. In May, the Russian Foreign Secretary retreated still further. An exchange of letters between William and the Tsar would suffice, he pleaded; anything would suffice which gave a written guarantee that Germany had not thrown her lot completely with the enemies of Russia. Caprivi again consulted the foreign office. The new Foreign Secretary, Marschall, concurred in Holstein's opinion that any written agreement would imperil relations with the other members of the Triple Alliance and with England. On June 4, the final German refusal was given to the Russians; two weeks later the treaty automatically lapsed.

Caprivi endeavored to convince the Russians that German policy had changed only in that it had become more honest. He was profuse with verbal assurances that Germany would not attack Russia, or join in an attack: Germany had nothing to gain by war with Russia, and much to lose; William II, no less than William I, cherished Russian friendship, and recognized the need of coöperation against the forces of revolutionary radicalism. The new Chancellor was pained to observe how little impression his words made in St. Petersburg. He refused to admit that the rapid shift of William II from support of the treaty to opposition gave any warrant for suspicion or for the accusation of unreliability. He remained convinced that relations between Russia and Germany would improve when the Tsar had time to observe the transparent honesty and loyalty of German policy under the new leadership.

Meanwhile the negotiations with England proceeded apace. Bismarck's successors wanted friendship with every country. Because of the Mediterranean Entente, good relations with England were especially prized. Colonial rivalry was thought to be the only barrier to intimacy, and Caprivi had, if possible a lower estimate of the value of colonies than his predecessor. In his first statements to the Reichstag he denied that colonies were of value to the nation as a whole, and ridiculed the phantasies of those who believed that "it was enough to stretch out one's hand to pick up nuggets of gold and ready-made cigars." National honor would not permit the abandonment of existing colonial possessions, but he promised that new territories would be taken only if useful as naval coaling stations.[2] Feeling as he did, it is not strange that Caprivi showed indifference to the fate of land in Africa which loomed large on the map, and which colonial enthusiasts thought essential to imperial greatness. In Africa, he insisted only on two concessions: South West Africa must have contact with the Zambezi which drained to the east coast; and German East Africa must at some point touch the Belgian Congo—must not, in other words, be "girdled" by British territory. As compensation for abandoned African claims, he asked that England surrender the tiny island of Helgoland in the North Sea. For years he had thought Helgoland essential to the naval defence of the Kiel Canal, which Germany was cutting across her territory at the base of the Danish peninsula, and he was willing to pay well to get the island. He was, as he knew,

[2] Reichstag *Stenographische Berichte* . . . 1890, II, 38–42.

offering good terms to England; but good relations were worth much, and Helgoland, while useless to England, was invaluable to Germany.

Salisbury knew a good bargain; he also welcomed a respite from colonial squabbles and the prospect of less effortful intimacy with Germany. The concessions offered by Germany would leave the sources of the Nile, and the territories giving access to the Nile from the east coast, in British possession. He fought hard to keep a corridor from Uganda to the British territories in south Africa so that there might be an "all red" route for the much talked of Cape-to-Cairo railroad and telegraph line; but since he saw enormous obstacles in the way of a railroad, or even telegraph line, running from one end of the continent to the other, he finally agreed to the German demand that East Africa touch the Belgian Congo. In the south, he agreed that a long narrow strip, later known derisively as Caprivi's finger, should jut out from German South West Africa to the Zambezi. Helgoland he yielded, despite the Queen's warning that it was bad ever to give up any territory.

On July 1, 1890, the treaty was completed. It had a mixed reception in both countries. Discerning men argued that each party had given up land of secondary importance in exchange for more vital concessions. Imperialists were outraged. In England, the Cape-to-Cairo dream was ended, and its ending provoked lamentation. In Germany, the dream of an East African empire extending to the Nile was ended, and again there was lamentation. Salisbury defended himself easily: the safety of the Nile was demonstrably vital to the safety of Egypt; the English gains were easy to see on the map, and the losses—especially Helgoland—were hard to see. Above all, his opponents were men of his own party. Liberals found it hard to criticize a Conservative premier for too great colonial concessions. Caprivi had a harder task. As a new man, he was vulnerable to the charge of indifference to imperial greatness, a charge which he scarcely tried to controvert. German newspaper readers were shocked, pleasantly or unpleasantly, by full-page advertisements attacking a major governmental action.[3] The Chancellor's task was complicated by the well-meant efforts of Salisbury's supporters to defend the treaty. Admiral Mayne, for instance, ridiculed the idea that Helgoland had value, even for Germany. In the improbable event of an Anglo-German war, he contended, any British boat passing by "would probably throw half a dozen shells into the place for a morning's entertainment, and, if the Teuton showed his usual sense, he would as promptly get into his steam launch and make for the nearest port on the mainland." [4] Wide of truth though history was to prove such prophecies, there were many in Germany who angrily accepted them, and who contrasted Caprivi's simplicity with Bismarck's sagacity. Possibly it was the memory of the ill-effects of his supporters' applause which a little later caused Salisbury to urge the necessity of popular discretion. "When it is my good fortune to conclude a treaty of course I desire that my fellow-subjects shall approve it, but I desire no less ardently that they shall abstain from saying so, because if they do it necessarily follows that the people on the other side think there is something very bad for them in it, and immediately resent it and the embarrassment is very difficult." [5]

Again it could not be said that the search for a simple policy had borne immediate fruit, but again the Emperor and his advisers were certain that their right intentions would eventually bring right results. On every possible occasion the desire for friendship with England, like the desire for friendship with Russia, was given marked expression. The limits of possible cooperation were also clearly marked. No less firmly than Bismarck, his successors refused to support English action against Russia in the Near East. In every way except one, the traditional foreign policy of Germany was to continue; and that one difference was the substitution of honesty for trickery.

The center of German policy remained the Triple Alliance.

[3] K.Z. June 28.
[4] Hansard, 3, v. 347, pp. 922–923.
[5] *Times*, weekly edition, May 22, 1891.

Negotiations for the renewal of the alliance were begun late in 1890, but were not brought to a successful conclusion until May, 1891. To Caprivi's distress, the Italians tried to make Germany assume responsibility for the preservation of the status quo in the whole Mediterranean basin as the price of renewal, even hinted that Italy might make terms with France if the desired changes were not made. In vain, the Germans argued that the old division of function exactly fitted real national interests: the Triple Alliance should safeguard Continental peace; the Mediterranean Entente should enforce stability in north Africa and the Near East. In the end he was forced to compromise by strengthening German obligations in the western Mediterranean and by acknowledging at least the interest of Germany in Near Eastern stability. He was also forced to take on the task of convincing England that a stronger entente between England and Italy, if possible an actual alliance, was needed to restrain French aggression. With this task he got nowhere. As always, Salisbury professed sympathy, but pleaded opposition in the House of Commons as an excuse, first for delaying, and then for entirely dropping the negotiations. Finally, the Italians demanded that their partners in the Triple Alliance make economic concessions which would counterbalance the unremitting campaign of France against Italian finance and commerce. Caprivi acceded to this demand enthusiastically. With a fervor unmatched since Cobden's day, he was convinced that economic peace in Europe was an essential preliminary to real political peace. From an exclusively German point of view also, he thought a lowering of tariff barriers would be beneficial. Every year thousands of Germans left the fatherland for the new world. Everyone agreed that this emigration was a drain on the national strength. Caprivi argued that the emigrant left because he could not find work at home: Germany must export men or goods. To export goods, it was necessary to permit other nations to send goods into Germany, in other words, to lower the high tariffs of the 'eighties.

In December, 1891, Caprivi laid before the Reichstag the first results of his policy of economic appeasement, reciprocal trade treaties with Germany's allies, Austria and Italy, and also with Switzerland and Belgium. In general, the treaties called for a lowering of German agricultural tariffs in return for the lowering of tariffs on industrial products. They were introduced at an auspicious moment. An economic depression had settled on Germany in 1890; there had been a crop failure in 1891 which was already producing distress and which in a few months was to produce food riots. In this situation, the urban and industrial classes found the prospect of increased exports and cheaper food doubly welcome. Agrarians, on the other hand, could not fight vigorously against lower agricultural tariffs when the food shortage was obvious and acute. The treaties were ratified without difficulty; but the conservative parties had misgivings for the future of agriculture in Germany if Caprivi's policy was extended, and the Chancellor promised it would be extended.

The reciprocal trade agreements were intended to serve the cause both of international and domestic appeasement. Other measures of the New Course were more exclusively directed towards the attainment of harmony at home. Here again the change was largely in tone. To replace strife by coöperation, the persecution of minorities was ended. In Alsace-Lorraine, restrictions on freedom of movement were relaxed. Financial concessions brought peace with the Hanoverians who resented the forced annexation of their country by Prussia a generation earlier. Polish loyalty was courted by cultural and religious concessions, culminating in the naming of a Polish leader as archbishop of Posen. In the Reich and in Prussia, legislation was drafted with the objective of teaching the lower classes to regard the state as a friend and protector. New social legislation went beyond the Bismarckian ideal of security, and undertook the more ambitious task of regulating hours and conditions of labor, more particularly for women and children. A graduated income tax shifted burdens to those classes able to bear them. Local government reform in Prussia was designed to give the lower classes a sense of participating in the making and execution of policy.

At every point, the program of the New Course showed a

common purpose. William II was inclined to define that purpose as generous honesty. Caprivi defined it as a desire to lead the German people from the epic age into the prose of everyday life. Whatever the words used, the driving impulse was to end strife in Europe and in Germany. And there could be no doubt that, judged by immediate results, the new leaders failed. The failure in foreign affairs was dramatically revealed when the French fleet visited Kronstadt in July, 1891, and the Tsar stood bareheaded during the playing of the revolutionary Marseillaise. After that it was obvious that France and Russia were on the verge of alliance. A very secret consultative pact was actually signed in August; the two governments promised to agree on a common policy in case war threatened. The festivities at Kronstadt were disturbing enough, but when the French fleet, on its voyage home, stopped at Portsmouth and was enthusiastically fêted by the British, a shiver of apprehension ran through German opinion. For two decades, Berlin had been the center of European politics. Kronstadt and Portsmouth suggested at least that Berlin was no longer in control, even suggested the possibility of dangerous isolation. Earlier, the prestige of a dominant position in Europe had made easy the task of government at home. Now, waning prestige abroad gave courage to internal critics, and seemed to justify the belief that the efforts of the imperial régime to win mass support were really an evidence of weakness. Many beneficiaries of the new program made this assumption: Alsatians, Poles, and especially socialists, confidently demanded further concessions. Conservatives, silenced at first by fear of losing William's favor, began to complain audibly, and found a leader in the deposed Chancellor. Bismarck still had friends in the newspaper world. The *Hamburger Nachrichten* was known to be his mouthpiece. For a time he was content with occasional random criticisms of the New Course, but at the beginning of 1892 the bombardment became more vigorous and sustained. Wisely, he centered his attack on foreign affairs, where criticism of his own policy had been slightest. Commencing with obscure hints, he intimated with increasing directness that his successors had sacrificed the essential and durable friendship with Russia in order to curry favor with weak Austria and treacherous England. Less openly, he suggested that the new internal policy was sacrificing agriculture, the real foundation of German power and virtue, in a vain effort to win the fickle and unpatriotic urban masses.

William II could, and did, defy his critics so long as they were limited to the followers of Bismarck, agrarians, and colonial enthusiasts. Early in 1892, however, the Emperor found to his dismay that the rest of the German people were not prepared to follow him without reserve. As the capstone of their efforts to win the masses from radicalism, his advisers introduced a bill for the reform of Prussian schools. The central feature of the bill was emphasis on religious education, to be given by denominational representatives. The ministers frankly stated their conviction that atheism and religious indifference were allies of socialism; religious faith was essential to patriotism. The middle and liberal parties, hitherto the strongest supporters of the government, promptly and violently rebelled; to them the bill meant the abandonment of everything they had fought for during the Kulturkampf. A majority could have been secured from the conservative and clerical parties, and Caprivi was for taking support where it could be found. William, however, was appalled by the break-up of his mass support. His distress soon drove him to the verge of physical and mental collapse. To the Chancellor's disgust, the Emperor surrendered and insisted that the bill be withdrawn.

The first bright hopes of the New Course had been dissipated, but neither Emperor nor Chancellor could formulate a new policy. The school program was abandoned. For the rest there was nothing to do but hold on grimly in the hope that time would vindicate faith in directness and simplicity. When Bismarck went to Vienna on the occasion of Herbert Bismarck's marriage in June, 1892, imperial displeasure was made obvious by the refusal of the German embassy to arrange the customary honors. The result was to enlist popular sympathy behind the fallen Chancellor, sympathy which Bismarck exploited in angrily critical speeches. In July a new blow fell. Elections in England brought Gladstone back to power, now as always full of hatred for the "foes of freedom." The discomfiture of the Germans at this turn of fortune was somewhat relieved by the fact that Lord Rosebery, an imperialist and friend of Germany, was made Foreign Secretary. Eagerly, the governments of the Triple Alliance sought from Rosebery assurances that the Mediterranean Entente was unimpaired by the change of government. Hatzfeldt, the German Ambassador in London, vainly discouraged these efforts, arguing that, while Rosebery could safely coöperate informally with the Triple Alliance, any effort to secure written guarantees would bring the Foreign Secretary into conflict with Gladstone and the many friends of France in the government. As Hatzfeldt prophesied, insistence forced Rosebery to say that he had not read the texts of the Mediterranean agreements—that is, did not acknowledge their binding force. The most that could be wrung from the uncomfortable Foreign Secretary were purely personal statements that he regarded Austria as England's "natural ally," that he desired to coöperate with the Triple Alliance, and that "in the event of France groundlessly attacking Italy, the interests of England as a Mediterranean and Indian power, would bring her naturally to the rescue of Italy." [6] This was, at best, less than Salisbury had promised in 1887; and it was, Rosebery emphasized, only his personal opinion, without any binding force whatever.

Thrown back on its own resources, supplemented only by two weak, discomfited allies, and confronted by allied, rapidly arming France and Russia, the German government prepared for the worst. In November, 1892, a new bill greatly increasing the size of the army was laid before the Reichstag. To placate public opinion, the term of service was reduced from three to two years, although many conservatives and some military men opposed this concession. Honestly and in sombre colors, Caprivi exposed the precarious military position of Germany, faced by

[6] G.P., VIII, 89.

the practical certainty that when war came it would be a war on two fronts against foes whose combined forces would be greatly superior even to the increased German army. Practically, his speech was a confession of defeat: the "simple" foreign policy of the New Course had made the nightmare of hostile coalitions a reality. The Bismarckian press complained that the expensive military reforms were necessitated by Caprivi's blunders. The liberal press refused to believe that the international situation necessitated increased expenditures. In May, 1893, the Reichstag rejected the bill. New elections were ordered, and, to secure a favorable majority, government spokesmen adopted a tone of blackest pessimism. By a slim majority—so slim that the Polish deputies held the balance—the bill was pushed through in July.

The cost was heavy. At home, the prestige of the government was damaged by the admission, which Bismarck had always avoided, that war on two fronts was an immediate danger. The international position of Germany had also been worsened. Denunciations of Russian aggression had won votes for the army bill; they also aroused anger in Russia. To win votes, it had been necessary to awaken fear of Franco-Russian power; statesmen in Paris and St. Petersburg naturally concluded that the intimacy between their countries had already accomplished much in making Germans fearful. The obvious moral seemed even greater intimacy. So in the summer of 1893, Germany and Russia drifted further apart. Antagonism found open expression in a tariff war of unprecedented vigor. Simultaneously, France and Russia drew closer together. The climax came in October, when the Russian fleet visited Toulon and was received by the statesmen and people of France with extravagant enthusiasm. It was no longer possible to doubt that the alliance was a reality. As after Kronstadt, a secret agreement followed the public demonstration. A military convention providing for armed assistance in case of a German attack on either country had been drafted by the French and Russian general staffs in 1892. At the end of 1893, the Tsar formally approved the convention. The Germans remained ignorant of the exact nature of the bond between their neighbors; but a bond obviously existed.

One ray of hope lit the gloom which settled over Berlin in 1893: the Franco-Russian alliance menaced England at least as much as Germany, probably more. The new army reforms would discourage attack; besides, why should Russia, the dominant partner in the new alliance, wish to attack Germany? Possibly to win supremacy in the Balkans, but a war over the Balkans would almost certainly bring England in on the side of the Triple Alliance. France would be glad to fight for Alsace-Lorraine, but Russia would not sacrifice men and money for a cause which would bring her no profit. More probably, the Germans concluded, England would first feel the united pressure of France and Russia. In the colonial field, the new allies could hope to extort many concessions without war, and even if war came, a naval fight with England offered the possibility of more sweeping victory and less disastrous defeat than a clash with the German army.

In July, 1893, it seemed for a brief moment that the accuracy of this analysis would be demonstrated when England and France came to the verge of war over Siam. The two countries had long been quarrelling over French encroachment on this buffer state between Burma and Indo-China. At last Rosebery showed a disposition to take a firm stand; the French showed no disposition to halt. Caprivi pondered the right course for Germany if hostilities began. "From the standpoint of domestic politics, a war would not be unwelcome, if it was for a popular cause," he concluded. "From a military point of view, it would be as good now as later. . . . For us, the ideal way for the next great war to begin is by the firing of the first shot from an English boat. Then we have the certainty of being able to enlarge the Triple Alliance into a Quadruple Alliance. . . . Therefore: first make sure England is irrevocably involved, then—whether Russia takes part or not—bring in all the powers of the Triple Alliance, or Italy + Germany. That is, strategically, the right plan, and must therefore be carried out diplomatically."[7] The Siam crisis subsided almost as quickly as it had risen; a truce was made, leaving France in possession of territory already occupied. The German government was convinced, however, that there would be new crises; the French and Russians had discovered how cheaply victory could be won. Holstein worked out the implications of the new European line-up in one of his rigidly logical draft dispatches. England had been safe, he argued, so long as France was weak and had no allies; both these assurances of safety had now disappeared. As soon as France and Russia began really to coöperate, England must choose between perpetual retreat and firm defence of her interests. Now that France and Russia were allied, however, England could not defend herself unaided; she could do so only with the help of the Triple Alliance. Considering the traditional duplicity of England, the members of the Triple Alliance would be foolish to help her before she was so deeply involved in war that escape was impossible. Then help would probably come too late; the French and Russian fleets would probably overwhelm the unaided British fleet. Obviously, the Triple Alliance could not risk English desertion. Therefore, the vital interests of all parties demanded that a definite alliance be made before war began. In short, England should join the Triple Alliance.[8] The German Ambassador was to explain the logic of the situation to Lord Rosebery.

Holstein's reasoning seemed irrefutable to German statesmen. Now that France and Russia were united, they maintained, the arguments against admitting England to the Triple Alliance, arguments which Bismarck had so often and so cogently urged, no longer had validity. Alliance with England had been dangerous while there was hope of keeping the eastern and western neighbors of Germany apart; alliance with England, in the Europe of 1893, was the logical answer to the Franco-Russian threat of a war on two fronts. The members of the Triple Alliance would be more secure if they could count on the aid of the Brit-

[7] G.P., VIII, 110.
[8] *Ibid.*, VIII, 113–115.

ish fleet. England had even more to gain—in fact, England could not hope to defend herself against France and Russia without aid from the Triple Alliance. William II and his advisers were convinced that these basic facts of the international situation must be as clearly seen in London as in Berlin. The only question in their minds was, whether England would face the facts and conclude the alliance, or hold back in the vain hope of diverting the aggressive ambitions of France and Russia against the Triple Alliance. If England could set the Continental powers to fighting each other, she would do so; that, no one doubted. German newspapers and diplomatic dispatches were alike filled with warnings against British perfidy. The eagerness with which Rosebery and a large part of the English press had affirmed solidarity of interest with the Triple Alliance during the Siam crisis encouraged the belief that Britain was prepared to act honestly. Therefore, the German government proposed an alliance, at least between England and Italy, if possible, a quadruple alliance.

The result was disappointing. No sooner had the crisis over Siam subsided than Rosebery became more than usually aloof, pleading difficulties with Gladstone and the radicals as an excuse for his inability to continue the intimacy so marked during the crisis. The Germans saw their suspicions confirmed: England wanted, not allies, but lightning conductors. After frightening France with the threat that a war with England meant war also on the Rhine, Rosebery was lapsing into silence, fearful lest the Triple Alliance ask guarantees of assistance in case of attack from France or Russia. The Germans concluded that they and their allies must adopt a no less reserved attitude, not only because England was unwilling to promise aid in return for aid, but because friendliness towards England might actually turn French and Russian antagonism against the Triple Alliance. France knew well that England would not intervene in a Continental war. If it was believed that Germany would intervene when England was attacked, then France would naturally conclude that the safest course was to fight Germany before engaging England, that "the shortest route to Cairo was along the Rhine." As long as England sought to save herself by jeopardizing the safety of others, the Triple Alliance must avoid all appearance of seeking English friendship; when England had come to realize the hopelessness, either of combating France and Russia single-handed, or of diverting their enmity against the Central Powers, then loyal alliance would be possible. And that day would surely come.[9]

To German statesmen, the existence of the Franco-Russian alliance made an alliance with England desirable, but also made informal coöperation with England dangerous. An alliance would mean security; coöperation without an alliance involved the risk of a war on two fronts without the assurance of British support. Internal political considerations fortified the belief that anything less than a binding promise of armed assistance would be perilous. The Bismarckian press throughout 1893 repeated over and over, with monotonous but effective insistence, its attack on the supposed objective and result of the foreign policy of the New Course. The objective was asserted to be friendship with England, a worthless objective because England was weak and burdened by the hostility of France and Russia; an unobtainable objective, because England never had been and never would be loyal to anyone. The result of Caprivi's policy, the indictment continued, had been to drive Russia into the arms of France. That was bad, but, the German public was warned, a still worse result would follow unless the effort to win England was abandoned: to save herself, Britain would lead the Triple Alliance into war with France and Russia, and then herself draw back into profitable neutrality, rejoicing that dupes had once more rescued her vulnerable empire.

The apologists of the New Course were hard pressed to answer this indictment. The Franco-Russian alliance had come after the change of chancellors, and after repeated demonstrations of German desire for English friendship, notably, the colonial agreement of 1890; it was plausible to see a cause and effect relationship between these events. An alliance with England had

[9] *Ibid.*, 125–126.

not been secured, and few Germans, least of all the advisers of William II, believed that anything less than a written guarantee would insure English support in case of war. The Bismarckian contentions concerning the past could not be directly met; it was, however, possible to argue that there was no ground for fear or suspicion about the future. There was no ground for fear, because the Franco-Russian alliance was directed against England, not against Germany; there was no ground for suspicion, because the Emperor and Caprivi were not dupes, and would not fight England's battles. By these reassuring arguments, the attacks of the Bismarckian press were countered. "Toulon changes nothing along the Vosges or the Alps," the *Vossische Zeitung* complacently asserted; "it changes much in India. England is the power which will suffer from this union." While France and Russia were divided, their thrusts could be parried; united, they could be resisted only by force. Some English newspapers were advocating union with the Triple Alliance as a means of escape; but the *Vossische Zeitung* could only say this was impossible. "It is unthinkable that Germany should promise to protect India against a Russian attack, or to take up her shield if France and Russia attacked the Suez Canal!" Why should Germany surrender her comfortable security to repair the weakness of England? "Russia's real enemy is not the Triple Alliance—and least of all is it Germany—England is the real enemy." English praise of isolation had a hollow sound, now that Russian ships floated beside the French in the Mediterranean, England's weakest and most vital line of communication. Possibly by new naval construction and by coöperation with Italy, England might yet save herself; certainly Germany was not going to rush to the rescue.

Over and over, the same reasoning was developed in this and other papers during the months between the Siam crisis and the Franco-Russian festivities at Toulon: the new alliance was directed against England; only with difficulty, if at all, could England resist the pressure of her foes. The areas where British interests conflicted with French and Russian interests were meticulously described. Relative military and naval strength was authoritatively analysed. The British army was dismissed as too weak for real use—if indeed, the *Frankfurter Zeitung* ironically remarked, this crowd of half-grown boys could be called an army. Even the British navy came off badly in these analyses. Some experts thought it might barely win, others thought it would lose, if matched against the combined fleets of France and Russia. With relief, the tranquility of Continental politics was contrasted with the troubled imperial scene; against British danger was set German security. The certainty that Britain would try to make the Triple Alliance fight her battles was demonstrated by detailed histories of British perfidy; the certainty that the Triple Alliance would not act as a cat's paw was duly emphasized. So far the public discussion was in harmony with governmental beliefs and policies. What was conspicuously absent from the press discussion was a reflection of the official conviction that alliance with England was desirable, if attainable. There was some belief expressed that Germany could not afford to see England materially weakened; more often, however, the belief that England was facing defeat and humiliation seemed to occasion real pleasure. There was some hope expressed that Italy and England would coöperate in the Mediterranean; but usually the thought of any union between England and the whole Triple Alliance was expressly repudiated.[10] The publicists who defended the New Course differed from the Bismarckian press only in refusing to believe either that the Franco-Russian alliance menaced German security, or that the Emperor would be foolish enough to court danger by subservience to England. Whether—as Caprivi seemed to believe in July, 1893—public approval could have been won for a war in support of England, or for a quadruple alliance, may be doubted, although the Chancellor apparently had no such doubts. The German government was, however, zealous to avoid the accusation of undue deference to English wishes.

In 1890 the German government had been willing to make

[10] *Cf.* the comments and press summaries in K.Z. July 29, Aug. 1, Nov. 3, Nov. 25; V.Z. July 26, July 31, Oct. 13, Nov. 10; F.Z. March 13.

extensive colonial concessions in order to insure political harmony with England. By 1893, to silence opponents of the government, it was necessary to take a determined stand on colonial questions, even at the risk of impairing political harmony. In January, the British Ambassador at Constantinople was reported to be coöperating with his French colleague to block German railroad concessions in Asia Minor. Without waiting for an explanation of this "unfriendly" action, the foreign office in Berlin gave a violent turn to the Egyptian screw. The consul at Cairo was instructed not to vote for increased military appropriations desired by England because "the offensively hostile attitude of the British Ambassador at Constantinople . . . was not in accord with the steady support which English interests had received for many years from Germany." The British promptly gave way, pleading that there had been some misunderstanding; but, although quickly settled, the episode was long remembered in both countries.[11] Soon other disputes arose. Now it was a question of restrictions on the transportation of coolies from Singapore to New Guinea; now, British South Africa was accused of encouraging rebellion in German South West Africa; now, officials in Nigeria were said to be encroaching on territory rightfully a part of Kamerun. Each question was eventually solved, the most important single act being the treaty signed on November 15, 1893, delimiting the frontiers of Kamerun on the west and setting the watershed of the Nile as the eastern limit of expansion for the colony. But although settled, each dispute left a residuum of bad feeling which was made greater by angry press comments. The Bismarckian press saw evidence of the desire to prevent German colonial expansion in the slightest reluctance of the British government to make concessions. British imperialists demanded a firm stand against the "unreasonable" demands of Germany, while English radicals, who cared little about the questions at issue, were quick to point out that if France and Russia were placated it would not be necessary to pay blackmail to Germany.

[11] G.P., VIII, 185, 186; Grey, *Twenty-Five Years*, I, 9–11.

Count Hatzfeldt in London, compelled to set forth the advantages of a union between England and the Triple Alliance, and simultaneously to secure the redress of colonial grievances, protested vainly that the two commissions nullified each other: colonial quarrels increased British unwillingness to make binding promises of coöperation; the knowledge that the Triple Alliance wished to secure promises of political support made the British feel colonial concessions were unnecessary. Statesmen in Berlin continued confident that the English would eventually realize it was necessary to give way to both demands, because there was no alternative. "While all other armies, as a result of universal military service, can summon the whole national strength to arms, England can scarcely raise what is necessary for the defence of India and Egypt in case of war," Caprivi explained; "and while the growth of the French and Russian navies during the last two decades has been rapid, England has been forced to give up her claim to control over the seas. This situation can change little within the foreseeable future, even if England builds more ships; because of her antiquated recruiting system she will lack sailors and soldiers." [12] Helpless to defend herself, Britain must turn to the Triple Alliance; but she could expect aid only in return for binding agreements, and only after German public opinion had been conciliated by colonial concessions.

In time Caprivi argued, all this would become obvious—unless England was able to provoke a fight between the Triple Alliance and France or Russia. That was the one danger. It was a danger which could be averted only by eternal vigilance and at some expense. When the hopes aroused by the Siam crisis were finally dissipated, the Emperor and his advisers turned to the essential, though temporary, problem of insuring Continental tranquility. In February, 1894, the tariff war with Russia was ended by a commercial treaty containing the customary exchange of reductions on manufactures and foodstuffs. It took courage to make the treaty, because an Agrarian League had been recently formed

[12] G.P., IX, 135.

in Germany for the express purpose of blocking any tariff reductions on Russian grain. The founders of the League were influential aristocrats, and they were able to count on the mass support of peasant organizations. Any gain in prestige among conservatives at home which might follow better political relations with Russia would, therefore, be more than offset by the anger of the same groups at the injury to their economic interests necessary to obtain political appeasement. William tried to outmanœuvre the opposition by a dramatic reconciliation with Bismarck. The move proved a dismal failure. Imperial favors to the fallen Chancellor were interpreted as evidence that Caprivi no longer enjoyed the Emperor's confidence; the critics of the New Course attacked with greater confidence. The commercial treaty was ratified in March, but only after a stiff fight in the Reichstag, a fight which welded the conservative parties into a firm, unbending opposition. Once again a question of foreign policy had provoked dissension at home; the contrast to the days when Bismarck had been able to exploit success abroad in order to facilitate his control over domestic politics was painfully obvious.

The reciprocal trade agreement lessened the possibility of trouble with Russia. Real friendship with France was scarcely possible, but it was possible to prevent colonial quarrels from intensifying the craving for revenge. The Anglo-German treaty delimiting the frontiers of Kamerun threatened to produce such a quarrel. By that treaty, England left the vast tract of land between Lake Chad and the watershed of the Nile in German possession, in return for a promise not to advance beyond the watershed. The British had been willing to make the agreement because France also coveted this land as a means of obtaining access to the Nile. French imperialists dreamed of pushing their empire right across Africa. They also dreamed of jeopardizing British rule in Egypt by control over the sources of the Nile: according to current scientific opinion, Egypt could be flooded or turned into a desert if the waters of the upper Nile were controlled by easily erected dams. These French hopes seemed doomed when England acknowledged the claims of Germany to the territory which gave access to the Sudan. The British congratulated themselves on a very clever move in the African chess game—until Germany surrendered her claims to France by a treaty signed in March, 1894. The German action was probably legal; the land was theirs to keep or give away as they chose. The action was also understandable; why should Germany assume the burden of blocking French ambitions? It is easy, however, to understand why the British felt they had been cheated when they learned that the result of their move to eliminate the French had been to put the French in possession. The Germans were not at all perturbed by accusations of double-dealing. They had avoided a fight with France, and they had made an Anglo-French fight over the Sudan more probable. By comparison with these achievements, the anger of England was unimportant. The British might bluster, but their dependence on Germany had been increased.

In Europe also, Caprivi believed it was necessary to guard against British efforts to push the Triple Alliance into a war. Austria and Italy, in their eagerness to revive the Mediterranean Entente, seemed strangely blind to Rosebery's scheming, and no less blind to the fact that England needed their aid much more than they needed England. In February, 1894, the Austrian Foreign Secretary stumbled into what Caprivi thought a crude trap. After being repeatedly begged to acknowledge the validity of the Mediterranean Entente, Rosebery countered with the proposal that Austria and her allies promise to hold France in check if England was forcibly resisting a Russian attack on the Straits. England, he said, could take care of the Russian fleet, but must have the assurance that the French fleet would not intervene. If the Triple Alliance would promise to keep France quiet, all would be well. Austria was delighted; England had abandoned her alarming reserve, and was friendly once more. Caprivi, however, promptly and emphatically refused to consider the proposal. England, he pointed out, promised nothing and asked a great deal. If the British fleet was fighting the Russians—

England was to choose the moment for action—then Austria "and her friends" were to hold France in check! Who, he asked, was able to restrain France? Austria, without a fleet worth mentioning, could not; Italy would risk suicide by challenging France on land or sea. The British Mediterranean fleet was smaller than the French fleet at Toulon. Once the British went into the Black Sea, probably no threats would deter France from seizing the opportunity to achieve mastery in the Mediterranean. Certainly, threats from Austria or Italy would not suffice. "There remains as a means of pressure only Germany, who must show herself ready to mobilize. Whether this threat would not prompt France to join in the war even more readily may be debatable. In any case, a war on two fronts, a war in which we have absolutely nothing to gain, is too serious a business for us to provoke over the Straits question. . . . Under the Rosebery proposal we would allow England to decide when we would become involved in a war in which we would risk our last man and our last mark, and in which our very existence would be at stake, while England would risk only a dozen or so battleships, would probably increase her commerce, and certainly would not endanger her existence. If England wants to make sure of our coöperation, let her make a binding agreement with the Triple Alliance, in which the reciprocal obligations would be independent of the duration of Lord Rosebery's or any other administration, and in which we could attempt to obviate the possibility of a premature and isolated treaty of peace by England." Failing such a binding agreement, Germany must preserve her freedom of action "until the first shot has been fired from a British ship." [13] The Austrians repeatedly and desperately urged that Rosebery's proposals be taken at least as a basis for negotiation. Gladstone had by now resigned, and Rosebery was Prime Minister; the way was open for a renewal of the old intimacy between England and the Triple Alliance. Caprivi remained firm. He would consent to no agreement. Germany was trying to separate Russia from France, and success seemed possible. "We might jeopardize this

[13] G.P., IX, 134–137.

success if we gave England the opportunity to report to Russia any words of ours unfavorable to her on the Dardanelles question." [14]

The New Course had come full circle: beginning with the attempt to coöperate with all powers on the basis of loyal frankness, the Emperor and his advisers had tried first to win England, and now were attempting to regain Russian friendship, even at the risk of antagonizing not only England, but the other members of the Triple Alliance. German statesmen were far from admitting that these shifts reflected instability on their part. The alliance of Russia with France had suggested the wisdom of alliance with England; the refusal of England to recognize the need for alliance had necessitated a conciliatory policy towards Russia at least until, as Caprivi was fond of saying, England had fired the first shot and was therefore irrevocably committed to action. Whether or not consistency might be rightly claimed, however, it was not perceived by the statesmen of other countries, or by the German people. To the uninitiated it seemed that the New Course was a zigzag course, shooting off towards England, then moving with equal violence towards Russia, and meeting with little encouragement in either direction. More damaging from the point of view of domestic prestige, was the fact that German policy now seemed dictated by the actions and policies of other powers; this was not what Bismarck had taught Germans to expect, and it was not comforting to German pride.

The decision to abandon temporarily the hope of alliance with England did not imply the abandonment of the belief that England must make colonial concessions in order to conciliate German opinion. On the contrary, at the very time when attempts to find a basis for coöperation in the Near East were being rebuffed, new concessions were being demanded. For years, the Samoan Islands had been administered jointly by England, Germany, and the United States. The Americans were tiring of the disputes consequent on joint administration. They expressed their intention to take one of the islands and to withdraw from

[14] *Ibid.*, IX, 144.

the others. Promptly, the Germans asked for the other islands. The trade of the islands was, they argued, already in German hands; besides, the islands were useful only as naval bases, and England had many bases in the South Seas; finally, the German people would be much pleased by the acquisition of these islands which had been almost the first center of their overseas activity. The arguments were not without foundation. The islands were actually of little value except as coaling stations, and England did have more than enough of such spots on the map. As Sir William Harcourt said: "We have already got the lion's share; why should we insist upon taking the tiger's also? Not to say the jackal's." [15] The difficulty was, however, that New Zealand and Australia objected strenuously to the acquisition of naval bases in the South Seas by European powers, and the Samoan group was only a trifling matter of some fifteen hundred miles from New Zealand. Harcourt might think it absurd that dominions which refused to contribute a farthing to the imperial naval budget should expect England to quarrel over "this Samoa grain of sand." But Rosebery had neither the courage nor the desire to risk the charge of betraying imperial interests; he stood out for a continuance of joint control.

Again Count Hatzfeldt found himself pressed to attain the unattainable. Rosebery, he reported, would certainly not give up the islands in his present mood. The new Prime Minister was more friendly than most Liberals, but even he thought small gestures, such as securing permission to ship coolies from Singapore, were enough to placate Germany. Furthermore, Rosebery had been piqued by the refusal of Germany to accept Cecil Rhodes' plan for a Cape-to-Cairo telegraph line, to give steady support in Egypt, or to join in a new Mediterranean agreement. There was, Hatzfeldt thought, one way to convince the English that small favors were not enough to win Germany and that opposition to Germany was dangerous. Why not give the British a good scare by combining with the French to reopen the whole question of the Nile valley, using the recently concluded treaty

[15] Gardiner, *Harcourt,* II, 326.

between England and the Congo Free State as an excuse for this action? [16]

The Congo treaty to which Hatzfeldt drew attention had been concluded on May 12, 1894. It is one of the most amazing agreements in the whole history of colonial bargainings. Disregarding minor provisions, by the treaty England leased to the Congo Free State a huge wedge of territory along the left bank of the Nile, known as the Bahr el Ghazal; in return, the Free State leased to England a strip of territory twenty-five kilometers wide along the frontier of German East Africa from Lake Albert Edward to Lake Tanganyika. Although in actual extent the Free State gains were many times greater than the British, it was easy to see why Rosebery was glad to effect the exchange of territory. The Bahr el Ghazal was technically part of Egypt. Actually it was a wilderness without settled government. England did not want to undertake the expense of military occupation; but so long as there was no settled government, the French were tempted to push their frontiers east to the Nile. Above everything else, the British wished to keep the French out. The Congo was a neutral state whose integrity was guaranteed by all the powers. If the Free State could be put in possession of the Upper Nile then the French advance would be blocked, and there would be no danger that the flow of the Nile would be impeded or diverted from Egypt. It was a clever scheme, if it worked. The corridor between Lake Albert Edward and Lake Tanganyika was no less to be desired. German East Africa would be separated from direct contact with the Congo, and the way would be open for an "all red" telegraph or railroad line from the Cape to Cairo. Again, a very clever scheme, if it worked. It is hard to see, however, how Rosebery thought either scheme could work. The powers had guaranteed the territory of the Congo Free State, *as that territory was delimited when the guarantee was made.* Could a neutral state alienate territory, or acquire new territory? It was at least a debatable question; and the fact that the territory was leased, not acquired or alienated outright, did not settle

[16] G.P., VIII, 435–439.

the question, because the lease had no definite time limit. King Leopold was, therefore, in a very vulnerable position. England also had acted with doubtful propriety. The Bahr el Ghazal was technically Egyptian, but it was not effectively occupied, and legally England did not own Egypt. England merely was occupying Egypt, and her title to occupation had not been recognized by the powers. Even granting that the Bahr el Ghazal was Egyptian, therefore, had England the right to give away, or lease, Egyptian territory? This question also was at least debatable. Finally, had England the right to take the corridor between the Congo and German East Africa? When the Anglo-German colonial agreement was being negotiated in 1890, as Salisbury had told the House of Lords, "Germany absolutely declined to be hemmed in by our territories to the sea, and insisted on communication at some point or other with the Congo State." [17] To obtain that communication, Germany had made concessions elsewhere. Now England was trying to evade her share of the bargain by acquiring a corridor between the Free State and East Africa. When, earlier in 1894, Germany had surrendered the territory east of Lake Chad to France, the English had been quick to make a charge of duplicity, asserting that they would not have recognized the German claim to the land had they known it was to be given to France. But the Germans had not promised to keep this land, and in 1890 the English had admitted the German claim to contact with the Congo. If the Germans could be accused of doubtful honesty in making the cession to France, then the English were hard put to evade a charge of dishonesty in nullifying the concession made four years earlier.

Whether judged from the standpoint of international law or of ethics, the Congo treaty was hard to defend. Newspaper opinion in France and Germany quickly reached the boiling point; the French government emphatically refused to recognize the validity of the agreement. Possibly because the prospect of a new Anglo-French quarrel was welcomed, the German government at first took a mild position, merely asking that the corridor be

[17] Hansard, 3, v. 346, p. 1268.

moved back a few miles from the frontier between East Africa and the Congo. Hatzfeldt's suggestion that the treaty be used as a means of convincing England that it would be wise to conciliate Germany produced a violent and complete change. In a note so abrupt that even Caprivi thought it erred on the side of rudeness, the German Foreign Secretary demanded that the lease of land along the frontier of East Africa be cancelled. Simultaneously, Marschall got in touch with the French Ambassador and suggested coöperative opposition to the treaty; the Ambassador agreed with alacrity. A week later, Marschall went even further: only by the prompt withdrawal of the whole treaty could European complications be avoided. "England will learn that she cannot treat us as she pleases, and that our friendship is preferable to our anger." [18] The English response was vigorous, but it was not at first what the Germans had hoped. Rosebery protested that Germany was taking a tone "which she might properly use in addressing Monaco." He, in his turn, resorted to menace, warning the Austrians "that the style of the German note, though not unusual in communications from Berlin, was insufferable, and that if Germany were going to side with France or appear to side with France in this and other African questions, we must reconsider our position as regards our general attitude in Europe, more particularly in the Mediterranean and the East." [19] Similar threats were made to Italy, with much effect. The Italian Prime Minister lamented the quarrel between England and Germany: "From the point of view of maintaining the balance of power in the Mediterranean, the coöperation of the Triple Alliance with England was a vital question for Italy." [20]

Very quickly, both the English and German governments were forced to draw back from their extreme positions. Rosebery admitted that the acquisition of the corridor was incompatible with the Anglo-German agreement of 1890, and agreed to its abandonment. Somewhat lamely, he claimed ignorance of the

[18] G.P., VIII, 442–443, 454.
[19] *Letters of Queen Victoria*, 3, II, 405.
[20] G.P., VIII, 463.

earlier engagements. The ignorance, if real, was hard to understand in view of Salisbury's public statement in the House of Lords, and in view of Salisbury's later statement that he had left a memorandum on the subject in the foreign office.[21] Be that as it may, Rosebery's surrender permitted the Germans to retreat from their insistence that the whole treaty be given up, a retreat made advisable by the alarm of Austria and Italy at the prospect of losing English support completely. Despite French anger at the refusal to stand firm until the lease on the Bahr el Ghazal had been cancelled, Germany drew back to safety. Eventually France won out singlehanded, but success did not remove resentment at German desertion.

The ostensible objective of Germany had been achieved, but the real objective had not been achieved. After the success of 1894 the British were even less willing to admit their dependence on Germany and the consequent need for making concessions. The fate of the Samoan question, which had prompted the effort to coerce England, was sufficient to demonstrate failure: Rosebery persisted in his refusal to surrender the islands. More than that, Rosebery now held ostentatiously aloof from the Triple Alliance, and was ostentatiously friendly to France and Russia. Italy and Austria said with increasing frankness that the Triple Alliance could not survive if Britain was permanently antagonized. Although the effort to coerce England into friendship had failed, however, the German government could get some satisfaction from the applause the effort had won at home. England had been challenged, and forced to give way; Germany and France had coöperated on an important colonial question; Germany had shown a flash of Bismarckian independence and decision—even newspapers with little sympathy for imperialism cheered. For the first time an action of the New Course won unanimous approval.

More such popular actions were needed, many of them; for the German people obviously needed something which would force them to think and act together. Throughout 1894 the in-

[21] *Ibid.*, XIV, 300.

ternal disintegration increased, and the prestige of the government declined proportionately. Almost every decision of the New Course had alienated some group, or aroused dissension between groups. Conservatives were angered by the reciprocal trade agreements, and through their Agrarian League attacked indiscriminately the Caprivi administration and "Jewish" finance and industry. The attempt to give the churches control over religious education in the Prussian schools had revived liberal anticlericalism and made the liberal parties suspicious of other official proposals; conversely, the clerical parties struck out at "godless" liberalism and remembered the failure of the government to force through the school bill. Nationalists regarded the concessions to Poles and other minorities as little short of treason; the minorities, particularly the Poles, were alarmed by the demand that they give up their political aspirations in return for cultural concessions. Many conservatives thought social legislation was serving as a stimulant to socialism; socialists warned the workers not to be seduced by bribes from a capitalist government. Over the whole German scene hung the pall of economic depression, exacerbating nerves, creating fears and hates; since depression had come with the New Course, depression was blamed on the New Course. Increasingly, the German government was isolated from the German people. Criticism of official action became habitual and was encouraged and sustained by the fallen Bismarck, whose prestige in retirement became greater than during his last troubled years of office. Caprivi had no cure. He had tried to govern in the national interest without regard for party; now he found it ever more difficult to mobilize a majority from the quarrelling Reichstag parties. The Emperor also had spurned the thought of party rule; now he was frightened by his isolation and determined to find a means of escape.

The reconciliation of the Emperor with Bismarck in January, 1894, effected without consulting Caprivi, was the first sign that William was abandoning his determination to rule without regard to faction. The reconciliation was not sincere on either side, and brought little respite from attack; but thereafter William moved slowly if hesitantly towards alliance with men of property and wealth who might be expected to support authority. He was alarmed, physically alarmed, by the epidemic of anarchist outrages in Europe, outrages which could plausibly be blamed on socialist agitation. He lost faith in conciliation as a means of winning the loyalty of the city worker, and listened more readily to those who counselled repression. He suggested the revival of the Bismarckian laws against socialism; Caprivi feared a majority could not be secured in the Reichstag. Repeatedly, William returned to the thought of legislative remedies. Always the Chancellor warned of defeat, and argued that a Prussian law was the best obtainable; the liberal parties were less strong in the Landtag. In September the Emperor discussed the problem with some of the rulers of the lesser German states. They had a way out: if the Reichstag refused to pass repressive legislation, force a showdown; alter the constitution, restrict the suffrage, if necessary to secure a favorable majority. In other words, they advocated a coup d'état, the desperate remedy with which Bismarck had toyed more than once. William was impressed. He asked Caprivi's advice. While waiting for the Chancellor's decision, he made peace with the Prussian aristocracy, so long in rebellion against the Chancellor's tariff policy. It was unthinkable, the Emperor said at a state banquet, that noblemen should oppose their ruler, just as unthinkable as royal action contrary to the interests of his loyal nobility. He was cheered, because he was thought to have seen the light. Humiliated, Caprivi offered his resignation. In October, 1894, it was accepted.

CHAPTER X

TOWARDS CONFLICT

SUCH WAS the history of the first four years of the New Course. During these years Germany, and Europe, had changed. In 1890 Berlin had been, in a very real sense, the capital of Europe. The Triple Alliance, the one solid diplomatic alignment, was controlled from Berlin. Through the Reinsurance Treaty, Russia was linked to Germany. Through the Mediterranean Entente, England was brought to serve German purposes. France alone stood aloof; but, devoid of allies, France was powerless. By 1894 the lines of force had shifted. The Reinsurance Treaty was gone. The Mediterranean Entente had lapsed. The Triple Alliance no longer had the assured contact with Russia and England which these two agreements had given. The Triple Alliance itself was changed. Italy and Austria no longer accepted German leadership unquestioningly; both powers were alarmed by the aloofness of England, which they blamed on Germany. While the Triple Alliance was weakened by dissension, the alliance between France and Russia gained strength. In the old Europe, all lines of force had converged on, and radiated from, Berlin; to be outside this magnetic field was to be outside the field of effective action. In the new Europe, there was no center. The Triple Alliance, the Franco-Russian alliance, and the British Empire were the centers of force. The relative strength of the three, and the relations between the three, were as yet undetermined. But there were three competing centers, not one. Within Germany, also, the precarious but effective balance of the Bismarckian age had been lost. If the outcome of the new international alignment was impossible to foresee, the confusion at home was even greater. The uncertain or nonexistent Reichstag majorities, which tempted William to scrap the constitution, were the reflection of destructive paralysing competition in every part of German national life.

The attempt to follow Bismarck's policy of security and stability without Bismarck and without Bismarck's methods, had failed. Undoubtedly the attempt failed partly because of the deficiencies of his successors, indeed the strongest evidence of defective capacity was their belief that the attempt could succeed. When the Emperor forced Bismarck to resign, he tossed away not merely an unmatched combination of ability and experience, he also tossed away the fear and respect which the old Chancellor's name commanded. Others were quick to see what had been lost. In 1890, the ambassadors to Russia and Austria were among those questioned concerning the advisability of renewing the Reinsurance Treaty. They replied that the treaty had been useful in Bismarck's day, but now it was dangerous.[1] Many things which had been possible for Bismarck were impossible for men who had not his prestige. The Emperor refused to see, however, that the task which Bismarck had accomplished only by unremitting toil, must be far harder for anyone else to accomplish; William was certain that the toil had been necessary because the methods had been wrong. Simple honesty could do easily what chicanery had barely been able to do.

The loss of prestige explained much that followed; the loss of concentrated ability explained more. The new rulers of Germany were a strange and ill-assorted group, united at the outset only by boundless goodwill and equally boundless ignorance. William, relying on intuition and improvisation; Caprivi, relying on the rules of military strategy, counting men and resources, seeing only the obvious, seeking clear definition and finality; Marschall, the Foreign Secretary, an obscure bureaucrat whose influence is hard to discern in these years. All realized their ignorance, and therefore turned to experts for information. Experts on questions of domestic administration were not hard to find; Bismarck's relative indifference to the details of domestic policy had

[1] Radowitz, *Aufzeichnungen*, II, 321.

permitted the energies of able men to find exercise. Over foreign affairs, however, the rule of the fallen Chancellor had been so despotic that there was place only for passive instruments of his will. Probably a few of the ambassadors who had retained some freshness and independence of judgment might have made good counsellors. But the directors of the New Course showed no realization that foreign policy required more than enthusiasm, honesty, and organization for success. Unhesitatingly they turned for advice to the most learned member of the foreign office staff, Baron von Holstein. The choice was natural enough. Through long service, Holstein had acquired an inexhaustible fund of information on political questions, and the ability to marshal his facts in memoranda which were models of lucidity. Under Bismarck, he had been a useful servant, supplying information which the Chancellor could interpret. The difficulty now was that the responsible directors of German policy were unable to interpret the meaning of the facts and, consciously or unconsciously, often relied on Holstein's judgment as well as his knowledge. This was dangerous because Holstein's judgment lacked breadth and flexibility; moreover, it was often warped by prejudice.

Such was the group which light-heartedly took up the burden Bismarck had carried so long. Studying them and their actions, it is impossible not to echo Salisbury's conclusion: "One misses the extraordinary penetration of the old man." [2] With Bismarck, singleness of purpose was disguised by a bewildering multiplicity of expedients; with his successors, the details of action are easier to describe than the purpose of action, or the relation between different actions. Often there was, as Hohenlohe said, no unity of will; usually no allowance was made for the unexpected, the Bismarckian imponderables; always, a deceptive appearance of logic concealed inability to understand, much less control, the total drift of events.

Possibly the change in the character of German leadership suffices to explain the rapid shift in domestic and international affairs. Even before Bismarck's fall, however, there were power-

[2] Cecil, *Salisbury*, IV, 375.

ful forces working against his policy of stability and security within Germany, forces which he had controlled only with increasing difficulty, and which by 1894 were uncontrollable. Since the commanding position which Germany had won in Europe had been predicated on the lack of desire for new conquests, it is hard to see how that position could have remained unchallenged once Germany resolved on expansion. This is particularly true of relations with England. Anglo-German coöperation had been based on the possession of common enemies and on the absence of competing interests. Even while these foundations were intact, coöperation had been made difficult by popular prejudice. By 1894, the foundations were crumbling, and popular prejudice had been intensified. Better leadership in the two countries might conceivably have averted the conflict which impended; how, it is difficult to see even in retrospect. Lacking able statesmen, and the lack was painfully obvious in both countries, events moved relentlessly towards conflict.

When Caprivi gave up, weary and disgusted, it was obvious that the New Course had missed its goal of harmonious internal coöperation under imperial leadership. His removal did not still the wrangling of faction or criticism of the government. Neither William nor the new Chancellor, Prince Hohenlohe, had a clear vision of the road to domestic unity or unchallenged leadership. They could, however, hope to accomplish much by continuing and making more definite the foreign policy which Caprivi had inaugurated during his last months of service. He had set out to improve relations with Russia, and he had adopted a reserved, even challenging, attitude towards England. His tactics had been condemned by Italy and Austria; there was much talk in these countries of the approaching demise of the Triple Alliance. The British had been thoroughly angered, and were threatening to make terms with France and Russia. But the German people were pleased. They refused to take seriously the complaints of Germany's allies; they were sure Russia could soon be separated from France; they were relieved that the indifference to colonial expansion and the deference to England which their government had shown in 1890 had been only transitory. The *Kölnische Zeitung* earlier had been a cautious critic of Caprivi. It had only praise, however, for the last phase of his foreign policy, and dismissed the supposed mistakes and dangers of that policy with contemptuous irony: "Strange siren songs are wafted from England to our shores. We hear the lament that Germany is becoming increasingly isolated, that the Triple Alliance is about to collapse, that Austrian statesmen, convinced that the Triple Alliance needs British support, cannot understand the policy of the German Emperor, which shows scarcely concealed hostility to England." England, said these siren voices, wanted to coöperate with Germany, but could not discover what Germany wanted; England regretted German isolation, but to save herself, England must make terms with Russia even though the result was greater danger for Germany. All these warnings, the *Kölnische Zeitung* retorted, were too obviously inspired by self-interest. What were the real facts? The Triple Alliance was really as strong as ever, and as ready as ever to coöperate with England, though without overvaluing the support of a country which had no army, and whose naval supremacy was imperilled by the union of France and Russia. Anglo-German relations, the editors admitted, had not improved of late, but the fault was England's. In the first place, England had been quick to ask assistance, but had refused to make binding promises of support. Naturally, the Triple Alliance had refused a one-sided bargain; "so England is now seeking to induce some other power to pull English chestnuts out of the fire." Lord Rosebery thought he had discovered this power in Russia; luck to him! The second cause of Anglo-German estrangement had been the fact that "from the first days of German colonial policy, England has sought to bar German progress in the most petty ways." Meticulously, the history of British opposition was set forth as justification for a ringing conclusion: "Too long Germany tolerated this opposition. Today our patience is exhausted. England went too far. The English government can no longer doubt that Germany has the strength and the will to prevent further obstruction of her colonial development. There is no question here of enmity, or of hatred towards England. It is a question only of protecting German interests. The rulers of England should recognize clearly that they can accomplish more by altering their colonial policy, than by trying to frighten us by the supposed isolation of Germany."[3]

There is a remarkable similarity between this editorial opinion and a very confidential report which Hatzfeldt had made a week earlier. Hatzfeldt described a conversation with Rosebery, who had expressed regret at the increasing weakness of the Triple Alliance and the increasing unfriendliness of Germany towards England. Both of these changes, Rosebery intimated, were forcing England to attempt an understanding with France and Russia. Hatzfeldt rejoined that for years he had urged that, instead of making platonic declarations of sympathy, England should place herself definitely beside the Triple Alliance. By such action, the preservation of peace would be made more certain, and, in the improbable event of war, the fate of the British colonies would not be decided in distant parts of the world, but in the Mediterranean and the battlefields of Europe. To this, Rosebery gave the old reply: a binding alliance was impossible; informal coöperation was the most that the British people would permit. Hatzfeldt's comment was equally stereotyped: the German people naturally suspected the sincerity of a nation which was not willing to accept definite obligations. Suspicion was strengthened, he continued, by the selfish attitude of England on all colonial questions; even when territory had no value for England, as in the case of Samoa, German expansion was blocked. Until this attitude changed, no improvement in the relations between the two countries was possible.[4]

Hatzfeldt's firm language was approved by the German Foreign Secretary, who went on to analyse the possibility of a successful understanding between England and France or Russia. He saw no chance that England could grant enough colonial

[3] K.Z., Nov. 20, 1894.
[4] G.P., IX, 153–159.

concessions to satisfy both these powers; if she bought off one, Germany would make terms with the other. What would probably happen, he thought, was that England would toss some morsels to her rivals, and thereby whet their appetite. "The general situation in Europe would remain very much the same, except that England, through her onesided generosity, would have sacrificed another bit of her historical prestige which, founded on long-past deeds, has served for decades to conceal her lack of real strength." [5] Once again, the secret views of German statesmen were echoed in the press within a few days, when the *Kölnische Zeitung* published a long leading article entitled "Can England Wage War?" An answer to the question was sought from the history of past maritime empires, Athens, Carthage, and Holland. The conclusion reached was that England's overseas empire could be saved only by alliance with a Continental power like Germany. Whether the British would recognize the true path to safety was thought dubious in the light of their history, and the history of earlier maritime empires. "The newest effort of the ever-shifting British policy to flirt with Russia and France, her real enemies, is a bad omen. Just so there was a Spartan party in Athens, and a Roman party in Carthage—before their fall." [6]

Possibly these echoes of official views were not accidental; the press bureau of the foreign office may have served as a sounding board. Even if inspired, however, such editorial expressions showed that a newspaper which had earlier criticized the foreign policy of the New Course was now prepared to support that policy. And the *Kölnische Zeitung* was not alone in advocating a stiff attitude towards England. Rosebery complained that the German press as a whole, by its attacks on England, was making good relations difficult. If, at a time when grumbling was popular, the official foreign policy was praised, it is impossible to disregard this praise because it may have been officially inspired. Rather, it would seem that on foreign affairs alone were the Ger-

[5] G.P., IX, 160–164.
[6] K.Z., Nov. 27, 1894.

man people substantially united, and in substantial agreement with their government—as the policy of the government was understood.

The reservation is important. Undoubtedly the official German policy towards England had shifted between 1890 and 1894. At the outset, the Emperor and his advisers had sought coöperation between England and the Triple Alliance. To secure that coöperation, they had been willing to make colonial concessions. By the time Caprivi left office, all appearance of intimacy was shunned, and colonial concessions were demanded with belligerent insistence. It was this obvious shift that the German public saw and applauded. The German government, however, regarded the estrangement and the colonial demands as necessary but temporary preliminaries to alliance with England. Fear of incurring Russian enmity, without having the certainty of British armed support, made coöperation on the old terms impossible. It was thought necessary to be brusque so that England would recognize the necessity for an alliance. Colonies must be secured so that German public opinion would welcome an alliance. These were temporary expedients; eventually, England and the Triple Alliance would unite to withstand their common enemies, France and Russia. Whether the German people understood the ultimate official objective is doubtful; certainly there was little expressed desire for the attainment of this objective. There seemed, rather, a disposition to accept the temporary expedients as the desirable and permanent German policy.

If the German view of England had altered markedly between 1890 and 1894, the English view of Germany had also changed. The Mediterranean Entente, the formal basis of coöperation with the Triple Alliance, had been ended by Lord Rosebery. To be sure, he continued to speak of his desire for common action, but on terms less favorable and less definite than those which Salisbury had accepted. By the Mediterranean Entente, England had agreed to work for the preservation of the status quo in concert with Austria and Italy, and to discuss common action in case that status was threatened with disturbance.

In other words, there had been equal and reciprocal obligations, and Germany had not been forced to accept the onus of blocking Russian ambitions. Having shelved this agreement, Rosebery proposed that if England decided to resist a Russian attack on the Straits, then the whole Triple Alliance was to prevent France from interfering. He was not willing to promise definitely that England would resist a Russian advance. He wished to bind the Triple Alliance—including Germany—but would not bind England. Caprivi's refusal to proceed on this basis was understandable. On colonial questions, also, Rosebery was less accommodating than Salisbury had been. The Conservative had resented the German use of Egypt as a lever for extorting colonial concessions. The Liberal not only showed greater resentment at the old "blackmailing" tactics; he even expected Germany to aid in the task of securing French recognition of the British occupation of Egypt! A flagrant indication of indifference to German wishes was provided by the Congo Treaty. Even if, as he maintained, Rosebery did not know that Germany had insisted on contact with the Free State in 1890, he must have realized that the attempt to secure a British girdle around German East Africa would be resented. Even Hatzfeldt, who earlier had counselled moderation, was driven by 1894 to the conclusion that it was time to bring home forcefully the necessity of a more accommodating attitude. His advice was accepted, and the Congo Treaty was successfully challenged, but the British attitude was changed only for the worse. Instead of recognizing the need for political and colonial concessions, Rosebery began to explore the possibility of a settlement with France and Russia.

The drift was ominous. Germany had lost faith in informal understandings and insisted on alliance; England was unwilling to continue even the old political obligations. Germany, from indifference to colonial expansion, had advanced to the point where territory was demanded, as in the case of Samoa, without reciprocal concessions; England was less inclined than ever to grant these demands. German policy proceeded on the assumption that the Franco-Russian Alliance was directed primarily against England, and that England was not strong enough to hold her own without the aid of the Triple Alliance; aid which was to be given at a price. British policy assumed that Germany was the real enemy of France and Russia, and that the Triple Alliance was dependent on English support; when a crisis arose, the British would decide whether or not their interests would be furthered by helping the Triple Alliance. In the English judgment, decision before a crisis arose was unnecessary, while the antagonism between the two Continental alliance systems was so deep that it was no longer necessary to buy German favor.

If these conflicting assumptions and conclusions had represented merely the judgment of a few statesmen they might have been of transient significance. They were, however, deeply rooted in traditional convictions of the English and German peoples, convictions which had earlier been successfully resisted, but which now the governments permitted, even encouraged, expression.

Two conflicting traditions were represented in the Liberal governments which held office precariously from 1892 to 1895 in England. Until his final retirement in 1894, Gladstone was the leader of those who, as Rosebery put it, "early in their careers imbibed the sanguine and futile gospel of Mr. Cobden," or who, as the old Premier would prefer to say, remained faithful to truly liberal principles.[7] His followers, and they were many, clung to the hope that the Europe of rival alliances, balance of power, and frenzied military preparations might yet awaken from folly, that a real concert of Europe could be attained by a spirit of generous compromise. They clung also to the conviction that the ultimate triumph throughout the world of what they called free government was certain, although they could not deny that the hope of orderly progress which had seemed so certain of fulfilment a generation before had not been fulfilled. Germany, to such Englishmen, was the great enemy of right, both in domestic and international government: when Bismarck appeared, progress had been halted. Europe had not yet chastened German pride, but men like Gladstone could neither

[7] *Letters of Queen Victoria*, 3, II, 299, 300.

forgive nor forget. Rosebery was confident that these convictions were "evanescent and doomed," but as Foreign Secretary until 1894, and even as Premier in the year following, he was forced to make concessions to the still-powerful adherents of the old liberal creed. The most conspicuous concessions were his refusal to continue the Mediterranean Entente, and his half-hearted efforts to find some basis for compromise with France and Russia, actions which convinced the Germans that a tacit understanding with England was worthless and dangerous. In a more subtle way, the dying liberal creed still affected, and never ceased to affect, the English picture of Germany. That picture was a composite image, made by laying several imaginary portraits, one on top of the others. From the 'sixties was inherited the picture of a brutal, militaristic, and untrustworthy Germany, the Germany of blood and iron. The perpetuation of the image was the legacy of men like Gladstone, and it was seen by Englishmen who, on questions of domestic politics, or even on other questions of foreign policy, no longer saw through liberal eyes.

Rosebery was the leader of the growing Liberal Imperialist faction in the government. Liberal Imperialism is hard to define, because it was compounded of remnants of older faiths and of new half-realized convictions. Moral earnestness and faith in progress were salvaged from the age of the Great Exhibition, but both were divorced from their earlier association with individualism and cosmopolitanism, and related almost exclusively to the British Empire. The parliament of man no longer held the gaze of Englishmen; Rosebery preferred to contemplate "the future of the race of which we are at present the trustees." To the Liberal Imperialists, opponents of the chosen British race, opponents real or supposed, domestic or foreign, were enemies of God, morality, and progress. From the older liberalism was also salvaged faith in democracy, but a democracy imperial in extent. "We must recognize," Rosebery admonished Englishmen, "that our foreign policy has become a colonial policy, and it is in reality dictated much more from the extremities of the Empire than from London itself." In this emphasis on Greater

Britain, Liberal Imperialism was the heir of Dilke and Seeley and Disraeli's Tory Democracy, but these men had been, by comparison, prophets of narrow and static creeds, content to live within the territorial limits already established. To Liberal Imperialists, morality and progress demanded that the British race secure as much of the world's surface as possible. "We are engaged at the present moment, in the language of the mining camps, 'in pegging out claims for the future,'" Rosebery told the Colonial Institute in March, 1893. "We have to consider, not what we want now, but what we shall want in the future. We have to consider what country must be developed either by ourselves or by some other nation, and we have to remember that it is a part of our responsibility and heritage to take care that the world, so far as it can be moulded by us, shall receive the Anglo-Saxon, and not another character." [8]

The strength of the Liberal Imperialists, in number and influence, explains the seeming anomaly that the change from Salisbury to Gladstone in 1892 resulted in a quickened and more hysterical imperial advance. Salisbury was no Little Englander, and he had added vast tracts to the Empire, but he had managed to retain some scepticism and objectivity himself, and he did try to check popular greed. He was, as Hatzfeldt admiringly reported, a shrewd bargainer who made no attempt to conceal the fact that Britain had a good appetite; but he admitted the right of others to share in the spoils, and he sought to take wisely rather than largely. Above all, he realized that the popular appetite for expansion needed restraint rather than stimulus, and that if the resentment at home and in the colonies against the expansionist ambitions of other powers was not curbed, England would drive her neighbors into concerted opposition. Occasionally, he was driven to action against his will, as in the contest over the Somali coast. "In my eyes," he remarked, "it seems a coast without harbors, trade, produce, or strategic advantage. But as everybody else is fighting for it, I suppose we are bound to think it valuable." Occasionally, fear of repudiation by British opinion pre-

[8] Crewe, *Rosebery*, 254. Thruston, *Rosebery*, 182.

vented him from making concessions. He had at one time been willing to give Samoa to Germany, but before he left office the protests from Australia and New Zealand had forced him to withdraw the offer. Usually, however, he was able to satisfy the other powers by concessions which were not of vital importance to England, and usually he was able to take down the temperature of opinion at home by large doses of scepticism. He tossed the Sahara to France, and stilled the complaints of his supporters by remarking: "This is what agriculturists would call very 'light' land." He settled the fate of other parts of Africa with Germany, and defended the results by an indirect attack on colonial enthusiasts: "We have been engaged in drawing lines upon maps where no white man's foot has ever trod: we have been giving away mountains and rivers and lakes to each other, only hindered by the small impediment that we never knew exactly where the mountains and rivers and lakes were." [9]

Even during the earlier Gladstone ministry of 1880 to 1885, colonial problems had been made more difficult of solution because foreign powers had been encouraged to advance by belief in Liberal pacificism, while imperialists at home had compelled strong action by playing on the popular conviction that Gladstone would disrupt the Empire if given a chance. In 1892, there were the same delusions at home and abroad, but now British imperialists could count on strong support within the government, and particularly from Rosebery. His own almost religious enthusiasm for empire, and the necessity of enlisting popular support against the anti-imperialists of his party, drove Rosebery to the side of those who believed England should take everything while other powers should be allowed to take nothing. Gladstone's eagerness to disarm French and Russian hostility forced the Foreign Secretary to tread softly in his dealings with these countries, and even to give ground on occasion, as in Siam. Gladstone had no love for Germany, however, while Rosebery had no realization of, much less sympathy for, the colonial aspirations of Germany. He, and most of his countrymen, still

[9] Cecil, *Salisbury,* IV, 92, 323, 324.

pictured Germany as a Continental power. French and Russian imperialism, while objectionable, had existed so long that it was accepted in England as an irremediable evil. But Germany had few colonies, and Bismarck and even Caprivi had repeatedly said that Germany could not afford the luxury of more. Englishmen were only too willing to accept these assurances as evidence of a settled policy, and to brush aside evidence of a change in that policy, whether the evidence was clamor in the German press or demands of the German government. Even if Germany wished to become an imperial power, Englishmen thought the aspiration foolhardy. Experience had destroyed the mid-century image of Germany as a poor relation dependent on English help for existence in face of French and Russian hostility, but the belief survived that the hostility of these neighbors necessitated the husbanding of every ounce of German strength for use on the Continent. Since Germany obviously had all she could do to protect herself, she obviously could not afford the luxury of colonies; Bismarck had been right, whether or not his wisdom was appreciated by his countrymen.

Englishmen had not lost all hope of coöperation with Germany by 1894, but they were aggrieved, as so often in the past, by the failure of Germany to act according to English predictions. Until Bismarck appeared, they had been confident that central Europe would, inspired by the example of England, eventually become a liberal federation; even in 1870, they had hoped that the grant of universal suffrage presaged a liberal North German Confederation; in the 'eighties again, the impending accession of Frederick III was expected to inaugurate a liberal régime. On each occasion the British prediction had been wrong, and although the conviction remained that the German Empire was a political anachronism, this was poor consolation. On German foreign policy, Britain repeatedly guessed wrong. From the days of Palmerston, Englishmen had been sure that Germany was dependent on them for aid against France and Russia, but the Germans had persistently refused to recognize their dependence. Bismarck had oscillated bewilderingly; his successors seemed to vacillate even more. William II was the embodiment of inconsistency. To the British, the moral seemed to be, not that their picture, or pictures, of Germany were false, but that Germany was perverse and untrustworthy, a dangerous member of the family of nations, and a friend who would desert or turn blackmailer in a crisis. The temptation was strong to escape from such an unsatisfactory friend by making terms with France and Russia. It was an escape continuously advocated by Gladstonian Liberals, and at the end of 1894 Rosebery was exploring the possibilities of success. As yet, however, England offered her rivals too little, and they asked too much.

The Germans could justly plead that they were misunderstood by their English cousins, but it is hard to believe that relations between the two countries would have been improved had the English vision been clearer: the Germany which was taking form, now that the restraining hand of Bismarck was removed, was to prove far more dangerous for England than the images held over from the past and taken for reality by Englishmen. Neither can it be said that Germans had a clear understanding of England; they also were cherishing pictures of a vanished age and mistaking them for reality.

Economically, Germany had not been a "satiated" nation even in Bismarck's day. A story, probably apocryphal, tells of the visit of the fallen Chancellor to Hamburg. He looked out at the harbor, felt the strong pulse of the city, and turned away muttering: it was a new world, a world he could not understand. The incident is true in spirit, if not in fact. He never understood the world of modern finance, commerce, and industry, or what that world meant to his policy of stability. The first successful use of the Thomas process for making steel from phosphoric ore in 1879 was of comparable importance in the history of Germany to the formation of the Austro-German alliance in the same year. On the Thomas process was built the metallurgical industry of Germany which, within a few years, carried German production up beyond even that of Britain. Probably the meeting between Emil Rathenau and Thomas Edison at the Paris

Exhibition in 1881 was of more lasting import than the renewal of the Dreikaiserbund. Out of that meeting came the German Edison Company, later expanded into the Allgemeine Elektrizitäts-Gesellschaft; and the A.E.G. gave Germany a practical monopoly of electrical development on the Continent. Angra Pequena, Kamerun, and Togo were names made familiar to Germans in the middle 'eighties; less familiar, but of greater significance economically and even politically, were the branches which German banks were installing in cities all over the globe in these years. The intimate connection between finance capital and commerce and industry, later to be a commonplace everywhere, grew up earlier and more completely in Germany than in other European countries. Finance, concentrated from the outset in a few giant banks, brought new industries and commercial connections into existence, fostered their growth, found new markets, controlled policies and prices, compelled amalgamation into cartels. Like disciplined armies, the agents of German economic interests moved out into the world, with the branch banks as field headquarters, and the banks at home as general headquarters where strategy was planned. Concentration did not, as the British prophesied, dull initiative. Years before, Prince Metternich had described Prussia as an upstart, and therefore a gambler. The gambler's touch was apparent in the policy even of the greatest German banks. Investments which an English banker, trained to habits of caution, would scorn to deal in, were taken up in Germany without question. The risks were great, losses were great. The curve of German economic change read like a fever chart—but the general direction was up. Daring, added to minute preoccupation with detail, was proving no less successful in economic than in military warfare.

Bismarck could not see what this new adventure meant. At home it meant new social strains and a new way of looking at life. He saw the social structure of his young manhood, preindustrial, semifeudal. The appearance of a new class—rich, ambitious, self-confident—was subtly altering the relation between classes. The middle class was now divided sharply. The aristocracy of birth and land was set against an aristocracy of wealth. This new, dynamic aristocracy was increasingly imposing its moral and cultural standards on all German society. Disraeli, at the Congress of Berlin, saw and described one specimen of a group which was strange even to him. Interspersed with receptions and dinners by members of the old aristocracy, was a banquet given by the Berlin banker, Bleichröder, originally Rothschild's agent, but risen to independence through his financial services to Bismarck during the wars of the 'sixties. Now the upstart had built himself a palace and was entertaining the diplomats of Europe. "The banqueting hall, very vast and very lofty, and indeed the whole of the mansion, is built of every species of rare marble, and, where it is not marble, it is gold." After dinner the guests were shown the full richness of the palace—"the splendid saloons and picture galleries, and a ballroom fit for a fairy tale, and sitting alone on a sofa was a very mean-looking little woman, covered with pearls and diamonds, who was Madame Bleichröder and whom he had married very early in life, when he was penniless." [10] Here was a way of life very different to Varzin, a world of quick success, success which must be flaunted, a glittering world unconscious of limits on action, on thought, on achievement. The gambler and the cynic in Bismarck could touch this world sympathetically. He could admire daring and he valued Bleichröder's information and advice. But in the comments of men like Bismarck on men like Bleichröder, Jew or Gentile, there was a note of contempt, contempt for a class outside, contempt sometimes mingled with fear of these powerful barbarians. Conversely, the bourgeois giants spoke of the Junkers with mingled awe and contempt, awe of effortless prestige, contempt for refusal to recognize the real source of all power—money; contempt also for men who looked to the past rather than the future.

The new men were not content to rest within the framework established in 1871. Their imaginations leaped to a new Germany, a world power, not a Continental power. A territorial

[10] M. & B., II, 1202–1203.

empire across the seas might or might not be a part of their vision. More often than not, economic domination was thought of greater importance than political domination. At home, Junkers governed, but wealth had power. So in the world, let England take the land; Germany would take the markets, and the market was what counted. In the shaping of their vision of world power, the state was thought a potent tool, but emphatically a tool, shielding the business man, forcing open doors shut by other states, pursuing an internal and foreign policy designed to make smooth the path of the really constructive worker, the man of affairs.

All this, had he understood it, would have seemed an inversion of values to Bismarck. For him, the state was the master, business was merely one of many auxiliaries. Just as he protected agriculture so that Germans might not starve in war, so he encouraged industry and commerce so that the state might be strong. Political purposes were not subservient to economic purposes. Quite the contrary. He took up colonial expansion when politically expedient, and discarded imperialism when expansion became politically inexpedient. The explorer Eugen Wolf sorrowfully recorded an attempt to secure political support for an expedition to East Africa in 1888. Bismarck pointed out that a quarrel with England would result, and Germany now needed England. " 'Your map of Africa is very beautiful, but my map of Africa is in Europe. Here is Russia, and here'—pointing to the left—'is France, and we are in the middle. That is my map of Africa.' "[11] Imperialism, whether territorial or economic, was an instrument of policy, now used, now put aside for other instruments, all passive and controllable weapons in Bismarck's armory.

He had no knowledge of the half-conscious aspirations of the new aristocracy, he had no knowledge of the power of the new aristocracy. That power was not to be measured by the influence money could buy. Increasingly the well-being of the German people, even the possibility of their existence, was becoming de-

[11] *Ges. Werke*, VIII, 646.

pendent on commerce and industry. In the territory which Bismarck had set out to unite in 1862, only one German out of three lived in a city; when Bismarck fell in 1890, the cities held two out of every five Germans; by 1900, more Germans were living in cities than in the country. Roughly, the rural population remained stationary during these years; the jump in population from forty millions to more than fifty-five millions was an increase in urban population. The new industry was concentrated in the cities. Industry drew essential raw materials from the world outside Germany, and sent abroad the produce of factory and mill. The map of Germany which Bismarck had studied at Frankfort, the changes he had made in that map, these were no longer the whole story. He had drawn lines radiating from Berlin to the other capitals of Europe. Banks and ships and traders were drawing other lines, not only in Europe, but to the fartherest corners of the world. These new lines were growing in number, and in significance for the national life of Germany. They bore no relation to Bismarck's ideal pattern, the pattern of a satiated Continental power. A new pattern was becoming visible, contrasting sharply with the old, the pattern of an expanding world power. The contrast was invisible to eyes trained to see the facts of a vanished age; when Bismarck helped to draw the new, his intent was to make secure the old and progressively obsolete pattern. Finance, commerce, and industry could hope that one day the old political design would be swept aside because the lines radiating from a hundred German cities to the world outside could not be broken without mortal damage to the whole nation. Time was on the side, not of Bismarck, but of business.

Caprivi's reciprocal trade agreements were a tribute to the importance of the new economic forces, though in part an unconscious tribute. The primary purpose of the agreements was political, to insure European political peace by lessening economic friction and increasing economic coöperation. Even in this statement of purpose, however, there was a recognition that international relations were in part determined by trade relations. Tariff policy was no longer an exclusively domestic concern, but must be adapted to the needs of foreign policy. To placate the neighbors of Germany, it was necessary to lessen the protection which Bismarck had given agriculture. Caprivi was far from admitting, however, that in lowering the tariff on foodstuffs he was impairing the defensive strength of the country. He argued that the damage done to agricultural self-sufficiency was more than compensated for by the openings which the treaties gave to exports. The ability of Germany to support her expanding population was dependent on the expansion of German industry; to grow, industry must be helped to find markets abroad. More clearly than Caprivi, the agrarians realized that his agreements had revolutionary implications. If agriculture was to be sacrificed to industry, the wealth and the power of the aristocracy was jeopardized. Therefore the agrarians organized to fight the treaty with Russia. They were defeated on that issue, but they continued to fight with the tenacity of men who had succeeded in identifying their selfish interests with the ideal interests of the state. And in the end they were largely instrumental in forcing Caprivi from office.

In an open fight between agrarians and industrialists, there could be little doubt of the victor. Since the collapse of middle class liberalism two decades before, opposition to the aristocratic, hierarchical ordering of German society and government had been largely confined to the hated socialists and, less vigorously, to the Catholic Center. These were not allies upon whom urban industry could or would want to rely. Indeed, there was little desire on the part of business men to alter the existing political or social structure, provided they could get room for expansion without challenging the authoritative state. That room they did get, less from their own efforts, and less from popular sympathy with industry, than from allies who had little conscious sympathy for plutocrats, who often had contempt for the new urban culture.

The long drift of German opinion favored the interests of the parvenu aristocrats of the cities rather than the interests of the agrarian aristocrats. The agrarians craved stability, and wished only to safeguard the Continental position of Germany. Industry, commerce, and finance craved new fields to conquer, in Europe and in the world. From 1871 to 1894, security was the central aspiration of the German government, and, apparently, of the German people. Even during these years, however, the rulers of Germany had been forced to make concessions to another and older aspiration, the desire for growth. In the middle 'eighties, Bismarck had picked up colonies, at least in part to increase his popularity at home. In the second half of his administration, Caprivi also had sought colonies, frankly to placate public opinion. Both Chancellors had regarded overseas expansion as transient, subordinate phases of national policy. But in the light of German history in the nineteenth and twentieth centuries, the decades of stability were to seem an interlude; in that history, the right to live and the right to grow are inseparably connected. The connection was obvious in the 'sixties. After 1871, Bismarck had sought to put limits on growth, and while he ruled the limits were not oppressively felt. His dramatic speeches, his ringing dispatches, his meetings with other statesmen, all recalled the change from the old days of German impotence, and all testified to the fact that Berlin was the diplomatic capital of Europe. Thus aroused and flattered, Germans felt that living was achievement enough. The enthusiasm evoked by the colonial movement in the 'eighties showed, however, that the belief in growth as a law of national life was not dead. Bismarck could make Germans forget their hunger for new achievements, their conviction that 1871 was the beginning, not the end, of the epic; but could anyone else? William II and Caprivi at first showed no realization that they must answer this question. Even in 1894 they thought the national hunger could be easily and permanently satisfied, but they did know their earlier indifference to expansion was no longer possible.

In one way, Bismarck had helped to prepare opinion for a world policy. For his own political purposes, he had set out to destroy the admiring affection which Germans had earlier felt for their English cousins. Certainly his efforts did less to accomplish this purpose than did the English themselves; the memory of earlier English ridicule and abuse was cherished and kept alive by many who were not Bismarck's agents. Certainly also the old feelings were not destroyed. Admiration was made clear by imitation, even by jealous efforts made to detect some weakness in England. Affection remained, too, but accompanied by a sense of injury, an exasperated determination to win recognition as an equal from these island kinsfolk, and a conviction that recognition would come only after successful rivalry in fields where England had long been preëminent. Few expected the rivalry would end in war. Despite the violence used in denouncing England, the objective was obscure. Colonial propaganda readily found an audience, and the colonies obtained by Bismarck were valued only as a beginning; but there seemed little desire to seize any part of the British colonial domain, and there was no agreement on the other territories Germany should take. There was only a feeling that Germany should have a colonial empire, that England should help her to get that empire because England had all, and more than all, she needed herself—and that England would not help Germany unless forced to do so. Similarly, the thought of sea power was popular, but most German writings on sea power reflected jealousy of British maritime supremacy rather than desire to end that supremacy single-handed or by an alliance with other powers.

Somehow, without really hurting these cousins they admired, the Germans wished to force from Britain a recognition of the power and greatness of Germans. Just what they wanted was obscure, but they felt half-consciously that one crowning victory had eluded them, and the feeling was a persistent source of irritation, and hope. For England was old; Germany was young. And the young alone had ground for confidence in their future. That was the German refrain. It was not by any means the tune Bismarck had called. His jackals were ordered to create mistrust of England; that was an easy task, made easier by the English themselves. But admiration had merely been turned into the desire to emulate, and affection had been converted into a determination to force a recognition of equality from the British. Here also, the popular temper was much more in harmony with the needs of expanding capitalism than with the Chancellor's static policy, though this fact did not become obvious until the glamor of Bismarckian hegemony in Europe had faded. By 1894, Germany hegemony had faded. Bismarck maintained that it had been lost because his successors had driven Russia into the arms of France by their vain efforts to win English favor. The argument was of doubtful validity, but it was cleverly chosen, with an eye to popular prejudice. The colonial agreement of 1890, the Emperor's visits to England and his speeches advocating Anglo-German intimacy were received with murmurs of discontent. When, however, Caprivi adopted a harsh tone in the controversy over the Congo Treaty, he won applause. Ignorant of the fact that their rulers thought harshness merely a temporary necessity, a means of awakening the English to the desirability of an alliance, the German people accepted the changed tone as evidence of a changed policy.

Unwittingly, the German government had started on a path which seemed both safe and short, but which was to prove dangerous and impossible to change. The temper of the English people obviated the possibility of obtaining either extensive colonial concessions or alliance. The temper of the German people made difficult either the cessation of colonial demands or a more conciliatory tone in negotiations with England. Finally, the revival of internal strife, and the inability of the Emperor's advisers to find a domestic policy which would create unity, made a vigorous and successful foreign policy essential. Even Bismarck had been forced to rely on the prestige which he had won for Germany in Europe as a means of maintaining his authority at home. The "simple" policy of William II had destroyed the delicate balance between competing interests and permitted the clash of creed and class to break all restraints. In some way, the German people must be brought to affirm once more their unity. The easiest way to obtain unity was by concerted action against the world outside. The traditions and aspirations of the German people, as well as the interests of expanding capitalism, demanded that concerted action be directed to the growth of Germany from a European power to a world power, in emulation of, and competition with, England. Caprivi's fumbling efforts to chart a course which would give safety in Europe and satisfaction to what he thought the removable prejudices of his compatriots, had put Germany on a road from which there was no turning. Whether there was any other course, is one of the great riddles of history.

Certainly, the past two generations had made easy the conflict which was certain after 1894. Blinded by the past, the English people refused to see the necessity of making room for German imperialism, as they made room, reluctantly to be sure, for French and Russian expansion. Blinded by the past, the English people found it easy to ridicule, or to condemn as immoral, the aspiration of Germany to grow in the world outside Europe, as England had herself grown. Between English eyes and the restless ambitious Germany of 1894 there hung like a cloud the memory of those years when Germany had been weak because divided, and the memory of those years when Germany had won unity and power by means which, to Englishmen, were abhorrent to nature's god and fatal to the progress of Germany and the world. Between German eyes and the harassed but confident England of 1894 there were no less blinding memories—memories of the shattered hope that England would give sympathy and support to the aspirations of German nationalism, memories of Bismarck's contemptuous defiance of Palmerston and Russell, memories of Granville's resistance to German colonization and of his retreat, memories of Gladstone's strictures on German political morality, memories of snubs innumerable, snubs real or fancied.

Memory, and the refusal to admit the validity of political standards or practices foreign to their own experience, prevented Englishmen from making those concessions which might have brought peace, might have prevented destructive conflict. The past, the arrogant self-confidence, and the desire to pay back old scores created by the past, only partly explained the eagerness with which Germany was advancing to challenge England. The Germans were driven on also by the necessity of demonstrating anew to themselves the unity and power of their country. Here also, however, was a legacy of the past, of the disunity and lack of calm assured purpose, left over from the centuries when Germany had no national center.

No one man could embody the confused and confusing currents of thought which the leaders of the New Course were still trying to chart and to follow in 1894. Much could be learned, however, at a lecture hall of the University of Berlin where Heinrich von Treitschke was, in that year, completing his long and illustrious academic career. Since the day he began as a Privatdozent at Leipzig in 1858, the loud but half-strangled voice of this deaf man had held the attention of students in German universities. At Berlin, his audience included not only young men destined for service in the army, the bureaucracy, and the professions, but older men who crowded his evening classes. For all, his lectures were unforgettable milestones in their intellectual development. So great was his fame that newspapers reported his lectures as events of public interest. Evidently this professor had something to say which his countrymen wished to hear. Through his life and his writings much of German history in the nineteenth century can be relived.

At the beginning of his career in the 'fifties, Treitschke was, like most academicians of that day, a liberal and a nationalist; like many other German historians, he studied the past in order to prophesy the future. For his students at Leipzig and later at Freiburg, he drew verbal pictures of the past glories of Germany, anguished pictures of contemporary Germany, and great cloud pictures of a future Germany, strong and glorious, united under the leadership of Prussia. To show what was possible for Germany, he drew idealized pictures of England, describing her as a Germanic country which, by good fortune and good sense, had won the blessings of unity, strength, and liberty; a country loyal to its historical traditions, yet able peaceably to adapt these traditions to new conditions of life; a country whose citizens were filled with national pride without being arrogant, neither denying the virtues of other nations nor seeking to impose English ways on other peoples. Here was a country Germans might study as a model, a national life which Germans might set as a goal. Germans, he argued, could even aim higher, because Germans had virtues denied to Englishmen—more penetrating and personal moral vision, intellectual capacity more akin to ancient Greece than to the pragmatic, limited thought of England. When to these virtues of mind and spirit was added life in a free, united state, Germany would herself be the model which others would study.

In the 'sixties, again like his contemporaries, Treitschke was forced to choose between his liberalism and his nationalism. At first, he tried to remain loyal to both ideals. In 1866, on the eve of the war with Austria, Bismarck offered him a chair at the University of Berlin if he would act as a scholarly press agent. The offer was tempting, not only because a post at Berlin was the goal of every nationalist scholar, but because Treitschke's approaching marriage made financial security essential. Nevertheless, he refused; he would not serve Bismarck until the Prussian constitution was respected. He was a nationalist, but he was also a liberal. As a liberal, he rebuffed Bismarck. As a nationalist, he resigned his chair at Freiburg when Baden joined Austria in the war. When, however, Austria had been ejected from Germany, and when it became obvious that German unity was near, Treitschke hastened to forgive Bismarck's defiance of the Prussian constitution, and to convince himself that the strong Prussian monarchy was far better for Germans than the liberal government he had earlier desired. Nationalism had conquered liberalism. Thereafter, in his lectures and his writings, Prussian history became a God-inspired preparation for German unity. France became the villain of modern history. England faded into the background. When the war with France came, he drew arguments for the seizure of Alsace-Lorraine from his store of history. The provinces must be German because God had placed on Germany the obligation of securing the future peace of the world, and because the Alsatians were lost children who must be reclaimed. That the people of Alsace-Lorraine had no wish to be Germans was irrelevant. "We have seen with joyful wonder the undying power of the moral forces of history, manifested far too frequently in the immense changes of these days, to place much confidence in the value of a mere popular disinclination. The spirit of a nation lays hold, not only of the generations which live beside it, but of those which are before and behind it." [12]

During the Franco-Prussian war, when German political unity was being completed, Treitschke laid on himself the task of aiding in the consolidation of victory. Germany now had a state, but Germans were, he felt, not yet aware of their greatness and their destiny. So far as the "weak pen" and his voice could serve, he would awaken his countrymen. His vehicle would be history. In 1871 he began work on the *History of Germany in the Nineteenth Century*, which was to occupy a large part of his time during the remainder of his life. The preface to the first volume clearly stated his purpose. Germany lacked a national historical tradition; he would lay the foundation for this tradition. "No nation has greater cause than we to hold in honor the memory of its struggling fathers, or recalls so seldom how through blood and tears, this labor of brain and of hand, the blessing of its unity has been achieved."

The nationalist purpose of the *History* is apparent from the first page to the last. Always Prussia was right; always her opponents, whether the other German states or foreign powers, were wrong. It was not strange that he should make villains of Metternich and of French statesmen; but the venomous hatred shown for England and Englishmen reflected the disillusionment of the years of unification. To him, Palmerston embodied English arrogance and English duplicity. Using the catchwords of liberalism and conservatism as a means of dividing the Continental powers against each other, Palmerston was long able to prevent concerted opposition to Britain; but fortunately for Europe, he overreached himself. "Ultimately the boundless arro-

[12] Treitschke, *Germany, France . . .*, 105

gance of England became intolerable to the pride of her neighbors." Mistrust, then hatred, then contempt for British statesmanship spread as the Continental powers came to understand "the most sacred principle of the British, the principle that England alone is entitled to deceive other powers." By Palmerston's death, Treitschke triumphantly pointed out, England scarcely ranked as a great European power.[13] This supposed decline of Britain made a good foil for the main theme of the *History*, the rise of Germany; with equal dramatic effect, Treitschke contrasted the internal decay of England against the triumph of German virtue. In centuries past, he argued, England had been the altogether admirable country which many Germans still thought her, but trade had rotted away the old virtues. "While the German gentry remained poor but knightly, in England old conceptions of honor and established prejudices of caste were undermined by the potency of money." The duel, "the indispensable and ultimate recourse against the degradation of society," died out. Tradesmen's ideals became the national ideals. On the one hand, there was the false optimism of Adam Smith "which completely ignored the two great forces of universal history, the force of stupidity and the force of sin." On the other, was Bentham's utilitarianism. "This gospel of the service of Mammon threatened to mutilate mankind, to lop off from the emotional life all heroic elements, everything that was sublime and beautiful, everything that was ideal." [14]

In Germany, Treitschke's *History* had the success he hoped for. Many of his colleagues were antagonized by his violence and his frank bias, but for the German people this became *the* German history. They were enthralled by the humor, by the pictorial power, and by the patriotism which breathed through every page. Foreigners were outraged, but Treitschke was unperturbed. "I write for Germans. Much water will flow down the Rhine before foreigners will permit us to speak of our country with the pride that has ever characterized the treatises on national history com-

[13] Treitschke, *History*, V, 34–37; VII, 547.
[14] *Ibid.*, VII, 220, 256 *ff*.

posed by Englishmen and by Frenchmen. But even the foreign world will some day have to accustom itself to the sentiments of New Germany." [15]

The *History* served to nourish German national pride by recounting the past. In the columns of the *Preussische Jahrbücher* Treitschke fought the contemporary enemies of the German spirit with an even sharper pen. Jews, Catholics, socialists, and democrats were the enemies at home. Abroad, Germany's Continental position seemed secured against French revenge by Bismarck's alliances and by the great German army. Germany's one dangerous opponent was across the North Sea. England was dangerous, Treitschke contended, partly because so many Germans still foolishly admired her government and trusted her policy, partly because of the skill with which England played the Continental states against each other to her own advantage. Germans must be made to understand that a conflict between Britain and Germany lay in the nature of things: two such great powers could not live side by side peaceably until they had measured their strength, one against the other. "We have already had our reckoning with Austria, France and Russia. The final reckoning with England will apparently be the longest and hardest, because here we are confronted with a policy which for centuries, almost unimpeded by other powers, has moved towards the objective of maritime world supremacy." Fortunately, Germany entered the lists against England with advantages earlier Continental contestants had not possessed. The "mountain of evil and cruelty" built during her imperial expansion weighed heavily on Britain; the very size of the empire made it increasingly difficult for England to exert effective power in Europe; above all, Germany had on her side "the great and well-formed hate which all peoples have slowly come to feel for England." In an age of national states and national armies, the British Empire was "an obvious anachronism," a relic of the days of sea fights and mercenary armies. He thought it inevitable that the Mediterranean must come under the control of Mediterranean states, led by national

[15] *Ibid.*, V, 611.

Italy. Inevitably also, the Continental states must insist on a larger voice in maritime and colonial affairs. "Over-rich and over-satisfied, vulnerable at a hundred points of their far-flung possessions," the British sought only to keep things as they were, opposing the forces of progress, opposing every new and hopeful power or idea in world politics. In his opinion, it was neither necessary nor probable that rivalry would lead to war. Germany asked only for a balance of power in the colonial field. The other Continental states had the same objectives. England, he concluded, must retreat before this united front.[16]

The *History*, and Treitschke's publicist writings, were designed to overcome what he thought the too-weak national pride of the German people. The same purpose is apparent in his lectures. In 1874 he obtained the coveted professorship at Berlin. There, as earlier in Saxony and Baden, his students regarded him as more than a teacher of past history; to them he was a prophet. Treitschke's own favorite was the course on politics, lectures upon which he worked for thirty years in the hope that out of them would grow a definitive work on political science. The hope was never realized, but after his death the lectures were published from students' notes. Despite the unevenness and the inaccuracies inevitable in volumes based on lectures as reported by students, the *Politics* is Treitschke's most important work for those who would understand German thought at the end of the nineteenth century.

Only in Germany, Treitschke argued, was it possible to create a science of politics, and even in Germany such an achievement had only become possible during the past century. Between the days of ancient Greece and eighteenth-century Germany, thought about politics had been dominated by catchwords without relation to reality: natural law, state of nature, social contract. These catchwords still held the allegiance of western Europe outside Germany, and their sway explained the monstrous political conceptions of the west. Two fallacious theories he had already disposed of in his *History*. The rationalistic system of Adam Smith

[16] *Deutsche Kämpfe*, II, 349–352; *Germany, France . . .*, 13–15.

blithely disregarded the fact that human stupidity and wickedness existed and must be controlled; laissez-faire would permit the evil in man free play. At the other extreme was Jeremy Bentham, with his mole-like view of human nature. To Bentham and the other utilitarians, the richness of human nature was invisible; they saw only pleasure and pain, and these in their lowest forms. Smith and Bentham he used to illustrate the futility of western thought, with its belief that the universe was governed by fixed natural laws, laws which the human reason could discover, laws which must inevitably bring the greatest possible happiness to man if they were obeyed. Belief in natural law, he contended, had been fatal to political science. Western thinkers produced out of their heads a model state, the model state for all peoples; they said this state existed only by virtue of a contract, and that no one need obey the state if the contract were broken; they prescribed for their model state obedience to the same "natural" laws which individuals were bound to obey.

Where in history did such a state exist? When German thinkers asked this one question, Treitschke declared, the whole natural law school of political science was shown to be futile logic-chopping. For the answer to the question was obvious. Nowhere in history could such a state be found. Here he saw the first great achievement of German thought: truth was to be found, not in the fictitious creations of the human mind, but in experience as recorded in history. Since the days of Herder in the eighteenth century, true German scholarship had accepted the testimony of experience as its only guide; politics, like all other humane studies, became applied history. In history, Treitschke continued, not only was the natural law state to be sought in vain, the very idea of a universal, unchanging law was seen to be without foundation. History showed, not uniformity, but endless variety, individuality. The second achievement of German thought was to break the neat mould of law into which the natural law school had tried to force all human experience, and to show instead that every individual was a law unto himself.

The greatest achievement of the Germans, in his opinion, was the demonstration that groups of men had personalities no less real and no less individual than men taken separately. The Catholic Church, the Anglican Church, the Reformed Church, each was an individual personality with its own wants, fears, hopes, in short, its own law of life. Individuals had certain common characteristics as human beings, and were at the same time peculiar, distinct persons; so groups like churches each had resemblances to other churches, but each also had a distinct personality.

The State as personality—"the most supremely real person, in the literal sense of the word, that exists"—was the central theme of the *Politics*. The stamp of personality was deep and lasting, Treitschke maintained, independent of the wills and purposes of the men who happened to be the government at any time, independent too, of transient national passion or even revolutionary disturbance. The personality grew out of the whole history of the national society, out of past triumphs and disasters as well as the present size, moral and physical resources, and world position of the national society. He saw the world peopled by these great personalities, each limited, but each in some way representing the highest reach of man's efforts, and in the great drama of the lives of states he saw objectively revealed the Will of God. "The rays of the Divine light are manifested, broken by countless facets among the separate peoples, each one exhibiting another picture and another idea of the whole. Every people has a right to believe that certain attributes of the Divine reason are exhibited in it to their fullest perfection." [17]

The essence of state personality was, according to Treitschke, the will to live and to grow; and the sole means to give effect to this will was power. Just here lay the greatness of Machiavelli. While political thought was still shrouded in error, Machiavelli had the genius to see, and the courage to say, "the State is Power." Over and over, Treitschke came back to the central importance of power. Weakness was the unforgivable sin of politics. The first duty of the statesman was to preserve and strengthen the power of the state, no matter what the cost. Growth, existence it-

[17] *Politics*, I, 17–19.

self, was impossible without power. Every aspect of national life must be so guided as to strengthen the national power, but the army was the great reservoir of power. Therefore the army must be a truly national army, recruited by universal service, and no expense must be spared to keep the army at the highest peak of efficiency. The very existence of a strong, national army was assurance that the power of the state would be recognized both at home and abroad, but he insisted that the cardinal fact must not be evaded—armies were for use in war. War was the ultimate argument, the *examen rigorosum,* in which peoples must show their mettle. "Brave peoples alone have an existence, an evolution or a future; the weak and cowardly perish, and perish justly. The grandeur of history lies in the perpetual conflict of nations." [18]

Much more Treitschke learned from history in his quest for generalizations on the nature of the state and on those forces in national life which make for the strength of the state. But as the reader proceeds he becomes aware of a curious fact: all history testified that, potentially, Germany was the ideal state. A survey of all known constitutional forms of government ends with the conclusion that the triumph of Prussian institutions in Germany was justified, not only because they were the most perfect German institutions, but because they were the most perfect institutions yet devised by man. The constitution of 1871 could be improved only by eliminating remnants of the institutions of other German states and extending Prussian institutions over a completely unified Empire. Similarly, the German people possessed every virtue necessary for the health of the state except confidence in their qualities. Germans, he complained, had not yet developed real national pride, were still too willing to think of other peoples, particularly the English, as better than themselves. In the hope of overcoming that defect, he ceaselessly extolled German valor and the German mind, often at the expense of other nations: the French were born calculators, while the German was a hero born; the excessive cosmopolitanism of Ger-

[18] *Ibid.,* I, 21, 84, 89, 94–104; II, 395, 396.

many was preferable to English narrow insularity. "The Latin has no feeling for the beauty of a forest; when he takes his repose in it he lies on his stomach, while we rest on our backs." "The climate, this want of wine, and lack of beautiful scenery have all been obstacles in the way of English culture."[19]

History revealed to Treitschke the future needs of Germany also. The drift of history was towards the domination of the world by a few great powers, a progressive trend because the large state was in every way more noble than the small state. Territorial growth must be largely overseas, colonial. Other nations were fast appropriating the free spaces; Germany must join in the movement or be relegated to a minor place in the council of nations. "The outcome of our next successful war must be the acquisition of colonies by any possible means." To be ready a fleet must be built: "This Germany of ours was once the greatest of the sea powers and, God willing, so she will be again." For a fleet, adequate sea-coast was essential; here was another task. It was intolerable that the mouths of the German Rhine were in alien hands; therefore Holland must be forced to enter the German customs union. "Nowhere in the world is there so much declamation about chauvinism as in Germany, and nowhere is there so little of it to be found. We hesitate to express even the most natural demands that a nation can make for itself."[20]

Here was a coherent view of life and a thoroughly German view of life. History was the story of the life and death of states, state personalities created and guided by the Will of God; each state seeking to live and grow, battling with other states for the chance to live and grow; to the powerful went victory, but power was from God, so that victory or defeat, domination or extinction, were alike the verdict of God. Both in his conclusions and in the premises upon which he built his conclusions, Treitschke was working in a tradition which, as he said, had been growing in Germany for a century. Germans firmly believed that history was the only guide to truth about human affairs. Before Darwin

[19] *Ibid.*, I, 206, 223, 230, 231, 274, 275.
[20] *Ibid.*, I, 33–36, 116–119, 213, 219.

was born, the idea of evolution was a commonplace in Germany. While Bentham was rearing his system on the confident belief that all men thought and felt alike, Germans were so preoccupied with the discovery of individuality in history that common, uniting characteristics threatened to disappear. Finally, in the heyday of English cosmopolitanism, Germans applied the idea of individuality to groups of men, seeing personalities no less real than those of individual men and women in these groups. In general, Germans believed through the nineteenth century that the national society, animated by a common view of life, the Volksgeist, was the highest group. There was much debate as to whether the national group was itself a group-person, or whether a state was necessary as the embodiment of the group personality; but that groups were persons few Germans doubted.

So far, German ways of thinking about politics, as reflected in Treitschke's writings, form a consistent whole. Underlying the main theme of the *Politics*, however, are minor themes of uncertainty and doubt, usually muted, but sometimes rising to challenge discordantly the dominant praise of all things German. When Treitschke first gave these lectures the German nation had no state. Before he had delivered them the last time, old Emperor William was dead; another, but very different William reigned in his stead, and William II no longer had Bismarck by his side. In face of events from 1888 to 1890, it was hard to maintain tranquil confidence that the persons who administered the state were of little importance. The contest between agrarian and industrialist for control over policy made it difficult to believe that the state personality was independent of party or group. Belief in the stability of the national will was challenged by the strife of parties, and most emphatically by the rise of the Catholic Center and socialist parties, parties which to Treitschke seemed more international than German. In the field of thought also there were disconcerting developments. Evolutionary biology, at first welcomed as confirmation of German ideas of development, was threatening to engulf the spiritual as well as the material world, to encompass the history of man as well as the history of animal species. Historians, economists, and sociologists were centering their studies increasingly around mass movements which were impersonal not only in their disregard of the individual in history, but in their purely mechanistic operation. Man was being drawn inexorably into the scientist's test tube, like everything else in a mechanistic universe.

Neither political strife nor the triumphant rush of mechanistic science was peculiar to Germany, but the habits of thought which were natural to Germans made the impact of both peculiarly hard. Germans had proudly pinned their faith to history as a guide. From history they had drawn two generalizations: individuality is everywhere to be found in history, uniformity is rarely if ever to be found; history shows groups of men to possess a personality no less real than individual men. These historical laws were earlier thought harmonious, but by the end of the nineteenth century they were seen to have many points of opposition, while it seemed that the logical consequence of both was to extinguish morality and to impose a rigidly mechanistic determinism. Those who chose to emphasize the absence of uniformity in history found themselves faced with moral anarchy. If every individual had his own law of life, where was there room for a general moral code? Many Germans faced this question without flinching, and moved, some to complete moral scepticism, some to a glorification of their own desires, a glorification for which they thought they found sanction in the writings of Nietzsche. Those who fled from moral anarchy, and sought to find general standards of conduct by emphasizing the personality of groups, were beginning to realize that the logical conclusion of their search was complete subservience to a state which itself knew neither freedom nor morality. While Germany had no state, glorification of the state personality had been easy, and had been a welcome escape from the wretched facts of German political life; even while William I and Bismarck ruled, the blinding light of victory made the state seem like a great miracle. As 1871 receded into history, however, the Germans saw with increasing clearness that belief in the personality of the state left the individual helpless in face of any demands the state might make, while the state itself was a helpless tool of God's will. Many Germans tried to conceal from themselves the pit into which they had landed, as Hegel and Ranke had done earlier. Others gloried in their servitude and burned incense before the great and irresponsible Leviathan; almost Byzantine adulation of the state spread rapidly, particularly in German military, official, and academic circles.

Catchwords from biology and from social and economic history were easily assimilated to the growing cults of the irresponsible individual or the irresponsible state. Biology, and the belief that history was the record of impersonal mass movements, encouraged belief in determinism. Loose talk about the survival of the fittest served to discredit moral standards, whether private or international, as snares set by the weak to fetter the strong. Life was a struggle in which victory went to the strongest and the shrewdest: the business man who refused to grasp a profit because of moral scruples, and the statesman who honored a treaty at cost to his country, were alike dupes. Belief in the all-importance of economic trends justified the capitalist who perfected the structure of capitalism, no matter what the cost in human suffering; economic trends made imperialism the one right national policy, again without regard to present consequences. Against the economic biology of the rich, was set the economic biology of the poor, socialism, which in its most popular form was a strange mixture of Marxian economics, analogies from biology, and remnants of humanitarianism and patriotism. Early in the century "Realpolitik" had meant a recognition that power was a dominant factor in international affairs; now Realpolitik meant the mixture of fraud and force by which workmen fought the rich, the rich fought their workers and competitors, and states fought other states. Looking back in 1922, a great German student, Ernst Troeltsch, admirably characterized the conflicting beliefs of the German mind as they were taking form at the close of the century: "Look at one of its sides, and you will see an abundance of romanticism and lofty idealism; look at the other, and you will see a realism which goes to the verge of cynicism and of utter indifference to all ideals and all morality; but what you will see above all is an inclination to make an astonishing combination of the two elements—in a word to brutalize romance, and to romanticize cynicism." [21]

The irresponsible individual or the irresponsible state, free will and morality impossible for either—these equally unattractive alternatives loomed as the logical conclusion of German faith in history as a guide to truth. Few Germans were willing to submit to either alternative without a struggle; even a cursory study of German literature confirms this conclusion. Only the heroic or the abject submitted; by far the larger number of Germans affirmed that somehow, even by the desperate measure of self-contradiction, free will and morality must be saved.

The *Politics* shows that Treitschke was keenly aware of the doubts and uncertainties of his countrymen. The harmony and symmetry of his hymn to the German state and the German people is continually broken by efforts to fit the facts of 1890 into the vision he had had a generation before. Biology and socialism gave him surprisingly little trouble. By a labored distinction between a personality and an organism, he rescued the state and the individual from the grasp of mechanistic evolution, at least to his own satisfaction. He was more harsh with socialism, because this specious doctrine threatened to undermine the loyalty of workmen to the state, but his diatribe against socialism may be reduced to a few dubious aphorisms: "The masses must forever remain the masses. There would be no culture without kitchenmaids." The very flimsiness of these arguments is testimony to the slight realization Germans yet had of the implications of mechanistic evolution and of economic determinism. To Treitschke, the decline of the national spirit as evidenced by the quarrels of political factions and by the spread of moral scepticism was more dangerous. At times he was disposed to attribute the contrast between the heroic Germany of his dreams and the divided Germany about him to the rise of commerce and industry.

[21] Gierke, *Natural Law* . . . 214.

The chivalric conception of life with its simple certainties was being attacked by sordid business morality which had produced "that most perverse form of human stupidity . . . that dreamworld of the intellect, which may be shortly defined as the Berlin temperament." At other times he sought a more specific culprit in the Jew, who was, he claimed, always a disintegrating force in whatever nation he resided, never amalgamating with the national tradition, turning by instinct to non-national activities like international finance. Treitschke would awaken Germany to the danger of "this uncanny phenomenon of an inferior race, ever thrusting its way further into a more advanced civilization." Jews resident in Germany must abandon their aloofness, must assimilate, not undermine, German culture; otherwise, Germans would take the cruel recourse of anti-Semitism to protect themselves. Whatever the cause, whether business in general or only Jewish business, Treitschke saw German culture everywhere under attack. "The foundations of our ancient and noble culture are crumbling; everything which once made us an aristocracy among the nations is mocked and trodden under foot." In these moods he willingly surrendered control over man's fate to God. "The God above us will see to it that war shall return again, a terrible medicine for mankind diseased." [22]

Here is one discordant note which ran through Treitschke's lectures: history showed Germans to be the greatest of peoples; German life since 1871 by no means showed the harmonious perfection which should logically have followed the creation of a guiding, controlling state. The jarring contrast could be disregarded if it could be argued that God in his time would bring the ideal and the actual into harmony. And if repetition could be accepted as evidence of settled conviction, it would be possible to say, as many have said, that Treitschke was content to let individuals and states drift on the God-directed stream of history. "There is no need for us to become critics of history, for the real point is to understand how the Divine plan has unfolded itself little by little in all the variety of actual experience"—over and

[22] *Politics*, I, 42, 69, 217, 227, 299–302.

over he reiterated the belief that history is the record of the inevitable.[23] In reality, however, he could not bring himself to accept the implication of inevitability: the loss of free will for individuals and states. How could belief in free will and moral responsibility be reconciled with belief in history as the guide to truth, and in the state personality as the objectively realized Will of God? Throughout his lectures, Treitschke was wrestling to effect the reconciliation. He was too honest to evade the problem as his colleague, the great historian Ranke, had done. Neither could he follow Hegel in sacrificing freedom and moral responsibility to history and the God-inspired state. He clung to history as a guide, and to the state as the highest personality; but he also insisted that there was an eternal moral law outside the flux of history, a truth which individuals and states must alike believe in, and follow. Logic could not reconcile faith in the ever-moving, ever-changing stream of history, and faith in timeless truth; only contradiction, open or covert, could reconcile these beliefs.

As one studies his lectures it becomes evident why Treitschke never wrote the definitive treatise on politics which he had planned. Try as he would for harmony, his blunt and honest mind revealed the contradictions in his thought. Side by side stand assertions that history was the only guide to truth; and that eternal truth was revealed in the Christian religion. Side by side stand assertions that history showed a world of individuals and groups, each with its own law of life; and that the fixed Christian moral law is binding on all men and all groups of men, including the state. Recoiling from his own demonstration of the state as power and of the glories of the struggle for power, he cited the growth of international law as proof of man's reason, and envisaged "a harmonious comity of nations" based on treaties freely signed and honorably observed. No less eagerly, he fought against the complete subjection of the individual to the will of the state, again by contradicting himself. He had said that Prussian history showed "the secret forces of Nature themselves at work"; but he also said that Prussian history, and all history, was

[23] *Ibid.*, II, 619.

made by individual men, not by historical necessity. He had said that the state brought justice and mercy into the world of man, and that without the state every man's hand would be against his neighbor; but he also said "there are great moral treasures belonging to man which stand so high that the Constitution of States is a little thing in comparison." The sum of these scattered contradictions is a view of life which is the antithesis of the dominant theme of the *Politics*. Here truth was found, not in the flux of history but in eternal moral law; here morality challenged power as the guide of state action; here the will of the individual, far from being enslaved by the state, stood ready to defy the state in the name of higher loyalties. To find an anchorage for freedom and morality in the rushing waters of history, Treitschke fell back unconsciously on the natural law which he had dismissed as a fiction. Despite his boast that politics was applied history, and history was the biography of states, when the logic of history drove him to the conclusion that truth was relative and freedom an illusion, and when the personality of the state threatened, not only to swallow all lesser personalities, but itself to be swallowed in the mind of God—when the implication of the vaunted German ways of thought became apparent, he was forced back on the liberal beliefs of his youth.[24]

Like Montaigne, Treitschke could say that he might contradict himself, but the truth he never contradicted. The difficulty after 1890 was that truth seemed so much more shadowy and elusive than a generation before. In his youth it had seemed certain that if Germany was once united in a powerful liberal state, then the virtues of the German people would find free expression in the life of their state. Under the spell of Bismarck's victories, he had abandoned liberalism and surrendered himself to historical necessity as revealed in the growth of the perfect Prussian state. The years since 1871 had not vindicated his buoyant confidence. On all sides doubts assailed him, doubt that any truth worthy of the name could be discovered in the shifting currents of history, doubt that the personality of the state and the state as power

[24] *Ibid.*, I, xxxvii, 13, 17, 28, 47, 193; II, 367.

could be reconciled with freedom and morality for either state or citizen, doubt that the German people had been regenerated by unity, doubt even of the God-inspired German state, now that Bismarck had fallen. Around him many of his countrymen were surrendering to the drift of history, some to the economic determinism of the socialists or of the economic imperialists, some to moral scepticism or moral anarchy, but more to the all-embracing state with its insatiable appetite for power, power at home and power abroad. Treitschke could not surrender his sovereign will. In his own successful fight against the handicap of deafness he had experienced the existence of a free, courageous will. He could not see in the gigantic efforts of a Bismarck merely the automatic reactions of a puppet. Christian consciousness of moral responsibility forced him to judge himself, his fellow-men, and his state by a moral code which the current of history could not wash away. Finally, he could not believe that his dream of German mind and German virtue perfected by the guidance of the Prussian state had been only a dream. When, in 1894, increasing blindness was added to deafness, he had only one thought, to finish the *History of Germany*. If he could complete that monument, he would have told the German people what great deeds their fathers had wrought; and if Germany could, by understanding her history, attain a really unified national life, then the greatness of the German spirit must triumph over the confusion besetting the nation. Even this boon was denied the indomitable old fighter. When he died in 1896 the *History* had reached only to the beginning of the Year of Revolutions, 1848.

Treitschke had not created a self-consistent science of politics, but he had held up a mirror in which was reflected the arrogant pride and the confused doubt of post-Bismarckian Germany. Germans were, as Bebel said, still drunk with victory, still awaiting a resumption of the triumphs temporarily ended at Versailles in 1871. Bismarck had understood how to exploit and how to control the unsated appetite for foreign adventure. Caprivi began his chancellorship with the chilling announcement that the epic age was over; Germans must accustom themselves to the prose of everyday life. That language Germans found it hard to speak after a century of more exalted speech. Further, the facts of everyday life made a poor showing when contrasted with the hopes of earlier years, above all the hope that unity would bring internal harmony. History had been minutely explored to discover the Volksgeist, the characteristic German way of living and of looking at life. Each explorer triumphantly returned with his own description of the Volksgeist, and hurled the terrible epithet "un-German" at those who disagreed with him. German faith in history, and in logical systems based on the lessons of history made amicable difference of opinion impossible. There was a right way for Germans to think and act; other ways of thinking and acting might be appropriate for Latins or Britons, but were probably inferior, and were certainly not German. Concession or compromise were next to impossible when every problem and every proposal was relentlessly scrutinized in the light of a fixed body of doctrine. Differences between sections, classes, political parties, even schools of poetry, became questions of loyalty or treason to the German Volksgeist. In this atmosphere harmony was a vain hope. The strident clamor of heresy-hunters confused and alarmed the neighbors of Germany, and Germans themselves. Only when Germans turned their eyes away from the internal scene and looked across their frontiers did the babel of voices cease, and strife give way to harmony. Like Treitschke, most Germans found rest from disheartening doubt in contemplation of the past glories and the still more glorious future of their countrymen in the world outside Germany.

It was the old story. In 1848, Germans had attained peace with each other only by concentrating on Schleswig-Holstein; and when the powers had halted the expedition against Denmark, the war of factions had begun again. Bismarck's career as Minister President after 1862 had proceeded from the premise that peace at home could be won only by exploits abroad. As Chancellor also he had repeatedly hushed domestic strife by appealing for united action against foreign foes. And now his successors were discovering that the harmony they had vainly sought could be won by challenging imperial Britain. Since Friedrich List had expounded his National System, and even before, as far back as the Wars of Liberation, patriots had hoped to attain through nationalism that peace which earlier Christian centuries had believed the world cannot give. Always, the barriers of class, creed, and tradition had proved too strong, except when the German nation had been set against other nations. The craving for peace at home had been Bismarck's strongest ally in his fight to make Prussia a great Continental power; the craving for peace was now to furnish the emotional support for the new industry in its determination to make Germany a world power. The men of the 'nineties, like the men of the 'sixties, including Bismarck, used the easy evasion of foreign affairs to escape from the domestic problems which could repeatedly be evaded, but never really escaped.

Since the Germans themselves refused to see the forces driving them into a world policy, it is not strange that Englishmen could not see what was going on across the North Sea. And yet, did not the catchword Greater Britain conceal an effort to escape from similar problems in Great Britain? The rise of democracy and the simultaneous loss of a monopoly on colonial and industrial power were threatening England with internal strains, weaker to be sure, but similar in character to those which repeatedly threatened to bring down the precarious structure of German unity. Out of office, Disraeli had laid equal stress on imperialism and Tory Democracy. In office, he speedily found it expedient to concentrate on imperialism, a program commanding general support; the problem of the two nations, the rich and the poor, was scarcely touched. Similarly, of the Liberals who revolted against Gladstone, it was the Liberal Imperialists, not the social radicals, who won power in the 'nineties. Because the foundations of British unity were more deeply and solidly laid, extravagant emphasis on nationalism was not necessary; but Greater Britain, like Weltpolitik, was in part an escape, or, as men thought, an answer to domestic discontent. Given understanding, the world might have been big enough to hold imperial Britain and imperial Germany, but how, in the light of history since the days of Cobden and List, could understanding be hoped for?

SELECTED BIBLIOGRAPHY

The lists which follow are, of necessity, incomplete. As the lesser of two evils, a few representative lists have been given, rather than samples of all kinds of material used. Literature, although of great assistance, has been omitted. Only a few items illustrative of "public opinion" have been included, and these for special reasons. In this category, aside from other contemporary books, the chief periodicals and annuals were used systematically. Newspaper materials were, however, only partially explored. The *Kölnische Zeitung*, the *Vossische Zeitung* and *The Times* of London were read for almost every day; the *Frankfurter Zeitung* was read much less completely; other newspapers were consulted only for periods of crisis. Although these four papers contained copious extracts from other journals, this is the largest gap in my study. A forthcoming work by Professor E. M. Carroll will close this gap, and compel some changes in the conclusions suggested by my partial study.

Except for a few British economic reports which were very extensively used, only recent official publications are listed. The contemporary official publications were covered fairly completely, although in general more time was spent on economic than on diplomatic reports.

More British than German biographical materials are listed, partly because the student of British history before 1898 is more dependent on this class of material in default of publications like *Die Grosse Politik*, partly because good English biographies are more numerous. Here, and in the list of General Studies, some works are included which are valuable for the understanding of developments affecting Anglo-German relations, even though there is little direct reference to these relations.

To reduce the list of General Studies, works which have been largely superseded by later publications have been omitted. There are a great many German doctoral dissertations on various phases of Anglo-German relations. Most of them are based on materials which I have used, and it seemed unnecessary to list these.

Although only works which have been of material assistance have been listed, I have starred those publications to which I am most indebted.

Official and Semi-Official Publications

France

*Ministère des Affaires Étrangères.—*Documents Diplomatiques Français (1871–1914)*, 24 vols., Paris, 1929–37.

*——, *Les Origines Diplomatiques de la Guerre de 1870–71: Recueil de Documents.* 29 vols., Paris, 1910–32.

Germany

**Die Grosse Politik der Europäischen Kabinette, 1871–1914*, ed., Johannes Lepsius, Albrecht Mendelssohn-Bartholdy, Friedrich Thimme. 40 vols., Berlin, 1922–27.

*Reichsarchiv.—*Die auswärtige Politik Preussens, 1858–71.* 6 vols., Oldenburg, 1932–36.

——, *Kriegsrüstung und Kriegswirtschaft.* 1 vol. in 2, Berlin, 1930.

Great Britain

**British Documents on the Origins of the War, 1898–1914*, ed., G. P. Gooch and Harold Temperley. 11 vols., London, 1926–38.

House of Commons Sessional Papers:

*"Reports of the Royal Commission Appointed to Inquire into the Depression of Trade and Industry," V. 23, 1886.

"Correspondence Respecting the Question of Diplomatic and Consular Assistance to British Trade Abroad," V. 60, 1886 [c.—4779].

*"Statistical Tables Relating to the Progress of the Foreign Trade of the United Kingdom, and of Other Countries, in Recent Years: with Report to the Board of Trade Thereon" [by R. Giffen], V. 93, 1888 [c. —5297]. Continued in V. 80, 1894.

*"Trade of the British Empire and Foreign Competition. Despatch from Mr. Chamberlain to the Governors of Colonies . . . and the Replies Thereto," V. 60, 1897 [c.—8449].

*"Foreign Trade Competition. Opinions of H. M. Diplomatic and Consular Officials on British Trade Methods," V. 96, 1899 [c.—9078].

*"British and Foreign Trade and Industry" [First Series], V. 67, 1903 [Cd. 1761]; Second Series, V. 84, 1905 [Cd. 2337].

Contemporary Works Alluded to in the Text

Bernard, Montague.—*Four Lectures on Subjects Connected with Diplomacy.* London, 1868.

"Borussen."—*Was für einen Kurs haben wir?* Gotha, 1891.

[CHESNEY, George].—*The Fall of England. The Battle of Dorking . . . By a Contributor to "Blackwood."* N.Y., 1871.

DAWSON, W. H.—*Bismarck and State Socialism.* London, 1890.

DILKE, Sir Charles.—*The Present Position of European Politics, or, Europe in 1887.* London, 1887.

*——, *Greater Britain.* N.Y., 1869.

*——, *Problems of Greater Britain.* London, 1890.

*DUNSANY, Lord. *Gaul or Teuton?—Considerations as to Our Allies of the Future.* London, 1873.

[ECKARDT, Julius].—*Berlin, Wien, Rom.* Leipzig, 1892.

*FARRER, Sir T. H.—*Free Trade Versus Fair Trade.* London, 1886.

*GRANT DUFF, M. E.—*Studies in European Politics.* Edinburgh, 1866.

*SEELEY, J. R.—*The Expansion of England.* London, 1925.

*SPENCER, Herbert.—*Social Statics; or, The Conditions Essential to Human Happiness Specified and the First of Them Developed.* London. 1851.

BIOGRAPHY, AUTOBIOGRAPHY, LETTERS, ETC.

For convenience of reference, the titles are listed by subject wherever possible.

ALBERT, PRINCE CONSORT. Bolitho, Hector, *The Prince Consort and His Brother*, London, 1933.

*——. Martin, Theodore, *The Life of His Royal Highness the Prince Consort*, 5 vols., N.Y., 1875–80.

ALEXANDER OF BATTENBERG. Corti, E. C., *Alexander von Battenberg, Sein Kampf mit den Zaren und Bismarck*, Vienna, 1920.

ANDRÁSSY. Wertheimer, Eduard, *Graf Julius Andrássy*, 3 vols., Stuttgart, 1910–13.

*BAGEHOT. Barrington, R., ed., *The Works and Life of Walter Bagehot*, 10 vols., London, 1915.

BALFOUR. Dugdale, Blanche, *Arthur James Balfour*, 2 vols., N.Y., 1937.

BECK. Glaise von Horstenau, Edmund, *Franz Josephs Weggefährte: Das Leben des Generalstabschefs, Grafen Beck*, Vienna, 1930.

BERNHARDI. *Aus dem Leben Theodor von Bernhardis*, 9 vols., Leipzig, 1893–1906.

BERNSTORFF. Ringhoffer, Karl, *The Bernstorff Papers: The Life of Count Albrecht von Bernstorff*, 2 vols., London, 1908.

*BISMARCK. *Bismarck, the Man and the Statesman, Being the Reflections and Reminiscences of Otto, Prince von Bismarck*, 2 vols., N.Y., 1898.

*——, *Die Gesammelten Werke*, 15 vols., Berlin, 1924–35.

BISMARCK. Busch, Moritz, *Bismarck, Some Secret Pages of his History*, 2 vols., N.Y., 1898.
——. Lenz, Max, *Geschichte Bismarcks*, Munich, 1913.
——. Lucius von Ballhausen, R. S., *Bismarck-Erinnerungen*, Stuttgart, 1921.
——. Marcks, Erich, *Bismarck, Eine Biographie*, Stuttgart, 1910.
——. ——, *Otto von Bismarck, Ein Lebensbild*, Stuttgart, 1915.
——. Meinecke, F., "Gerlach und Bismarck," *Historische Zeitschrift*, LXXII, 44–60 (1894).
*——. Meyer, A. O., *Bismarcks Kampf mit Oesterreich am Bundestag zu Frankfurt (1851–1859)*, Berlin, 1927.
——. Robertson, C. Grant, *Bismarck*, N.Y., 1919.
——. Wertheimer, Eduard von, *Bismarck im politischen Kampf*, Berlin, 1930.
BLUNT, Wilfred Scawen, *My Diaries . . . 1888–1914*, London, 1932.
BRIGHT. Trevelyan, G. M., *The Life of John Bright*, London, 1913.
BUNSEN. Bunsen, Frances, *A Memoir of Baron Christian Bunsen*, 2 vols., London, 1868.
CAPRIVI. Gothein, Georg, *Reichskanzler Graf Caprivi*, Munich, 1918.
CARNARVON. Hardinge, Sir Arthur, *Life of the Earl of Carnarvon*, 3 vols., London, 1925.
CECIL, Algernon, *British Foreign Secretaries, 1807–1916*, London, 1927.
CHAMBERLAIN, Joseph, *Speeches*, 2 vols., Boston, 1914.
——. Garvin, J. L., *The Life of Joseph Chamberlain*, 3 vols., N.Y., 1932–34.
CHURCHILL. Churchill, W. S., *Lord Randolph Churchill*, 2 vols., London, 1906.
*CLARENDON. Maxwell, Sir Herbert, *The Life and Letters of . . . Fourth Earl of Clarendon*, 2 vols., London, 1913.
COBDEN, Richard, *Political Writings*, London, 1878.
——, *Speeches on Questions of Public Policy*, 2 vols., London, 1870.
——. Dawson, W. H., *Richard Cobden and Foreign Policy*, London, 1926.
——. Hobson, J. A., *Richard Cobden, the International Man*, N.Y., 1919.
*——. Morley, John, *The Life of Richard Cobden*, 2 vols., London, 1881.
CRISPI, Francesco, *Memoirs*, 3 vols., London, 1912–14.
CROMER. Zetland, Marquis of, *Lord Cromer*, London, 1932.
CURZON. Ronaldshay, Earl of, *The Life of Lord Curzon*, 3 vols., N.Y., n.d.
DELANE. Cook, Sir Edward, *Delane of "The Times,"* N.Y., 1916.
——. Dasent, A. I., *John Thadeus Delane*, 2 vols., N.Y., 1908.
DILKE. Gwynn, Stephen, and Tuckwell, Gertrude M., *The Life of . . . Sir Charles Dilke*, 2 vols., N.Y., 1917.

DISRAELI. Zetland, Marquis of, ed., *The Letters of Benjamin Disraeli to Lady Chesterfield and Lady Bradford*, 2 vols., N.Y., 1929.
——. Hutcheon, W., ed., *Whigs and Whiggism*, N.Y., 1914.
*——. Monypenny, W. F., and Buckle, G. E., *The Life of Benjamin Disraeli, Earl of Beaconsfield*, 2 vols., London, 1929.
DUFFERIN. Lyall, Sir Alfred, *The Life of the Marquis of Dufferin and Ava*, 2 vols., London, 1905.
ECKARDT, Julius von, *Aus den Tagen von Bismarcks Kampf gegen Caprivi*, Leipzig, 1920.
EDWARD VII. Lee, Sir Sidney, *King Edward VII, A Biography*, 2 vols., London, 1925–27.
ELLIOT, Sir Henry G., *Some Revolutions and Other Diplomatic Experiences*, N.Y., 1922.
ERNST II, DUKE OF COBURG, *Aus Meinem Leben und aus Meiner Zeit*, 3 vols., Berlin, 1887–89.
EULENBURG. Haller, Johannes, *Philip Eulenburg, the Kaiser's Friend*, 2 vols., N.Y., 1930.
FRANCIS JOSEPH. Redlich, Joseph, *Emperor Francis Joseph of Austria*, N.Y., 1929.
FREDERICK III. Engel, E., ed., *Kaiser Friedrichs Tagebuch*, Halle, 1919.
——. Meisner, H. O., ed., *Das Kriegstagebuch von 1870–71*, Leipzig, 1926.
FREDERICK, EMPRESS. Ponsonby, Sir F., ed., *Letters of the Empress Frederick*, N.Y., 1930.
GAVARD, Charles, *Un Diplomate à Londres; Lettres et Notes, 1871–1877*, Paris, 1895.
GLADSTONE. Guedalla, Philip, ed., *Gladstone and Palmerston*, London, 1928.
——. ——, *The Queen and Mr. Gladstone*, 2 vols., London, 1933.
*——. Morley, John, *The Life of William Ewart Gladstone*, 3 vols., London, 1903.
GOLTZ. Dorn, Arno, *Robert Heinrich, Graf von der Goltz*, Halle, 1929.
GOSCHEN. Elliot, Arthur R. D., *The Life of . . . First Viscount Goschen*, 2 vols., London, 1911.
*GRANVILLE. Fitzmaurice, Lord Edmond, *The Life of . . . Second Earl Granville*, 2 vols., London, 1905.
HAMILTON, Lord George, *Parliamentary Reminiscences and Reflections, 1886–1906*, 2 vols., London, 1916–22.
HAMMANN, Otto, *Bilder aus der letzten Kaiserzeit*, Berlin, 1922.
——, *Der Neue Kurs: Erinnerungen*, Berlin, 1918.
HARCOURT. Gardiner, A. G., *The Life of Sir William Harcourt*, 2 vols., London, 1923.

HARDEN, Maximilian, *Köpfe*, 2 vols., Berlin, 1910–11.
HOHENLOHE, *Memoirs of Prince Chlodwig of Hohenlohe*, 2 vols., London, 1906.
HOLSTEIN. Rogge, Helmuth, *Friedrich von Holstein, Lebensbekenntnis*, Berlin, 1932.
——. Trotha, Fr. von, *Fritz von Holstein als Mensch und Politiker*, Berlin, 1931.
HUTCHINSON, H. G., *Portraits of the Eighties*, N.Y., 1920.
LASSALLE. Oncken, Hermann, *Lassalle, Eine politische Biographie*, Stuttgart, 1923.
LEININGEN. Valentin, Veit, *Fürst Karl Leiningen und das deutsche Einheitsproblem*, Stuttgart, 1910.
*LIST, Friedrich, *The National System of Political Economy*, London, 1904.
*——, *Schriften, Reden, Briefe*, 10 vols., Berlin, 1927–35.
——. Hirst, M. E., *The Life of Friedrich List*, N.Y., 1909.
——. Lenz, Friedrich, *Friedrich List, der Mann und das Werk*, Munich, 1936.
LOFTUS, Lord Augustus, *Diplomatic Reminiscences*, 4 vols., London, 1892–94.
LOWE, Charles, *The Tale of a "Times" Correspondent*, London, 1927.
LÜDERITZ. Schüssler, Wilhelm, *Adolf Lüderitz, Ein Deutscher Kampf um Süd-Afrika, 1883–86*, Bremen, 1936.
LYONS. Newton, Lord, *Lord Lyons, A Record of British Diplomacy*, 2 vols., London, 1913.
MARSCHALL. Schütte, Ernst, *Freiherr Marschall von Bieberstein*, Berlin, 1936.
MCCARTHY, Justin, *British Political Portraits*, N.Y., 1903.
MACCOLL. Russell, G. W. E., *Malcolm MacColl, Memoirs and Correspondence*, London, 1904.
METTERNICH. Bibl, Viktor, *Metternich*, Paris, 1935.
——. Meyer, A. O., "Der Streit um Metternich," *Historische Zeitschrift*, CLVII, 75–83 (Oct., 1937).
*——. Srbik, Heinrich, Ritter von, *Metternich, der Staatsmann und der Mensch*, 2 vols., Munich, 1925.
MILL, J. S., *Autobiography*, N.Y., 1924.
——, *Utilitarianism, etc.*, London, 1936 (Everyman).
*MORIER. Wemyss, Rosslyn, ed., *Memoirs and Letters of Sir Robert Morier*, 2 vols., London, 1911.
PALMERSTON. Ashley, Evelyn, *The Life of Viscount Palmerston*, 2 vols., London, 1876.
*——. Bell, H. C., *Lord Palmerston*, 2 vols., London, 1936.

PALMERSTON. Bulwer, Sir Henry Lytton, and Ashley, Evelyn, *The Life of Viscount Palmerston*, 5 vols., London, 1870–76.
——. Guedalla, Philip, *Palmerston*, N.Y., 1927.
PEEL. Parker, Charles Stuart, *Sir Robert Peel*, 3 vols., London, 1891–99.
——. Ramsay, A. A. W., *Sir Robert Peel*, London, 1928.
PETERS, Karl, *Lebenserinnerungen*, Hamburg, 1918.
——. Schorn, H. F., *Dr. Karl Peters, Ein Lebensbild*, Hamburg, 1920.
RADOWITZ. Holborn, Hajo, ed., *Aufzeichnungen und Erinnerungen aus dem Leben des Botschafters Joseph Maria von Radowitz*, 2 vols., Berlin, 1925.
RAYMOND, E. T., *Portraits of the Nineties*, London, 1921.
RIPON. Wolf, Lucien, *The Life of . . . First Marquess of Ripon*, 2 vols., London, 1921.
RODD, Sir James Rennell, *Social and Diplomatic Memories*, 3 vols., London, 1922–25.
ROSEBERY. Crewe, Marquess of, *Lord Rosebery*, N.Y., 1931.
RUMBOLD, Sir Horace, *Recollections of a Diplomatist*, 4 vols., London, 1902–5.
RUSSELL, G. W. E., *Portraits of the Seventies*, London, 1916.
RUSSELL, Lord John, *Recollections and Suggestions, 1813–73*, London, 1875.
——. Gooch, G. P., ed., *The Later Correspondence of Lord John Russell*, 2 vols., London, 1925.
RUSSELL, Lord Odo. Taffs, Winifred, *Lord Odo Russell, Ambassador to Bismarck*, London, 1938.
SABUROV. Simpson, J. Y., ed., *The Saburov Memoirs, or Bismarck and Russia*, N.Y., 1929.
SALISBURY, Robert, Marquis of, *Essays*, 2 vols., London, 1905.
*——. Cecil, Lady Gwendolen, *Life of Robert, Marquis of Salisbury*, 4 vols., London, 1921–32.
——. Penson, L. M., "The Principles and Methods of Lord Salisbury's Foreign Policy," *Cambridge Historical Journal*, V, 86–106 (1935).
SCHWEINITZ, General von, *Briefwechsel*, Berlin, 1928.
*——, *Denkwürdigkeiten*, 2 vols., Berlin, 1927.
SMITH. Maxwell, Sir Herbert, *The Life and Times of William Henry Smith*, 2 vols., Edinburgh, 1893.
STAAL. Meyendorff, Baron A., ed., *Correspondance Diplomatique de M. de Staal*, 2 vols., Paris, 1929.
STANLEY, Lady Augusta, *Letters*, N.Y., 1927.
STOCKMAR, Baron E. A. C., *Memoirs*, 2 vols., London, 1873.
TREITSCHKE, Heinrich von, *Briefe*, 3 vols., Leipzig, 1914–20.

TREITSCHKE, *Briefe an Historiker und Politiker*, Berlin, 1934.
——, *Deutsche Kämpfe*, neue folge, Leipzig, 1896.
——, *Germany, France, Russia, and Islam*, London, 1915.
*——, *Historische und Politische Aufsätze*, 4 vols., Leipzig, 1897–1903.
*——, *History of Germany in the Nineteenth Century*, 7 vols., N.Y., 1915–19.
*——, *Politics*, 2 vols., N.Y., 1916.
——. Leipprand, Ernst, *Heinrich von Treitschke im deutschen Geistesleben des 19. Jahrhunderts*, Stuttgart, 1935.
——. ——, *Treitschkes Stellung zu England*, Stuttgart, 1928.
*VICTORIA. *The Letters of Queen Victoria, 1837–1861* (First Series), Benson, A. C., and Esher, Viscount, eds., 3 vols., N.Y., 1907.
*——, *1862–85* (Second Series), Buckle, G. E., ed., 3 vols., London, 1926–28.
*——, *1886–1901* (Third Series), Buckle, G. E., ed., 3 vols., N.Y., 1930–32.
VITZTHUM, Count, *St. Petersburg and London in the Years 1852–64*, 2 vols., London, 1887.
WALDERSEE, Alfred, Graf von, *Aus dem Briefwechsel*, Stuttgart, 1928.
*——, *Denkwürdigkeiten*, 3 vols., Stuttgart, 1923–25.
——, *A Field-Marshal's Memoirs*, London, 1924.
WILLIAM I. Marcks, Erich, *Kaiser Wilhelm I*, Munich, 1918.
WILLIAM II. *Ereignisse und Gestalten aus den Jahren 1878–1918*, Leipzig, 1922.
WOLFF, Sir Henry Drummond, *Rambling Recollections*, 2 vols., London, 1908.

GENERAL STUDIES

ARIS, R.—*History of Political Thought in Germany from 1789 to 1815*. London, 1936.
AYDELOTTE, W. O.—*Bismarck and British Colonial Policy. The Problem of South West Africa, 1883–1885*. Phila., 1937.
BARKER, Ernest.—*Political Thought in England from Herbert Spencer to the Present Day*. N.Y., n.d.
BASCH, V.—*Les Doctrines Politiques des Philosophes Classiques de l'Allemagne*. Paris, 1927.
BECKER, Otto.—"Bismarck und die Aufgaben deutscher Weltpolitik," in Emil Daniels, ed., *Am Webstuhl der Zeit*. Berlin, 1928.
BERGSTRASSER, L.—*Geschichte der politischen Parteien in Deutschland*. Mannheim, 1921.
BINKLEY, R. C.—*Realism and Nationalism, 1852–1871*. N.Y., 1935.

BODELSEN, C. A.—*Studies in Mid-Victorian Imperialism.* Copenhagen, 1924.

BRANDENBURG, Erich.—*Die Reichsgründung.* 2 vols. Leipzig, 1916.

*BRINTON, Crane.—*English Political Thought in the Nineteenth Century.* London, 1933.

BRÜNS, G.—*England und der deutsche Krieg,* 1866. Berlin, 1933.

*CLAPHAM, J. H.—*Economic Development of France and Germany, 1815–1914.* Cambridge, 1936.

*——, *An Economic History of Modern Britain.* 3 vols., Cambridge, 1926–1938.

*CLARK, Chester W.—*Franz Joseph and Bismarck. The Diplomacy of Austria before the War of 1866.* Cambridge, Mass., 1934.

*DAWSON, W. H.—*The German Empire, 1867–1914.* 2 vols., N.Y., 1919.

DEWEY, John.—*German Philosophy and Politics.* N.Y., 1915.

EISENHART ROTHE, W. von, and Ritthaler, A., ed.—*Vorgeschichte und Begründung des deutschen Zollvereins 1815–1834. Akten der Staaten des deutschen Bundes und der Europäischen Mächte.* 3 vols., Berlin, 1934.

ENSOR, R. C. K.—*England, 1870–1914.* Oxford, 1936.

ERGANG, R. R.—*Herder and the Foundations of German Nationalism.* N.Y., 1931.

FAY, S. B.—*Origins of the World War.* 2 vols., N.Y., 1928.

FRANKFURTER ZEITUNG,—*Geschichteder, 1856–1906.* Frankfurt, 1911.

FRANZ, Eugen.—*Die Entscheidungskampf um die wirtschaftspolitische Führung Deutschlands (1856–1867).* Munich, 1933.

FRIEDJUNG, Heinrich.—*Historische Aufsätze.* Stuttgart, 1919.

——, *Der Kampf um die Vorherrschaft in Deutschland, 1859 bis 1866.* 2 vols., Stuttgart, 1916–17.

FULLER, J. V.—*Bismarck's Diplomacy at Its Zenith.* Cambridge, Mass., 1922.

*GIERKE, Otto.—*Natural Law and the Theory of Society, 1500 to 1800 . . . with a lecture on The Ideas of Natural Law and Humanity by Ernst Troeltsch;* translated with an introduction by Ernest Barker. 2 vols., Cambridge, 1934.

GOOCH, G. P.—*Germany and the French Revolution.* London, 1920.

——, *Studies in Modern History.* London, 1931.

GORIAINOV, S. M.—*Le Bosphore et les Dardanelles.* Paris, 1910.

GUILLAND, A.—*Modern Germany and Her Historians.* London, 1915.

HAGEN, Maximilian von.—*Bismarcks Kolonialpolitik.* Stuttgart, 1923.

HALÉVY, E.—*The Growth of Philosophical Radicalism.* London, 1928.

HALLGARTEN, W.—*Vorkriegsimperialismus.* Paris, 1935.

HARRIS, DAVID.—"Bismarck's Advance to England, January, 1876," *Journal of Modern History,* III, 441–456 (Sept., 1931).

HARRIS, DAVID.—*A Diplomatic History of the Balkan Crisis of 1875–1878. The First Year*. Stanford, 1936.

HAUSER, Henri, ed.—*Histoire Diplomatique de l'Europe, 1871–1914*. 2 vols., Paris, 1929.

HAYES, Carlton J. H.—*Essays on Nationalism*. N.Y., 1926.

*——, *Historical Evolution of Modern Nationalism*. N.Y., 1931.

HERRMANN, W.—*Dreibund, Zweibund, England, 1890–1895*. Stuttgart, 1929.

*HOFFMAN, Ross J. S.—*Great Britain and the German Trade Rivalry, 1875–1914*. Phila., 1933.

HOLBORN, Hajo.—*Deutschland und die Türkei 1878–1890*. Berlin, 1926.

HOOK, Sidney.—*From Hegel to Marx*. N.Y., 1936.

HOSKINS, Halford L.—*British Routes to India*. N.Y., 1928.

IBBEKEN, R.—*Das aussenpolitische Problem Staat und Wirtschaft in der deutschen Reichspolitik 1880–1914*. Schleswig, 1928.

KANTOROWICZ, H.—*The Spirit of British Policy*. N.Y., 1932.

JENKS, Leland H.—*The Migration of British Capital to 1875*. N.Y., 1927.

KEHR, Eckart.—"Englandhass und Weltpolitik," *Zeitschrift für Politik*, XVII, 500–526; also, the comment of A. Grabowsky, *ibid*., 527–542.

KIEWIET, C. W. de.—*The Imperial Factor in South Africa*. Cambridge, 1937.

KLEIN-HATTINGEN, O.—*Geschichte des deutschen Liberalismus*. 2 vols., Berlin, 1911–12.

KNAPLUND, Paul.—*Gladstone and Britain's Imperial Policy*, London, 1927.

——, *Gladstone's Foreign Policy*. N.Y., 1935.

*LANGER, W. L. *The Diplomacy of Imperialism*. 2 vols., N.Y., 1935.

*——, *European Alliances and Alignments*. N.Y., 1931.

——, *The Franco-Russian Alliance, 1890–94*. Cambridge, Mass., 1929.

LASKI, H. J.—*The Rise of European Liberalism*. London, 1936.

——, *Studies in the Problem of Sovereignty*. New Haven, 1917.

LEE, Dwight E.—*Great Britain and the Cyprus Convention Policy of 1878*. Cambridge, Mass., 1934.

LEGGE, J. G.—*Rhyme and Revolution in Germany, 1813–1850*. N.Y., 1919.

LEUPOLT, E.—*Die Aussenpolitik in den bedeutendsten politischen Zeitschriften Deutschlands 1890–1909*. Leipzig, 1933.

LORD, R. H.—*Origins of the War of 1870*. Cambridge, Mass., 1924.

LOVELL, R. I.—*The Struggle for South Africa, 1875–99*. N.Y., 1934.

*MARCKS, Erich.—*Der Aufstieg des Reiches; Deutsche Geschichte von 1807–1871/78*. 2 vols., Stuttgart, 1936.

Marcks, Erich.—*England and Germany*. London, 1900.
——, "Die europäischen Mächte und die 48er Revolution," *Historische Zeitschrift*, CXLII, 73–87 (1930).
Medlicott, W. N.—"The Mediterranean Agreements of 1887," *Slavonic Review*, V, 66–88 (1926).
Meine, K.—*England und Deutschland in der Zeit des Überganges vom Manchestertum zum Imperialismus 1871–76*. Berlin, 1937.
Meinecke, F.—*Die Entstehung des Historismus*. 2 vols., Munich, 1936.
*——, *Die Idee der Staatsräson in der neueren Geschichte*. Munich, 1929.
——, *Preussen und Deutschland im 19. und 20. Jahrhundert*. Munich, 1918.
——, *Staat und Persönlichkeit*. Berlin, 1933.
*——, *Weltbürgertum und Nationalstaat*. Munich, 1919.
Merriam, C. E., and Barnes, H. E., eds., *A History of Political Theories, Recent Times*. N.Y., 1924.
*Meyer, A. O.—*Deutsche und Engländer*. Munich, 1937.
*Michael, Horst.—*Bismarck, England und Europa* (*vorwiegend von 1866–1870*). Munich, 1930.
Muncker, F.—*Anschauungen vom englischen Staat und Volk in der deutschen Literatur der letzen vier Jahrhunderte*. 2 vols. [to 1840's], Munich, 1918–1925.
Nolde, Baron Boris.—*L'Alliance Franco-Russe. Les Origines du Système Diplomatique d'Avant-Guerre*. Paris, 1936.
*Oncken, Hermann.—*Das deutsche Reich und die Vorgeschichte des Weltkrieges*. 2 vols., Leipzig, 1933.
——, *Die Rheinpolitik Kaiser Napoleons III. von 1863 bis 1870*. 3 vols., Stuttgart, 1926.
Precht, Hans.—*Englands Stellung zur deutschen Einheit 1848–1850*. Munich, 1925.
Pribram, A. F.—*England and the International Policy of the European Great Powers, 1871–1914*. Oxford, 1931.
*——, *The Secret Treaties of Austria-Hungary 1879–1914*. 2 vols., Cambridge, Mass., 1920–21.
Ramsay, A. A. W.—*Idealism and Foreign Policy; A Study of the Relations of Great Britain with Germany and France, 1860–1878*. London, 1925.
Raphael, L. A. C.—*The Cape-to-Cairo Dream*. N.Y., 1936.
Raymond, Dora N.—*British Policy and Opinion during the Franco-Prussian War*. N.Y., 1921.
Rheindorf, K.—*England und der deutsch-französische Krieg*. Bonn, 1923.

ROSENBERG, Hans.—*Die nationalpolitische Publizistik Deutschlands, vom Eintritt der neuen Ära in Preussen bis zum Ausbruch des deutschen Krieges.* 2 vols., Munich, 1935.

ROTHFELS, Hans.—*Bismarcks englische Bündnispolitik.* Stuttgart, 1924.

RÜHL, Hans.—*Disraelis Imperialismus und die Kolonialpolitik seiner Zeit.* Leipzig, 1935.

*RUGGIERO, Guido de.—*The History of European Liberalism.* London, 1927.

*SARTORIUS VON WALTERSHAUSEN, August.—*Deutsche Wirtschaftsgeschichte 1815–1914.* Jena, 1923.

*SCHMITT, Bernadotte E.—*England and Germany, 1740–1914.* Princeton, 1916.

SCHMOLLER, Gustav von.—*Grundriss der allgemeinen Volkswirtschaftslehre.* 2 vols., Leipzig, 1901–19.

*SCHNABEL, Franz.—*Deutsche Geschichte im neunzehnten Jahrhundert.* 4 vols., Freiburg, 1929–37.

SCHUYLER, R. L.—"The Climax of Anti-Imperialism in England," *Political Science Quarterly*, XXXVI, 537–560 (1921).

SETON-WATSON, R. W.—*Britain in Europe, 1789–1914. A Survey of Foreign Policy*, N.Y., 1937.

*——, *Disraeli, Gladstone and the Eastern Question, 1875–1878.* London, 1935.

SOMBART, Werner.—*Die deutsche Volkswirtschaft im neunzehnten Jahrhundert.* Berlin, 1921.

SPIES, H.—*Das Moderne England.* Strassburg, 1911.

*SRBIK, H., Ritter von.—*Deutsche Einheit. Idee und Wirklichkeit vom Heiligen Reich bis Königgrätz.* 2 vols., Munich, 1936.

STADELMANN, R.—*Das Jahr 1865 und das Problem vom Bismarcks deutscher Politik.* Munich, 1933.

*STEEFEL, Lawrence D.—*The Schleswig-Holstein Question.* Cambridge, Mass., 1932.

STERN, Alfred.—*Der Einfluss der französischen Revolution auf das deutsche Geistesleben.* Stuttgart, 1928.

——, *Geschichte Europas* [*1815–1871*]. 10 vols., Berlin, 1894–1924.

SUMNER, B.H.—*Russia and the Balkans, 1870–1880.* Oxford, 1937.

TAFFS, Winifred.—"The War Scare of 1875," *Slavonic Review*, IX, 335–349, 632–649 (1930, 1931).

TAUBE, A. von.—*Fürst Bismarck zwischen England und Russland.* Stuttgart, 1923.

TEMPERLEY, Harold.—*Victorian Age in Politics, War, and Diplomacy.* Cambridge, 1928.

THIMME, F.—"Das Memorandum E. A. Crowes vom 1. Januar 1907; Das 'berühmte Schwindeldokument' E. A. Crowes," *Berliner Monatshefte*, VII, 732–768, 874–879 (1929).

THORP, Willard L.—*Business Annals*. N.Y., 1926.

TOWNSEND, Mary E.—*Origins of Modern German Colonialism*, 1871–1885. N.Y., 1921.

——, *Rise and Fall of Germany's Colonial Empire, 1884–1918*. N.Y., 1930.

TROELTSCH, Ernst.—*Der Historismus und seine Probleme*. Tübingen, 1922.

*VALENTIN, Veit.—*Geschichte der deutschen Revolution von 1848–1849*. 2 vols., Berlin, 1930–31.

*——, *Bismarcks Reichsgründung im Urteil englischer Diplomaten*. Amsterdam, 1937.

VEBLEN, Thorstein.—*Imperial Germany and the Industrial Revolution*. N.Y., 1915.

——, *The Place of Science in Modern Civilization*. N.Y., 1919.

VOSSLER, Otto.—*Der Nationalgedanke von Rousseau bis Ranke*. Munich, 1937.

*WAHL, Adalbert.—*Deutsche Geschichte von der Reichsgründung bis zum Ausbruch des Weltkriegs*. 3 vols., Stuttgart, 1926–36.

WARD, A. W.—*Germany, 1815–1890*. 3 vols., Cambridge, 1916–18.

*WARD, A. W., and Gooch, G. P., eds.—*The Cambridge History of British Foreign Policy, 1783–1919*. 3 vols., Cambridge, 1922–23.

WENTZCKE, Paul, and Heyderkoff, Julius, eds.—*Deutscher Liberalismus im Zeitalter Bismarcks. Eine politische Briefsammlung*. 2 vols., Bonn, 1925–26.

WERNER, L.—*Der Alldeutsche Verband 1890–1918*. Berlin, 1935.

WERTHEIMER, M. S.—*The Pan-German League, 1890–1914*. N.Y., 1924.

YOUNG, G. M.—*Victorian England. Portrait of an Age*. Oxford, 1936.

YOUNG, G. M., ed.—*Early Victorian England, 1830–1865*. 2 vols., London, 1934.

ZIEKURSCH, J.—*Politische Geschichte des neuen deutschen Kaiserreiches*. 3 vols., Frankfurt, 1925–30.

INDEX

(1)